Carnegie Endowment for International Peace

DIVISION OF ECONOMICS AND HISTORY

John Bates Clark, LL.D., Director

ECONOMIC AND SOCIAL HISTORY

OF THE WORLD WAR

(*BRITISH SERIES*)

JAMES T. SHOTWELL, Ph.D.

GENERAL EDITOR

WITH THE COLLABORATION OF THE BRITISH
EDITORIAL BOARD

OXFORD

AT THE CLARENDON PRESS

ECONOMIC AND SOCIAL HISTORY OF THE WORLD WAR

BRITISH EDITORIAL BOARD

For List of other Editors and the plan of the Series see end of this volume.

WAR GOVERNMENT OF THE BRITISH DOMINIONS

BY

ARTHUR BERRIEDALE KEITH, D.C.L., D.Litt.

OF THE INNER TEMPLE, BARRISTER-AT-LAW
REGIUS PROFESSOR OF SANSKRIT AND COMPARATIVE PHILOLOGY AT THE UNIVERSITY
OF EDINBURGH ; FORMERLY OF THE COLONIAL OFFICE

OXFORD: AT THE CLARENDON PRESS
London, Edinburgh, New York, Toronto, Melbourne and Bombay
HUMPHREY MILFORD
1921

PRINTED IN ENGLAND
AT THE OXFORD UNIVERSITY PRESS

EDITOR'S PREFACE

In the autumn of 1914 when the scientific study of the effects of war upon modern life passed suddenly from theory to history, the Division of Economics and History of the Carnegie Endowment for International Peace proposed to adjust the programme of its researches to the new and altered problems which the War presented. The existing programme, which had been prepared as the result of a conference of economists held at Berne in 1911, and which dealt with the facts then at hand, had just begun to show the quality of its contributions; but for many reasons it could no longer be followed out. A plan was therefore drawn up at the request of the Director of the Division, in which it was proposed by means of an historical survey, to attempt to measure the economic cost of the War and the displacement which it was causing in the processes of civilization. Such an ' Economic and Social History of the World War ', it was felt, if undertaken by men of judicial temper and adequate training, might ultimately, by reason of its scientific obligations to truth, furnish data for the forming of sound public opinion, and thus contribute fundamentally toward the aims of an institution dedicated to the cause of international peace.

The need for such an analysis, conceived and executed in the spirit of historical research, was increasingly obvious as the War developed, releasing complex forces of national life not only for the vast process of destruction but also for the stimulation of new capacities for production. This new economic activity, which under normal conditions of peace might have been a gain to society, and the surprising capacity exhibited by the belligerent nations for enduring long and increasing loss—often while presenting the outward semblance of new prosperity—made necessary a reconsideration of the whole field of war economics. A double obligation was therefore placed upon the Division of Economics and History. It was obliged to concentrate its work upon the problem thus presented, and to study it as a whole; in other words, to apply to it the tests and disciplines of history. Just as the War itself was a single event, though penetrating by seemingly unconnected ways to the remotest parts of the world, so the analysis of it must be developed according to a plan at once all embracing and yet adjustable to the practical limits of the available data.

During the actual progress of the War, however, the execution of this plan for a scientific and objective study of war economics proved impossible in any large and authoritative way. Incidental studies and surveys of portions of the field could be made and were made under the direction of the Division, but it was impossible to undertake a general history for obvious reasons. In the first place, an authoritative statement of the resources of belligerents bore directly on the conduct of armies in the field. The result was to remove as far as possible from scrutiny those data of the economic life of the countries at war which would ordinarily, in time of peace, be readily available for investigation. In addition to this difficulty of consulting documents, collaborators competent to deal with them were for the most part called into national service in the belligerent countries and so were unavailable for research. The plan for a war history was therefore postponed until conditions should arise which would make possible not only access to essential documents but also the co-operation of economists, historians, and men of affairs in the nations chiefly concerned, whose joint work would not be misunderstood either in purpose or in content.

Upon the termination of the War the Endowment once more took up the original plan, and it was found with but slight modification to be applicable to the situation. Work was begun in the summer and autumn of 1919. In the first place a final conference of the Advisory Board of Economists of the Division of Economics and History was held in Paris, which limited itself to planning a series of short preliminary surveys of special fields. Since, however, the purely preliminary character of such studies was further emphasized by the fact that they were directed more especially towards those problems which were then fronting Europe as questions of urgency, it was considered best not to treat them as part of the general survey but rather as of contemporary value in the period of war settlement. It was clear that not only could no general programme be laid down *a priori* by this conference as a whole, but that a new and more highly specialized research organization than that already existing would be needed to undertake the Economic and Social History of the War, one based more upon national grounds in the first instance and less upon purely international co-operation. Until the facts of national history could be ascertained, it would be impossible to proceed with comparative analysis ; and the different national histories were themselves of almost baffling intricacy and variety. Consequently the former European Committee of Research was dissolved, and in its place it was decided to erect an Editorial Board in each of the larger countries and to nominate special editors in the smaller ones, who should concentrate, for the present at least, upon their own economic and social war history.

The nomination of these boards by the General Editor was the first step taken in every country where the work has begun. And if any justification was needed for the plan of the Endowment, it at once may be found in the lists of those, distinguished in scholarship or in public affairs, who have accepted the responsibility of editorship. This responsibility is by no means light, involving, as it does, the adaptation of the general editorial plan to the varying demands of national circumstances or methods of work ; and the measure of success attained is due to the generous and earnest co-operation of those in charge in each country.

Once the editorial organization was established there could be little doubt as to the first step which should be taken in each instance toward the actual preparation of the history. Without documents there can be no history. The essential records of the War, local as well as central, have therefore to be preserved and to be made available for research in so far as is compatible with public interest. But this archival task is a very great one, belonging of right to the governments and other owners of historical sources and not to the historian or economist who proposes to use them. It is an obligation of ownership ; for all such documents are public trust. The collaborators on this section of the war history, therefore, working within their own field as researchers, could only survey the situation as they found it and report their findings in the form of guides or manuals ; and perhaps by stimulating a comparison of methods, help to further the adoption of those found to be most practical. In every country, therefore, this was the point of departure for actual work ; although special monographs have not been written in every instance.

This first stage of the work upon the war history, dealing with little more than the externals of archives, seemed for a while to exhaust the possibilities of research. And had the plan of the history been limited to research based upon official documents, little more could have been done, for once documents have been labelled ' secret ' few government officials can be found with sufficient courage or initiative to break open the seal. Thus vast masses of source material essential for the historian were effectively placed beyond his reach, although much of it was quite harmless from any point of view. While war conditions thus continued to hamper research, and were likely to do so for many years to come, some alternative had to be found.

Fortunately such an alternative was at hand in the narrative, amply supported by documentary evidence, of those who had played some part in the conduct of affairs during the war, or who, as close observers in privileged positions, were able to record from first or at least second-hand knowledge the economic history of different phases of the great war, and of its effect upon society. Thus a series of monographs was planned consisting for the most part of unofficial yet authoritative statements, descriptive or historical, which may best be described as about half way between memoirs and blue-books. These monographs make up the main body of the work assigned so far. They are not limited to contemporary, war-time studies ; for the economic history of the war must deal with a longer period than that of the actual fighting. It must cover the years of ' deflation ' as well, at least sufficiently to secure some fairer measure of the economic displacement than is possible in purely contemporary judgments.

With this phase of the work, the editorial problems assumed a new aspect. The series of monographs had to be planned primarily with regard to the availability of contributors, rather than of source material as in the case of most histories ; for the contributors themselves controlled the sources. This in turn involved a new attitude towards those two ideals which historians have sought to emphasize, consistency and objectivity. In order to bring out the chief contribution of each writer it was impossible to keep within narrowly logical outlines ; facts would have to be repeated in different settings and seen from different angles, and sections included which do not lie within the strict limits of history ; and absolute objectivity could not be obtained in every part. Under the stress of controversy or apology, partial views would here and there find their expression. But these views are in some instances an intrinsic part of the history itself, contemporary measurements of facts as significant as the facts with which they deal. Moreover, the work as a whole is planned to furnish its own corrective ; and where it does not, others will.

In addition to this monographic treatment of source material, a number of studies by specialists is already in preparation, dealing with technical or limited subjects, historical or statistical. These monographs also partake to some extent of the nature of first-hand material, registering as they do the data of history close enough to the source to permit verification in ways impossible later. But they also belong to that constructive process by which history passes from analysis to synthesis. The process is a long and difficult one, however, and work upon it has only just begun. To quote an apt characterization, in the first stages of a history like this one is only ' picking cotton '. The tangled threads of events have still to be woven into the pattern of history ; and for this creative and constructive work different plans and organizations may be needed.

In a work which is the product of so complex and varied co-operation as this, it is impossible to indicate in any but a most general way the apportionment of responsibility of editors and authors for the contents of the different monographs. For the plan of the History as a whole and its effective execution the General Editor is responsible; but the arrangement of the detailed programmes of study has been largely the work of the different Editorial Boards and divisional Editors, who have also read the manuscripts prepared under their direction. The acceptance of a monograph in this series, however, does not commit the editors to the opinions or conclusions of the authors. Like other editors, they are asked to vouch for the scientific merit, the appropriateness and usefulness of the volumes admitted to the series; but the authors are naturally free to make their individual contributions in their own way. In like manner the publication of the monographs does not commit the Endowment to agreement with any specific conclusions which may be expressed therein. The responsibility of the Endowment is to History itself—an obligation not to avoid but to secure and preserve variant narratives and points of view, in so far as they are essential for the understanding of the War as a whole.

J. T. S.

PREFACE

THIS work is an attempt to describe the influence of the war on the activities of the governments of the Dominions and on their relations to the government of the United Kingdom. The question has been treated in the main in its political aspect; it would have been impossible within the limits of space available to deal in any adequate detail with the economic problems which faced the Dominion governments, or the modes in which they were handled, and these topics will form the subject of special monographs. Even in the case of political issues it has been necessary to select only those items which are of chief practical importance, and to pass over problems whose interest is predominantly legal. Attention has in the main been concentrated on the events in the period prior to the ratification of the peace with Germany; it would be premature yet to estimate the effect on Imperial relations of the proceedings at the Geneva meeting of the League Assembly.

It has been necessary to assume for the purpose of the discussion of war conditions those views as to the legal and constitutional position of the Dominions, for which arguments and authorities are adduced in my *Responsible Government in the Dominions* and *Imperial Unity and the Dominions*.

To the High Commissioners for the Dominions I am indebted for valuable information, and to my wife for criticism and other aid. I desire also to express my appreciation of the action of the Carnegie Endowment for International Peace in including this work in their series and of the care bestowed by the Clarendon Press in its production.

A. BERRIEDALE KEITH.

UNIVERSITY OF EDINBURGH.

CONTENTS

CHAPTER I

THE FRAMEWORK OF EMPIRE GOVERNMENT
BEFORE THE WAR

1. POLITICAL INSTITUTIONS.
  The characteristics of responsible government in the Dominions — The Federations — The Legislatures — The Executive Governments — The Judiciary — The legal limitations on Dominion authority — Constitutional restrictions on exercise of Imperial powers of control.

2. IMPERIAL CO-OPERATION IN BUSINESS AFFAIRS.
  The Colonial Conferences from 1887–1907 — The Imperial Conference of 1911 — The Dominions Royal Commission.

3. DEFENCE AND FOREIGN AFFAIRS.
  Military defence — Naval defence — The Committee of Imperial Defence — Foreign affairs — Discussions at the Imperial Conference of 1911 and the Defence Committee — The Imperial proposals of 1912 for closer co-operation in matters of defence and foreign affairs.

1. POLITICAL INSTITUTIONS

THE territories comprising the British Empire fall, as regards their political institutions, into two well-defined groups ; in the one division are India, the Crown Colonies, and the Protectorates, such as Nigeria; in the other the United Kingdom and the five Dominions, the title formally accorded in 1907 to the Dominion of Canada, the Commonwealth of Australia, the Dominion of New Zealand, the Union of South Africa, and Newfoundland. The territories of the former group possess much variety of government, and India and Malta have both progressed in regard to certain matters of internal concern beyond the normal restrictions of their status ; but with these exceptions the rule prevails that the Executive Government is carried on by officers whose tenure of office depends on the pleasure of the Imperial Government, and whose duty it is to obey the instructions of that Government in the exercise of their functions. Though the assistance of non-official representatives of the people, either nominated or elected, is obtained in legislation, the Executive Government in almost every case has power to secure the passing of any legislation which

1569·32   B

it holds essential to the interests of the territory. While, therefore, the territory is administered in the interests of its population,
the decision as to the true character of its needs rests, not with
the people but with the Imperial Government and Parliament.

In the United Kingdom and the Dominions the Executive
Government is immediately responsible to Parliament, representing the will of the people in each territory. The concession to the
Colonies from 1840 onwards of the system of the control of the
executive by Parliament was undoubtedly the only means by
which the continuance within the Empire of Canada, Australasia,
and South Africa could have been secured. But it raised at once
a problem which contemporary opinion deemed insoluble : how
can there be unity in an Empire if the Governments of the component parts are not ultimately responsible to a single authority ?

But the issue did not press hardly in the early days of
colonial self-government, especially as the colonies were numerous
and thinly peopled, and engrossed in local affairs. It became,
however, more real when in 1867 the Dominion of Canada was
formed by the federation of the most important of the North
American colonies, in 1900 the six colonies of Australia formed
a federal Commonwealth, and in 1909 the four South African
colonies were merged in a Union, for thus there came into
existence powerful Governments representing large areas with
important and rapidly increasing populations and possessing both
the resources and the desire to take part in other than merely
local affairs.

By 1914 in this way there existed in addition to the Executive
Government and Parliament of the United Kingdom, similar
forms of government in the five Dominions. In New Zealand and
Newfoundland the form of government was purely unitary ; in
the Union of South Africa the Parliament had full powers of legislation, but, as a concession to local feeling, when it was decided
not to create a Federal Government, limited powers of legislation
were assigned to Provincial Councils and corresponding administrative functions were assigned to Executive Committees in the
Cape of Good Hope, Natal, Transvaal, and the Orange Free State.
In Canada and Australia, on the other hand, true federal constitutions were created with a careful division of powers between the

federal and local governments and legislatures. There were, however, marked distinctions between the aims of the statesmen who brought into being the federations of the Canadian Provinces and the Australian colonies; the former aimed at securing as great a measure of unity as was practicable, influenced in no small degree by the lessons of the war of secession in the United States, and anxious to consolidate British power in North America against the possibility of conflict with the States. In Australia local autonomy was more strongly demanded, fear of foreign attack was less felt, and it was necessary to leave as much authority as possible to the local legislatures. In the division of powers, therefore, between the Dominion Parliament and the Provincial Legislatures the principle adopted was that the latter should have strictly defined authority over all merely provincial matters while in all other matters power would be vested in the Dominion Parliament. In Australia, on the other hand, the State Parliaments retained all the authority they had as colonial Parliaments, save where it was specifically taken from them as in the case of customs and excise and defence, while the Commonwealth Parliament was given exclusive powers in a few matters, and concurrent, but paramount, authority in a large number of questions of common interest. A further security to the States was provided, in the fact that their legislation was not made subject to disallowance by the Commonwealth Government, their Governors were appointed by the Imperial Government, and not by the Commonwealth Government, and they remained in direct communication on all matters within their sphere of authority with the Imperial Government. On the other hand, in Canada provincial Acts might be disallowed by the Dominion Government only, the Lieutenant-Governors were appointed by the Dominion Government, and direct communication with the Imperial Government was not permitted.

In the Dominions, the States, and the Provinces of Quebec and Nova Scotia, the legislatures were bi-cameral; in the other Canadian Provinces single chambers were held sufficient. The lower houses were elective, practically on adult suffrage, but only in Australia and New Zealand were women eligible to vote; in Canada the term House of Commons was adopted in imitation of the British usage ; in the Commonwealth and New Zealand House of Representatives, and in the others, Legislative Assembly or House of Assembly. The upper houses or Legislative Councils were nominee in Quebec, Nova Scotia, Newfoundland, New South Wales, and Queensland, elective in Victoria, South Australia, Western Australia, and Tasmania ; in the Dominion of Canada, the Commonwealth, and the Union of South Africa, the Senates were chosen so as to secure due representation of the different parts of these Dominions ; that of Canada was nominee, that of the Commonwealth purely elective, that of the Union four-fifths elective and one-fifth nominee. In New Zealand nomination as the mode of choice was abandoned before the war, but the change did not become effective during its course. The relations between the upper and the lower houses, when the former were nominee, were supposed to follow the principles applicable in the United Kingdom as regards the relations of the House of Commons and the House of Lords prior to the enactment of the Parliament Act of 1911 ; since, however, in Canada, Quebec, and Nova Scotia, the number of members was limited and the tenure was for life, no constitutional means of overcoming a deadlock existed. In the case of the elective upper houses legal attempts were made to define their relationships, but without achieving complete success. In practice the lower house possessed the monopoly of initiating expenditure, but the upper claimed the right of free criticism and an equal share in all other legislation.

The Executive Governments followed closely the British model. The place of the King, in whose name the Government was conducted, was taken by the Governor, styled in the case of the federations, the Union, and New Zealand Governor-General, and in the Canadian Provinces Lieutenant-Governor. In his actions, whether in exercise of the royal prerogative or under statutory authority, he was guided by his ministers, who held office nominally at his pleasure, really at the pleasure of the majority of the lower house of the legislature. Collectively the ministers constituted the Cabinet, which normally included all holders of ministerial office, contrary to the British practice under which only the more important ministers were included in it, a divergence explained by the small numbers of ministers in

Dominion Governments. The Cabinet constituted the Executive Council (in Canada styled Privy Council) of the Governor, and by its advice were issued Orders in Council, just as in the United Kingdom Orders of the King in Council are issued on the advice of the Privy Council. At these formal meetings of the Council the Governor might preside, but like the King he never took part in Cabinet meetings. A distinction, however, must be noted between the Executive Council and the Privy Council; the latter included besides ministers past and present many high officials who might take part in the passing of formal Orders, but in the Dominions none but ministers actually in office were summoned to meetings of the Executive Council. The unity of the Cabinet depended on the person of the Prime Minister, who was commissioned by the Governor to form an administration; on his resignation or death it was dissolved and it became incumbent on the Governor to select a new Premier. The obligations of ministers to the Premier and the Cabinet were similar to those recognized in the United Kingdom; while a minister was entitled to carry out the routine administration of his office without reference to other ministers, he must obtain their concurrence in any legislative proposals, and must not adopt any important step in policy without their sanction.

While the relation of the Governor to his ministers had been closely assimilated to that of the King and his ministers in the United Kingdom, the assimilation was not complete in 1914; a Governor could not, it was held, carry on the Government save with ministerial advice, but he could decline to accept that advice if he were prepared, in the event of his ministers resigning as the outcome of his refusal, to find other ministers to carry on the Government and to take responsibility to Parliament for his refusal. The measure of authority thus recognized was, it may be noted, very restricted; it merely permitted a Governor, if he thought that the ministry had ceased to represent the will of the people, to refuse to act on its advice, and the power was admitted because the people on the whole regarded it desirable that such a safeguard should exist.

Under the direction of ministers the detailed work of administration was entrusted to civil servants, whose position was secured in Australia, New Zealand, and the Union, by the institution of Civil Service Commissions in order to obviate political intervention ; in Canada and Newfoundland, on the other hand, despite efforts at reform, the civil service was largely affected by political influences. In all cases the civil service lacked in some degree the status of the service of the United Kingdom ; ministers were expected to give more detailed attention to business than was possible in the latter case, and it was difficult to induce Parliaments to recognize that adequate remuneration must be offered in order to attract men from the more tempting careers offered in the professions and commerce.

The Judiciary, on the other hand, maintained the best traditions of the United Kingdom. Security of tenure for the judges of the Supreme Courts was assured under the constitutions by requiring the assent of both houses of Parliament to their removal from office, and, while the removal of judges of the lower courts was simpler, the fact that decisions lay from their decrees to the Supreme Court provided an effective barrier to any executive interference with the course of justice. The Judiciary had, moreover, a function not exercised by the ordinary courts of the United Kingdom. The latter were constantly called upon to interpret Acts of the Parliament of the United Kingdom, but they could not call in question the validity of any such Act. In the Dominions the Courts were bound to decide whether the Acts of the Dominion Parliaments were within the constitutional powers of these legislatures, and, if so, whether they were nevertheless invalid because they were inconsistent with an Imperial Act, applicable to the Dominion. This function was of the highest importance in the case of the federations and the Union, in which the courts were constantly invoked to declare the validity or invalidity of legislation on constitutional grounds.

Closely parallel as was the structure of Dominion administration to that of the United Kingdom, it differed from it in one essential—the Parliament of the United Kingdom was possessed of full sovereign authority of legislation, while the Dominion Parliaments held only a derivative authority granted by the Imperial Parliament or in the case of Newfoundland by the Crown under the prerogative, to legislate for the peace, order, and good government of the Dominion. Similarly the Government of the United Kingdom was an Imperial Government, while Dominion Governments were Governments of dependencies. From these considerations it necessarily followed that the legislation of Dominion Parliaments, though extremely wide in scope, was subject to certain definite restrictions. In the first place, its operation was limited to the territorial limits of the Dominion, including its territorial waters, while the Imperial Parliament could legislate for British subjects throughout the world. Secondly a Dominion Parliament might not pass legislation inconsistent with its position as a dependency ; thus it could not authorize a declaration of war, or annexation of territory, or the secession of the Dominion from its subordination to the United Kingdom. Thirdly, Dominion legislation could not over-ride Imperial legislation applicable to the Dominion nor take away the power of the Imperial Parliament to pass Acts binding the Dominion, a principle in itself obvious but expressly enacted in the Colonial Laws Validity Act of 1865. Fourthly, Dominion legislation might be disallowed by the Imperial Government after it had been enacted by the two houses of the legislature and assented to by the Governor, or the Governor might be required to reserve the Bill for the consideration of the Imperial Government, in which event it would lapse unless expressly assented to within a limited period. Similarly a Dominion Executive had no *locus standi* in international affairs ; a Dominion Government could not accredit or receive a diplomatic representative from a foreign country or conclude a treaty of any kind ; if its citizens had grievances in foreign countries, representations must be made by the Imperial Government on which devolved the protection of British subjects abroad ; if foreigners had grievances against a Dominion, they had to be put forward to the Imperial Government. The Judiciary in the Dominions was also subject to Imperial control, for from decisions in civil matters—and exceptionally also in criminal questions—an appeal might be brought to the Judicial Committee of the Imperial Privy Council, which thus obtained the opportunity of securing the due observance by Dominion courts of the supremacy of Imperial over Dominion legislation.

In practice, of course, the full exercise of Imperial supremacy would have nullified the concession of self-government, and it became the task of the Secretary of State for the Colonies, the minister of the Imperial Government charged with the control of Dominion affairs subject to the general supervision of the Cabinet, to decide in what cases it was essential to assert the rights of the Imperial Government and Parliament. By 1914 the rule had been effectively established that in all matters of internal government the Dominions must be allowed the decision of the action to be taken, however much their policy might diverge from that which was adopted by the Imperial Government for the United Kingdom, whether as regards fiscal matters, social legislation, or family relations. Even the right of free amendment of the constitution was recognized as belonging to the Dominions; in the case of Canada, however, the right was severely limited because of the fact that the constitution represented a federal pact which could not be varied save by the consent of the parties concerned, so that change was impossible unless the provinces and the Dominion were in agreement to ask the Imperial Parliament to amend the British North America Act. In the case of the Commonwealth authority to change was granted to the Parliament, or either house, supported by a majority in a referendum to the electorate, but the power of change was limited to alterations consistent with the federal structure of the constitution in accordance with the intention of the framers of that document. For any further change an Imperial Act was requisite as in the case of the Dominion of Canada. Within the limits of the federal constitutions, however, the Provinces and the States were left free to alter their constitutions as they thought fit, subject, of course, to the Imperial right of disapproval of any change hostile to the continuance of the unity of the Empire. The constituent powers of the Parliaments of the Union of South Africa, New Zealand, and Newfoundland, were absolute, subject only to the same contingency.

2. Imperial Co-operation in Business Affairs

The extraordinary completeness of the freedom from Imperial control of the Dominions in all internal affairs rendered co-operation between the Dominions and the Imperial Government a matter of pressing importance, and an effective means to this end was presented in periodical Conferences between representatives of the different governments. The first of these Conferences was held in 1887 to celebrate the Jubilee of Queen Victoria's reign, and membership of it was extended to representatives from some of the Crown Colonies. It was followed in 1894 on the invitation of the Canadian Government by a Conference at Ottawa confined to representatives of the Governments of the self-governing colonies, which discussed problems of Imperial preference and communications. Further Conferences followed in 1897 on the occasion of the Queen's Diamond Jubilee, and in 1902 at King Edward VII's coronation; at the latter meeting it was agreed that Conferences should be held every four years. In 1905 Mr. A. Lyttelton, as Secretary of State for the Colonies, suggested that the work of the Conference—which might be styled in future Imperial Council—should be supplemented by the creation of a permanent body representative of the United Kingdom and the Colonies, which would carry out on the instructions of the Conference such inquiries as were referred to Royal Commissions or departmental committees in matters affecting the United Kingdom alone. The suggestion was coldly received by Canada, and the Liberal Government which took office in the United Kingdom at the close of 1905 did not endorse Mr. Lyttelton's proposal. At the Colonial Conference of 1907 which followed, the title of the Conference was altered to Imperial Conference, and a formal constitution was prescribed ; the Conference would consist of the Prime Ministers of the United Kingdom, Canada, the Commonwealth of Australia, New Zealand, the Union of South Africa, and Newfoundland, and the Secretary of State for the Colonies, who would preside in the absence of the Prime Minister of the United Kingdom. Other Imperial and Dominion ministers might attend meetings; but, save with special permission, only two ministers should speak for any unit on one topic, and each unit should have one vote only. The full Conference was to meet once in four years ; subsidiary Conferences might be held to deal with important questions arising between the regular meetings, or matters of minor importance requiring expert investigation. The resolutions of the Conferences, however, were to be merely advisory ; they were not to bind even those Governments which supported them to adhere to them if on further investigation they proved to present difficulties of execution.

No restriction was laid down as to the subjects of discussion, and at the first meeting of the Imperial Conference in 1911 a wide range of topics was discussed, including Imperial relations, the treatment of British Indians, an Imperial Court of Appeal, international relations, naturalization, commercial relations, Imperial steamship communications, postal and telegraph reforms, emigration and labour exchanges, shipping conferences and rebates, coinage, weights and measures, uniformity of law as to companies, trade marks, patents, copyright, compensation for accidents, income tax and death duties, legislation as to destitute and deserted persons, recognition of Imperial and Dominion judgements, the law of conspiracy, Suez Canal dues, Imperial Exhibitions, and the celebration of the King's birthday. From the point of view of commercial relations the most important step taken was the decision to secure the appointment of a Royal Commission, representative of the Governments concerned, charged with the duty of investigating the natural resources of each part of the Empire represented at the Conference, ' the development attained and attainable, and the facilities for production, manufacture, and distribution ; the trade of each part with the others and the outside world, the food and raw material requirements of each, and the sources thereof available, to what extent, if any, the trade between the different parts has been affected by the existing legislation in each, either beneficially or otherwise, and by what methods consistent with the existing fixed policy of each part the trade of each part with the others may be improved and extended.' The resolution served a double purpose : since the Conference of 1894 the Dominions had passed resolutions approving the principle of Imperial preference, but the Imperial Government had been unable to accept any obligation to give colonial products a preference in the British market. In 1903 Mr. Chamberlain, then Secretary of State for the Colonies, had been converted to a belief in Tariff Reform as the most secure means of effecting Imperial unity ; but the Unionist Prime Minister, Mr. A. J. Balfour, was unable to adopt in full his colleague's point of view, partly because a strong section of the Unionists manifested distinct hostility to any policy of tampering with freedom of trade. At the Conference of 1907 the Liberal Government, which had largely derived its majority from its vigorous defence of Free Trade, was unable to make any concession, and the refusal was the cause of some dissatisfaction, especially in Australia. In 1911, therefore, the Government of the United Kingdom was anxious to avoid disturbing the harmony of Imperial relations by an acrimonious controversy on this issue, and the Dominion Governments had no wish to insist on a discussion which could not be fruitful. At the same time it was held that great value would attach to a systematic investigation of inter-imperial commercial relations by a Commission charged with ascertaining facts and making recommendations, subject to the principle that in their suggestions they must respect the fixed policy of each part of the Dominions.

The labours of the Commission began in 1912; the inquiries on which they embarked were exhaustive, and had not been brought to a conclusion before the outbreak of the war. They were completed while hostilities were yet in progress, and though the value of the recommendations of the Commission was seriously reduced by the changes in conditions produced by the war, much material of value was collected and made available for the guidance of the Imperial and Dominion Governments.

3. DEFENCE AND FOREIGN AFFAIRS

The grant of self-government in internal affairs necessarily involved the duty of each colony to make provision for maintenance of internal order and, so far as its resources permitted, for its protection against external aggression, though the Imperial Navy assumed the main burden of safeguarding the colonies from hostile attacks. Imperial troops were, therefore, withdrawn from the Colonies save in so far as their presence was rendered desirable for the protection of naval bases such as those of Halifax and Esquimalt in Canada, from which Imperial troops were not finally withdrawn until 1905, when Canada spontaneously accepted the burden of supplying the necessary men. In the Union of South Africa Imperial troops remained up to the outbreak of the war of 1914. The local forces of the Colonies were wholly under the control of their Governments and legislatures, and the Imperial

Army Act expressly provided that colonial legislation should be applicable to colonial forces even beyond the limits of the colony if the colonial legislatures so desired. The system adopted depended on the choice of each Dominion ; while Canada up to the outbreak of war remained faithful to a militia system which in practice was entirely voluntary, Australia and New Zealand, apprehensive of danger from Japan, adopted in 1909–10 a system of compulsory training for boys and youths, and the Union of South Africa in 1912, in order to secure safety against a native rising, adopted a system under which training was compulsory, but only a certain number of those liable were actually called upon. In all these cases, however, only local defence was contemplated in the application of compulsion, and Newfoundland had no military force of any kind.

While no attempt was made by the Imperial Government to secure control of the military forces of the Dominions, it was agreed, as the outcome of the Colonial Conference of 1907 and a subsidiary Naval and Military Conference in 1909, that an Imperial General Staff should be created to study military science in all its bearings and to collect and disseminate to the various Governments military intelligence. It was to work in communication with General Staffs created in the Dominions, which, though under the control of the Dominion Governments, were to correspond direct with the Imperial General Staff and to prepare in conjunction with it schemes for the training, education, and war organization of the military forces of the Dominions. No obligation, however, was accepted by the Dominions to supply troops in war time, and when the war broke out little had been done to plan concerted action.

In regard to naval defence provision was made as early as 1865 by the Colonial Naval Defence Act for colonies to maintain local flotillas for harbour and coast defence, and the Australian colonies took advantage of the authority thus conferred. The acceptance of a share of the burden of Imperial defence on a wider basis was delayed until 1887 when, in return for an increase in the British squadron on the Australian station, small subsidies were promised by the Australasian Colonies. The policy of subsidy was reaffirmed in 1902 by the Colonial Conference. But the principle of contribution was disliked in the Commonwealth and a suggestion was made instead for the creation of a Commonwealth fleet. This proposal raised at once the difficult problem of legal control and international relations, and it was not until the Naval and Military Conference of 1909, held as the outcome of the un-easiness created in the Empire by revelations of German naval ambitions, that the principle of the creation of a Commonwealth fleet was conceded, while Canada at the same time adopted a similar policy, New Zealand, on the other hand, preferring the older plan of a pecuniary contribution and undertaking to present a battle-cruiser to the Empire. In 1911 the legal and international difficulties, inherent in the creation of units not under direct Imperial control in time of peace, were removed by an agreement which secured that Dominion fleets should normally be confined to definite areas and should in matters of international intercourse act under Imperial instructions, while in time of war it was con-templated that full control would be conferred by the Dominion Governments on the Imperial Board of Admiralty. In 1913 New Zealand, consequent on the fall of the Liberal Government in the preceding year, changed her naval policy, and decided to create a small unit under her own control.

For the co-ordination of the consideration of problems of naval and military defence there existed the Committee of Im-perial Defence. This body owed its existence to the interest taken by Mr. Balfour, as Prime Minister, in defence questions ; its constitution was elastic, the Prime Minister being, in Mr. Balfour's view, the only essential member, but the ministers in charge of Army and Navy affairs, the Chancellor of the Exchequer, and the Secretaries of State for Foreign Affairs and the Colonies were among those often summoned, while military and naval experts were normally present. The functions of the Committee were essentially advisory, not executive, and it was called into being to deal as a whole with the problems of home, colonial, and Indian defence. Its elasticity of composition permitted the summoning of Dominion ministers to discuss questions involving Dominion interests, and the Colonial Conference of 1907 formally agreed on the principle that the Committee should advise on any local question if it were invited to do so by the Government interested, and that a Dominion representative should be summoned to any meeting at which such questions were discussed if the Dominion Government so desired. It was, of course, clearly understood that the advice given by the Committee was not binding on the Dominion Government, which remained free to accept or reject it at pleasure.

Little use was made by the Dominions of the arrangement agreed to in 1907, but in 1911 the Imperial Government endeavoured to convert the Committee of Imperial Defence into an important element in the conduct of Imperial relations, by using it as a means of keeping the Dominions in touch with foreign affairs in their bearing on defence problems. It had been conceded from the beginning of the self-government of the Dominions that foreign affairs rested with the Imperial Government, but it was assumed that in her conduct of Imperial foreign policy the United Kingdom would have due regard to the needs of the Dominions. The assumption was justified by the practice of the Imperial Government. From the first it admitted that any colony should be consulted before any transaction affecting it was concluded, and by 1880 it was agreed that no commercial treaty should be made binding on a colony without its consent, and that special commercial agreements would be negotiated if possible with foreign powers when desired by the Colonies. In pursuance of these principles commercial treaties entered into by the United Kingdom were made applicable to the colonies only if they expressed a desire to adhere, and the right of separate withdrawal was obtained in treaties concluded in and after 1899, while, as the result of the Imperial Conference of 1911, clauses were introduced into treaties concluded under the old system permitting their termination separately in respect of any Dominion which so wished. The first separate commercial treaty in the interest of a colony was concluded in 1893 regarding Franco-Canadian trade, and in 1894 and 1907 general principles regarding such negotiations were laid down, which effectively secured the position of the Dominions in tariff negotiations.

Colonial Governments were also interested in political questions directly affecting their immediate concerns; but to the larger issues of foreign policy they displayed no little indifference, a fact easily explicable from the absorbing character of their struggles to settle the vast territories under their control. The results, however, of this indifference were embarrassing, for colonial Governments failed to appreciate the interconnexion of general and local issues, and thus resented with undue bitterness the sacrifices which the United Kingdom was forced to make in Africa and in the Pacific in the period from 1881–6 in order to avoid conflict with Germany at a time when the occupation of Egypt had strained relations between France and the United Kingdom almost to breaking point. The fear, indeed, of being involved in the maelstrom of European politics induced statesmen in Victoria in 1870 to suggest that the Imperial Government should be asked to concede the right of treaty-making to the colonies and to obtain from other states their recognition as neutralized territories in order to prevent their being compelled to take part in any Imperial war. When the movement for Imperial Federation offered the colonies a share in moulding the foreign policy of the Empire in exchange for the surrender of a portion of their local autonomy, the suggestion was emphatically rejected. In vain did Mr. Chamberlain, as Secretary of State for the Colonies, seek at the Colonial Conferences of 1897 and 1902 to induce the colonial Governments to share in the control of the foreign policy and the burden of the defence of the Empire. At the Colonial Conference of 1907 Mr. Deakin protested against Imperial policy in the New Hebrides as un-satisfactory to Australia and New Zealand, while Sir Robert Bond denounced Imperial policy regarding the rights of United States fishermen in Newfoundland under the treaty with the United States of 1818, but these criticisms also followed the traditional line of local interests.

The national self-consciousness of the Dominions was, however, developing, and, though no protest was made against the fact that the Dominions were not consulted with regard to the Hague Peace Conferences of 1899 and 1907, the conclusion in 1909 of the Declaration of London regarding Naval Warfare, without consultation with the Dominions, elicited a formal protest from the Commonwealth of Australia. At the Conference of 1911 Mr. A. Fisher, Prime Minister of the Commonwealth, secured, with the ready acquiescence of the Imperial Government, the passing of a resolution to the effect that the Dominions should be consulted when the instructions to the British delegates at future meetings of the Hague Conference were being framed, and that conventions provisionally agreed to at such meetings should be circulated to the Dominions for consideration before final signature, and that a similar procedure, as far as time and opportunity and subject-matter permitted, should be followed as regards instructions to British delegates for the negotiation of other international agreements affecting the Dominions. Mr. Fisher made the further suggestion that the Dominion Governments should be placed in direct communication with the Foreign Office, but this suggestion was not pressed. The Imperial Government, however, invited the Dominion delegates to take part in a meeting of the Committee of Imperial Defence, at which the Secretary of State for Foreign Affairs explained the principles affecting the foreign policy of the United Kingdom and their bearing on defence. But, although the gravity of the existing situation in Europe was fully realized by those present at this meeting, no proposal was made on any side by which the Dominion Governments might keep in effective touch with the progress of events. The time, in fact, was not ripe for the Dominions to take a continuous interest in foreign affairs ; indeed it was made clear by Sir Wilfrid Laurier during the discussions at the Imperial Conference that Canada did not desire to see established any general rule requiring the consultation of the Dominion on foreign issues not immediately affecting her, since consultation involved responsibilities which Canada was not prepared to accept. It was agreed, however, at the meeting of the Committee of Imperial Defence that one or more representatives of the Dominion Governments should be invited to attend meetings of the Committee when naval and military questions affecting the Dominions were under consideration, and that steps should be taken to set up in each Dominion a Defence Committee.

The defeat of Sir Wilfrid Laurier's Government at the close of 1911 on the issue of reciprocity with the United States was in large measure due to the fear, encouraged by rash predictions of the President of the United States, that reciprocity might attract Canada into the sphere of the political influence of the United

States, and Sir Robert Borden's accession to office was marked by his display of a desire for more effective Imperial co-operation. When visiting London in 1912, he asked that Canadian and other Dominion ministers, when in London as members of the Committee of Imperial Defence, might be given in confidence knowledge of the policy and proceedings of the Imperial Government in foreign and other affairs. This elicited from the Secretary of State for the Colonies on behalf of Mr. Asquith's Government an assurance that the Imperial Government would welcome closer co-operation in matters of defence and foreign policy, and a suggestion that a Dominion minister should be stationed in London with personal access to the Prime Minister, the Foreign Office, and other departments of state, as a means of keeping the Imperial and Dominion ministries in close touch on all matters of common concern, though it was, of course, made clear that the Imperial Government did not desire to divest itself of any of its ultimate responsibility for foreign affairs and Imperial defence. The offer thus made to Canada was extended to all the Dominions on December 10, 1912. The response was disappointing. Canada did nothing until 1914, when, on the death of Lord Strathcona, who since 1896 had been High Commissioner for the Dominion in London, Sir George Perley, a minister in the Dominion Government, was sent to act as Dominion representative. South Africa emphatically declined to adopt the proposed procedure, and New Zealand more guardedly refused the offer. The Commonwealth of Australia ignored the proposal, but instead asked that a Conference on Naval Defence should be summoned, a proposal which proved impracticable of execution owing to the difficulty of ministers from other Dominions visiting England at the time proposed by Australia, and later to political difficulties in the Commonwealth itself which precluded the dispatch of a minister. To some extent the needs of the situation were met as far as concerns New Zealand and the Union of South Africa by the visit to London and full discussion with the Imperial Government of defence affairs by individual ministers in 1913, but no further steps were taken to communicate with the Dominions regarding foreign policy. On the other hand, the Committee of Imperial Defence urged the advantages to be obtained by the Dominions following the example of the United

Kingdom and preparing ' War Books ', detailing the steps to be taken by the naval, military, and civil authorities in the event of the outbreak of war, and this advice was more or less carried out by the Dominion Governments, in special by Canada, where under Sir Robert Borden's direction careful consideration was given to the procedure to be followed in the event of hostilities.

CHAPTER II

THE DOMINIONS AND THE UNITED KINGDOM, 1914–16

Responsibility of United Kingdom for declaration of war in 1914 — Legal effect of declaration — The War Prerogative of the Crown — Non-interference with Dominion autonomy — Postponement of Imperial Conference in 1915 — Gradual recognition in United Kingdom of necessity of closer co-operation with Dominions.

THE pre-war organization of the Empire rendered it inevitable that when, on August 4, 1914, the necessity of protecting the liberty of Europe and vindicating public right compelled the Imperial Government to declare war against the German Empire, the decision to take part in hostilities rested on the sole responsibility of that Government, though its action vitally affected the whole of the British Empire. It is true that the Dominion Governments in the days immediately preceding the final decision had spontaneously sent messages assuring the Crown of their readiness to afford such aid as the crisis might render necessary, but it was impossible for these Governments to form any deliberate opinion on the details of the issue or to intervene with any suggestions as to means of securing the maintenance of peace. Fortunately for the unity of the Empire in the struggle the wrongdoing of Germany was flagrant and unabashed, so that it was impossible for serious doubt to be felt as to the justice of the British action. Moreover, nowhere was the falsity of the German accusation that the British Government had been meditating the encirclement of Germany more clearly realized than in the Dominions, in which no serious attempt had been made to prepare even for a defensive war.

The outbreak of war revealed in an interesting and somewhat unexpected manner the extent to which the Imperial Government was responsible for the issues of war and peace and the legal consequences in the Dominions of the existence of a state of war, while at the same time it also emphasized the degree of autonomy attained by the Dominions. The declaration of war by His Majesty on the advice of the Imperial Government immediately created a state of war as between the whole of the British Empire and Germany, while subsequent Declarations added Austria-Hungary, the Ottoman Empire, and Bulgaria, to the list of foes. But no demand was made for assistance naval, military, or financial, from the Dominions, whose autonomy was rigidly respected. Their offers of aid were naturally accepted with much warmth, and when invited suggestions were made as to the most effective form in which help could be rendered, but no effort was made to put pressure on the Dominions.

The same respect for Dominion autonomy was exhibited in the war legislation of the Imperial Parliament and in the prerogative orders issued by the Imperial Government in virtue of the royal prerogative regarding war. Scrupulous care was taken to secure that no powers should be exercised which were not already vested in the Crown as an essential part of the war prerogative; thus the Proclamations of August 5, 1914, regarding trading with the enemy [1] and warning British subjects throughout the Empire that persons contributing to German loans or contracting with the German Government would render themselves liable to the penalties of high treason as abetting the King's enemies, created no new offences ; they merely reminded British subjects, wherever resident, of the common law of the Empire, arising from their allegiance, which renders trade with the enemy criminal and aid given to the enemy treason. On the war prerogative rested similarly the whole series of Proclamations and Orders in Council dealing with the days of grace allowed for the departure of German merchant vessels from British ports throughout the Empire, the carriage of contraband of war by British ships between foreign ports, the definition from time to time of contraband goods, and the operation, with restrictions, of the Declaration of London and its final abandonment in favour of more rigid rules of war. Under a combination of the prerogative and statutory powers contained in the Colonial Courts of Admiralty

---

[1] For South African cases under the common law see Keith, *Imperial Unity*, pp. 359, 360 ; for the common law in the Commonwealth the exhaustive judgement of the High Court in *R.* v. *Snow*, 23 C.L.R. 256.

Act, 1890, prize courts in the Dominions were called into activity
to exercise their jurisdiction under Imperial enactments. In New
Zealand, Newfoundland, and the six Australian States, the jurisdiction was exercised by the Supreme Courts; in Canada by the
Exchequer Court of the Dominion, and by local judges in Admiralty
at Halifax, Quebec, St. John's, Victoria, and Charlottetown; and
in the Union of South Africa by the Cape and Natal Provincial
Divisions of the Supreme Court. Procedure in prize cases was
regulated by Imperial Acts of 1914 and 1915, and the full extent
of Imperial authority was manifested when the prize jurisdiction
of the local judge in Admiralty at Victoria, British Columbia, was
revoked by the Admiralty on the ground of his failure properly
to carry out the duties of his office.[1]

In all matters, however, in which Dominion autonomy could
be respected, this was done. When restrictions were imposed on
the transfer of ships from British ownership by Acts of 1915 and
1916, the measures were not made applicable to British ships
registered in the Dominions. The obligation to compulsory
service imposed on certain classes of persons resident in Great
Britain by the Acts of 1916–18 contained explicit exclusion from
their operation of persons who, though resident for a time in Great
Britain, were ordinarily resident in His Majesty's Dominions
abroad. Moreover, this privileged position was extended when
conventions were concluded with allied powers regarding the
reciprocal liability of British subjects resident in their territories
to compulsory service and of allied subjects resident in Great
Britain, for steps were taken to ensure that British subjects
ordinarily resident in Dominions which had not adopted compulsion were not included.[2] When it was desired to extend the
operation of the common law, and fresh disabilities were imposed
in the United Kingdom on aliens and trading with the enemy
was further penalized, the Acts passed were not made applicable
to the Dominions, but the Dominion Government were informed
of the terms of the legislation, and were left to legislate in similar
terms if they thought fit, as was usually the case, though action
was sometimes tardy as in the case of Union legislation as to

[1] See *Canadian Law Times*, xxxvii. 296–308.
[2] See Military Service (Conventions with Allied States) Act, 1917.

enemy trade.   It remained, however, absolutely within the discretion of the Governments to take what action they thought
fit, and the variety of treatment possible was well illustrated in
the various efforts made by the Government of the Commonwealth to free Australian trade in metals from German domination.[1]
So completely was local autonomy respected that no interference
was attempted by the Imperial Government even in regard to
the military expeditions conducted by the Dominions and their
occupation of enemy territory.   The terms of the capitulation of
German New Guinea, which were much too favourable to the
enemy, were concluded on the authority of the Australian officer
commanding the expeditionary force, and were acquiesced in by
the Imperial Government, although, in view of the fact that the
fleet which rendered the expedition possible was under Imperial
control, it might have claimed a voice in the decision.   Similarly
the capitulation of Samoa was arranged by the New Zealand
commanding officer, and General Botha decided the generous
terms on which the German forces in South Africa laid down
their arms.[2]   Even on the vital question of naturalization, affecting
allegiance to the Crown, the Imperial Act of 1918 left the Dominions
unaffected.   The military and naval forces of the Dominions
which served in the war were raised either voluntarily or under
Dominion Acts applying compulsion ; not a single person in the
Dominions was compelled to serve in any form by Imperial
legislation.

While the autonomy of the Dominions was thus rigorously
respected, no effective effort was made in the first two years of
the war to bring the Dominion Governments into any form of
partnership with the Imperial Government in the control of the
forces of the Empire, though with the passage of time the numbers
of men contributed by the Dominions became sufficiently large
to make the problem worthy of serious consideration.   The
Dominion Governments accepted with loyalty the position.   At
the beginning of 1915 strong suggestions were made in the United
Kingdom that the Imperial Government should summon the
Dominion Governments to a Conference ; it was pointed out

---

[1] *The Round Table*, vi. 175–80 ; *Official Year Book of the Commonwealth*, xii.
471–4.   [2] See below, Chap. VI, § 1.

that the Imperial Conference fell to meet in that year, and while
the normal Conference with its many and not very important
resolutions was obviously not suitable for an emergency such as
then prevailed, a full consultation between the Dominions and
the Imperial Government could not fail to be of the utmost public
advantage, and would give the Dominions fresh interest in the
conduct of the war. The idea was keenly supported in public
utterances by the Prime Minister of the Commonwealth, then on
a visit to New Zealand, who urged that such a Conference would
be of more value than any of its predecessors. But the suggestion
was treated coldly in Canada, where ministers were too deeply
immersed in their normal work to care for absence from it, only
Mr. Rowell, leader of the Liberals in Ontario but not then in
federal politics, championing the idea. In the House of Commons
on April 15, 1915, Mr. Harcourt revealed the fact that the holding
of a Conference had been suggested by Mr. Fisher in December,
but that the other Dominions had been unfavourable to it, so
that in January he had intimated to the Governors-General that
the Conference would not be held, but had added an intimation
that it was the intention of His Majesty's Government to consult
each Prime Minister 'most fully and if possible personally when
the time arrives to discuss possible terms of peace'.[1] The stress
laid on the readiness to consult on the peace issue is significant ;
it was then the view of the Imperial Government and of the
majority of Dominion statesmen that this was the one point of
importance to the Dominions, which need not trouble themselves about the employment of their forces, but might be con-
tented to devote themselves to the sufficiently perplexing problem
of keeping them up to strength by reinforcements. Probably, too,
there was underlying the decision the erroneous belief in the
possibility of early victory which, despite Lord Kitchener, persisted in the United Kingdom and even more in the Dominions
for many months. The Dominion Governments were not moved
from this attitude even when the failure of the Gallipoli expedition,
which deeply involved Australia and New Zealand, became
evident ; they accepted with loyal resignation the decision to
withdraw the troops without accomplishing their object and after

[1] *The Times History of the War*, xii. 282 ff.

most cruel losses, nor did they base on the fiasco any claim to be consulted in the direction of the war.

On the other hand, the Imperial Government showed itself ready and willing to act on the terms of the offer of December 1912, and to communicate freely with any Dominion minister resident in London or visiting the United Kingdom. Canada alone acted on the principle of keeping a minister in England, Sir George Perley in the first instance, and afterwards Sir E. Kemp, being in close communication with the Imperial Government on military and cognate affairs. Sir Robert Borden himself visited the United Kingdom in July 1915, when the unprecedented step was taken of inviting him to meet and confer with the Cabinet. The same procedure was followed on the occasion of Mr. Hughes's visit in the following year. Mr. Hughes, however, created a new precedent : *en route* to England he visited Ottawa and was sworn of the Dominion Privy Council and took part in a meeting of the Canadian Cabinet. His stay in England was also marked by a new feature ; representing as he did the views not only of Australia but in some measure those of New Zealand or even of Canada, he carried on an energetic campaign in favour of the principles which he deemed necessary for success in the war, and even more for securing freedom from German domination of British industry after the war. It must be remembered that he had already found great difficulty in fighting in Australia German influence on trade and industry, and he was undoubtedly disappointed to find some lukewarmness in the Government at home on the issue. Much to his gratification he found a legitimate means of furthering his aims ; invited to represent Australia at the Economic Conference of the Allies held at Paris on June 14–17, 1916, he found a hearty supporter in Sir George Foster, who represented Canada, and their influence was not negligible in its effect on the terms of these resolutions. In addition to proposals for the period of the war, they embodied the principle of the obligation of the allies in the post-war period to refuse for a period of years most-favoured-nation treatment to enemy powers ; to conserve for allied countries before all others their natural resources during the period of commercial, industrial, agricultural, and maritime reconstruction ; to protect their commerce, industry, agriculture, and navigation, against economic aggression arising from dumping or any other mode of unfair competition, by the use of the prohibition of importation of enemy goods ; and to prevent enemy subjects from exercising in their territories industries or professions prejudicing national defence or economic independence.[1]

Mr. Hughes's mission was fraught with consequences of great importance to the political life of Australia, as he returned to the Commonwealth convinced of the necessity of conscription in order to maintain the strength of the Australian forces. His visit to London was followed by that of Mr. Massey, the Prime Minister of New Zealand, and Sir Joseph Ward, Minister of Finance and his colleague in the control of the Coalition Government formed in the preceding year. The presence of Dominion statesmen, and especially the activities of Mr. Hughes, had brought home to the public in the United Kingdom the vital interest which the Dominions had in the war and in the terms of settlement, while Sir Robert Borden had on more than one occasion emphasized the fact that the participation of the Dominions in the war had created a new epoch in the relations of the Empire, for, as comrades in arms, the Dominions must expect also to be comrades in peace and sharers in a policy which, as the event had proved, might lead them all unexpectedly to a crisis. It is noteworthy that in no case was any suggestion made by a Dominion minister that the policy which had led to the war could, or should, have been modified, or that the Imperial Government were in any degree responsible for the calamity. Nor was there any general complaint that the Dominions had not been warned betimes ;[2] Dominion ministers were doubtless only too well aware that before the event it would have been even harder to persuade the Dominions of the danger than it was to bring it home to the people of the United Kingdom despite their proximity to Germany.

Gradually the view gathered force that in the failure to convene a meeting of Dominion statesmen as early as possible after the outbreak of war to take counsel together for the development of the strength of the Empire a great opportunity had been

[1] *Parl. Pap.* Cd. 8271.
[2] Cf. Commonwealth *Debates*, 1919, pp. 1405, 1406.

allowed to pass away, and Mr. Massey expressed this view with much force and felicity on more than one occasion in November 1916. It is easy to understand the motives which induced the statesmen of all the Dominions, save Mr. Fisher, to think it more important to concentrate their energies on their immediate tasks, and yet easier to excuse the ministers of the United Kingdom, immersed in the grave preoccupations of a struggle so doubtful and difficult, for lacking the imagination to realize the possibilities of the situation. Mr. Massey himself, engaged in the early months of 1915 in a somewhat petty contest with Sir Joseph Ward, showed then no eagerness to accept a summons to a Conference. The visits of the Dominion ministers had been, it was clear, at least as instructive to them as to the British public, and by the end of the year the way was open to a new and important development in the relations of the Dominions and the United Kingdom.

CHAPTER III

THE IMPERIAL WAR CABINET AND THE WAR CONFERENCES

1. THE IMPERIAL WAR CABINET

As part of the proposals of the new Government formed in the United Kingdom in December 1916 for the more effective conduct of the war, there figured naturally a project of securing further assistance from the Dominions, and on December 14 telegrams were sent to the Dominions, conveying a suggestion of somewhat novel character. The idea of an ordinary Imperial Conference of the pre-war type was negatived, but the Prime Ministers were invited ' to attend a series of special and continuous meetings of the War Cabinet in order to consider urgent questions affecting the prosecution of the war, the possible conditions on which, in agreement with our allies, we could agree to its termination, and the problems which will then immediately arise '. For the purpose of these meetings, it was added, the Prime Ministers would be members of the War Cabinet. At the same time India, which was excluded by a resolution of the Colonial Conference of 1907 from inclusion in the Imperial Conference, was invited to be represented on similar terms to the Dominions. The invitation was accepted by all the Dominions, but Australia was not actually represented. Mr. Hughes, then in office with the support of the Liberal Party and a fragment of Labour, was not prepared to leave the Commonwealth at a time when a general election was due ; he therefore secured the assent of the House of Representatives to the proposal that the Imperial Parliament should be asked to extend the duration of the existing Commonwealth Parliament ; but the suggestion was rejected by the Senate, in which Labour had a small majority. Mr. Hughes, accordingly, decided to remain in Australia and to devote his attention to the impending elections. The other Dominions, however, were effectively represented. Sir Robert Borden, the Canadian Prime Minister, was accompanied by Sir George Perley, Minister of the Overseas Military Forces, the Hon. R. Rogers, Minister of Public Works, and the Hon. J. D. Hazen, Minister of Marine, Fisheries, and Naval Service.[1] New Zealand sent the Prime Minister, Mr. W. F. Massey, and Sir Joseph Ward, Minister of Finance and Posts. General Botha could not leave the Union, but his place was taken by Lieut.-General Smuts, and Sir Edward Morris represented Newfoundland.

Though it seems to have been contemplated, when the invitation was issued, that nothing in the nature of an ordinary Imperial Conference should be held, events proved too strong for the carrying out of this intention. On the contrary it was found necessary to divide the proceedings into two parts. On the one hand, there were held between March 20, 1917, and May 2, fourteen meetings of the Imperial War Cabinet, consisting of the oversea representatives and the members of the British War Cabinet, as reconstituted by Mr. Lloyd George, sitting together for deliberation about the conduct of the war and for discussion of the larger issues of Imperial policy connected with the war.[2] Over this body, of course, the British Prime Minister presided, and, though the Secretary of State for the Colonies was a member of the War Cabinet, he represented in it only the Crown Colonies and Protectorates. On the other hand, there were held meetings of the Imperial War Conference, presided over by the Secretary of State for the Colonies, and not, as was provided for in the constitution of the Imperial Conference proper, by the Prime Minister, in which the oversea representatives discussed with members of the British Government non-war problems or questions connected with the

[1] The two last mentioned were not members of the War Cabinet proper, and similarly in 1918 only two Ministers were normally admitted to it.—*The Times*, June 15, 1918.

[2] *Parl. Pap.* Cd. 9005, pp. 5–9.

war, but of minor importance. The proceedings of the War Cabinet were secret; those of the War Conference were as usual held in private, but a selection of the results arrived at and of the discussions was made public. But it is certain that much of the energy of the War Cabinet was devoted to the grave question of increasing the number of troops available, and the most important outcome of its deliberations was the decision taken by Sir Robert Borden to face the unpopularity inevitable in Canada of the adoption of the policy of maintaining by conscription the Dominion forces.

An important resolution was unanimously agreed to at the last session of the War Cabinet, to the effect that meetings of an Imperial Cabinet should be held annually or at any intermediate times when matters of urgent Imperial concern required to be settled, and that the Imperial Cabinet should consist of the Prime Minister of the United Kingdom and such of his colleagues as dealt specially with Imperial affairs, of the Prime Minister of each of the Dominions or some specially accredited alternate possessed of equal authority, and of a representative of the Indian people to be appointed by the Government of India. The exact significance of the War Cabinet as an institution was explained by the Prime Minister in the House of Commons on May 17; it was intended that the responsible heads of the Governments of the Empire ' should meet together at regular intervals to confer about foreign policy and matters connected therewith, and come to decisions in regard to them which, subject to the control of their own Parliaments, they will then severally execute'. What further developments might arise it was left to the future to decide, ' the whole question of perfecting the mechanism for continuous consultation about Imperial and foreign affairs ' being reserved for the consideration of a special conference to meet after the termination of the war to readjust the constitutional relations of the Empire. Sir Robert Borden, in an address on April 3 to the Empire Parliamentary Association, laid great stress on the equality of the Dominions with the United Kingdom in the deliberations of the Cabinet; the First Minister of the United Kingdom presided over its proceedings, but only as *primus inter pares*; each nation preserved unimpaired its perfect autonomy, its self-government, and the responsibility of ministers to its own electorate.

After the meetings of the Imperial War Cabinet had terminated, in June 1917, the Prime Minister invited General Smuts to attend the meetings of the War Cabinet of the United Kingdom during his stay in the United Kingdom, which he consented to prolong for this purpose. The position of General Smuts during the remainder of his stay in England until 1919 was somewhat anomalous. He was not acting as a representative of the Union of South Africa in the strict sense of the term ; on the other hand he was not a minister of the United Kingdom without portfolio, and was not described officially as a member of the War Cabinet, though he attended its meetings.

The Imperial War Cabinet, after an interval of over a year, reassembled on June 11, 1918, at a crisis in the fortunes of the allies.[1] The United Kingdom was represented by the Prime Minister, the members of the War Cabinet, the Secretaries of State for Foreign Affairs, the Colonies, War, and the Royal Air Force, and the First Lord of the Admiralty. Canada sent Sir R. Borden and Mr. N. W. Rowell, President of the Privy Council ; Australia Mr. Hughes and Sir J. Cook ; New Zealand, as in 1917, Mr. Massey and Sir J. Ward ; the Union of South Africa General Smuts and Mr. H. Burton ; and Newfoundland its new Premier, Mr. W. F. Lloyd. India, on this occasion, was represented not merely by the Secretary of State for India, with assessors, as in 1917, but by the Secretary of State, and Mr. S. P. Sinha, Member of the Executive Council of the Governor of Bengal, as representative of the Indian people, while the Maharaja of Patiala attended as the spokesman of the Princes of India.

The Cabinet, which held its first meetings at the moment when the German offensive had gained its way to the Marne, did not terminate until the tide had definitely turned, the German offensive had been checked, and the great allied counter-offensive was well under way. The discussions, therefore, which began with the anxious investigation of military problems, were gradually turned to questions of foreign policy and the war aims for which the British Commonwealth was fighting. It is also definitely

[1] *Parl. Pap.* Cmd. 325, pp. 7–11.

recorded that not only did the oversea members of the Imperial War Cabinet help to determine the line of policy to be adopted by the British Government at the important session of the Allied Supreme War Council at Versailles in July, but they were actually present [1] at one meeting of the Council on July 5.

The meetings of the Cabinet led to two important decisions as to constitutional practice. In the first place, the Prime Minister of the United Kingdom readily conceded what had been suggested but dropped at the Imperial Conference of 1911, the right of the Dominion Prime Ministers as his colleagues on the Cabinet to communicate direct with him ; such communications were, it was agreed, appropriate only to questions of Cabinet importance, but the Prime Ministers were to be the judges of what questions should thus be treated. Moreover, while it was agreed that telegraphic communications should normally be sent through the machinery of the Colonial Office, this arrangement was not to exclude the adoption of more direct means of communication in exceptional circumstances, a concession which was obviously essential if the right of direct communication were not to become nugatory. In the second place, in order to secure continuity in the work of the Imperial Conference, and a permanent means of consultation during the war on the more important questions of common interest, the Prime Minister of each Dominion was accorded the right to nominate a Cabinet minister, either as a resident or visitor in London, to represent him at meetings of the Imperial War Cabinet to be held regularly between the plenary sessions, and it was also arranged that India should be represented on such occasions. This arrangement was a revival adapted to the altered circumstances of the suggestion made by Mr. Asquith's Government in 1912 that in order to keep the Dominions in touch with the Imperial Government each Dominion should depute a minister to reside in London who should have free access to the Prime Minister, the Secretary of State for Foreign Affairs, and other ministers in order to discuss questions of common interest and to acquire full information on the aims and tendencies of the foreign policy. That proposal, as has been seen, received but a cold

[1] Not, of course, as full members. The Council included only two British members ; see *The Times History of the War*, xvii. 182.

reception at the hands of the Dominion Governments, though after the death of Lord Strathcona, the Canadian Government sent to represent them in London a minister who remained a member of the Dominion Cabinet, and the new arrangement never came into operation through the rapid progress of events.

The meetings of the Imperial War Cabinet terminated at the end of July when the Prime Ministers dispersed in order to return to their Dominions. Those Dominion representatives who remained for a time in England[1] attended several meetings of the British War Cabinet, but the further development of the arrangement agreed to by the Imperial War Cabinet was precluded by the swift collapse of German power. As soon as its imminence was realized, warning was sent on October 27 to the Prime Ministers of the Dominions of the necessity of their early return to England to take part in the discussion between the allies as to the peace settlement. By November 20 the meetings of the third session of the Imperial War Cabinet had begun, though representatives of New Zealand and India were lacking, and General Botha arrived to represent the Union of South Africa only on December 16. On December 3 the Imperial War Cabinet had an important conference with M. Clemenceau and Marshal Foch, representing France, and with Signor Orlando and Baron Sonnino, representing Italy, and both before and after Christmas meetings took place with President Wilson. It was during this session of the Cabinet that general agreement was arrived at on the policy to be adopted in the discussions at the Peace Conference proper.

With the removal to Paris of the Prime Ministers in January 1919 and the recognition of the separate representation of the Dominions at the Peace Conference a new stage was opened in Imperial relations, markedly diminishing the unity achieved in the Imperial War Cabinet. The exact nature of the Cabinet as it existed before this change took place is well indicated in a speech made by Sir Robert Borden to the Empire Parliamentary Association on June 21, 1918, in which he explained that the

[1] Mr. Hughes did not return to Australia, and General Smuts continued to attend War Cabinet meetings.

summoning of the Cabinet in 1917 marked an epoch in the history of the Empire. Prior to that date the Dominions had lacked full national status, because the British Government exercised a trustee-ship for the Dominions in respect of foreign affairs, which was sometimes exercised without much consultation of their Govern-ments. That state of affairs had disappeared, since the Govern-ments of the Dominions had been admitted to the discussion on equal terms with the British Government of matters of common interest, and above all foreign affairs. Answering the objection that the term ' Cabinet ' as applied to such an assembly was a misnomer, he dwelt on the fact that the term had changed in significance from time to time, and there was no incongruity in its application to a meeting of ministers to debate and determine the various needs of the Empire. ' If I should attempt to describe it,' he added, ' I should say it is a Cabinet of Governments. Every Prime Minister who sits around that board is responsible to his own Parliament and to his own people ; the conclusions of the War Cabinet can only be carried out by the Parliaments of the different nations of our Imperial Commonwealth. Thus each Dominion, each nation, retains its perfect autonomy. I venture to believe, and I thus expressed myself last year, that in this may be found the genesis of a development of the constitutional relations of the Empire which will form the basis of its unity in the years to come.' The Prime Minister of New Zealand expressed his sense of the importance of the arrangement in a speech in the New Zealand Parliament on November 7, in which he laid especial stress on the proposal for the appointment of a resident minister in London with the right of sitting on the Imperial War Cabinet, and after the war the Imperial Cabinet. This meant, in his view, that the Imperial Cabinet, instead of meeting once a year, could be convened whenever there was business for it to do. Such a plan was preferable to any attempt to force through a system of federation for the Empire. Sir Joseph Ward also welcomed the scheme as a prelude to that federation which as in 1911 he considered to be the inevitable goal of the Empire.

Although Sir R. Borden's defence of the terminology applied to the new institution is ingenious, it may be doubted whether the application of the name ' Cabinet ' has not been misleading, even to some of those who participated in its proceedings.[1] It has been regarded as an Executive Government of the whole Empire, exercising in respect of the Empire the same functions as are exercised by the Cabinet of the United Kingdom in respect of the British Isles. The divergences between the two institutions, are, however, as important as the similarities ; the Imperial War Cabinet had no Prime Minister ; the President was only a *primus inter pares* ; its members sat not by virtue of his selection but as representing their own Dominions. There was no collective responsibility ; each representative had to answer to his own Parliament. There was no possibility of majority decisions ; matters agreed to by the Dominion representatives were accepted subject to the concurrence of their colleagues and the approval of their Parliaments, and failure to carry them out involved no penalty, such as would await a member of a British Cabinet who declined to comply with a Cabinet decision. Nor in any exact sense of the term was the Imperial War Cabinet an executive body. If the members of the British War Cabinet who were also, as a matter of course, members of the Imperial body, adopted a course of action after consultation with the Dominion representatives, it was open to them to have the matter carried into effect, in so far as it could be done without fresh legislation, by the issue of orders to the British departments of state who had the requisite means to carry out what was ordered. Thus, so far as the Cabinet was able to arrive at decisions on military movements after the constitution of a single allied command in March 1918, it was possible to make them effective by directions issued through the responsible minister of the British Government. As the forces of the Dominions had come by arrangements with their Governments under the control of the British Government, consultation at the Imperial War Cabinet in some measure served the purpose of giving the Dominions a share in the direction of the movements of their own forces. But the ultimate decision and the legal power of control alike rested with the British Government. Similarly executive action in the Dominions could be taken only

[1] Cf. *The Times History of the War*, xii. 298–304 ; *The Round Table*, vii. 452–6, 836–40 ; Keith, *Canadian Law Times*, xxxviii. 495–505 ; J. S. Ewart, *Kingdom Papers*, i. 268 ff. ; G. M. Wrong, *Canada and the Imperial War Cabinet* (1920).

by the authority of the Dominion Government concerned, and the Dominion Prime Ministers were not in a position to secure such action save through representations to their colleagues sufficient to secure their approval of the steps proposed.

In effect, therefore, the Imperial War Cabinet differed in no essential respect from the Imperial War Conferences which were held contemporaneously, meetings of the two bodies usually alternating during the first two sessions of the Imperial War Cabinet. The real distinction between the two bodies lay not in their powers, but in the nature of the questions discussed ; the Cabinet dealt only, like the British War Cabinet, with the most important aspects of the war and the possible terms of peace, while the Conference was concerned with various questions regarding the less important aspects of the war, and a few topics of some interest but not of first-class rank, not immediately concerned with the war. The comparatively secondary nature of the proceedings of the Conference was signalized by the absence from its deliberations of the Prime Minister, whose place was taken by the Secretary of State for the Colonies by derogation from the normal constitution of the Imperial Conference.

The essentially war character of the Imperial Cabinet left it without any clear *raison d'être* as soon as the conclusion of the peace negotiations left the Dominion ministers at liberty to return to their Dominions. The resolution of 1918 regarding the right of the Prime Ministers to appoint ministers to attend in their place any meetings of the Imperial Cabinet, which might be summoned, was, indeed, technically in being ; practically it remained a dead letter through the failure of any one of the Dominions to take advantage of its terms. Nor was this unnatural ; the prospect of the holding of a special conference on the constitutional issue, at first projected for 1920, then postponed by agreement until 1921, and later further delayed,[1] rendered it needless to insist on perpetuating without fuller discussion an arrangement agreed to under emergency conditions which had disappeared, and one moreover which, through various causes, had never actually come into formal operation.

[1] Mr. Bonar Law, House of Commons, November 17, 1920. Cf. below, Chap. VI, § 5.

2. THE IMPERIAL WAR CONFERENCE OF 1917

The meetings of the Imperial War Conference of 1917 [1] fell
between March 21 and April 27, and the most important part of
their proceedings, dealing as it did with matters immediately
affecting the war, was kept secret.   Of those resolutions which
were made public the most important was that on the constitution
of the Empire, on April 16 :

' The Imperial War Conference are of opinion that the readjustment of the constitutional arrangements of the component
parts of the Empire is too important and intricate a subject to be
dealt with during the war, and that it should form the subject of
a special Imperial Conference to be summoned as soon as possible
after the cessation of hostilities.[2]

They deem it their duty, however, to place on record their
view that any such readjustment, while thoroughly preserving all
existing powers of self-government and complete control of
domestic affairs, should be based upon a full recognition of the
Dominions as autonomous nations of an Imperial Commonwealth,
and of India as an important portion of the same, should recognize
the right of the Dominions and India to an adequate voice in
foreign policy and in foreign relations, and should provide
effective arrangements for continuous consultation in all important
matters of common Imperial concern, and for such necessary concerted action, founded on consultation, as the several governments
may determine.'

The debate which preceded the passing of the Resolution was
interesting in the clearness with which it revealed the determination of the Dominion statesmen to achieve equality of status for
the Dominions.   Sir Robert Borden admitted that in the main
the old predominance of the Imperial Government and Parliament
had passed away, though he mentioned that during the war a case
had arisen of divergence of view as to whether a prerogative of
the Crown was to be exercised by the Governor-General in accordance with the wish of the Imperial Government or that of the
Dominion Government.   General Smuts was even more emphatic

---

[1] *Parl. Pap.* Cd. 8566. In Cd. 8673 are given discussions as to the admission
of Canadian live cattle to the United Kingdom, which, refused originally on grounds
of risk of disease, is now withheld as a matter of protection.

[2] This Conference is still uncertain as to date.

on the necessity of the change. 'Whatever we may say,' he argued, 'and whatever we may think, we are subject provinces of Great Britain. That is the actual theory of the constitution, and in many ways which I need not specify to-day,[1] that theory still permeates practice to some extent.' The Resolution recognized that all this must be ended, and it very wisely added that all existing powers of self-government must be respected in any new arrangements. It followed that 'one theory, one proposed solution of our future constitutional relations, is negatived by this Resolution. If this Resolution is passed, then one possible solution is negatived, and that is the federal solution.' The federal solution, he maintained, would lead to disaster when the nations proposed to be federated were spread over the whole world, speaking different languages, and belonging to different races with entirely different economic circumstances. The experiment of federal government in America had been a success, but, apart from possibilities of doubt as to its future, the circumstances were different in vital respects; there was on the one hand half a continent with a compact population developing along common lines, on the other young nations growing each in its own way to be great powers. The only future for such nations was autonomy with unity of action engendered by continuous consultation and interchange of ideas, and this could be brought about, whether through the machinery of the Imperial Cabinet suggested by Sir Robert Borden or in some other equally effective way. For the federal solution as ultimately necessary for the unity of the Empire, a plea was put in by Sir Joseph Ward, who insisted that a necessary preliminary to any such result must be the setting up of separate legislatures for the different parts of the British Islands, in order to relieve the United Kingdom Parliament of a congestion already serious, and one likely to be increased by the grant of female suffrage.

Pending the reconstruction of Imperial relations, the Conference agreed to recommend the modification of the Resolution of the Colonial Conference of 1907 so as to permit of the representation of India at future Imperial Conferences, and a further

[1] See Keith, *Imperial Unity*, pp. 589-92. Cf. General Smuts, *The British Commonwealth of Nations* (1917).

concession was made to Indian sentiment by the acceptance of the principle of reciprocity in the treatment of Dominion subjects in India and Indian subjects in the Dominions.[1] They agreed also in the principle that there should be uniformity of policy and action with regard to naturalization throughout the Empire, and commended a memorandum by the Home Office to the consideration of the Dominion Governments.

The question of Naval Defence led to a Resolution requesting the Admiralty to work out immediately after the war what they considered the most effective scheme of naval defence for the Empire for the consideration of the several Governments summoned to the Conference, with such recommendations as the Admiralty considered necessary in that respect for the Empire's future security. They also pronounced in favour of the assimilation of the military stores and equipment of the military forces of the Empire, and urged that the ordnance personnel of these forces should be trained on the same method and according to the same principles. To effect these ends they recommended the appointment of an expert committee to consider patterns of equipment, and the attachment of selected officers from the various parts of the Empire for adequate periods to the Imperial Ordnance Department. Stress was also laid on the importance of developing an adequate capacity of production of naval and military material, munitions, and supplies in all parts of the Empire, including the countries bordering on the Pacific and Indian Ocean where such facilities did not exist. Measures were urged upon the British Government in order to secure more adequate protection against the temptations to which Dominion soldiers while on leave in England were exposed. Gratitude was expressed to France for her action in allotting in perpetuity the land in which British soldiers were buried, and the King was requested to constitute by royal charter an Imperial War Graves Commission in accordance with the scheme drawn up by the Prince of Wales in a memorandum to the Prime Minister of March 15. The Commission, when constituted, was asked to draw up an estimate of the probable cost of the work entrusted to their care, and to submit it to the Imperial and Dominion Governments with their

[1] See below, Chap. XII.

recommendations as to the mode in which the cost should be shared. Due provision was made in the Charter for the representation on the Commission of the whole of the Empire.

The Resolutions on trade were in the main directly prompted by the war. The most important adopted the principle of Imperial Preference :

' The time has arrived when all possible encouragement should be given to the development of Imperial resources, and especially to making the Empire independent of other countries in respect of food supplies, raw materials, and essential industries. With these objects in view this Conference expresses itself in favour of :

(1) The principle that each part of the Empire, having due regard to the interests of our allies, shall give specially favourable treatment and facilities to the produce and manufactures of other parts of the Empire.

(2) Arrangements by which intending emigrants from the United Kingdom may be induced to settle in countries under the British flag.'

The Conference reported also in favour of placing restrictions on importations from enemy countries for twelve months after the war, in order to prevent dumping or other unfair modes of competition by these countries. In connexion with the development of natural resources in the Empire they recommended for the consideration of the Governments concerned the questions of the production of an adequate food supply and arrangements for its transportation when and where required under any conditions that might reasonably be anticipated ; the control of natural resources available within the Empire, especially those that were of an essential character for necessary national purposes, whether in peace or in war ; and the economical utilization of such natural resources through processes of manufacture carried on within the Empire. It was agreed to recommend the creation of an Imperial Mineral Resources Bureau charged with the duty of collecting information as to the mineral resources of the Empire and of advising as to the development of such resources. Satisfaction was also expressed at the decision of the Board of Trade to extend the system of Trade Commissioners charged with assisting the development of inter-imperial trade, and the Dominion Governments were advised to co-operate with the Board of Trade in making the project a success. Various proposals as to patents and trade marks, rendered a burning question by the war, were considered, and agreement was reached in favour of the consideration after the war of the vexed question of double income tax which, through the increase of rates of taxation throughout the Empire, had become a matter of serious concern both to British firms carrying on business in the Dominions and to private individuals resident in the United Kingdom who drew their income from monies invested in the Dominions or depended on remittances from the Dominions.

3. THE IMPERIAL WAR CONFERENCE OF 1918

The Conference of 1918 held its meetings between June 12 and July 26, usually alternating with meetings of the Imperial War Cabinet. As in 1917 much of its proceedings were kept secret, and none of those which were published equalled in importance the constitutional pronouncement of 1917. A discussion of some length took place on the channel of communication between the Dominions and the Imperial Government consequent on the altered status allotted to them, which rendered communication through the Colonial Office no longer suitable. It was pointed out by the Secretary of State for the Colonies that it would not be practicable for the Prime Minister to undertake the immense burden of controlling all communications with the Dominions, and that the position of the Governors-General should not be overlooked. But he admitted that it was not to be thought that the existing arrangements should stand indefinitely, and in the result it was referred to the Imperial War Cabinet to decide the matter in the manner mentioned above.[1] The Conference also reiterated and amplified its declaration of 1917 on the question of the treatment of British Indians in the Dominions and vice versa. On the question of naturalization it was agreed that a special Conference should be summoned to examine questions of naturalization in the light of the resolution in favour of uniformity passed

---

[1] See above, p. 31.

in 1917. But the further proposal that it was desirable that for a period of years after the war subjects of former enemy countries should not be permitted to become naturalized or to acquire any political rights or obtain privileges as to lands or mines was coldly received by the Dominion of Canada,[1] which abstained from voting, while the representatives of the Union of South Africa formally dissented. At the instance of Mr. Hughes the question of the creation of an Imperial Court of Appeal on which he had prepared a memorandum in 1916 in anticipation of the Conference of 1917 at which he was unable to be present, was discussed, but no progress towards agreement was made and the matter was allowed to stand over for a future Conference.[2]

The prospect of demobilization, rendered imminent by the British and allied successes on the western front, was the cause of the passing of a Resolution in favour of the establishment of an advisory and executive committee, known as the Military Demobilization Committee of the British Empire, consisting of representatives of the Dominions and Colonies, the War Office, the India Office, and the Ministry of Shipping, charged with the duty of considering all military questions of demobilization affecting the Governments concerned. The Committee was empowered to take decisions in matters of detail, to submit questions of principle to the Governments affected, and to arrange for the fullest interchange of information regarding plans for demobilization. Appreciation was expressed of the labours of the Imperial War Graves Commission, which had been granted a royal charter in accordance with the recommendations of the Conference of 1917, and it was agreed that the cost of its operations should be defrayed by the Governments concerned in proportion to the number of graves of their dead.

Much consideration was given to the important question of securing for the Empire after the conclusion of hostilities adequate supplies of raw materials, and for the supply of raw materials to allied countries on a basis of reciprocity. The terms of the Imports and Exports (Temporary Control) Bill then before the Imperial

---

[1] Because of the holding of land by aliens already settled in Canada ; see the Dominion Lands Act Amendment Act, 1919, and Naturalization Act, 1920.

[2] See below, Chap. X, § 8.

Parliament were examined,[1] but it was recognized that no uniformity of action would be possible and instead it was agreed that the Governments concerned should discuss with representatives of the trades concerned the best means of obtaining command of the essential supplies. It was also agreed that the report of the Committee on Raw Materials, which was laid before the Conference, should be communicated to the Dominion and Indian Governments in order to ascertain their views on the appropriate steps to be taken, and that the allied powers should be asked to state their needs and resources in regard to the materials dealt with in the report. A memorandum on the subject of petroleum was laid before the Conference which, having regard to the great and growing importance of petroleum and its products for naval, military, and industrial purposes, recommended the memorandum to the careful consideration of the Governments concerned. In pursuance of the policy of freeing the Empire from dependence on German-controlled organizations in respect of non-ferrous metal and ores, the Conference endorsed the principle of the Non-ferrous Metal Industry Act, 1918, of the United Kingdom, and recommended the adoption by the other Governments of the Empire of effective measures to carry out the policy. Explanations were given to the Conference of the steps already taken, and the further measures contemplated by the Government to free the industry of the United Kingdom from dependence on German dyestuffs, and the Conference agreed to recommend co-operation by the other Governments of the Empire with the Imperial Government in its efforts to promote the development of the dye industry in the British Empire and thus to free British industry from enemy domination. A memorandum by the Minister of Reconstruction on the constitution of an Imperial Mineral Resources Bureau as agreed upon at the Conference of 1917 was laid before the Conference, which approved the proposal that a royal charter of incorporation should be applied for, agreed to the suggested allocation of expenditure, and concurred in the increase of the number of members of the mineral, mining, and metal industries on the Governing Body of the Bureau from four to six. The Conference also accepted a proposal brought forward by the Colonial Office for the establishment of a Bureau of Mycology, to deal with

[1] This measure failed to become law in the United Kingdom.

questions affecting fungoid diseases of plants, thus supplementing the work of the Bureau of Entomology established in 1909.

Much attention was paid by the Conference to the question of inter-imperial communications, raised on the initiative of the Board of Trade. It was agreed that, in order to maintain satisfactorily the connexions and at the same time to encourage commercial and industrial relations between the several parts of the Empire, shipping between the United Kingdom and the Dominions and India should be brought under review by an inter-imperial board on which the United Kingdom, the Dominions, and dependencies should be represented. For this purpose the appointment of an Imperial Investigation Board was approved, with power to inquire into and report on all matters connected with ocean freights and facilities, and on all matters connected with the development and improvement of sea communications between the different parts of the Empire with special reference to the size and type of ships and the capacities of harbours, the Board to include, in addition to representatives of the Governments concerned, persons with an expert knowledge of the problems involved, including representatives of the trading and shipping interests. The Board of Trade also submitted proposals for the enlargement, improvement, and co-ordination of facilities for parcel deliveries between the United Kingdom and the various parts of the Empire, and the Conference commended the scheme to the examination of the Governments concerned. Great stress was also laid on the necessity of the material reduction of cable rates between the United Kingdom, Canada, Australia, South Africa, and India, and the United Kingdom, Canada, Australia, and New Zealand were urged, in order to secure the cheapest and most reliable telegraphic communication, to co-operate in the acquisition of a state-owned Atlantic cable. Favourable consideration was also given to a memorandum by the Minister of Information in which stress was laid on the necessity of securing from British sources an adequate news service for all parts of the Empire, and the Imperial Government was commissioned to formulate a scheme on the basis indicated in the memorandum, and to submit it for the consideration of the Dominion Governments. The question of statistics, which was dealt with in the Report of the Dominions Royal

Commission, elicited a recommendation in favour of the holding of a Conference of Statisticians after the war, at which there should be considered the establishment of an Imperial Statistical Bureau.

The Conference reaffirmed their resolution of 1917 in favour of encouraging emigrants from the United Kingdom to settle within the Empire, and favoured the establishment of a consultative committee on which Dominion representatives should sit, as the best means of keeping the Dominions in touch with the organization set up by the Imperial Government to supervise emigration.

The effect given to the resolutions was more rapid and complete than is normally the case with conference resolutions. The Imperial Mineral Resources Bureau was duly incorporated by royal charter in June 1918, its personnel was completed in July, and by 1919 it had already accomplished a considerable amount of useful work. The Bureau of Mycology was also brought into being, and after considerable delay a Commission to investigate questions of shipping came into being in 1920. The most striking sequel to the Conference, however, was the decision of the Imperial Government to carry into effect the principle of Imperial preference approved in 1917 and enforced by the resolutions of 1918. The Finance Act, 1919, adopted the principle of according a reduction of one-sixth of the duty on tea, coffee, chicory, currants, dried or preserved fruit, sugar, glucose, molasses, saccharin, motor spirit, and tobacco ; of one-third of the duty on motor cars, musical instruments, clocks, watches, &c., and cinematograph films ; of 40 per cent. on wines not exceeding 30 degrees of proof spirit and $33\frac{1}{3}$ per cent. on wines exceeding 30 degrees. Reductions were also allowed on the additional duties imposed on wines, and no increase was made in the rates on spirits the produce of the Empire, while large increases of duty were imposed on foreign spirits. The new policy, though it had been recommended for adoption by a Committee in 1917 [1] before the meeting of the Imperial War Conference, met with strong opposition from supporters of free trade principles, and some annoyance was caused in the Dominions through the conversion of the matter into a party issue. In the finance legislation of 1920 the same policy was adopted, and again strong protests were elicited from the opposition, who con-

[1] *Parl. Pap.* Cd. 8472.

tended that the value of the preference was slight to the Dominions, and that it could only be made of value to them by violation of the policy of freeing food and raw material imports from taxation other than that absolutely essential for revenue purposes, which had been laid down in the manifesto issued by the Prime Minister and the leader of the House of Commons before the general election of 1918.

Control of emigration from the United Kingdom, so as to divert it from foreign countries to the Dominions, is regarded as impracticable by the Imperial Government, but the reorganization of the Emigrants' Information Office into the Overseas Settlement Committee indicates an increased realization of the importance of directing British emigration to settlement within the Empire.[1] Substantial assistance has also been provided to aid ex-service men and women to proceed to the Dominions, and in many cases effective co-operation between local authorities and the Committee has been established. A Statistical Conference met in 1920,[2] and by the Finance Acts of 1919 and 1920 substantial relief against double income tax was given.

But of far greater importance was one sequel of the Conference of 1918 which was foreshadowed on July 26, when the members of the Conference presented in person to His Majesty a loyal address assuring the King of the determination of the British people to maintain the Empire ' against a barbarous and perfidious enemy without, while drawing closer within the bonds which tie each part to the rest in a unity of which the Throne is the outward and visible symbol'. In his reply the King alluded to the hope he had expressed in the preceding year that his children would follow in the footsteps of the Queen and himself in acquiring the priceless experience of visiting the Dominions, and assured the Conference that the Prince of Wales contemplated with eagerness the prospect of visiting the Dominions whenever the cessation of war rendered this possible. Effect was given to this aspiration in 1919 when the Prince proceeded to Canada, and in the following year when he travelled

---

[1] *Parl. Pap.* Cmd. 573. A Bill of 1918 to supervise emigration agencies was unhappily worded and had to be withdrawn, Agents-General protesting that their propaganda work might be penalized.

[2] *Parl. Pap.* Cmd. 648. Dominion delegates also took part in Entomological and Forestry Conferences.

widely in Australia and New Zealand. The welcome which was extended everywhere to His Royal Highness was beyond expectation cordial. Labour in the Commonwealth had been suspicious and inclined to be hostile, but the spontaneous loyalty of the people was not affected by doctrinaire objections to monarchic institutions or capitalism. Not the least striking of the successes of the Australian tour was the visit to Queensland, where ministers and many of their supporters distinguished themselves during the war by sentiments the reverse of imperialistic. 'The Australian people', said Mr. Hughes, ' have taken the Prince to their hearts, and feel for him a strong personal affection, which, in these days of toppling Thrones in other lands, is the best assurance that the British Empire, unlike others that rest upon force, will endure throughout the ages.'

There is, it is certain, no possible doubt as to the significance and importance of the Crown as the point of unity in the Empire. The recognition of this aspect of the Throne is of comparatively recent origin, and is a clear indication of the growth of Dominion autonomy. The Dominions have come to claim and be accorded equal status within the Empire, and the sovereign therefore appears to them in a new light, not as part of a dominant Government, but as the symbol of a unity which depends ultimately on sentiment. If it were possible for the sovereign to pay periodic visits to the Dominions, the value of such a procedure would be extremely high, and, since public considerations in the present state of foreign and domestic affairs render the absence of the King from the British Isles a matter of extreme difficulty, the value of the visits of the Prince can hardly be exaggerated. Nor should it ever be forgotten that the respect commanded by the Crown is largely due to the recognition that the King has accepted with absolute loyalty the restrictions imposed on a constitutional monarch.

CHAPTER IV

THE ECONOMIC ACTIVITIES OF THE DOMINION GOVERNMENTS

1. CANADA AND NEWFOUNDLAND.

Contrast between Imperial and Dominion conditions — The Imperial Munitions Board — Co-operation of the Dominion Government — The War Trade Board — The Canadian Trade Missions — The Siberian Economic Commission — Encouragement of Agriculture — Control of food prices and cost of living — The Canada Food Board — Advisory Council for Scientific and Industrial Research — War Purchasing Commission — Governmental shipping policy — Dominion railway policy — Acquisition of the Canadian Northern Railway — Acquisition of the Grand Trunk Railway — Hudson Bay Railway — Newfoundland control of fish export industry — Prohibition.

2. AUSTRALASIA.

Queensland control of meat for the Imperial forces — Commonwealth arrangements for metal industries — The Australian Wheat Board — The Central Wool Committee — Other governmental trade activities — Commonwealth governmental shipping — State and Commonwealth control of food prices — The Railway War Council — New Zealand and Imperial purchases — Control of food prices — The mining industry — Prohibition.

3. SOUTH AFRICA.

Munitions — Wool — Control of food prices — Cost of Living Commission — Parliamentary Select Committee — The marketing of gold — The Commission on low-grade mines.

1. CANADA AND NEWFOUNDLAND

IN the United Kingdom the war evoked not merely the most remarkable development of the energies of the administration in the raising of troops for the front and for home defence, but it elicited also efforts on an unparalleled scale for the development of the productive activities of the country both as regards the output of munitions of war and the increase in the supply of food grown locally. The attempt to increase food production was seconded by a system of control of distribution and consumption of ever-increasing complexity and efficiency, which served in no small measure to provide that security with regard to food supplies on which rested confidence of the favourable termination of the war. In the Dominions, on the other hand, these problems never assumed the same importance, nor did they affect deeply the structure of the Dominion Governments.

In Canada alone were circumstances favourable for the development of munition industries on a large scale, and in this case the fact that the control of the movement was vested in the hands of a body created by and responsible to the Imperial and not the Dominion Government minimized the effects of the enterprise on the administration, despite its importance in the economic development of the Dominion. The other Dominions were without the necessary experience or material in the shape of factories for the production of munitions on a large scale, and, though they developed their local output to the best of their ability in order to make good the supplies which normally would have reached them from the United Kingdom, it was out of the question for them to make any serious attempt to produce for export, even if questions of shipping had not rendered such a course inexpedient. On the other hand the war increased the importance of the food exports of the Dominions and gave every incentive to increased production as at once profitable and patriotic, rendering it unnecessary for the Dominion Governments to take such direct steps as were adopted in the United Kingdom to secure an extension of the area of cereal cultivation. Two problems, however, arose which demanded their intervention : the profits of export were such as to induce serious increases in the cost of local supplies, which had to be encountered by measures intended to check the rise in the cost of living, and the importance of dealing effectively with local output led to the activity of the Governments in securing arrangements with the Imperial Government for the purchase of supplies on a wholesale scale.

At the outbreak of war Canadian manufacturers were wholly without experience in the manufacture of shrapnel and had never made a cartridge case or fuse, but shortly after hostilities commenced they were induced by the Imperial Government, acting through the Shell Commission, a body set up to secure Canadian co-operation, to undertake manufacture of munitions, and by the end of 1915 their exports amounted to over 57,000,000 dollars in value. The activities of Canada increased enormously in the three remaining years of the war under the control of the Imperial Munitions Board, which replaced the Shell Commission. The Board was essentially an Imperial body ; it was an integral part of the Ministry of Munitions, and was directly responsible to the Minister, while the Imperial Government accepted full financial responsibility for all its expenditure. Within the Board itself full authority and responsibility rested with the Chairman, Sir Joseph Flavelle, who was assisted by the other members of the Board whose functions were partly advisory, partly executive. The Board acted as sole purchasing agent not only for the Ministry of Munitions, but also for the War Office, the Admiralty, the British Timber Controller, and the Department of Aeronautics, while the Ordnance Department of the United States made use of its services in arranging contracts for munitions and supplies placed by the United States Government in Canada. The Board not merely let out contracts to existing firms; it promoted the creation of companies, whose stock it held, to operate national munition plants in Montreal, Renfrew, Trenton, Toronto, and Parry Sound, and a copper-refining plant was established, at a cost of 2,500,000 dollars, at Trail, British Columbia. Employment was given to from 250,000 to 300,000 persons, while 50,000 more were handling supplies or engaged in other indirect services to the Board. By the close of the war the national plants were making steel and forgings, cordite and cordite powder, acetone and methyl-ethyl, nitro-cellulose powder, gun cotton, and T.N.T., loading live fuses and producing shrapnel forgings, and turning out aeroplanes, including bombing planes for the United States navy. In 1918, despite grave difficulties as to labour, the Board launched 23 steel ships and 45 wooden vessels with a deadweight carrying capacity of 253,463 tons. The total exports of the Board for the war period reached over 1,012,000,000 dollars, and, when the armistice led to the winding up of the work, total orders of 1,300,000,000 dollars from the United Kingdom and 400,000,000 dollars from the United States had been entrusted to the Board.

In its operations the Board had the sympathetic approval of the Dominion Government, but in no degree fell under its control. An important step in furtherance of the activities of the Board was taken by the Power Comptroller of the Dominion, Sir Henry Drayton, on April 18, 1918, when an Order in Council was issued on his recommendation regulating the supply of electric power at Niagara to Canadian munition plants, United States munition plants, and contracts for industrial or lighting requirements in Canada, in order to secure that munition plants received a preference in all matters of supply. The labour question presented throughout a difficult problem ; indirectly aid was rendered by the Order in Council of April 4, 1918, which provided that every male person residing in the Dominion must be regularly engaged in some useful occupation, unless under 16 or over 60 years of age, a student in training, temporarily unemployed, physically unfit, or unable to obtain suitable work, while just before the armistice an Order in Council of October 11 enacted a code of rules regarding labour in war time, and prohibited strikes or lockouts for the period of the war.

The Dominion Government itself undertook in 1918 a closer supervision of the direction of industry in Canada in order to further production for war purposes. On February 8, a War Trade Board was created as a Sub-Committee of the War Committee of the Cabinet, though the only minister appointed to it was Sir George Foster, Minister of Trade and Commerce, who acted as Chairman. The Board was entrusted with the control of licences for export from Canada and import into Canada ; the supervision of industrial and commercial enterprises with a view to prevent waste of labour, of raw materials and products ; the direction of priority in the distribution of food, electrical energy, raw materials and partially finished products, and the investigation of the conditions of trade, industry, and production, other than the production of food. It was also required to make recommendations for the maintenance of the more essential industries, and for curtailing the use of fuel or electrical energy in the less essential industries. Its duties were to be carried out in co-operation with the Canadian War Mission at Washington and with the War Trade Board of the United States. The activities of the Board were of the highest importance in securing co-operation with the United States in matters of war supplies and in the utilization of the resources of the two countries in raw materials. Lists of prohibited and permitted imports were published, and the question of wool exports and imports was among the important issues disposed of by the Board.

The conclusion of the armistice evoked another important

step. Simultaneously with the departure of Sir George Foster for London in order to share in the peace negotiations, a Canadian Trade Mission under the chairmanship of Mr. Lloyd Harris, who had acted earlier in the year in a similar position at Washington, was dispatched to London in order to co-operate with the minister in advancing the interests of the Dominion during the period prior to the establishment of normal trade relations when British requirements in agricultural products and manufactures would largely be procured through governmental channels. To co-operate with the mission in London a Canadian Trade Commission was established on December 10 at Ottawa, authorized under Order in Council to act in the purchase of Canadian products for other governments, to distribute contracts or orders among Canadian producers, to confer with inter-allied Boards and other bodies, and to add to its numbers by appointing associate members from specific industries or groups of industries. Earlier in the year, on October 21, the Siberian Economic Commission had been appointed charged with the duty of co-operating with the allied powers in re-establishing the productive industries and re-organizing the commercial activities of Siberia, and of investigating local conditions as to transport, agriculture, trade, and finance with a view to the development of Canadian trade. The mission, however, was withdrawn in the following year on the failure of the allied effort to effect a political re-organization of Siberia.

The activities of the Dominion Government in the promotion of the agricultural industry were from the outset devoted to increased production for export, and became of greater intensity with the progress of the war. At the close of 1916 Sir George Foster had discussed with the Wheat Commission in London the purchase of the Canadian wheat crop of 1917, in view of the decision of the Imperial Government to guarantee home producers a minimum price and to acquire the surplus crop in Australia, India, and Egypt. Negotiations began between the two Governments in February 1917, but the first offer made by the Imperial Commission, through the Dominion Government, of 1·30 dollars a bushel was rejected on March 3 by the grain growers of the west and of Ontario, who declined to accept the suggestion that they should prefer patriotism to profit. Their position was strengthened by the decision of the Dominion Government, effected by Order in Council of April 16, under the War Measures Act, to accept the standing offer in the United States customs tariff of free import into that country of wheat, wheat flour, and semolina, from countries which permitted the similar entry of these products from the United States. This step, which had long been pressed on the Government by the Liberal opposition and the farming interests of the west, raised prices in Canada by opening an alternative to the British market, and encouraged further extension of production and immigration. The Government followed up their policy by the appointment on June 11 of a Board of Grain Supervisors to control the grain production and the trade in grain. It was empowered to fix grain prices on shipment from storage elevators, but not the price paid to farmers, to take grain from elevators without the consent of owners, to prevent the restriction of marketing, and to arrange sales to the British and Allied Governments. The prices fixed by the Board were 2·40 dollars for the remainder of the 1916 crop, 2·21 for 1917, and 2·24 for 1918, prices which undoubtedly conferred a great benefit on Canadian grain growers, while, if imposing a heavy burden on Imperial finances, they ensured a large export. The effecting of the necessary increase in production was facilitated in considerable measure by the operations of the Seed Purchasing Commission, which was appointed late in 1916 with headquarters at Regina, and which in 1917 purchased 829,000 bushels of seed wheat, and 408,000 bushels of seed oats for distribution to the farmers of the west and the east. In 1918 arrangements were made under an Order in Council of October 7 for loans at 7 per cent. through local banks to farmers in need of seed wheat and without means to purchase, the Government guaranteeing the principal and interest up to 5 per cent. on these advances, while another Order of November 28 instructed the Commission to requisition seed oats at three western points in view of the shortage of such seed.

The Government also intervened in the negotiations of the Imperial Commissioner who was sent to secure the Canadian output of cheese for the British Government, and the arrangements decided upon in May 1917 for the purchase of the output were facilitated by an advance of 40,000,000 dollars from the Dominion Government to finance the transaction. The Imperial Government also secured large supplies of bacon and other products, and the Live Stock Branch of the Department of Agriculture took measures to impress on the public the necessity of increasing the output of hogs and other forms of animal food, while it gave active assistance by arranging with the railway companies for the transport of cattle, sheep, and swine from points where feed was scarce to more favourable conditions. Efforts were also made by the Minister of Agriculture when in London in 1917 at the Imperial War Conference to induce the Imperial Government to permit the landing of live cattle from the Dominion in the United Kingdom, but all that was obtained was an admission that the exclusion of Canadian cattle could be justified only on grounds of agricultural policy, and not on the score of disease, the ground alleged for many years.[1] On the other hand the Imperial Government agreed to the formation by the Dominion Government of a Canadian Wool Commission, which was entrusted with the distribution of such amounts of Australasian wool as could be made available for the use of Canadian manufacturers, after meeting Imperial needs. In 1918 Imperial encouragement was given to flax production for manufacture into aeroplane linen.

The vast activity in agriculture, which raised the exports of its products from 251,569,000 dollars in 1914 to 740,456,000 dollars in 1918, resulted in the growth of food prices in Canada, where indignation was especially directed against the high profits earned by cold-storage companies. An Order in Council of June 16, 1917, accordingly provided for the appointment of a Food Controller, authorized, with the approval of the Governor in Council, to fix the prices of food, and the cost of its storage, distribution, and sale ; to provide for the conservation of food and the prevention of waste ; and to purchase, requisition, store, sell, and deliver food. It was at the instance of the Food Controller that the export of Canadian flour to the United States was prohibited by Order in Council of August 17, and various other regulations of similar character were enacted, but on January 24, 1918, the Food Controller resigned, and on February 11 the Canada Food Board was created, invested

[1] See *Parl. Pap.* Cd. 8673. The controversy was still being waged in 1921.

with the powers of the Food Controller, and placed under the control of the Minister of Agriculture. The Board was authorized to ascertain the food requirements of Canada and to facilitate the export of the surplus to the United Kingdom and to allied countries ; to direct the production, conservation, and distribution of foodstuffs in the interests of Canada and other British possessions and allied countries ; to co-operate with the Provincial Governments in co-ordinating the activities of all local bodies for these purposes, and to enter into agreements for the cultivation of idle land and to mobilize and utilize on a voluntary basis the farm labour resources of Canada. The co-operation of the Women's Organizations of Canada was invited at a Women's War Conference held on the initiative of the Dominion Government at Ottawa from February 28 to March 2.

The policy of the Board rejected the proposal of rationing, on the ground of the impossibility of making it effective in so vast an area of productive consumers and on the score of expense involved. On the other hand the use of grain in the making of liquor was forbidden and voluntary conservation was encouraged in every way ; millers were required to increase the percentage of flour extracted from wheat ; efforts were made to encourage the use of non-wheaten flours in Canada, despite popular objections ; the export of food suitable for consumption by livestock was prohibited ; manufacturers of food and public eating places were placed under control. The prices of milk, flour, bread, and sugar were regulated, and dealers' profits were limited by a series of Orders. Food in storage was commandeered and sold, if there was danger of deterioration. The necessity of meeting the United Kingdom demand for wheat in 1918 was recognized and effectively provided for by a series of measures under which control was taken of flour mills by the Board and their profits regulated ; and bakers and restaurants were put under licence and their profits limited. The use of sugar was limited ; hoarding of food was penalized. At the same time the Board favoured energetic efforts to attract labour to the land, and to encourage every form of production. In August 1918 it was estimated by the Board that wheat exports had been increased by 30 per cent. during twelve months of economy and increased production, that 200,000 barrels of flour had been saved monthly, and 100,000 tons of sugar had been saved in the year.

Important work was also done by the Advisory Council for Scientific and Industrial Research, whose first report was issued in October 1918, and bore evidence of wide activity. It dealt with such war topics as the production of flax suitable for making the linen required in aeroplanes ; munition plants and their post-war uses ; the production of industrial alcohol from wood and toluene from sulphite liquor, as well as with forestry questions and the vexed issue of salmon fishing in the Fraser River and in British Columbia waters,. the Council formulating the conclusion that, unless arrangements could be arrived at with the United States, the fish would be in danger of extinction.

Of greater importance was a body which, at first intended to direct the purchase of war supplies, became under an Order in Council of February 7, 1918, the purchasing authority for all supplies required by the Government. This body, the War Purchasing Department, represented one side of the endeavour of the Union Government in Canada to eliminate the evils of patronage from public life, which contemporaneously was carried out as regards civil servants by a measure placing the whole of the Outside Service of the Federal Civil Service under the control of the Civil Service Commission, whose authority had hitherto in the main been restricted to the civil servants at Ottawa. Under the new arrangement as to purchases all stores had to be obtained through the Commission, save as regards supplies for the Government railways, articles of small value which might be urgently required from time to time at places distant from Ottawa, and special purchases where the provisions of the Order could not be fulfilled without detriment to the public interest.

While the Imperial Munitions Board was concerned with the production of ships for the Imperial Government, the Union Government in Canada announced through the Minister of Marine on January 4, 1918, an imposing policy of construction of ships on Government account, intended partly as a contribution to the solution of the problem of wartime transportation, and partly as a means of furthering Canadian trade interests at the close of the war. On the return of peace the ships were to be operated in conjunction with the governmental railway system. All the existing ship yards were to be brought into full operation, and a mill for the production of steel plates was immediately to be provided at Sydney, Nova Scotia. The estimated total of the expenditure to be undertaken was placed at 50,000,000 to 60,000,000 dollars. Not until December 3, 1918, was the first ship of the governmental fleet launched at Montreal, but by the close of 1919 15 further ships had been delivered, and the total ready or under construction had risen to 60 with a tonnage of about 350,000. The working of the fleet is in the hands of the Canadian National Railways, and a wide range of services has been undertaken.

The importance of this enterprise in maritime transport was largely enhanced by the steps taken by the Union Government to extend widely the control of the Government over the Canadian railway system. The way for such action had been paved by the events of the war, which added enormously to the cost of operating the railways without securing them adequate returns.[1] In 1916 the Dominion Government found it necessary to afford special aid to the Grand Trunk Pacific and the Canadian Northern Railway in order to enable them to meet current obligations and payments of interest. A Royal Commission was accordingly appointed to inquire into the whole question of railway transport, including questions of re-organization or state acquisition. The majority of the Commission, Sir Henry Drayton, Chairman of the Railway Commission of Canada, and Mr. W. M. Acworth of London, reported in favour of the transfer of the three great lines, the Canadian Pacific, the Grand Trunk Railway, and the Canadian Northern Railway, together with the Inter-colonial and the National Trans-continental Railways, to the control of an independent Board of Trustees, which should be constituted on a permanent, non-political, self-perpetuating basis, exempt from direct governmental or Parliamentary control, while the Government should assume responsibility to this body for the interest on the existing securities of the railways. The minority report, by Mr. A. H. Smith, President of the New York Central

---

[1] An increase of 5 per cent. only was allowed by the Dominion Railway Commission in 1916 ; further increases of 15 and 20 per cent. took place in 1918.

Railway Co., deprecated the proposal and suggested in lieu detailed reforms in the working of the lines.   Public opinion, however, especially in the west, manifested itself strongly in favour of the principle of nationalization, and the Government on August 1, 1917, intimated that they had decided not to interfere with the Canadian Pacific Railway, which was completely solvent ; to assist the Grand Trunk Railway, which, in itself sound, was hampered by liabilities arising from the Grand Trunk Pacific, by a loan ; and to acquire by purchase at a price not exceeding 10,000,000 dollars the 600,000 shares of capital stock of the Canadian Northern Railway, which were still in private hands or pledged as security for loans, thus obtaining the full ownership of the Company, the remainder of whose stock had been in the possession of the Government since 1914.   The Bill was resisted stoutly by the Liberal opposition but was carried through both houses on a party vote.   The arbitration to decide the value of the shares was held next year, and in September the railway passed finally into Government hands.   On November 19 an Order in Council united all the Government railways, the Canadian Northern, the Inter-colonial, the National Trans-continental, and a number of minor lines, with a total mileage of 13,700, under the presidency of Mr. D. B. Hanna, and a Board of Directors.

In the meantime negotiations had been proceeding between the Government and the Grand Trunk Railway, the former desiring to secure the railway by purchase, the latter hoping to obtain advances to enable it to surmount the difficulties of the war period, since the control of rates by the Government prevented it recouping itself for increased working costs by higher charges. Nothing came from these discussions and in 1918 the Government under the War Measures Act appointed the Minister of Railways as Receiver of the Grand Trunk Pacific Railway.   The final settlement of the whole matter was completed in October 1919 when the Government carried through Parliament its proposals for the purchase of the Grand Trunk Railway system, the preference and ordinary stocks to be paid for at a rate decided by arbitration, while the Government undertook the liabilities of the Company in respect of its guaranteed 4 per cent. stock and its debentures.

A Committee of Management was agreed upon, two members to be appointed by the Grand Trunk, two by the Government, and the fifth by the other four members, and the Grand Trunk and the Canadian National Railways were to be operated as nearly as possible as one system. The mileage thus definitely brought into the Government system was 6,508 in Canada and 1,665 in the United States, representing the joint amount of the Grand Trunk and the Grand Trunk Pacific. The new lines were amalgamated with the existing lines under the Canadian National Railways Co., a corporation formed by statute for the purpose of operating all the railways under federal control. Of minor importance, but also of value was the steady progress made during 1918 in the completion of the Hudson Bay Railway, connecting the newly-created harbour of Port Nelson with the wheat fields of the west, and reducing the route from Saskatoon to Liverpool, during the short season of navigation, from 1,489 land miles and 3,359 sea miles to 697 land miles and 2,966 sea miles, with an important reduction in cost of export as well as a welcome relief to the congestion of transport eastwards.

The successful operation of the systems in 1918 both for war transport and domestic purposes was largely due to the control exercised by the Canadian Railway War Board, whose management greatly strengthened the case for nationalization.[1] The urgent problem of conservation of fuel for railway and domestic use was entrusted in 1917 to a Fuel Controller, whose powers were greatly increased in 1918.

In Newfoundland governmental activities during the war period were mainly concerned with measures to secure the food supply which, especially in February 1918, was menaced by losses of shipping. The more important step was taken, especially after the armistice, of endeavouring to control scientifically the disposal of the output of the Newfoundland fisheries, the means adopted including regulations for the grading of fish according to quality; the imposition of restrictions on the amounts to be exported to the various countries which consumed fish; and the making of arrangements by the Government as to the prices to be demanded for the fish. These measures, interfering as they

[1] See the Toronto *Globe*, January 2, 1919.

did largely with the freedom of action hitherto possessed by the fishermen and exporters, were not altogether popular, and, while successful at first when competition from other sources of supply was absent or reduced through the persistence of war conditions, failed to find favour when the gradual resumption of normal conditions in the markets of the world made the minimum prices fixed by the Government too high for prospective purchasers, and the whole scheme was widely relaxed at the end of 1920. The Government, for its part, complained that it had received no effective support from the Imperial Government in securing favourable terms for the entry of Newfoundland fish into foreign markets, with the result that Norway and Iceland captured these markets to the detriment of Newfoundland. It was suggested by Mr. W. F. Coaker, Minister of Marine, that the United Kingdom should accord Newfoundland cod a trade preference, and that, if this course could not be adopted, the Government must look to the conclusion of an arrangement with the United States for the absorption there of the cod catch in return for preferential treatment of American exports in the Newfoundland market even as against British exports.

The desire to further economy in consumption of food stuffs as well as to increase the efficiency of labour and diminish the temptations of soldiers in training played a part in the marked progress of the prohibition movement in the case both of Newfoundland and the Dominion. In the former, however, the unitary constitution permitted swift and effective action, and the régime of prohibition in the fullest sense became effective in 1917. In Canada the division of powers between the Provinces and the Dominion, as well as the conflict of sentiment between the British and the French population, accustomed to the free use of light intoxicants, rendered action slower and less perfect. The lead was taken by Alberta and Saskatchewan in 1915, and by the beginning of 1918 every province save Quebec had enacted prohibitory laws so far as the constitution permitted; Quebec followed suit in the same year with a measure which provided for the complete prohibition of the liquor traffic from May 1919, while in 1,097 municipalities of the Province prohibition was already in force. The Dominion legislated in 1916 to prohibit the sending

of intoxicants from one Province to another to be sold or used in
the latter Province contrary to the law of that province, and an
Order in Council of December 24, 1917, forbade the importation
into the Dominion of liquors over 2½ per cent. proof. A further
Order of March 11, 1918, introduced prohibition of inter-provincial
transport with effect from April 1 : manufacture was also prohibited by the Order, but this step was not actually put in force,
the existing restrictions under Provincial and Dominion enactments on sale and transport rendering immediate steps in this
sense needless. An Order of February 11, 1919, imposed severe
penalties on the sale of liquor to officers or men in uniform, and an
effort was made to enact as a permanent measure a statute
ratifying the Dominion Orders in Council, under the War Measures
Act, regarding the prohibition of the importation, transport, and
manufacture of liquor ; the Senate, however, so seriously amended
the Bill that it was withdrawn by the Government, and in lieu
an Act was passed forbidding the manufacture in a province of
any intoxicating liquor to be dealt with in violation of the law of
the province. The issue of prohibition, therefore, remains largely
a provincial matter, and in 1919 Quebec, and in 1920 British
Columbia, modified the strictness of their régime.

2. AUSTRALASIA

At the instance of Sir Thomas Robinson, then Agent-General
for Queensland in London, the Government of Queensland immediately on the outbreak of war procured the enactment of an Act
to secure supplies of meat for the use of the Imperial Government
during the war. Under this measure all stock and meat in any
place in Queensland were to be kept for disposal by the Imperial
Government in aid of the supplies for the armies in the war.
Provision was made for the appointment of a Board to fix the
amount of compensation to be paid to owners of stock and meat,
and arrangements were made with the Imperial Government for
the purchase of the meat, the total export in 1917–18 reaching
169,798,883 lb. The precedent thus set was followed in increasing
measure during the war, but the power was normally exercised
not by the State but by the Commonwealth Government, which
relied for this purpose on the extremely wide power to issue

regulations under the War Precautions Act which was ascribed to it by the High Court of Australia.[1]

The incentive to this development of activity by the Commonwealth came first from the problem of the control of industrial metals, which became one of pressing importance immediately after the outbreak of war revealed the extent to which the output in Australia had fallen under German control. After a period of difficulty and confusion, the Commonwealth Government succeeded in September 1915 in forming the Australian Metal Exchange with offices in Melbourne and Sydney, the membership being confined to British companies, British firms, or natural born British subjects, and a veto on membership being given to the Attorney-General for the duration of the war and for a year after the declaration of peace. No industrial metal might be exported save under a contract registered at the Exchange by a member, and, during the war, with the consent of the Minister for Trade and Customs. In May 1916 the Government secured the formation of the Zinc Producers' Association Proprietary Limited, to control and dispose of the Australian output of zinc concentrate and metals, fundamental principles being British control and equality of treatment for all the members. Representation on the Board was secured for the Commonwealth Government, while the Imperial Government was allotted a seat on the London Board of the Association. A contract was procured from the Imperial Government for the sale of the stocks on hand at December 31, 1917, of 250,000 tons per annum for the war and one year thereafter, and of 300,000 tons for the nine succeeding years, while a further agreement provided for the sale of the supplies available up to 45,000 tons of spelter and electrolytic zinc for ten years from January 1, 1918. In November 1917 followed the creation on similar lines of the Copper Producers' Association Proprietary Limited. By an agreement of September 1915 the Imperial Government agreed to take over practically all the wolfram, molybdenite, and scheelite produced in the Commonwealth for a period up to six months after the declaration of peace.

The abnormal conditions produced by the war rendered the question of the marketing of wheat of the highest importance,

[1] See below, Chap. XI, § 2.

and a wheat marketing scheme was accordingly entered into by the Commonwealth, and the States of New South Wales, Victoria, South Australia, and Western Australia with a view to the realization on the best terms of the wheat harvest of these states for 1915–16, and of making advances to farmers pending realization. The same general principles were subsequently adopted in respect of the harvests of 1916–17, 1917–18, and 1918–19, the outline of the scheme being that all growers should participate equitably in the realization of the harvest, and that the limited freights available should be allotted between the States in accordance with the exportable surplus of each. The distribution of freights and the realization of the crop were controlled by the Australian Wheat Board, consisting of ministerial representatives of the Governments of the Commonwealth and of the States, and a representative of the growers from each State. It was advised by a Committee of leading wheat shippers, while the overseas sales were arranged by a London Wheat Committee, consisting of the High Commissioner and the Agents-General of the States concerned. In each State a local Board or Commission controlled the operations of the scheme within the State, and effected all local sales, including sales to millers, while the Wheat Board fixed all prices at which wheat might be sold, save as regards poultry feed, which was left to the States. The farmers' crops were either acquired outright by the Governments of the States, or received by the Governments for sale on behalf of the farmers, and arrangements were made with the banks for advance payments to farmers on delivery of their wheat at railway stations to the agents of the State Governments.

Action as regards the wool clip was deferred until the season 1916–17, when owing to the demand for wool for British and Allied military clothing the Imperial Government offered to acquire the clip at an increase of 55 per cent. on the price ruling in 1913–14, and the arrangement was repeated in respect of the clips up to that of 1919–20 inclusive. The control of the scheme was placed in the hands of a Central Wool Committee, assisted by a Committee in each State. These Committees consisted of representatives of the wool growers, wool sellers, wool buyers, manufacturers, and scourers or fellmongers ; in addition the Central Wool-Committee had a governmental representative as Chairman. There was as little interference as possible with the normal course of trade, but in lieu of sale in the ordinary way there was appraisement by Government Wool Appraisers, and thereafter the wool became the property of the British Government to be shipped as freight space became available on the understanding that the allotment of freight should be based on the amount of wool appraised in each State. Similarly, with a view to assist the Imperial Government, a Flax Industry Committee, representing the Victorian Department of Agriculture, the flax growers, and the cordage manufacturers, was appointed in 1918 with executive powers, and arrangements made for the sale of the output to the United Kingdom.

The Commonwealth asserted also its control over minor branches of industry. Power was taken in 1916 to regulate the purchase or sale of rabbit skins or sheepskins or hides, and for the supervision of the distillation of coal tar, and to forbid the use of crude tar save with the permission of a minister. In 1917 local committees were set up by the Commonwealth to decide upon the quantities of hides to be used for tanning and export, and to determine the classes, quantity, and output of leather. A Committee was appointed in the same year to make recommendations as to what classes of goods should be refused admission to the Commonwealth on the ground of their being luxuries. Returns of livestock and meat owned by any person in the Commonwealth were demanded. Power was given to require returns of stocks of goods of such kinds as might be prescribed by notice in the Gazette, to forbid the purchase of such stocks, and to compel their sale to the Government.

Shipping naturally, under the constitution, fell to be regulated by the Commonwealth, and from February 16, 1917, the control of shipping was vested in a Commonwealth Shipping Board, whose policy was administered by two central committees, one charged with overseas and the other with interstate shipping. Authority was conferred on the Controller of Shipping to requisition at schedule rates any vessels registered in Australia or engaged in the coasting trade, and to determine what vessels should be made available for the overseas service. In October 1916 the

Prime Minister purchased fifteen ships for the Commonwealth at a cost of £2,047,900, and orders were later given in America for the construction of fourteen wooden vessels. Further a great programme of construction in Australia was inaugurated, the number originally aimed at being forty-eight, involving the establishment of new yards and the extension of existing yards. In addition orders for five large steamers have been placed in England, and a number of ex-enemy vessels has been allotted to the Commonwealth.

The general question of the regulation of the price of foodstuffs was at first dealt with by a conference of federal and State ministers which met shortly after the war and decided that, for the purpose of controlling food prices, uniform legislation should be passed in all the States. Western Australia had already legislated, and New South Wales, Victoria, Queensland, and South Australia proceeded to pass legislation, but in Tasmania the Legislative Council threw out the Control of Necessaries of Life Bill which was passed by the lower house. Even in the cases in which legislation was passed, the scheme failed to work satisfactorily. It had been supposed that the Commissions appointed in each State to fix prices would work in close harmony with one another, and in August 1914 the Commonwealth Government appointed a federal Royal Commission to consider the question of the food supply, with the intention that it should co-operate with the State Commissions in securing an effective uniform policy throughout the Commonwealth. But nothing came of this, and the Commission ceased to function after October 30, 1914. In Victoria legislation was delayed by objections on the part of the Legislative Council ; when passed, operations under the Act were ineffective, and as soon as the General Election was over the orders already made fixing certain prices were abandoned. In Western Australia the Commission ceased to operate in October 1915, while it was not until that year that the Commission in South Australia fixed any prices.

The lack of success in the efforts of the States induced action by the Commonwealth ; in March 1916 a Prices Adjustment Board was created with power to fix the prices of flour, bread, bran, and pollard. After investigations the Board fixed the prices of flour, bran, and pollard in every milling centre in Australia, and determined the price of bread in over a thousand separate towns, after inquiry as to the cost of manufacture, distribution, &c. Later the operations of the Board were widely increased, and an exhaustive list was drawn up of goods declared to be necessary commodities whose prices were to be determined by it. To assist in the process a Commissioner was appointed in each State to make investigations and to make recommendations to the Minister for Trade as to the maximum selling prices of various commodities. This step was, not unnaturally, followed by the resignation *en masse* of the members of the Board, whose action left the power of fixing prices in the hands of the Minister, acting on the recommendations of the Commissioners in the States, the Commissioner for Victoria acting as Chief Prices Commissioner. Prices were fixed accordingly by regulation for many commodities, until in May 1919 the Commonwealth Government decontrolled many articles, trade in which had been regulated during the war, and at the end of that month the branch offices in the States were closed, leaving only the Central Office of the Prices Commission at Melbourne to deal with the control of the few articles, including butter, cheese, and flour, trade in which was still regulated. With the relaxation of Commonwealth control, the legislation of the States has come again into force and action has to some degree been taken under it, while fresh legislation has also been undertaken.

The Commonwealth constitution provides that the Commonwealth has authority over the control of railways with respect to transport for the naval and military purposes of the Commonwealth, and in 1911 a Railway War Council, consisting of military and naval officers, was instituted, charged with the duty of furnishing advice and information regarding railway transport for military purposes and securing co-operation between the Commonwealth Defence department and the railway departments of the States owning the railways, in regard to the concentration and mobilization of troops. The functions of this Board became of importance with the outbreak of war and were executed with the aid of an Engineer and Railway Staff Corps which numbered forty-seven officers in 1918. The war brought into prominence the defects of the railway system which had been dwelt upon for years before its outbreak without producing any effective result. The objection to the lack of communication between South and Western Australia had been realized before the war, and construction of a line between Port Augusta and Kalgoorlie had been authorized by a federal Act of 1911, the States granting to the Commonwealth all the land necessary for the construction of the line. Construction began in 1912, being carried on from both ends, but only 167 miles had been completed by June 1, 1914. The progress of the work, though rendered all the more urgent by the war, was not facilitated by war conditions ; owing to the inability of contractors to supply rails, platelaying on the western section of the work had to be suspended from December 1915 to the beginning of July 1916, and from December 1916 to the following May. The eastern and western divisions finally met on October 17, 1917, at a point 621 miles from Kalgoorlie, the total distance between the two termini being 1,051.30 miles. The journey from Port Augusta is performed in 37 hours 20 minutes, at an average rate of 28.16 miles throughout inclusive of stoppages.

Although, however, one great military and economic difficulty has been removed by the completion of this important work, there remains, as has been insisted by the Railway War Council, the serious military objection to the present system of railway communication that the divergences in gauge in the different States impose serious delays and involve much labour in the transhipment of baggage and still more of implements of war. The problem, however, of making the necessary change, the importance of which on grounds of economics has long been recognized, still remains unsolved in view of the enormous cost which the alteration would involve. The Council has also favoured the connexion of the north of Australia at Port Darwin by railway with the south as a matter of military necessity, but this reform also has been held over on grounds of expense.

In New Zealand also a chief preoccupation of the Government was to secure the effective marketing of the output of the Dominion. On March 3, 1915, there came into being the Department of Imperial Government Supplies, constituted for the purpose of controlling the purchase of frozen meat, while later its activities were extended to include such other items as wool, butter, cheese, and hides. In addition the Department undertook a considerable amount of business on behalf of the New Zealand Government, including the purchase of butter and cheese for use in camps and on transports, and arrangements for the sale and shipment of kauri gum.

In securing the arrangement for the purchase by the Imperial Government of the New Zealand output of meat, the initiative was taken by the Prime Minister, who convened conferences attended by the representatives of the industry at which the whole terms of the agreements were definitely fixed; changes were made also by agreement in December 1917, and in January 1919 the arrangement was continued to June 30, 1920. During the season of 1915–16 a third of the first-grade cheese produced was also purchased, and the amounts were increased in subsequent years up to July 1, 1920. It was not until November 20, 1917, that the scheme of purchase was applied to butter, when in addition to fixed prices an undertaking was given for the distribution to producers of half the profits realized on United Kingdom sales. The sum thus obtained was later applied by agreement in order to remove the unfairness caused by the limitation of price enforced on the sale of butter for local consumption as compared with the price realized by oversea sale. Sheepskins, hides, and calfskins, rabbits, condensed milk, and glaxo were among other purchases, while during the period of active hostilities the small New Zealand output of scheelite was also purchased. As in the case of the Commonwealth the purchase of wool began with the clip of 1916–17 on the same basis of prices; in both cases it was also agreed that the growers should receive half of any profit realized by the Imperial Government on sales for other than military purposes.

The question of the increase in the cost of living evoked the passage in 1915 of the Cost of Living Act, which provided for the establishment of a Board of Trade, consisting of a Minister and three other members. The Board was required to investigate questions relating to the cost of living, and more particularly questions relating to the supply, demand, or price of commodities; questions relating to the trade, commerce, or business of New Zealand; and questions relating to markets for New Zealand

F 2

products and manufactures. They were also empowered to investigate alleged breaches of the Commercial Trusts Act, 1910, the provisions of which were at the same time extended to apply to all articles of food for human consumption or their ingredients. This extension made illegal any combination or association to control the price or the supply or demand of any article of food.

The powers conferred on the Board became of importance chiefly in 1918, when its sphere of operations, hitherto comparatively narrow, was considerably extended in practice. Thus at the end of 1917 an Order in Council was issued, providing for the regulation of the price of good milling wheat and its distribution among the millers, while in view of the anticipated shortage in the home-grown supply two purchases, each of two million bushels, were arranged for from the Commonwealth. In order to ensure an adequate local production in 1918–19 the Government guaranteed to the farmers a minimum price of 6s. 4d. a bushel with an open market, but, in view of the purchases of Australian wheat and the decision to control flour and bread prices, it was finally agreed to purchase the crop at 6s. 6d. a bushel. This increase in wheat prices rendered necessary the adjustment of the prices of bread and flour, and the Government, in lieu of permitting increases, adopted the policy of subsidizing the millers ; a further subsidy was accorded later, when it was decided to reduce by 10s. a ton the price of flour, in order to compensate for the rising cost of the baking and delivery of bread, the arrangement extending to February 28, 1920. From March 1918 the price of groceries was controlled, and increases of prices forbidden without the assent of the Board. Control was applied also to petrol, cement, bacon, fish, potatoes, and milk, and from an earlier period to sugar. From August 1918 the timber industry was placed under control and prices limited. On September 10, 1918, a most important inquiry into the coal industry in the Dominion was entrusted to the Board, eliciting an elaborate report, urging the introduction of economies in the production of coal, the conservation of the coal resources, the concentration of the industry in the most profitable fields, the removal of the causes of labour unrest, and the institution of proper housing for mine workers, the inauguration of an efficient system of distribution, and the regulation of coal prices in the interests of consumers. They did not, however, recommend state purchase and the direct management of the mines by the Government, but recommended the institution of a Dominions Coal Board, representing the coal-owning companies, their employees, and the Crown, the first two bodies appointing each two members, while the Crown should appoint the chairman. The Board should be empowered to take over the existing coal companies at a valuation, paying them in stock, and to manage the mines on enlightened and progressive lines.

In Australasia the movement for prohibition worked with much less effect than in North America, though in New Zealand a strong party already existed convinced of the merits of the scheme. The matter fell, under the constitution, primarily into the hands not of the Commonwealth in the case of Australia, but of the States, though the Commonwealth might have exercised its war powers had the matter been regarded as sufficiently vital to the conduct of the war to render this course justifiable. In point of fact a decided impetus to state action was provided in the case of New South Wales by the issue on February 17, 1916, by the Commonwealth Minister for Defence, under the War Precautions Act, of a proclamation ordering that licensed premises in the County of Cumberland and within a radius of five miles from any military camp should be closed at 6 p.m., a drastic measure altered a week later by fixing the hour at 8 p.m. The State Parliament then legislated, by the Liquor Referendum Act, 1916, to secure a referendum as to the hour of closing of licensed premises, and as a result from July 21, 1916, to the close of the war all premises were closed at 6 p.m.

In Victoria the Licensing Act, 1915, provided for a scheme of local option, the first polls to be held contemporaneously with the first general election after January 1, 1917, but by a further Act in 1916 the polls were postponed until the subsequent general election, and when held in 1920 proved that local option was opposed to prohibition. The hours for the sale of liquor were, however, reduced, from July 6, 1915, to from between 9 a.m. to 9.30 p.m., and from October 25, 1916, closing at 6 p.m. was made compulsory ; reduction of rent in the case of licencees affected by these orders was permitted and assessed by the Licences Reduction

Board created in 1906, which continued during the war the process of reducing superfluous licences on the payment of compensation. On the other hand by the Act of 1916 further facilities were accorded for the obtaining of new licences in the Mallee.

Even less support for reduction of licences was found in Queensland, in which local option polls were held in 1917, for in only four areas out of fifty-seven was reduction of licences carried, and in other two an increase was approved. In South Australia a referendum of March 27, 1915, decided in favour of closing of licensed premises at 6 p.m. In Western Australia an Act of 1915 fixed for the Metropolitan and Agricultural districts the hours of opening from 9 a.m. to 9 p.m. ; in the case of the Goldfields the matter was left to a referendum, and it reported in favour of keeping the former hour of 11 p.m. for closing. In Tasmania a referendum of March 25, 1916, decided in favour of 6 p.m. as the closing hour.

In New Zealand more drastic steps were taken. Treating was forbidden by an Order in Council of August 21, 1916, and the grounds for cancellation of licences were increased in number. An Act of 1917, made permanent in 1918, fixed the hours for the sale of liquor as between 9 a.m. and 6 p.m. In 1918 an Act was passed securing the taking on April 10, 1919, of a referendum on the issue of national prohibition of the liquor traffic with compensation to all those engaged in the industry or national continuation of the sale of liquor ; provision was made to secure the taking of the votes of all the soldiers abroad, and it was by their votes that the issue resulted in the small majority of 10,362 for national continuance. In December 1919 three issues were submitted, again under the Act of 1918, to the electorate, continuance, national prohibition without compensation, and state purchase and control, and again the poll showed that the prohibition party, though almost as strong as their opponents, could not command a majority for their proposals.

3. South Africa

The pressure of the necessity of improved facilities for the manufacture of munitions was brought strongly home to the Union of South Africa by the outbreak of the rebellion among the Boers, and by the preparations for the advance against German South-West Africa. The United Kingdom, the normal source of supply, was unable to send munitions, and it was, therefore, necessary to utilize the services of as many manufacturers and workshops as possible. Large demands were also made on the production of mechanical transport in order to secure effective communication across the Kalahari desert from Kuruman to Keetmanshoop.

The exigencies of the war and the shortage of shipping induced the Imperial Government in 1917 to negotiate with the Union Government for the purchase by the former of the surplus stock of wool in the Union at the same price as adopted in the case of Australasia, 55 per cent. over the prices for 1913–14. Unfortunately in this case the proposal was not accepted without considerable opposition and friction. The farmers had received much higher rates in proportion for the clip of the previous year, and they argued that the United Kingdom was using its control of freight to compel them to ship to the United Kingdom, losing the chance of higher profits in the markets of Japan and the United States. The terms, though finally accepted, remained throughout the war the source of agitation among the Republican adherents of the Nationalist party in the Union, who argued that the Union was thus subjected to economic exploitation in the interests of the Empire, ignoring the fact that the lack of ships would in any case have prevented the existence of a free market.

The other economic issue confronting the Government was the gradual rise in prices ; a Special Commissioner after inquiry in 1916 found that the cost of living in respect of foodstuffs and other necessaries had increased by 15 per cent. since 1914, while there had been no corresponding general rise in wages, and in the Cape Peninsula rents had risen by 10 per cent., though throughout the country generally they were stationary. In November 1917 an Advisory Committee on Food Supplies gave way to a Cost of Living Commission, charged with the duty of reporting on the sufficiency of the stocks, present and prospective, of essential foodstuffs, the increase in the cost of necessaries of life to the consumer, and the possibility of reducing such cost or preventing further increases, with special reference to the possibility of regulating prices, expropriating stocks, abolishing or controlling combines for the purpose of maintaining prices, suspending import duties, modifying railway rates, and the acceptance by the Government of a share of the cost of insurance against marine war risks on imported goods. The Commission was also required to report whether undue war profits were being made on necessary commodities. The Commission found that supplies were adequate except in the case of wheat, for which a maximum price of 16s. per 100 lb. was advocated. They also found in favour of the imposition of maximum prices for sugar, rice, matches, paraffin, and petrol. Recommendations of a wholesale character were also made to secure the development of house building and on the question of undue profits, which were stated to have been earned by wholesale merchants in foodstuffs, boots and shoes, soft goods, and hardware. It was also suggested that a meat investigation commission should be appointed to prepare a scheme for the re-organization of that trade, that maximum wholesale prices for beef should be fixed, based on the sum paid for meat purchased by the Imperial Government, and that the export of meat for the open oversea market should be prohibited until it was clear that the needs of the local consumer were being met at reasonable prices. A scheme was also suggested to secure that goods should pass as cheaply as possible from the importer or producer to the consumer, a system of licences being adopted under which traders would be required to conduct their businesses on fixed principles.

The proposals of the Commission were referred by the House of Assembly in April 1919 to a Select Committee which did not endorse the views of the Commission on the exaction of undue profits, holding that in the main high profits had been fortuitous, consequential upon rising prices in the markets of the world. They held also that no scheme for licensing traders so as to limit profits could be made a success, and did not approve the idea of limiting export of meat. There was also a divergence between the two bodies regarding an excess profits tax to absorb all profits above a defined limit, which the Commission advocated, and the Committee disapproved. They supported the views of the Commission on housing, and advocated assistance in various ways for co-operation among consumers, negating, however, a suggestion that this assistance should take the form of financial aid. The recommendations of the Committee were not given effect to in the session of 1919, but were in part carried out in the following year.

War conditions affected seriously the mining industry, and evoked a limited measure of governmental intervention. Prior to the war the output of the mines went to London, where it was disposed of at par value in British currency, less charges for shipment, insurance and refining, and when the war took place arrangements were made with the Bank of England to continue the practice though with increases in the charges. Towards the end of 1919 it was argued that payment in British currency at its nominal value was unfair in view of the depreciation in the value of that currency, and in 1919, on the depreciation of British currency in the United States, it became obvious that a substantial premium could be obtained if export to the United States were freely permitted, reversing the policy hitherto followed by the Government. To secure, however, the best terms it was essential that the establishment of a refinery and mint should be arranged for, and the adoption of this policy was successfully urged on the Government by the Chamber of Mines. An Act (No. 45) was, therefore, passed in 1919 providing for the establishment of a Pretoria Branch of the Royal Mint, negotiations being carried on with the Imperial Government to secure their acceptance of this mode of procedure. At the same time an arrangement was entered into with effect from July 24, 1919, providing for the shipment of all gold refined or unrefined, excepting only the amount requisite for local currency requirements, to the Bank of England, and for its sale by Messrs. Rothschild on behalf of the producers at the best price available, the Bank receiving authority from the Imperial Treasury to license the export of the gold at any time within five weeks after its receipt by the Bank.

The action thus taken in obtaining a premium on the sale of gold was largely motived by the importance of affording aid to the low-grade mines, whose representations resulted in the appointment of a Commission by the Union Government in June 1919. This body was charged with an inquiry into the position of the gold mines working at a loss or a small and diminishing profit;

the effect which would be produced by the closing down of such mines ; the measures possible to prevent closing down or alleviate the position created by closing down ; the position of native and coloured workmen in the industry ; and the more efficient utilization of the native labour force available. The report showed that no fewer than twenty-one mines, employing 10,503 white persons, and 81,734 natives, with an annual wages bill of £6,500,000 and a monthly output of £1,030,516, were working at a small annual loss, as a result of the increased cost of materials and supplies, higher wages for white employees, shortage of native labour, and curtailment of the hours of work. Costs had risen from 17s. 5d. per ton milled in 1914 to 22s. 9d. in 1919. The remedies suggested by the Commission, apart from the relief produced by the premium on gold, included greater co-operation between the employees and the management, to be secured by the setting up of works committees and joint committees, but with advisory powers only ; the readjustment of working conditions to extend the effective working hours of the natives ; and the introduction of additional native labour, to be obtained from territory north of 22 south latitude. It was pointed out that the excessive mortality among such labourers had resulted in the discontinuance of their recruitment in 1913, but the discovery of a pneumococcal vaccine and improved hygienic measures showed that the resumption of recruitment would be free from serious risk, and an experimental introduction of 5,000 natives was recommended.

CHAPTER V

THE EXPEDITIONARY FORCES OF THE DOMINIONS

1. THE CANADIAN FORCES.
   Recruitment and organization in Canada and England — Command in France — Problem of reinforcement in 1916 — Sir R. Borden's decision as to conscription in 1917 — Sir W. Laurier's opposition — Difficulties in Quebec in 1918 — Canadian control of army administration in England and France.

2. THE COMMONWEALTH FORCES AND THE REFERENDA.
   Recruitment and organization — Necessity of increased reinforcements in 1916 — Failure in referendum of October 1916 — Formation of Coalition Government — Unsuccessful referendum of December 1917 — Failure of recruiting conference of 1918 — Peace views of Labour.

3. NEW ZEALAND AND THE COMPULSORY DRAFT.
   Recruitment and organization — National registration in 1915 — System of compulsory draft adopted in 1916 — Further efforts in 1918.

4. THE UNION OF SOUTH AFRICA.
   Volunteers for overseas service — Question of payment — Native labour battalions.

5. THE ROYAL NEWFOUNDLAND REGIMENT.
   Voluntary enlistment — Forestry corps — Adoption of compulsion.

6. THE MILITARY CONTRIBUTION OF THE DOMINIONS.
   Comparative number of enlistments and casualties — Value of Dominion troops — Military organization in Dominions after the war.

1. THE CANADIAN FORCES

ON the outbreak of the war Canada immediately promised the dispatch of a contingent of 20,000 men, almost at once increased to 33,000, for service overseas, and the promise was forthwith made good.[1] The real magnitude of the struggle received prompt recognition; a second contingent soon followed the first; early in 1915 there were two Canadian divisions in the field, and by July 1916 Canada was maintaining four divisions, supplemented by a cavalry brigade, and considerable forces of forestry and railwaymen. To produce these contingents the Dominion had at the outset to rely on only the small regular establishment (under 4,000) and the trained men of the Militia;

[1] Ex-regulars in Canada formed a separate corps, Princess Patricia's Canadian Light Infantry, which immediately joined the imperial forces but later was re-attached to the Canadian troops.

all others were volunteers without previous military training of any kind.

The mode of formation of the new army took at first the form of specially raised battalions, the men for which were recruited by the efforts of men of outstanding local influence, mayors, prominent business men, or Members of Parliament. Thus battalions were recruited from University men or from particular trades or localities, and the command of the newly-raised battalion was naturally often enough conferred on the man responsible for its recruitment, his assistants receiving rank as officers. The system produced eager and willing recruits, but from the military point of view it had grave disadvantages. The officers commanding were often ignorant of their duties, recruits were accepted without sufficient scrutiny, necessitating the discarding in England of many, found unfit for serious soldiering, after much money and time had been wasted on training them, and no provision was made for keeping up the strength of the battalions under the conditions of modern war. It was, therefore, often necessary after arrival in England to break up the new battalions, keeping the senior officers unemployed, while the men went as drafts to battalions already in the field, a process which produced great discontentment in Canada and hampered recruiting. Eventually the procedure was revised; the system of raising independent divisions was abolished, and in lieu of it was substituted a territorial system with a number of divisions for each province. These divisions were supported by special reserve troops in France and by special reserve battalions in camp in England, and the battalions at the front were thus kept up to strength despite the grave losses sustained by them.

The responsibility for the organization of the Army rested in the first months of the war largely with Major-General Sir Sam Hughes, Minister of Militia, whose efforts before the war at the improvement of the Canadian forces had been unflagging. But the Minister was of an imperious temperament ill-brooking opposition and, when it became necessary for him to work in close co-operation with the British military authorities on the arrival of the Canadian forces in England, friction became incessant, the issue being aggravated by the fact that Sir Sam

Hughes was a convinced supporter of the merits of the Ross rifle which had been rejected by the British War Office, and which in the course of the war showed more and more glaring defects. After a period of strain in the relations between the War Office and Canada, the matter was solved by the resignation of the Minister, who failed to find sufficient support for his views among his colleagues. His resignation was the preliminary to an important change in the Ministry; the office of Minister of Militia was now in effect expanded into two ministries, the Minister of Militia whose head-quarters were at Ottawa and who sat in the Dominion Cabinet, and the Minister for Militia Overseas, with head-quarters in London. In the first instance the duties of the latter post were undertaken by Sir George Perley, who had come to London in 1914 to perform the duties of High Commissioner on Lord Strathcona's death, while the post in Canada was filled by Sir Edward Kemp, a man of much business experience. A year later, in October 1917, Sir George Perley was relieved of the additional duties which he had assumed and which were plainly excessive, and Sir Edward Kemp [1] assumed office in November in London, his place in Canada being taken by General Mewburn, a distinguished Liberal soldier, whose entry into the Cabinet was one of the results of the formation of the Union Government as a coalition of Conservatives and Liberals. England was made a base from the first for the training of the Canadian army, and on the reorganization by Sir George Perley of the establishment in London at the close of 1916 Lieut.-General Sir R. Turner, V.C., was given control of the work.

In France the work was divided into three main sections, the Army Corps, the Cavalry Brigade, and the additional services, including the Railway Corps and the Forestry Corps. The Army Corps, which consisted from July 1916 of four divisions, a fifth which was formed and equipped having been broken up before dispatch to the field in 1918, had a nominal strength of about 75,000 men. There were 52 battalions of infantry, over 10,000 artillery, from 3,000 to 4,000 engineers, and about 2,000 Army Service Corps. The artillery comprised one horse artillery and

---

[1] On May 27, 1919, he gave in the Canadian House of Commons a record of his work.

12 field artillery brigades, 9 siege batteries, 12 trench mortar batteries, 2 heavy artillery batteries, an anti-aircraft battery, and 5 divisional ammunition columns. There were 24 companies of engineers and 20 machine-gun groups, as well as the Signalling Service, the Army Service, and the Medical Service. The command of the Army Corps, originally held by General Alderson, passed in the spring of 1916 to Lieut.-General Sir Julian Byng, on whose promotion after the battle of Vimy in 1917 to an Army Command, the wish of the Dominion was gratified in July by the selection of a Canadian officer, Lieut.-General Sir Arthur Currie, who had enlisted at the beginning of the war as a gunner, and by his great military ability had succeeded in attaining the command of the first Canadian division. Of the commanders of the divisions three were professional soldiers, two with a long record of service in the permanent forces of Canada, one an imperial officer seconded to the Canadian forces before the war, while the fourth was under the command of a Canadian who before the war was in civil life as a newspaper editor and proprietor in Quebec. The officers commanding brigades were largely drawn from civil life, and the Canadian intelligence system, which reached a high degree of perfection, owed much to the ability of Colonel C. H. Mitchell, one of the leaders of the development of hydro-electric power in Canada. Commissions in the battalions, which originally were given by nomination, were later filled by promotion from the ranks, and cadet schools were established both in England at Bexhill, and in France.[1]

As in England the ready flow of recruits which marked the opening months of the war gradually slackened, while at the same time the necessities of the situation increased. At the beginning of 1916 Sir Robert Borden definitely adopted the ideal of raising half a million men in Canada. At that time some 225,000 men had been enrolled, of whom 60,000 were on the continent, about the same number in England, and the rest in the Dominion. Both Sir R. Borden and Sir Wilfrid Laurier as

[1] The troops were apparently enlisted at first under the Army Act of the United Kingdom, not under the Canadian Militia Act, though the officers were given commissions in the Militia; as late as April 1916 their legal status in Canada was questioned. *The Round Table*, vi. 547. Cf. *Fournier* v. *Price*, R. J. Q. 60, S.C. 489.

leader of the opposition had asserted that compulsion was impossible, but the latter at least had realized that the new aims of the Government involved a great strain. Anxiety soon began to be felt as to the progress of recruiting, the voluntary system endangering the supply of men essential for agriculture and industry, while enabling many who could be spared to evade service, and early in 1916 the Legislature of Ontario appointed a war committee, representing both political parties, to see what steps could be taken to regularize recruiting and render the effort of the province more fruitful. By July the claim of munitions for workers had become of great importance, over 400,000,000 dollars worth of contracts having been placed in the Dominion and 200,000 men absorbed in the work. Strong appeals were issued by the Prime Minister, and a national Recruiting Commission was appointed on October 25 with the title of the National Service Board and with Mr. R. B. Bennett as Director of Recruiting, assisted by associate directors in the provinces. The Commission was specially charged with the duty of inducing manufacturers to substitute female for male labour and to persuade Labour to co-operate in such substitution, there being reluctance on both sides to make the sacrifice involved. But the position remained unsatisfactory; the English population had contributed the vast majority of the recruits; in addition to 500,000 Germans and Austrians there were 700,000 or 800,000 Americans, who could not be expected to yield volunteers for service, and the two million French-speaking people, mainly of Quebec, showed an almost total unwillingness to serve. The latter result was fomented by the denouncement by Nationalist leaders such as M. Bourassa of any participation in the wars of the Empire, and of the forging round the neck of Canada of ' a militarism unparalleled in any civilized country, a depraved and undisciplined soldiery, an armed rowdyism, without faith or law, and as refractory to the influence of individual honour as to that of their officers '. Sympathy with France, which might *a priori* have been expected to exercise influence on the people of Quebec, was wanting; as Sir Wilfrid Laurier pointed out, immediate ties of family connexion with France were comparatively rare in Quebec, and of immigrants from France many were priests imbued with a strong dislike of the religious policy of the French republic.

It was not, however, until his return from the Imperial War Cabinet of 1917 that the Prime Minister resolved finally on the necessity of conscription, well aware as he was of the difficulties in the way. By that time, however, it was absolutely clear that nothing short of conscription would enable Canada to reach the numbers she had decided to be necessary, and the adoption of the system of the selective draft in the United States had placed the Dominion in an invidious position while at the same time diminishing the danger of men leaving the Dominion for the republic to evade military service, a treaty being proposed between the United Kingdom and the United States providing for the drafting of subjects of either country resident in the other.[1] Only 400,000 recruits had been obtained, and of the 1,600,000 people of French speech in Quebec only 6,979 had enlisted, while the English-speaking population of a quarter that number had given 22,000 men to the army, and the French resident outside Quebec, though only a sixth of the number in that province, had yielded 5,904 soldiers. The demand for conscription came not merely from the supporters of the Government; Mr. Rowell, the leader of Liberalism in Ontario, though not in federal politics, and a formidable body of Liberal opinion demanded the step despite the objections of Sir W. Laurier. Sir R. Borden determined on alliance with such Liberals as would unite on a policy of conscription, and introduced a Military Service Bill. The measure provided for compulsion for the purpose of securing reinforcements up to 100,000 men from the ages of 20 to 45.[2] The men were divided into ten (later six) classes, the first of which was to be called up forthwith, and comprised any British subject normally resident in Canada, or resident there since the beginning of the war, who had attained the age of twenty and was not born earlier than 1883 and was unmarried or a widower without a child. There were excepted from the operation of the measure members

---

[1] *Parl. Pap.* Cd. 9101 gives the definitive text only of the general agreement. The special Canadian-United States agreement was not published. Both only became operative on July 30, 1918.

[2] It was estimated that there were 630,000 unmarried men between 20 and 34.

of the Imperial forces or of the forces of any Dominion, men who had served in the war and been discharged honourably, clergy including members of any recognized religious order, ministers of religious denominations, and Mennonites and Doukhobors who had been granted exemption from military service on settling in the Dominion, and persons granted exemptions. Men of alien birth who retained their old nationality were not affected by the measure, while aliens of enemy origin naturalized since 1902 were by the War Times Election Act disfranchised and allowed until May 1918 exemption from liability to serve on application. Appeals for exemption were regulated on a threefold basis ; the first tribunal consisted of two persons, one nominated by the senior County Court Judge in the district and one by a board of selection chosen by Parliament, over 1,250 of these tribunals being set up. From their decision either the man or the military representative might take an appeal to the appellate tribunal, consisting of a judge nominated by the Chief Justice of the province in which the appeal was brought, and there was a final appeal to a Judge of the Canadian Supreme Court. No special class, occupation, or trade was accorded exemption as such, but eight grounds were laid down on which appeals might be brought, importance of continuing in habitual occupation, of continuing employment for which the applicant was specially qualified, of continuing education or training, serious hardship due to exceptional financial obligations, or exceptional domestic position, ill health or infirmity, and adherence to a religious denomination the tenets of which forbade combatant service, provided in the last instance the applicant expressed willingness to serve as a non-combatant in the Army Medical Corps, Mechanical Transport, Army Service Corps, &c. The administration of the measure was entrusted to the Minister of Justice aided by a Military Service Council representing equally the two political parties.

The measure excited bitter opposition in Quebec, and Sir Wilfred Laurier on June 18 declined to admit that the House of Commons, in which there were over twenty vacant seats, while the western provinces were under-represented to about the same extent, was entitled, after its existence had been prolonged beyond the due period by an Act of the preceding year at a time when no proposal of conscription was in the air, to enact such a measure. He insisted that instead a referendum should be taken. But the second reading of the Bill was carried by 118 votes to 55, and the amendment proposed by Sir Wilfrid was rejected by 111 votes to 62. The Military Service Council proceeded to prepare a proclamation which was issued on October 13 calling up for service the first class, but slow progress [1] was made during the last months of the year, while the energy of the Government was diverted to a general election and the consolidation of a coalition Government. The triumph of the coalition at the polls placed them in a position to secure the carrying out of the Act, but the measures taken to enforce it in Quebec resulted in rioting in Quebec City from March 28, 1918, and on April 1 the troops which had been called upon by the Officer commanding the District, in default of action by the Mayor, to restore order and to protect property, were compelled to fire on the mob, killing four civilians and wounding many others. The Government acted effectively to vindicate the law ; an Order in Council was passed on April 4, and communicated on the following day to the House of Commons, authorizing the Governor in Council within any designated area to supersede either in whole or in part the jurisdiction and powers of the civil courts, and to render obligatory on the civil population within the area the orders of the Officer commanding the troops, power being given to try and punish by court martial offenders against the law and persons disobeying military orders. Fortunately, despite the bitterness of feeling in Quebec, Sir Wilfrid Laurier insisted on the necessity of respecting the law, and the Roman Catholics in the western communities impressed, through Archbishop Mathieu, on their co-religionists in the east the invidious situation created by the reluctance of Quebec to play its part in the struggle. Prominent members of the political world in Quebec lent their aid to recruitment, the Premier, Sir Lomer Gouin, especially distinguishing himself in this regard, and many young students from the Universities joined the colours.

Serious difficulty arose throughout the Dominion with regard to the exemption of agricultural workers. It was undoubtedly

[1] By January 1918, 404,395 men had been registered, 23,885 reported for service, the rest had applied for exemption, and 278,779 had been granted it.

the desire of Parliament and the Government that such workers should be excused military service, and an Order in Council of December 31, 1917, went so far as to permit the Minister of Militia to discharge at pleasure from military service any person engaged in agriculture, whose application for exemption had been rejected. Youths between 20 and 22 years of age were freely granted exemption if engaged on farm work, with the result that the flow of effective recruits was much slackened. This was the state of affairs when a telegram of April 1 was received by the Governor-General from the British Prime Minister consequent on the disasters suffered by the allies in the German offensive of March 21. 'As already announced,' it ran, 'we propose to ask Parliament to authorize immediate measures for raising fresh forces. I would also urge the Government of Canada to reinforce its heroic troops in the fullest possible manner, and with the smallest possible delay. Let no one think what even the remotest of our Dominions can now do can be too late. Before the campaign is finished, the last man may count.' The Dominion Government acted on this suggestion by asking the House of Commons on April 19 to sanction the issue of an Order in Council authorizing the immediate calling up of men from 20 to 22 inclusive, disallowing the right of application for exemption under the Military Service Act and cancelling the exemptions already granted. The legal authority for the enactment was given as the War Measures Act, 1914, but the proposal not unnaturally was objected to by Sir Wilfrid Laurier as an encroachment of the executive authority on the sphere of the legislature. The approval of the House of Commons was, however, accorded by 114 to 65 votes, and the Order issued on April 20. Its legality was at once disputed, and on June 28 a majority of the Supreme Court of Alberta held in the case of N. E. Lewis that the Order was invalid, on the ground that it could never have been the intention of Parliament when enacting the Military Service Act to leave it open to the Government to proceed by means of Orders in Council under the War Measures Act. Before the Superior Court at Montreal the case was argued on the basis that the Imperial Parliament alone could suspend the right of habeas corpus; that legal action on habeas corpus was governed by provincial legislation which the Dominion

Parliament could not override ; that even if Parliament could suspend the right it could only do so by legislation ; and that the War Measures Act did not sanction the suspension of habeas corpus, and on July 5 the Court accepted these arguments and declared the Order invalid. The Government replied to the Alberta decision by an Order in Council of July 5 ordering that the terms of the Order of April 20 should be carried out despite the Alberta judgement or any other judgement, and a contest between the Dominion Government and the Court followed, the Government refusing to obey a writ of habeas corpus for the production of a soldier named Norton, while the Court issued a writ of attachment against Colonel Moore, the officer who refused to produce Norton. On July 18–20, however, the Supreme Court decided the legal aspect of the issue in the case of G. E. Grey[1] of Nipissing, who had contested the validity of the Orders; it held by a majority of four to two that the terms of s. 6 of the War Measures Act were sufficiently wide to justify the issue of the Order, while a clause in the Military Service Act expressly provided that nothing in that law should be held to interfere with or detract from the powers conferred on the Governor in Council by the War Measures Act ; stress was also laid on the fact that the principle of the Order in Council had been submitted to Parliament before enactment. The decision, not being technically on appeal, was disregarded by some judges in Quebec, Mr. Justice D. Monet in the Superior Court at Montreal on August 6 denying that the Parliament of Canada could suspend the right of habeas corpus, but due respect for the decision was shown in the rest of the Dominion. In answer to strong appeals made by a huge delegation of 5,000 farmers from all over Canada Sir R. Borden replied firmly on May 14 insisting that, if the line in Europe was broken, food production in Canada would be unavailing. Innumerable methods of evasion, however, were invented, many men fled to inaccessible spots whence they defied the efforts of the Government to secure their arrest. By the close of the recruiting campaign with the armistice only 83,355 men had been secured under the Act for military service, while 24,933 men had been called up for service but released on compassionate or other

---

[1] Cf. *Canadian Law Times*, xxxviii. 671 ; Ottawa *Journal*, July 4, 1918.

adequate grounds. The Military Service Council, which at first aided the Minister of Justice in the administration of the Act, was disbanded on June 15, and its place taken by a Military Service Branch as a departmental organization. Boards of Review were also established in 1918 to revise the decisions of the Military Medical Boards, and from their judgements a final appeal lay to the Central Appeal Judge. The total enlistments under the voluntary system were 465,984, while 21,169 enlisted in the Royal Air Force or other Imperial services.

Important alterations were made in 1918 in the control of the Canadian forces in England and in France. By an Order in Council of April 11 an Overseas Military Council was formally created presided over by Sir E. Kemp as Minister of the Overseas Forces, and including his Deputy, a Chief of Staff, who took the place of the General Officer commanding in England, and Adjutant- and Quartermaster- and Accountant-Generals. The power of the minister was much increased by this step, and negotiations were entered into to secure the fuller control by Canada over its forces in France also. The matter was taken up by Sir Robert Borden on his visit to England to take part in the Imperial War Cabinet meetings in 1918, and a statement issued by him at Ottawa on August 24 explained that the organization of the Canadian Army was to be independent of the British Army except so far as the supreme command of Sir Douglas Haig and Marshal Foch was concerned, the internal management of the Canadian Army to be entirely under Canada. For this purpose arrangements were made for the existence of a Canadian section at General Head-quarters with specific authority over the various Canadian adminis-trative services and departments in the field, and empowered to supervise the carrying out of such executive action as might be decided upon from time to time in respect to the personnel of the forces. It was also authorized to supervise the many subsidiary Canadian organizations in France and Belgium. It was also agreed to create a Canadian Air Force to co-operate with the British Air Force, in which many Canadians had been serving under Imperial control, but the termination of the war left this project incomplete. A Canadian force, however, was sent to Vladivostock to co-operate with the Japanese and American forces, returning to Canada in June 1919, while Canadian troops fought at Archangel and in the Murmansk.

2. The Commonwealth Forces and the Referenda

On August 3, 1914, the Commonwealth Government [1] informed the Imperial Government of its readiness to send a force of 20,000 of any composition desired, and the Imperial Government in its acceptance suggested that the force sent should take the form of a division, of staff, three brigades, and divisional troops, but without howitzer brigade or heavy battery, and a light horse brigade. After this force had been raised, a measure facilitated by the adoption of compulsory training from January 1, 1911, under the Act of 1909, the Commonwealth Government notified their intention to dispatch further troops, including communications units, supply units, and hospitals (about 2,000 men), first reinforcements (about 3,000), two additional light horse brigades (about 4,000), an additional infantry brigade (4,500), and certain veterinary units. The first contingent left Australia under convoy on November 1, reaching Egypt on December 5, and the second convoy left late in December, troops thereafter sailing without convoy. The total number actually sent oversea numbered 329,862 up to December 31, 1918. They were organized chiefly in the following units : (1) Army Corps Troops, including 2 Army Corps Mounted Regiments, 3 Corps Cyclist battalions, 3 Army Field Artillery Brigades ; (2) a Mounted Division of 5 light-horse brigades, 5 machine gun squadrons, and auxiliary troops ; (3) 5 Divisions including 15 infantry brigades, 5 pioneer battalions, 5 machine gun battalions, 10 field artillery brigades, 35 trench mortar batteries, engineers, &c., and (4) a large number of miscellaneous units, including flying squadrons, an aeroplane squadron which served in Mesopotamia, railway operating companies, 3 battalions Imperial Camel Corps, and numerous hospitals. The administration of the force in the Commonwealth was carried out by the Minister of Defence with the assistance of the Council of Defence and the Board of Administration of the Military Forces, and the necessary business in the United Kingdom was performed subject to his control.

[1] A formal record of the Commonwealth part in the war was given by Senator Pearce in the Senate on May 5, 1920.

From the first the raising of the troops was by voluntary enlistment, for though, since 1911, compulsion has been applied in the Commonwealth for the purpose of training citizens to defend Australia, it is expressly provided that members of the military forces of the Commonwealth whether serving in the small permanent force or the Citizen forces cannot be called upon to serve beyond the limits of the Commonwealth or any territory under its authority except with their consent. The volunteers, however, were enlisted, not as at first in the case of Canada under the Imperial Army Act, but under the Australian Defence Act,[1] which, however, made applicable to them while on active service the terms of the Army Act subject to unimportant variations. Volunteers were plentiful in the early days of the struggle, interest running high in the extremely gallant struggle of the Australian troops in Gallipoli, and on November 26, 1915, the Commonwealth Government definitely offered the Imperial Government a further force of 50,000 in addition to the reinforcements for the troops already sent, amounting to 9,500 a month. On this basis the total number supplied by June 1916 would have reached the creditable total of 300,000 men, the figure given by the Prime Minister, Mr. Hughes, at Ottawa. On the other hand the Minister for Defence announced on March 23 that the number had been put too high, and that the British Government had reduced the demands for reinforcements, so that the number actually dispatched overseas by June would be only 209,500 with from 50,000 to 60,000 in training at home, the totals in the two categories being then about 150,000 and 60,000 respectively. Unhappily there was some misunderstanding in the announcement, which had a distinctly depressing effect on recruiting, the impression being created that there was no real necessity for volunteers. The recruiting committees, which had been working hard since the outbreak of war, condemned vigorously the minister's declaration, and some efforts were made to undo its effect but without substantial success. The movement for conscription, which had been suspended in order to allow free play to voluntaryism, regathered force, but at the same time the attitude of Labour began to be definitely anti-compulsion, or at most prepared to

[1] 1903–11, ss. 54 A, 55 ; amended by Act No. 36 of 1917, ss. 14, 15.

assent to it only if accompanied by the conscription or confiscation of wealth.

During his visit in 1916 to London the Prime Minister had the opportunity of informing himself fully of the state of the war requirements, and he expressed himself emphatically on the necessity of Australia playing her full part, despite arguments that her finances would not permit further expenditure, that the men were needed for home production, or that the war was in any case won by the allies. It was, therefore, with much disappointment that supporters of compulsion learned from his speech in Parliament on August 30 that the Government were not prepared to submit any conscription proposal to the legislature. On the other hand they had decided, after passing through Parliament a Referendum measure for this purpose,[1] to take at the end of October a referendum, asking whether the electors were willing that the provisions of the Defence Act which permitted the calling up of men for home service should be extended to permit of calling them up for service abroad. Pending the result of this referendum a determined effort was to be made to secure 32,500 recruits in September, that being the number necessary to keep the Australian forces up to strength, in view of the fact that in the last three months the average of recruits had fallen to 6,000. If the total were not reached, then the Government would call up for training under the powers given by the Defence Act all single men without dependents between 21 and 45, so that, if the referendum were answered in the affirmative, the men thus raised for home defence could be sent abroad after completing their training. This cumbrous method of procedure was motived by the strong dissent of a section of Labour, Mr. Hughes's party, from the doctrine that the voluntary system had ceased to be satisfactory, and the doubts of others whether, even if voluntary recruitment had failed, conscription was a suitable remedy. As a result there was certain to be a majority in the Senate against a Bill for the purpose of permitting compulsion for oversea service, and the Labour party in caucus was definitely by a majority against producing such a Bill, while, if the popular vote was in favour, it was reasonable to suppose that the Senate, despite its

[1] No. 27 of 1916.

Labour majority, would bow to their decision and accept without delay a Bill. The only alternative was to enact conscription by a regulation under the War Precautions Act, but, apart from the constitutional impropriety of such a step in a matter of so great importance affecting the liberty of the subject, it was very doubtful whether the other members of the Cabinet, who in the usual method of Labour governments had been chosen by the caucus and not by the Prime Minister, would have concurred in the proposal, and the Senate could by resolution have disallowed the regulation.[1] It is, however, possible that a bold course of action might have carried the day; a Bill for conscription could have been passed in the House of Representatives, and the Senate might have hesitated to reject the proposal in a concrete form.

The referendum was held on October 28, under the provisions of the Military Service Referendum Act passed for the purpose. The vote in favour of the proposal to apply compulsion for service outside Australia was 1,087,557, the vote against 1,160,033. There were majorities for in Victoria, Western Australia, and Tasmania, and the Federal Territories, but large majorities against in South Australia and New South Wales, and a substantial majority against in Queensland. The voting did not proceed rigidly on political lines; in South Australia and New South Wales the Labour leaders were on the whole in favour of conscription, but the vote against was conclusive; though all the Senators from Victoria were Labour, a fair majority in favour of compulsion was secured. It was clear that the farmers' vote was largely cast against a proposal which would mean loss of labour and of high profits; the Roman Catholic hierarchy as a rule were hostile, and in Queensland the Irish influence was strong. Many specious arguments were adduced against compulsion:[2] the allies were sure to win; Australia had sent more troops to the front proportionately than the United Kingdom—a grotesque absurdity; Indian troops should be used—a suggestion coming with very bad grace from men who excluded Indians from the Commonwealth; conscription was the negation of freedom; the men who

---

[1] Under the general power given by Act No. 1 of 1904, s. 10.
[2] *The Round Table*, vii. 378–94 ; *The Times*, December 15, 1917.

volunteered would find their places filled by cheap alien labour ; the women voters in particular were urged not to force men to the dangers of war. The device of calling men up for home defence proved an error ; much inconvenience was caused, and those called up were rendered bitterly opposed to the proposal and influenced their friends to defeat it. The Industrial Workers of the World started a vehement propaganda against it, and the New South Wales Labour party expelled the Prime Minister from its number. Mr. Hughes also was guilty of a grave error in tactics ; after three of his colleagues had declined to assent to the passing of a Regulation under which voters were to be asked when voting if they had fulfilled any duty incumbent on them of coming up for service under the summons issued under the Defence Act, he secured its passage at a meeting of the Executive Council from which they were absent. They immediately resigned as a protest against his irregular action, and, though the Regulation was cancelled, much harm was done to a cause which seemed to require support by so strange a method of procedure. Even more serious was the fact that the Prime Minister made no definite intimation that failure in the referendum would mean his resignation, leaving it to be inferred that, though the proposal for conscription was important, it was not in his view vital that it should be accepted. In any event, however, the use of a referendum on such an issue was wholly unwise, assuming as it did that the average elector in a country of adult franchise was in a position to form an effective opinion on an issue in which personal comfort came so obviously into contact with national interest.

The failure of the referendum was followed by a troubled period in Commonwealth politics from which there emerged a Coalition Government,[1] in which the Liberals played the numerically superior part, possessing effective majorities in both houses but definitely pledged not to introduce conscription either by statute or regulation during the life of the Parliament, but if necessary owing to the course of the war to refer the question again to the people. The strong position of the Government was doubtless due to this announcement, coupled with assurances of their intention to subordinate everything else to efforts to win the war,

[1] See below, Chap. IX, § 2.

for their attitude harmonized with the feeling of the Commonwealth, which was anxious for victory bùt disinclined to proceed to conscription. The defeat of the Italians brought into operation the consideration of urgency on which action by the Government depended. Sir William Irvine, distinguished alike in the political life of Victoria and of the Commonwealth, had during the struggle declined to be any party to the undertaking regarding conscription; he now urged upon the Government the only effective course of a dissolution and an appeal to the people to relieve the Government of its pledge. Unhappily his advice did not prevail; some members of the governmental party feared for their seats in the event of an election; others, though less apprehensive, deprecated the trouble and cost of a general election so soon after the victory of May 5, 1917, and a more specious argument was adduced by some of the Senators, whose seats would not be affected by a dissolution, and who argued that an election would not relieve them from their pledges, ignoring the obvious solution of resigning their seats and thus giving the electors a chance to release them. It was, accordingly, decided by the Cabinet on November 7 to adopt the method of a referendum to be taken under the authority of a regulation made under the War Precautions Act 1914–16, and not, as in the preceding year, under a special statute. On November 12 in an important declaration of policy at Bendigo the Prime Minister definitely stated that the events in Russia and Italy were such that without the power to ensure reinforcements the Government could not give effect to the Win-the-war policy which the country had so clearly approved in May. 'I tell you plainly', he added, 'that the Government must have this power. It cannot govern the country without it and will not attempt to do so.' The Government thus pledged itself to retire if the referendum failed, assuming a definite responsibility for the necessity of the proposals which the electors were asked to approve.

The proposals of the Government were carefully framed to render acceptance probable. Voluntary enlistment was to continue. The number of reinforcements was to be fixed at 7,000 a month. Compulsory reinforcements were to be called up by ballot to the extent to which voluntary enlistment failed to provide this number. The ballot was to be from single men only (including widowers and divorcees without dependent children) between 20 and 44 years. There were to be exempt persons physically unfit ; judges and magistrates ; ministers of religion ; persons whose employment in any particular industry was declared to be necessary for the supply of food and material essential for the war ; persons whose religious belief did not allow them to bear arms, subject to liability for non-combatant service ; and persons whose calling up would because of domestic circumstances entail undue hardships on their dependents. The Government was to determine the industries necessary for the successful prosecution of the war and the national welfare of Australia, and a special tribunal was to decide the amount of labour necessary for their successful operation. In selecting men consideration was to be had to any members of the same family already serving, so as to secure proportional sacrifices being required from each family, and ballots were to be taken by States on the basis of the proportionate number of eligible persons in each State. The tribunals for deciding exemptions were to be constituted of magistrates specially appointed, and an appeal would lie to a Supreme Court Judge.

Provision was made for excluding from the vote every naturalized British subject born in an enemy country, and every British subject whose father was so born, a regulation which excited a good deal of bitter protest. Further harm was done to the case of the Government by the indiscriminate use of the military censorship as a means, the opposition alleged, of preventing the true facts about the situation being put before the electors. Much play was made by the opposition with the fact that in October 1916 the Government had demanded 32,500 men and a monthly average of 16,500 thereafter, and now only asked for 7,000, and it was suggested that the 4,000 a month average obtained in 1917 by voluntary enlistment was really adequate. The Prime Minister damaged his case by indiscriminate charges of disloyalty against all his opponents and involved himself in a struggle with the Government of Queensland which in Labour hands was opposed to his campaign.[1] Statements, the circulation

[1] *The Round Table*, viii. 627–39.

of which was prohibited by the censorship, were given publicity by the Queensland Premier and Treasurer by communication to the Legislative Assembly, and the special edition of the State *Hansard* containing the reports of their statement was given wide circulation, a step counteracted by the Commonwealth Government seizing the stock of *Hansard* at the Queensland Government printing establishment. The Commonwealth Government then commenced a prosecution of the Premier and the State retorted by an action against the Commonwealth, proceedings happily in either case later dropped. But in connexion with this incident, and with an attack made on him at a Queensland meeting, the Prime Minister inaugurated a Commonwealth Police Force intended to protect federal interests when these might be in danger of suffering at the hands of the State police.[1] More serious, if possible, than the opposition of the Queensland Government was the bitter hostility of the Roman Catholic Archbishop of Melbourne, Cardinal Mannix, who as an out-and-out supporter of Sinn Fein was bitterly hostile to British success in the war, and whose influence weighed heavily in Victoria. The result of the voting was not unexpected; 1,015,159 votes were cast for the governmental proposals, 1,181,747 against. As in 1916 Western Australian, Tasmania, and the Federal Territories gave an affirmative reply, though in Tasmania the voting was almost equal; New South Wales, Queensland, and South Australia were as then hostile, and the efforts of the Archbishop carried Victoria over to the side of the opposition. An outstanding feature of the referendum of December 20 was the fact that the votes of the oversea soldiers were almost equally divided, 91,642 in favour, and 89,859 against; many of those who voted in the negative were actuated by motives of chivalry, being unwilling to expose others to the horrors of modern warfare, though themselves prepared to endure them. A considerable section of the negative vote was undoubtedly influenced by more full realization of war conditions and dangers, the women's vote often being decided by this consideration.

The Government did not, despite its pledge of November 12, effectively resign office, but cast about for new methods of

[1] Sydney *Daily Telegraph*, November 29 and 30, 1917.

meeting the situation, the discredit of which was keenly felt. The Chief Justice was commissioned to ascertain the quota of monthly reinforcements necessary to keep up to strength the forces at the front and fixed it at 5,400, a decision which was held by the opposition to have justified the scepticism which they had expressed as to the validity of the demand for 7,000 a month. A new minister, Mr. Orchard, was appointed in charge of Recruiting, better terms offered to wives and dependents of volunteers, and the system of insurance of the lives of volunteers, inaugurated by private action, was encouraged. Finally, on the suggestion of Captain Carmichael, an ex-minister of New South Wales, and a Labour leader, who, having returned wounded from the front, had thrown himself wholeheartedly into the recruiting campaign, a conference of politicians, employers, Trade Unionists, and others was convened by the Governor-General acting on the precedent of the Home Rule Conference called by the King. The Conference, invitations to which were accepted by all invited save the Trades Hall leaders in Victoria, met at Melbourne on April 12, and its labours extended over seven days. Two well-defined points of view were at once apparent: on the one hand the Federal Government and the Governments of the States where Labour was not in power, and the employers; on the other Mr. Tudor, leader of the Commonwealth opposition, Mr. Ryan, Labour Premier of Queensland, and the representatives of State Labour parties and trade unions. It soon appeared that Labour was determined to demand important concessions as the price even of co-operation in voluntary recruiting. It asked for the definite abandonment by the Government of any idea of conscription, and for the cessation of discharges by the Government or private employers of eligible men in order to induce their enlistment. It demanded that the unions which, as a result of the recent industrial strife in New South Wales, had lost the privileges conferred by registration under the State law, should be reinstated in their old rights; that all regulations under the War Precautions Act not vital to the prosecution of the war should be repealed and an assurance given that they would not be re-enacted; that the press censorship and limitations on freedom of speech should be abolished save as regards news of military advantage to the enemy ; that all political and industrial prosecutions under the War Precautions Act should cease and fines imposed be refunded ; and that all persons, not guilty of criminal acts, imprisoned in connexion with peace propaganda, industrial troubles, and recruiting should be released, while steps were to be taken at once against profiteering. The Prime Minister and Mr. Holman, Premier of New South Wales, proved willing to meet these claims to a large extent, but even so it was impossible for the Prime Minister to secure the acceptance by the Labour leaders of a resolution pledging full personal support and the use of their influence in promoting voluntary recruitment in the Commonwealth, and the Conference had to acquiesce in urging the people of Australia to ' unite in a whole-hearted effort to secure the necessary reinforcements under the voluntary system ', a very poor return for the definite concession by the Federal Government of an undertaking to drop conscription. Even so, however, the resolution proved unacceptable to the most important section of Labour concerned, the Labour Council of New South Wales, for, when its President, in loyalty to the agreement at the Conference, pressed the Council to approve it, his suggestion was defeated by 79 votes to 75. Much more effective was the realization of the seriousness in the position among the workers themselves ; the number of recruits accepted had fallen off in February and March to 400 a week ; the breaking of the allied line by the German offensive increased the number in the first week of April by fifty, and in the week ended May 18 the total of recruits attained 1,491.

Official Labour, however, was not affected by considerations which weighed with the rank and file of the movement. In June at its annual meeting the Labour Conference of New South Wales declared emphatically in favour of the immediate negotiation of peace, and the same policy was reaffirmed and expanded at the Interstate Labour Conference which began its session at Perth, Western Australia, on June 17. The resolutions of the Conference were pacifist in tone ; the outbreak of the war was attributed generically to commercial rivalry, territorial ambitions, and dynastic considerations, and the absence of sincere efforts to obtain a speedy peace was condemned. The example of the

Russian revolution was extolled, and imitation inculcated. Since an allied military victory would involve high sacrifices, the impoverishment of the workers, and the destruction of civilization, the holding of an international conference for the immediate arrangement of peace with separate representation for the workers of the Dominions was demanded. The actual peace terms proposed were much on the lines of the British Labour Party, but the Australian Labour Party was not prepared to fight in order to obtain them. At the same time it formulated a policy for Australian defence, which forbade the training of men who were not voters [1]—thus wholly transforming the defence system of the Commonwealth, which depends on progressive training commenced in early youth ; demanded the election of officers, and the abolition of salutes and other useless discipline, of military oaths and distinctions between commissioned and non-commissioned officers ; required the training of employees in employers' time and at their expense ; forbade the use of military forces in industrial disputes ; and provided for the right of the citizen to retain his arms after the expiry of his training, presumably as a necessary preliminary to the dictatorship of the proletariat. Further participation in recruiting was to be subject to the condition that the allies should clearly express their willingness to make peace without annexations or penal indemnities, and to priority being given to the requirements of Australia for home defence and industrial needs. Labour leaders practically ceased to aid in recruiting, and nothing but the early termination of the war saved Australia from inability to maintain her forces in France.

3. New Zealand and the Compulsory Draft

New Zealand had adopted the same policy of compulsory service for home defence as the Commonwealth, and she thus had available on the outbreak of war material which rendered it possible immediately to offer a force of 8,000 men to the Imperial Government, and this body, leaving New Zealand at the end of October, shared with the Australian contingent the journey to Egypt.

[1] The Labour party in 1920 has advanced the doctrine of the abolition of all compulsion. It has been alleged by a member of the party that preparations were made in 1917 to declare a republic if conscription were carried ; *The Times*, March 8 and 12, 1920.

Volunteers were numerous and eager ; the Maoris were also determined to share in the contest, and, when the news of the landing of Indian troops in France arrived, it was felt that their demand must be accepted, and a contingent left for Egypt. Similar provision [1] as in Australia had to be enacted regarding the control of the men when on active service under the terms of the Army Act, and the defence department was well organized and able to cope with an emergency which it had foreseen and for which it was in some degree prepared.

In the early days of the war the flow of recruits enabled the Government easily to keep up the reinforcements of 1,800 every two months which the War Office deemed adequate to meet the wastage of war. At the close of 1915, however, the intimation was received that the number requisite, on the basis which had been applied in the United Kingdom, should be raised to 2,500,[2] and the difficulty of attaining this figure became obvious. The inequality of voluntaryism was becoming more keenly felt ; public opinion was in advance of the Government in demanding conscription, and the widespread character of the demand was realized by the Minister for Defence when, on making a recruiting appeal to railwaymen at Dunedin, he was met by the demand that the Government should apply conscription, on the ground that the workers, while willing to do their duty, were not inclined to leave their well-paid posts in order to allow less patriotic men to fill them. On the other hand a conference called by the Federation of Labour protested against conscription of men without conscription of wealth.

The way for action had been partially prepared by the National Registration Act of 1915, which enabled the Government to secure the replies of the men between 19 and 45 to questions asking them if they were prepared to serve overseas. The result indicated that 110,000 men were willing to do so, including 33,127 single men and widowers without dependents, but also that 34,386 declined absolutely to serve on any conditions. Up to January 1916, however, the rate of reinforcements necessary had been

---

[1] Act No. 44 of 1915, amended by No. 9 of 1918.

[2] Reduced in August 1917 to 1,920, apparently under pressure from New Zealand ; *The Round Table*, viii. 217–19.

H

kept up, and the new Recruiting Board, composed of the Prime Minister, the Minister of Finance, and the Minister of Defence, which then took over charge had some preliminary success in their operations. Local bodies were urged to co-operate, the national registration returns were brought up to date, and recruiting encouraged. But the needs of the situation were obviously in excess of what could thus be effected, and the Government in May 1916, encouraged by the process of events in the United Kingdom, brought in proposals for conscription. Labour opposed the suggestion, but on the second reading on May 31 a Maori member rebuked their views as indicating more care for money than loyalty, and insisted that the Maoris were fully satisfied with their pay. The second reading passed by 49 votes to 5, the third by 44 to 4, and, though the Legislative Council secured changes in the Bill to provide for a central appellate tribunal and to make some concession to conscientious objectors, the measure was enthusiastically supported there, and became law in August.

The Act [1] established the Expeditionary Force Reserve, consisting of every male natural-born British subject resident in New Zealand between the age of 20 and 46 inclusive, except members of the Expeditionary Force, or men discharged from it, criminals, lunatics, and natives, power being reserved to apply it to natives by proclamation. The reserve was divided into two divisions; the first included unmarried men, men married since May 1, 1915, except those who had a child under 16 by a previous marriage, widowers and men divorced or judicially separated from their wives, if without children under 16. The second included all other reservists. Arrangements were made for the preparation of a register of the reserve, and for the calling up and selection from time to time of as many men as the Minister of Defence considered necessary, the method of selection to be by ballot. The names of the men called up were to be gazetted and thereupon the men became members of the Expeditionary Force as if they had voluntarily enlisted and taken the oath of allegiance. Apart, however, from the ballot, power was given to the Minister of Defence to give notice to a family consisting of two or more

[1] No. 8 of 1916; under Act No. 9 of 1918, s. 6, the reserve created by the Act was abolished by Proclamation of August 13, 1919.

brothers belonging to the first division of the reserve to show cause why they should not be called up for service. A man called up might appeal to a Military Service Board on the ground that he was not a member of the reserve or of the division or class called up, or that by reason of his occupation his calling up was contrary to the public interest, or that by reason of his domestic circumstances or for any other reason his calling up would be a cause of undue hardship to himself or others, it being sufficient evidence of such hardship that the appellant was the sole surviving son of his parents who was of military age, and that at least one of his brothers had been killed in the war, or that he was at the beginning of the war, and had remained, a member of a religious body, under whose doctrines, as well as his own conscientious religious belief, the bearing of arms and the performance of any combatant service were contrary to divine revelation, provided he was willing to perform non-combatant work at the rate of pay which might be fixed. Voluntary enlistment was to proceed contemporaneously until brought to an end by proclamation.

The passing of the Act led to an increase in voluntary recruiting, and, after some delay in making preliminary arrangements, the first ballots in each recruiting district took place on November 16, 1916, thereafter being held monthly, the principle being that persons whose names were drawn should have two months before joining camp in New Zealand for training. Opposition to the carrying out of the Act was not lacking; farmers were extremely apprehensive of the loss of their men or their sons, ignoring the fact that under conditions of transport as they existed great production was not of first-rate importance. There were complaints regarding the medical boards, and the exemption tribunals were hampered by lack of guidance as to the kinds of industry which were essential in the public interest. To meet this difficulty an Industrial Efficiency Board was established to advise the Government on this question, but, as originally constituted, it contained only representatives of business interests and only later, on protests from agriculturists, was a representative of their interests added. Among classes whose cases were adjourned indefinitely were shearers, miners, provided the output was kept up, a condition necessary to prevent reduction, seamen, marine engineers, railway servants, sanitary plumbers, slaughtermen, police, and civil servants. Little was attempted towards securing substitution of female for male labour, the Government taking no steps in the matter even as regards its own employees.

The events of 1918 produced a vital change in the situation, and the Government recognized that further efforts were demanded of New Zealand, which had postponed calling up members of the second division so long that the idea had become widespread that there was no real need for exertion in procuring men. Mr. Lloyd George's appeal[1] after the disaster of March for further aid was answered by an expression of readiness to meet any demands made, and on April 11 Mr. Massey announced that the British Government had asked that a Tank battalion might be formed out of the reserves available in England and that the Dominion Government had assented, and had also agreed that, if the military authorities and the general officer commanding the Army Corps thought fit, any surplus of reserves in England might be used at the front, and had offered again to increase the number sent monthly. On April 15 the Minister of Defence, Sir James Allen, announced the decisions of the Government as to the necessary action. The British Government had asked for a material increase in the number of infantry reinforcements, and to effect this 1,700 more men would be sent in April, May, and June. To secure the men Class B of the second division, comprising married men with one child, would be called up, and classes C and D, married men with two and three children respectively, would be opened for voluntary enlistment.[2] At the same time many first-division cases were reopened, and those affected in the second division took pains to secure that no fit unmarried men should escape service, but in the main the married men responded readily enough to the call. The Government also took power in the Finance Act[3] to make regulations for procuring, enforcing, controlling, and regulating national service during the war; for prohibiting or restricting any service, employment,

[1] *The Times*, April 1, 1918; see above, p. 83.
[2] Voluntary enlistment for the first division ceased on June 23, 1917.
[3] No. 2 of 1918, s. 25.

occupation, business, work or industry ; and for regulating the remuneration for national service, subject, however, to the Arbitration Act and any industrial award or agreement in force. The term 'national service' was defined very widely so as to include the use of any factory, premises, machinery, or the like. These great powers were viewed with much suspicion by the Labour party, but the only concession made by the Government was to promise that any regulations made under the Act would be laid before Parliament, and would be cancelled if disapproved by the House of Representatives. But as far as regards employment the Act remained a dead letter, the only regulations made dealing with restrictions on development works and the raising of new capital by companies, which were intended to divert expenditure into the war loan.

The administration of the Defence Department was, as might be expected, the object of numerous criticisms during the war, but a searching inquiry by a Commission under Sir Robert Anderson of Australia revealed, indeed, many errors in business methods, but no cases of fraud, while emphatic testimony was borne to absence of evidence of ministerial interference in appointments. On the whole also the Government showed commendable firmness in the administration of the Act, though the coalminers by a strike procured virtual exemption for themselves, a concession for which, however, much might be said on the merits of the case. In particular the Prime Minister declined to yield to great pressure brought upon him to intervene in the case of Mr. Webb, member of the House of Representatives for the Grey electorate, a convinced supporter of Labour and an anti-conscriptionist, who having been called up and refused exemption had declined to serve, and been sentenced to two years' imprisonment. It was contended on behalf of his constituency that they were entitled to have him released in order to speak for them in Parliament, but, though concession would have smoothed his path and might have been given on this ground, Mr. Massey declined to compromise on the issue. Mr. Webb's seat shortly after was vacated by his absence from a session of Parliament, and the electorate enabled to secure a spokesman in the House.

4. THE UNION OF SOUTH AFRICA

The energies of the Union of South Africa were at first entirely sunk in the conduct of the expedition against German South-West Africa, which was delayed by operations to suppress the rebellion of a section of the Boer population. Like the Commonwealth and New Zealand, the Union had adopted a system of compulsory service for the defence of the Union, but the operation of the scheme had been limited by financial considerations which resulted in making the scheme in operation in peace time practically a voluntary one. Not until the conclusion of the campaign in South-West Africa was it possible for the Union to consider the question of sending a contingent to Europe, and an unexpected difficulty then presented itself. As explained by the Minister of Defence in a minute of June 24, 1915, the cost of the expedition to South-West Africa would amount to at least £15,000,000, and for this Parliament had made provision.[1] But no provision had been made for any expenditure on an overseas force to be paid by the Union at Union Defence Force rates, which were roughly thrice as high as Imperial rates, and a special session of Parliament would have been requisite to authorize such expenditure. To call such a session would have been invidious, as Parliament was on the eve of expiring, while the Government could not pledge itself to it while it was not secure of a return to power. The only offer, therefore, which it could make was one of the formation of a contingent which, on leaving Africa, would at once become part of the Imperial forces and be paid by the Imperial Government at Imperial rates. The loyalty of the British community in South Africa showed itself in eagerness to accept these meagre terms, and before the end of the year an infantry brigade, five batteries of heavy artillery, an aviation squadron, a signalling company, and a general and field hospital had been sent to Europe.

This, however, was not the only step taken by the Government. On July 9 a pressing request emanated from the Imperial Government for the dispatch of 200 men as a garrison for Nyasaland, and the Union Government expressed readiness to comply

---

[1] Act No. 18 of 1915.

with this request, but held that Union rates of pay must be applicable to this contingent, and that in the absence of statutory authority the force must be maintained from Imperial funds. There was hesitation on the part of the War Office to attempt the differentiation of payment to Imperial troops, and the same question arose in a much more important form in the case of the troops which were asked for for service in East Africa [1] after the successes of the Germans had indicated that the forces, British and Indian, available at the time were inadequate for the purpose. The situation was in a measure cleared up after the general election had secured the Government in power ; General Botha then procured the approval by Parliament of the principle that the Union should bear the difference between Imperial and Union rates of pay in respect of the forces sent from the Union for service in East and Central Africa. The position of the forces sent to Europe thus became more and more anomalous, until it was finally disposed of by the agreement of the Imperial Government to pay them at Union rates from January 1, 1917, while the Union Government secured the grant of a sum of £1,000,000 to the Imperial Government as a contribution to war expenditure. The reason for the apparently ungenerous action of the Union was simple ; the Nationalist opposition was bitterly opposed to any expenditure and any assistance of any kind by the Government ; the Unionists were anxious that the Union should act in the same manner as the other Dominions, and bear the whole cost of the contingents, and the Government found it advisable to steer an intermediate course. On the one hand they lent to the Imperial Government the full aid of their military organization in securing troops, thus rendering it unnecessary for South Africans to proceed to Europe to volunteer for service, and on the other they compromised on the question of payment.

In addition to European troops, South Africa lent invaluable aid by the raising of coloured and native forces for non-combatant duties both in Europe and in East Africa,[2] while coloured forces were employed on combatant work in East Africa. The Defence

[1] Recruiting began in September 1915, and in November the Union Government undertook to organize a brigade which took the field in February 1916. These and all the other Union forces served under the Army Act.

[2] Cf. Sir H. Sloley, *Journal of African Society*, xvii. 199–211.

Act of the Union expressly excludes natives from the scope of its operation, and any proposal to arm them was obviously unaccept-able, especially as General Smuts in his command (from January 12, 1916) of the British forces operating in East Africa came with increasing rapidity to recognize the extreme efficiency attainable under African conditions of warfare by native troops, and to see in this possibility one of the gravest menaces to the future of Africa.

It was inevitable that as early as 1917 the shortage of recruits for Europe[1] should have been felt, but the possibility of compulsion was out of the question. In Canada the Government respected for long the objections of Quebec, though these were not to be compared in gravity to the attitude of a populace of which a con-siderable portion had been either in open rebellion or in active sympathy with rebels but a brief period before. The remarkable thing was not that the supply of recruits fell short of the number aimed at, but that men proved so ready to abandon their prospects in the Union to take effective part in the war, although they knew only too well that the losses suffered by the British popula-tion during hostilities could hardly fail to prove a grave handicap when those who escaped death returned to their homes.

5. The Royal Newfoundland Regiment

Newfoundland alone of the Dominions had at the outbreak of war no military resources of any kind, the last Imperial troops having been withdrawn in 1868, and since that date no effort having been made for an emergency which no one foresaw. But immediately after the beginning of hostilities the Government decided to secure the representation of the island in the Imperial forces, and an offer was made to provide by the end of October a battalion equipped as far as practicable locally. Volunteers[2] were secured, and sent to England, and the number was gradually increased until a full battalion had been made up. The men were enlisted in the first instance for a year only ; the expiry of that

---

[1] Up to May 1917, 66,150 had enlisted for overseas service and 4,000 had gone on their own account ; 44,214 had volunteered for service in Africa.

[2] Provision was made for its discipline under the Army Act by an Act (c. 4) of the War Session, and for its cost by c. 8.

time found the firstcomers still in England, and they were duly offered the choice of re-enlistment or return to their homes ; the acceptance of re-enlistment was unanimous, and the regiment shortly after began an honourable career at Gallipoli.

In 1917, in addition to the steps taken to keep the regiment at full strength, a new departure of importance was made in the dispatch to Scotland of a Forestry Corps. With the exception of the Adjutant, whose primary business was to maintain the military organization of the corps, the officers were practical lumbermen. Recruits were not accepted unless medically unfit for the field, or married men, not too young, with families. Among the 500 men whom the corps ultimately contained, there were old men of sixty, past fighting age, and lads too young to be recruited for the ordinary service, as well as men whose active service had been cut short by wounds received in France.

Not until 1918 was compulsion deemed necessary, but in response to the urgent appeals for aid which followed the March offensive, the two houses of the Legislature each passed unanimously at the beginning of May an Act for compulsory service.[1] It was immediately followed by the issue of a proclamation calling all unmarried men between 19 and 25 to the colours by May 24. But the total of voluntary enlistments from the beginning of April to the middle of May had risen to 600, showing emphatically the anxiety of the Newfoundlanders to render what aid they could, and within three weeks from the coming into force of the Act, 1,500 men enlisted.

The total of men recruited up to the date of the armistice reached 9,236; 1,082 men killed or died of wounds, and 2,314 wounded, attest the gallantry and services of the regiment. But the number should be increased by not less than 3,000 Newfoundlanders who enlisted in the Canadian forces, attracted by the high pay given by Canada. Moreover, the small population had also to supply men for the Royal Naval Reserve, and its scanty numbers rendered the proportion of men who for domestic reasons could not be spared, exceptionally high.

[1] C. 26. A home-defence force was also sanctioned by c. 25, and a Department of Militia provided for by c. 17 of 1917.

6. The Military Contribution of the Dominions

Throughout the war there were at times efforts made in the Dominions by those opposed to the process of recruitment for the oversea forces to criticize adversely the national effort of the United Kingdom, and to suggest that the Dominions were being called upon unfairly to contribute towards defence, and that their troops were unduly exposed to losses and danger. The actual figures [1] of the men raised and the losses suffered are an instructive commentary on these charges.

At the outset of the war the total forces of the United Kingdom were 733,514, and during the war no fewer than 4,970,902 men were recruited. As the estimated male population of the United Kingdom in July 1914 was 22,485,501, the percentage of serving troops to the male population was 25·36; if Ireland, which in its effort fell lamentably short of the rest of the United Kingdom, is omitted, the percentage rises to 27·28. The losses in killed were up to April 13, 1919, 549,967, wounded, 1,649,946, and missing, 253,353, giving a percentage of casualties to the male population of 10·91.

In the case of Canada the total forces sent oversea or in training at the armistice came to 458,218 men; the estimated white male population, including only those born in Canada or the British Isles, was in July 1911, 3,400,000, giving a percentage of serving troops to male population of 13·48. The killed numbered 55,175; wounded, 149,733; missing, 767; giving a percentage of casualties to male population of 6·04. The percentage of serving troops was nearly the same in the case of Australia, being 13·43, there being 331,814 men sent overseas or in training, to an estimated population in July 1911 of 2,470,000. The casualties were higher: killed, 55,585; wounded, 151,245; missing, 3,121; or a percentage of 8·50 to male population. The contribution of New Zealand in men was proportionately higher; from a total of 580,000 males, she sent or had in training 112,223 men, a percentage of 19·35; her casualties were: killed, 16,132; wounded, 40,749; missing, 5; a percentage to population of 9·80. South

[1] *The Round Table*, ix. 495–505. The figures given officially at various times differ slightly from those here adopted. Those for South Africa include service in East Africa.

Africa, from 685,000 male white population, sent or trained 76,184 men, or 11·12 per cent.; her casualties were: killed, 6,928; wounded, 11,444; missing, 33; a percentage of 2·7. In addition, however, 44,000 coloured and native troops were recruited in South Africa for service in labour brigades, and they suffered severe losses, mainly from epidemics.

The figures alone are sufficient to establish the severity of the strain put on the United Kingdom, but there are other factors to be borne in mind which emphasize its character. The proportion of older men past military service in the United Kingdom is larger than in the Dominions; the percentage of rural population is higher there, and the average physique better, while a considerable proportion of the male population of the Dominions consists of British emigrants, naturally drawn, especially in view of the rigid physical standards now enforced on entry by the Dominion Governments, from the fittest of their contemporaries. Moreover, the male population in the Dominions is certainly underestimated, in comparison with the British, the estimates being based on the figures of the census of July 1911, without allowance for the often considerable increase of population since. Nor can it be forgotten that in the United Kingdom a very large number of men physically fit for service was employed on munition work, that a smaller number was so employed in Canada, and that munition work in the other Dominions was on a much less considerable scale. In the case of Canada, allowance must also be made for the enormous population of French-speaking Canadians, whose holding back left more than a fair share to be borne by the British-speaking members of the people.

These facts are relevant, for it is the great strain which was imposed on the man power of the United Kingdom which explains the fact that in the later stages of the war the Dominion troops were clearly superior in physical power, and the resultant energy, to the British troops. Further, the number of divisions maintained by the United Kingdom was always proportionately higher than the number of Dominion divisions in relation to the total of troops available, and in the year 1918 it was found necessary to reduce British infantry brigades to three battalions each in lieu of the normal four which remained the Dominion number. British units were consequently often under strength as compared with Dominion units, and had less chance of relief and relaxation. The extent to which the Dominions' forces were picked men, volunteers for the greater part, is shown effectively in the number of casualties reckoned to the number of men sent overseas or in training in November 1918. The percentage in the case of the United Kingdom, which supplied a large number of low-category troops for work in the back areas, was 43 ; in the case of Canada, which supplied large numbers of technical troops, 44·88 ; in that of Australia, whose soldiers distinguished themselves by their extreme audacity and push, 63·36 ; and in that of New Zealand, 50·70 per cent. The value of the Dominion forces cannot, therefore, be overestimated, and, if the totals sent fell far short of the British effort, it would be idle to ignore how little possible it was to bring home to communities long indifferent to European affairs the essential character of the war as one for their own liberty as much as for that of the rest of the world.

It must be remembered also that the value of the Dominion troops was enhanced by the fact that from the first they served under the orders of the Commanders-in-Chief in the area in which they were stationed, that they had been trained largely upon British lines, and that, though in some cases differently equipped, they could easily enough be assimilated to British troops, considerations rendering them of much greater value than mere allied forces ever can be. On the other hand, as they were kept in distinctive units, they preserved a character of their own, and in a comparatively brief time were able to supply men fully fitted to lead them. Nor was their quasi-national character a disadvantage ; though Sir Arthur Currie, as the commander of the Canadian Army Corps, was under the superior command of a British officer, it was claimed, doubtless with justice, that he could exercise a greater degree of independence in suggesting considerations affecting operations to be carried out by his troops than would have been possible or natural in a British officer in a similar command, and that this position enabled him to afford material aid in the successful completion of the war, in the last stages of which Dominion troops played a part of rare distinction and value.

A question of some interest presents itself as to the extent to which the measure of distinction, which belonged to the Dominion forces as appertaining to territories possessing independent governments, came into operation during the war. The evidence, however, on this point is inadequate to permit of any definite conclusions. It is of interest, at any rate, to note that Sir Edward Kemp, as Minister of the Overseas Forces of Canada, stated that early in 1918 he had declined to reduce the number of brigades in a division at the period when the reduction was made in respect to British divisions, and that he had successfully made representations to Sir Douglas Haig and even to Marshal Foch, in order to secure the keeping of the Canadian Corps together at a time when reinforcements were wanted which did not include an entire Army Corps. The statement is interesting as indicating the possibility of more serious division of authority in cases where the numbers of troops supplied by the various portions of the Empire were more nearly equal in numbers to those of the United Kingdom.

Suggestions have, not unnaturally, been made that the lessons of the war should be turned to account by the adoption of more effective arrangements for military co-operation in time of war, and in 1919 three committees, with Dominion representatives, considered various aspects of military defence from this point of view. But the proposal has not received substantial support from the public of the Dominions, which rather deduces from the facts of the war and the formation of the League of Nations that wars in future should be few, and that voluntary co-operation after they have been initiated is sufficient for all practical purposes. Moreover the burden of unproductive expenditure is deeply resented in lands with enormous tasks of development before them, and there is on every hand indication of marked anxiety to curtail to the maximum public expenditure of an unremunerative character. Thus in Canada, though authority was formally given in 1919 for the increase of the permanent military force from a maximum of 5,000 before the war to 10,000, the Government made no effort to act on the authority, and in June 1920 the total stood only at 3,555. A reorganization of districts has been effected, their number being fixed at eleven, each with a small staff and a small force of the permanent corps, charged with the duty of training the Militia, organized as 110 infantry regiments and 75 batteries of artillery. Steps have been taken also to provide for an Air Force, a limited number of selected airmen being trained for a short period annually under the Air Board established by an Act of 1919. The Board is charged also with duties of scientific investigation and exploration, and provincial interest has been secured. Even, however, these moderate steps, which are in principle identical with the pre-war policy, were criticized by the opposition as involving unjustifiable expense.

In Australia also the Government has determined to adhere to its established military policy, despite the demands of the Labour Party for the abolition or restriction of compulsory service, but that policy is to be modified in respect of the precise period of training youths, the time of training now being restricted to four years. New Zealand has been equally conservative, and the requirements of the law as to compulsory training have been treated with much liberality in view of the absence of any immediate danger, and the existence in the Dominion of a large body of fully trained men, a factor which has also affected in important regards the military policy of the Commonwealth. One step of importance, however, was announced in the Prime Minister's financial statement on July 27, 1920 : in view of the fact that the defence of the country would in future require co-operation between naval, air, and land forces, the Government had decided to institute a Committee of Defence, as recommended by the Committee of Imperial Defence in 1911, to advise the Government on higher policy, and to co-ordinate the naval, air, and military defence of the Dominion.

In the case of the Union the war destroyed the plan of the Defence Act of 1912, which contemplated that the South African Mounted Rifles, the permanent force of the Union, should perform police and military duties combined ; the existing force at the outbreak of war had first to be called from the five districts into which the Union was divided, and stationed on the German frontier, while later it shared in the operations against that territory, and after that many of its members enlisted for service in East Africa or overseas. Its police functions were performed from 1914 by the South African Police, and on the termination of hostilities it was decided to let the South African Mounted Rifles revert to their primary duty of acting as police. It was also decided to resume the system of training in force before the war, but the suggestion to create a small permanent military force at least to bridge the period between the effective result of the resumption of training, evoked from the Nationalist party on July 23, 1920, a vehement protest against a system of militarization. The Prime Minister met the attack by a frank assertion that he was wholly opposed to militarization, and regarded money spent needlessly on defence as subtracted from the development of the country, but he indicated that, though the League of Nations might bring greater safety in future, for the time being it was impossible to dispense with some form of defence ; the question, however, could only be settled next year, when the whole matter would be open for examination in detail.

Needless to say the suggestion, favourably viewed in the report of Lord Esher's Committee on the Army in India, that there should be created a single Imperial General Staff, including Dominion representatives, which would determine the policy of the Empire Governments as to military defence, has received no approval in the Dominions from Governments or Parliaments.

CHAPTER VI

DOMINION WAR OPERATIONS AND NAVAL DEFENCE

1. THE CONQUEST OF GERMAN SOUTH-WEST AFRICA.
   Plan of campaign — Outbreak of rebellion — Renewal of operations and completion of conquest.
2. THE REBELLION IN SOUTH AFRICA.
   Parliamentary approval of Union attack on South-West Africa — Treachery of Maritz — Van Rensburg's vision — Death of de la Rey — Resignation of Beyers — Outbreak of rebellion — Efforts for reconciliation — Failure of negotiations — Death of Beyers and capture of de Wet — Leniency to rebels — Causes of the rebellion.
3. THE EXPEDITIONS IN THE WESTERN PACIFIC.
   Australian expedition against German New Guinea — New Zealand's occupation of Samoa.
4. THE DOMINION NAVAL FORCES AND THE WAR.
   Origin and development of Commonwealth fleet unit — Transfer to Admiralty control on outbreak of war — War service — Naval forces in the other Dominions.
5. THE FUTURE OF NAVAL DEFENCE.
   Discussions with the Admiralty in 1918 — Lord Jellicoe's visit to the Dominions and recommendations — Views of the Dominions.

1. THE CONQUEST OF GERMAN SOUTH-WEST AFRICA

GERMAN SOUTH-WEST AFRICA had been lost to the Empire, in the main owing to the delay of the Government of the Cape of Good Hope, in the period 1883–4, in accepting responsibility for the cost of the administration of the territory, if the United Kingdom would agree to its annexation. The failure of the German Government in the period of the Boer war to render the support which many Boers anticipated, and some claimed had been promised, cooled the relations of interest which had at one time existed between the Boers in the Republics and the Germans, as representing a great power which might be used against the extension of British power in South Africa. With the Government in German South-West Africa the Governments of the four colonies, and later of the Union, lived on good terms, and their goodwill was of distinct importance to Germany in her finally successful efforts to reduce to submission, though by barbaric methods, the natives of the territory. But it was obvious that in any war with Germany there would be presented to the Union an ideal opportunity for acquiring lands which should normally have formed part of the Union.

The initiative in an attack on German South-West Africa came, however, from the Imperial Government on August 6, 1914,[1] and was based not on a proposal of conquest but on the necessity of preventing the activity of the wireless installations of the Germans in the territory which menaced British sea-power. It was indeed made perfectly clear that, if the territory were conquered, the Union must be prepared to leave the disposal of it under the terms of peace in the hands of the Imperial Government. The Union Government gave a ready acceptance of the proposal, and Parliament, which was hastily summoned to ratify the decision, gave approval by a strong majority. The position of the Government had in the meantime been strengthened by the action of the German forces, which had crossed in aggression the extreme south-east corner of the frontier at Nakob, a fact on which the Government not unnaturally laid much stress as an argument to secure the adherence of their supporters to active measures.

The task undertaken by the Government was the heavier in that it was to be accomplished by the use of Union forces only, for the Union Government had assented immediately on the outbreak of war to the withdrawal of the small Imperial garrison in the Union. The permanent force of the Union under the Defence Act [2] was intended for the purposes of a mounted police, and was, of course, numerically far too weak for an attack on forces which included at least 5,000 trained soldiers. The citizen forces, however, were eager, and some of them had been well trained in volunteer corps before the war, or in formations under the Act, which, however, had only been a couple of years in operation, while there were many veterans, British and Boer, of the war of 1899–1902. The plan of attack was dictated by the communications of the territory ; from the ports of Swakopmund in the north and Lüderitzbucht on the south, railway lines run to join, at Karibib and Seeheim, the central railway which extended from Otavi (with branches to Tsumeb and Grootfontein) on the north

---

[1] *Parl. Pap.* Cd. 7873.   [2] No. 13 of 1912.

through Windhuk, the capital, to Ukamas, just short of the Orange River, the boundary between German and British territory on the south. Landings at the two ports could effectively be supported by advances against the southern extremity of the railway from Steinkopf, on the Namaqualand line from Port Nolloth to O'okiep, and from Prieska, the terminus of the line from De Aar. In accordance with this plan a force of infantry, light horse, and artillery under Colonel Beves of the permanent forces occupied Lüderitzbucht successfully on September 19, the safety of the convoy being secured by the escort of H.M.S. *Astraea*. At Lüderitzbucht it was joined by the force destined for Swakopmund, which had been diverted from that port on the news of the disaster which had just overtaken the force of Brigadier-General Lukin at Sandfontein. This body of troops had left Cape Town on September 2, and had established its base at Steinkopf, with the intention of advancing on German territory across Raman's Drift on the Orange River, contemporaneously with an advance on Schuit Drift from Upington by troops under Lieutenant-Colonel Maritz. Lack of caution and the defection of Maritz proved fatal to it ; the German Commander-in-Chief, Colonel von Heydebreck, on September 26, defeated, and captured the remnant of, a force of South African Mounted Rifles and Transvaal Horse Artillery at Sandfontein, the only real military success which the Germans were to attain in the war. It was necessary for the time being to meet the dangers created by the treachery of Maritz, and the combined force at Lüderitzbucht under the command of Colonel Sir Duncan McKenzie could undertake no offensive measures of importance until well on in the following year. Steps, however, were taken for the projected advance ; the railway which the Germans had destroyed on evacuating Lüderitzbucht was rebuilt, Sir George Farrar, who had lent his services for this purpose, losing his life by an unhappy accident, and the position of the British forces was gradually advanced first on December 13 to Tschaukaib, and on February 19, 1915, to Garub. The way for a further advance was in the meantime paved by the dispatch of Colonel Skinner to Walfish Bay, which he re-occupied, the port having been for a time in German hands, on Christmas Day, and to Swakopmund, which fell into his hands without fighting on

January 16, 1915. On February 11, General Botha, after inspecting the forces at Lüderitzbucht and Tschaukaib, arrived at Swakopmund and took over command. Four days later a flood on the Swakop River did some damage, but was of great value as facilitating the British operations throughout the rest of the campaign, for water was thus easily found close to the surface even after the flood had subsided, and the advance of General Botha's mounted troops most unexpectedly facilitated. On February 22 an advance from Swakopmund drove the enemy into the interior.

On the south, after the disaster of Sandfontein, General Lukin was compelled to abandon Raman's Drift, and the Germans held Schuit Drift and the whole of the southern and the eastern frontier, whence they, with the aid of the rebels under Maritz and Kemp, penetrated from time to time into British territory. Upington, which was commanded by Colonel van Deventer, was attacked on January 23, with disastrous results for the rebels, and soon after 40 officers and 517 men of Kemp's commando laid down their arms with their commander at Upington, while 4 officers and 46 men of Maritz's commando surrendered at the same time. The rest of Maritz's commando were expected to surrender in the various places where they were dispersed, but before the surrender was carried out the German forces made an attack on Kakamas, on February 3, but completely failed. Maritz, apparently as a result of this fight, did not surrender, but fled to Portuguese territory. The defeat of the rebellion, however, facilitated an offensive, and at the end of February and the beginning of March, van Deventer invaded German territory in three columns, by Raman's Drift, by Schuit Drift, and by Nakob, while a column under Colonel Berrangé left on March 6 Kuruman on a 600 miles march across a waterless desert in order to cross the eastern frontier near Rietfontein and take the German forces in the rear. To co-operate with Berrangé, van Deventer detached a force under his brother, in order that the combined forces should seize the railway in the rear of the German forces, who were holding a position of great natural strength at Noacheb, where the railway from Kalkfontein on the south runs through mountain ranges to Keetmanshoop on the north. On April 7 Kalkfontein was occupied, on April 11 General Smuts arrived to take over com-

I 2

mand, and a general advance was begun in which McKenzie's forces from Garub co-operated, being charged with the duty of seeking to cut the railway at Gibeon, before the main body of the German forces could retire north. This he just failed to do, though he won, after a reverse on April 25, a substantial victory on the following day at Gibeon, but the Germans had hastily to evacuate the whole of the south of the territory, the conquest of which was proclaimed by General Smuts on April 27 at Aus.

Events had moved too rapidly in the south to permit of steps being taken by General Botha in the north to occupy Karibib and thus prevent the German forces escaping north. But on May 5 Botha had occupied Karibib, and Windhuk was shortly afterwards surrendered without bloodshed, the wireless installation thus falling into British hands. The effect of the loss of the capital and the wireless installation, which was its chief possession, was seen in an overture for surrender which was now received from the German Commander-in-Chief Francke, Colonel von Heydebreck having been killed early in the war by a bomb explosion. Botha returned from Windhuk to Karibib, arranged an armistice of forty-eight hours from May 20, and met at Giftkop, 30 miles north of Karibib, the German Governor Seitz and the Commander-in-Chief. The German terms, however, proved absurd; they suggested that the forces should remain until the end of the war in Europe in the positions they then occupied. Botha, declining to prolong the armistice, immediately prepared to advance north in pursuit of the Germans as they retired along the railway line. The final march began on June 18, Botha in the centre with two mounted brigades and an infantry brigade and heavy artillery, Myburgh with a burgher column on the right wing, and Brits with a similar column on the left. The advance was extremely rapid, and the German resistance ineffective; on July 1 the mounted forces occupied Otavi, followed three days later by the infantry, who had marched 80 miles in four days through hot and waterless country. By that time a local armistice had been arranged, the German forces being given until the morning of July 9 to surrender. Myburgh, with equal energy, had occupied Tsumeb on July 4, after the Germans had fired on his troops during a parley, and had then tried to induce him to withdraw, on the plea that the armistice at Otavi applied to Tsumeb also. Brits on July 6 appeared at Namutoni, 40 miles north-west of Tsumeb, where the German commander and 170 officers and men surrendered to him. The German positions at Tsumeb were now completely untenable, but surrender was delayed until the last moment.

The terms granted were extremely generous, especially when it is remembered that the Germans had poisoned wells and had treated prisoners with much lack of humanity. The officers were allowed to retain their arms on giving their parole, and were to be permitted to live in any place that they selected. The non-commissioned officers and men retained their rifles without ammunition, and were to be interned in any place within South-West Africa chosen by the Union Government. The reservists, the settlers who having been settled in the territory had joined the forces on the outbreak of war, were allowed to return to their homes on parole, and permitted to keep their rifles. No other action was possible, for the misrule [1] of Germany had created such strong hatred against the Germans that, unprotected, their lives would have been in the gravest danger.

The leniency of the terms is obvious, and was freely criticized at the time. The argument that the losses, which further fighting would have involved, deterred General Botha from carrying the war to its logical conclusion of unconditional surrender is patently absurd, but the reflection that the prolongation of hostilities would have involved much pecuniary outlay was doubtless a most important factor in determining the Prime Minister's attitude. Moreover, it was obvious that the Union Government had a heavy task to face in winding up the rebellion among the irreconcilable section of the Boer population in the Union, and in proceeding with the difficult duty of restoring harmony in that population, and that everything which distracted the Premier from these duties was to be deprecated. A further consideration doubtless lay in the fact of the uncertainty of the future ; if the territory was to be returned to Germany after the war, no useful purpose lay in taking any steps beyond those necessary to render it unavailable for aid to Germany during hostilities, nor, if it

[1] *Parl. Pap.* Cd. 9146.

were to be retained, was it any part of the purpose of the Government to expel the German settlers who had made their homes there.

The whole of the credit for the campaign rested with the South African forces and their leaders, whose strategy was independent of Imperial suggestion or guidance. They were fortunate in so far as they possessed a great superiority of numbers, from 40,000 to 50,000 men being put in the field, and still more perhaps in the fact that the German leaders showed no capacity for command, and threw away many chances of harassing the attacks by cutting communications, defeating isolated parties of the British forces, and so forth.[1] But the value of the British victory was great, especially coming as it did after the defeat of the rebellion, for the distinguished part played in it by the Dutch went some way to effacing the mutual distrust of British and Dutch created by that episode. At the same time the campaign showed in a distinctive manner the importance of British sea power. It was only the complete command of the sea enjoyed by the British fleet which enabled men to be transported with guns and equipment to Lüderitzbucht and Swakopmund, and, had this possibility been shut off by the strength of the German naval forces, the contest would have presented almost unsurmountable difficulties owing to transport questions. It is doubtful, however, whether this fact was fully appreciated by the people of the Union.

2. The Rebellion in South Africa

It is doubtful whether, when ministers expressed on August 10, 1914, their readiness to act on the suggestion of the Imperial Government for an attack on German South-West Africa, they realized how grave would be the discontent which their decision would raise in certain quarters among the Dutch population. In Parliament, indeed, matters went satisfactorily in the special session which was promptly summoned to approve the policy of attack on German South-West Africa, announced by the Prime Minister on September 9. The House of Assembly, ' fully recognizing the obligations of the Union as a portion of the British Empire ',

[1] See W. Whittal, *With Botha and Smuts in Africa* (1917) ; R. Hennig, *Deutsch Sud West im Weltkriege* (1920) for divergent views of the strategy of the campaign.

passed a humble address, assuring His Majesty of ' its loyal support in bringing to a successful issue the momentous conflict which has been forced upon him in defence of the principles of liberty and of international honour, and of its whole-hearted determination to take all measures necessary for defending the interests of the Union and for co-operating with His Majesty's Imperial Government to maintain the security and integrity of the Empire ', and further requesting His Majesty to convey to the King of the Belgians sympathy with the Belgian people in their struggle. An amendment to this was moved by the Labour party, dealing with the necessity of the reduction of armaments after the termination of the war, but this was not pressed. On the other hand, Mr. Hertzog proposed an amendment that ' This house, being fully prepared to support all measures of defence which may be necessary to resist any attack on Union territory, is of opinion that any act in the nature of an attack, or which may lead to an attack, on German territory in South Africa would be in conflict with the interests of the Union and of the Empire '. But Mr. Hertzog could claim only 12 supporters against the 92 of the Government, including, besides General Botha's own followers, the Unionists and the Labour party. Even from the Orange Free State only nine of the members voted for the amendment, while six supported the motion. In the Senate, General de la Rey also opposed an attack on German territory, but his loyalty to the Government and to General Botha prevented him from voting against the governmental proposal.

There were others who, unlike Mr. Hertzog and de la Rey, were prepared to carry the matter to an armed revolt.[1] Maritz had served in the Boer War, and at its termination left the country, apparently apprehensive lest some of his proceedings during that conflict might bring him into trouble He tried his fortune in Madagascar and then in German South-West Africa, where by organizing a transport service among Dutch farmers he aided the Germans very substantially in their war of extermination against the Hereros. Later he returned to the Orange Free State and entered the Union Police there. On the organization of the Defence Force he was given a commission in the force, and in

[1] *Parl. Pap.* Cd. 7874.

1912 passed through the Military Training School at Bloemfontein. Early in 1913 he was placed in charge of Military District No. 12, comprising the north-western Cape districts on the German border. At the beginning of August 1914, on the urgent representations of General Beyers, the Commandant-General of the Defence Forces, he was appointed as Lieutenant-Colonel of the forces on the Union border in the direction of Kakamas and Upington. There can be no doubt of the motives which led him to seek this post. As early as the time of his study at Bloemfontein he appears to have been in communication with the Governor-General of German South-West Africa, with a view to the recovery at a suitable moment of the independence of the Boer Republics, and it can hardly be doubted that he secured his post on the frontier in order to facilitate a movement for which the war with Germany seemed to offer exceptional facilities. Whether General Beyers was already committed to this policy when he urged Maritz's appointment, cannot be known [1]; a rival of General Botha for power in the Transvaal, his opposition had been bought off on the concession of responsible government in 1906 by his appointment to the Speakership, and he had hoped for the Speakership of the Union when the colonies were amalgamated. He failed to obtain this ambition, as a result of one of the compromises necessary when the Prime Ministership went to General Botha, and not to Mr. Merriman, Premier of the Cape, and seems not to have been consoled by the honour conferred on him in 1912 in his appointment to be Commandant-General of the Defence Force. A visit to Europe, during which he was granted an audience by the German Emperor, possibly helped to impress upon his mind the possibility of German aid. What is certain is that the Government and Maritz alike trusted him; on August 11 Maritz visited him at Pretoria, and hastening back to his command was met by Joubert, who in July had been in German territory, and whom he made at once staff captain. Soon afterwards Joubert proceeded to Pretoria, where he interviewed Beyers. Maritz's designs must have been plain almost immediately, for when the German authorities ordered all cattle

---

[1] The Commission appointed to inquire into the causes of the revolt, which reported in February 1917, found no proof of treasonable relations with Germany.

in the south of the territory to be driven north, some Dutch
farmers took refuge with their herds over the British border, and
fired on German patrols who pursued them. Maritz proceeded on
August 21 to the border, had a conversation by telephone with
the German commanding officer at Warmbad, and on his return
denounced the farmers as murderers, his irritation doubtless arising from the difficulties which this episode might put in the way
of the co-operation which he expected from Germany.

Maritz, however, could expect to effect little without the aid
of more distinguished men, and the hopes of the rebels centred in
de la Rey, whose popularity in the Western Transvaal was un-
rivalled. De la Rey was sensitive to religious influences, and
a seer, van Rensburg of Lichtenburg, had seen in a vision the
number 15 on a dark cloud with blood issuing from it, and de la Rey
returning home without his hat, followed by a carriage covered
with flowers. It was thought that a great meeting of burghers
summoned at Treurfontein on August 15 would witness a definite
declaration of opposition to the Government by de la Rey, but
the hope was disappointed ; General Botha had interviewed
de la Rey, and the latter confined himself to advising his hearers
to await events. September 15 was chosen as the moment for
a better concerted plot. Major Kemp, in charge of the training
camp at Potchefstroom, was to be trusted, and the citizen forces
in the Western Transvaal would then be gathered there for training, and might be relied on to revolt if de la Rey addressed them ;
Beyers at Pretoria had prepared and handed to the press for
publication on September 15 a manifesto resigning his post and
denouncing the Government ; on the morning of the 15th, Joubert
arrived from Maritz with a message ' that all arrangements had
been made and all was ready '. De la Rey had been down at
Cape Town to protest in Parliament against the governmental
policy. The conspirators expected him to return via Kimberley,
arriving at Potchefstroom on the 15th, but he had taken the
route through the Free State, and reached instead Johannesburg.
Joubert was hastily sent in a motor car to fetch him to Beyers at
Pretoria, and he seems to have yielded to his persuasion to go to
Potchefstroom. The route of the motor in which Beyers and he
travelled lay through Johannesburg, and the police were on the

outlook for a gang of bandits, who were thought to have escaped in a motor car. Beyers' car was challenged, and probably in the belief that the conspiracy was known no reply was given ; the patrol fired, and de la Rey was killed instantaneously.

The movement for rebellion came thus to a standstill for the moment. Beyers's manifesto had been censored by the Government, and only appeared in the press on September 21, accompanied by a reply of great force by General Smuts, in which he exposed in full the treachery of the General. ' For the Dutch-speaking section in particular ', he wrote, ' I cannot conceive anything more fatal and humiliating than a policy of lip loyalty in fair weather and a policy of neutrality and pro-German sentiment in days of storm and stress.' Beyers in the meantime had perjured himself beyond forgiveness ; at de la Rey's funeral on September 20, he had declared that rebellion was far from his thoughts, and called the spirit of de la Rey to witness to the truth of his assertion. At a meeting held at Lichtenburg on the following day, when he, Kemp, and de Wet were present, he declared, when the flag of the old Orange Free State was unfurled by one of the audience, ' We don't want any of this nonsense here.' Maritz, however, was not prepared to recede from his plans, and indeed must have felt that it was too late to do so. General Smuts, to put the matter to the test, instructed him to co-operate in an advance on German territory, and on September 25 received the reply that his force was unfit to take the offensive, that he would do his best to support the Government on the British side of the frontier, but if there were further plans to attack German territory he desired his resignation to be accepted. An emissary from General Smuts found on September 27 Maritz's force at Upington totally untrustworthy, and on October 2 Maritz moved to Van Rooisvlei, 25 miles west of Upington, crossed the border with Joubert on the 6th, and on the 9th, after disarming the machine-gun section which was under British officers, persuaded the bulk of his commando of some 600 men to rebel. Sixty loyal officers and men were handed over to the Germans. General Smuts in the meantime had ordered Colonel Brits to take over the command from Maritz, and Colonel Bouwer had been sent by Brits to summon Maritz to surrender his command. On arrival he was arrested, but released in order to take back the ultimatum that, unless Maritz was allowed to meet Hertzog, Beyers, de Wet, Muller, and Kemp, he would invade the Cape. He was in possession of guns and small arms, ammunition, and money received from the Germans, had been given a German command, and, besides having correspondence with the German authorities dating back to September, was in possession of a treaty, signed by the Governor of German South-West Africa, guaranteeing the independence of the Union as a republic, and undertaking not to invade it save on Maritz's invitation, in return for the cession of Walfish Bay and other portions of Union territory. Maritz was flying the republican flag.

The Government had no option but to act promptly; on October 11 commandants in the Transvaal were ordered to commandeer 100 men in preparation for action, and on the following day the facts of the rebellion were made public and martial law proclaimed throughout the Union. The operations against Maritz were entrusted to Brits, who defeated him on October 15 and 26, dispersing his forces and driving Maritz to take refuge in German territory. In the meantime rebellion had broken out in the Transvaal; on October 13 the conspirators met at Kopjes in the Orange Free State to concert plans, and Beyers and de Wet met at Pretoria on the following day. On October 19, 150 men of the Lichtenburg commando under Veldkornet Claassen mutinied, and Beyers left Pretoria, and was next heard of on October 22, when he was at Damhoek in the Transvaal with a rebel commando. On the same day, at Kopjes, de Wet and Kemp held a meeting, at which a resolution was passed that ' Whereas the Dutch South African people in the Orange Free State and the Transvaal are oppressed, the meeting resolves to confide all further measures to General Beyers in the Transvaal and to General de Wet in the Orange Free State.' On the next day rebels occupied Heilbron in the Free State, and on October 24 trains were stopped at Treurfontein in the Transvaal, and men and material commandeered ' by order of Commandant-General C. Beyers '. The rebels also set to work in both provinces to collect men and commandeer property, in some cases deceiving loyal farmers by the use of the governmental forms. Moreover, they spread false accounts of all sorts ; Paris and London were occupied, Maritz had 30,000 men to restore the independence of the republics ; Botha was secretly in favour of the rebellion and was only biding his time to declare himself ; there would be no bloodshed, the movement was only one of passive resistance as in Ulster ; the Government would not fight if it knew they were in earnest. Van Rensburg had a vision of the English retreating to Natal carrying with them Smuts, while Botha deserted them to stay with his people. Given the simple and trusting disposition of the Boers where their leaders are concerned, the effect of these mis-representations was natural. Other methods, however, were not spared ; recalcitrants were menaced with condign punishment if they did not at least refrain from action against the rebels, and many men were far from willing participants in the rebellion.

The Government had from the moment of Maritz's treachery spared no efforts at conciliation. Ex-President Steyn, whose health had kept him in retirement ever since the conquest of the Free State, was appealed to on October 11 and asked to throw his unparalleled influence in the Free State against rebellion ; he demurred, alleging bad health, the difficulty of his position, and his strong disapproval of the expedition to German South-West Africa. In deference to renewed and urgent appeals he endea-voured on October 24 to get into touch with Beyers, de Wet, and Kemp, but, though Hertzog assisted in the effort, de Wet put off visiting his former chief ; the Government, however, refrained from action against him in the meantime. The Government had made it plain to Steyn that they were prepared to let the leaders and men in rebellion go quietly home, laying down their arms, and to refrain from prosecuting any of them, and their forces had orders not to fire first on rebel commandos. This forbearance was in vain, and on October 27, General Botha, who since Septem-ber 22 had assumed the office resigned by Beyers, fell at Commissie Drift on Beyers and routed his force. But the Government's patience was not yet exhausted. Beyers had reappeared after his defeat at Katbosfontein, and Mr. C. Meintjes, with instruc-tions from the Government, visited him there on November 4, and elicited from him a statement of willingness to lay down arms if the Government undertook only to use volunteers for the

German campaign and not to prosecute the rebels. The first point was needless, for the Government had never suggested the use of compulsion to secure men for the German campaign, and had called up troops only to deal with the rebellion of Maritz. But the insincerity of Beyers was patent; before a reply could be received, he moved 25 miles south and broke through the Government forces on the railway line at Kingswood, evidently in an endeavour to reach the Free State and join de Wet. In this plan he was defeated by the Government forces which on November 7 attacked his camp, capturing a third of his force. The Government had on November 5 promptly decided to agree to Beyers's terms, and had on the following day offered Beyers a safe conduct to interview Steyn. On his defeat, Beyers at last bethought himself of this offer, and by the generosity of the Government reached Steyn on November 10, and Steyn promptly asked the Government for a safe conduct for Beyers to interview de Wet.

De Wet's actions in the meantime had rendered it unwise for the Government to grant the request; he had on one excuse or another declined to see Steyn; on October 29 he looted and pillaged Vrede, where he delivered a famous speech in which he complained of a 5s. fine imposed on him for flogging a native, denounced ' the miserable, pestilential English, General Botha's ungodly policy, the dastardly act of robbery in attacking German territory, the oppression of the Dutch and the boycotting of their language by the English, the unfair distribution of governmental posts, and the disregard of old Boer customs '. More serious was a defeat which he inflicted on Commandant Cronje's force on November 8, which encouraged de Wet so much that he entered the important town of Winburg on the following day and seized the Mayor and others of the leading inhabitants. To permit Beyers to confer with him would merely have resulted in de Wet infusing into Beyers some of his courage and determination. It was necessary to convince de Wet that he could not defeat the Government, and on November 12 Botha met his forces at Mushroom Valley and routed them utterly. At the same time the Government expressly called on the rebels to surrender by November 21 on a promise of amnesty for all save the leaders or those who had violated the rules of civilized warfare, while warning those who failed to come in that they would be punished and their property made chargeable for the losses suffered by loyal citizens. Efforts were now made by Steyn to secure on November 16 safe conducts for a meeting between Beyers, whom the Government had permitted to rejoin the rebels, and de Wet, but on November 17 the Government resolutely declined the suggestion, demanding unconditional surrender. De Wet's power had indeed been broken ; with difficulty he succeeded in crossing the Vaal, but then fled towards the German border, which he was not destined to reach, being captured on December 1 at Waterburg, 110 miles west of Mafeking. Beyers on December 7 was routed at Bothaville ; seeking to escape he made for the Vaal, then in high flood, but the swift stream overwhelmed him, and two days later his dead body was taken from the river. The minor leaders sought still to bargain, but the Government insisted on absolute surrender, and the end was not long delayed. Kemp alone, after fighting engagements with chequered success with the Government forces, disappeared on November 25 in the Kalahari, to emerge two months later to attack with Maritz the Government forces at Upington. Their defeat there was followed by his surrender, and Maritz's flight to Portuguese territory, where he was ultimately captured by the Portuguese.

On the meeting of Parliament the Government asked for and received approval of an Indemnity and Special Tribunals Act,[1] which laid down the treatment to be ascribed to the rebels. A distinction was drawn between the leaders and the rank and file, though it was not embodied in a definition. If any person was, after a preparatory examination, indicted before a competent court and found guilty of high treason, he might be sentenced to imprisonment with or without hard labour for life, or for a term of years, or to a fine not exceeding £5,000, or to both fine and imprisonment. If found guilty only of seditious or rebellious acts not amounting to high treason, he might be sentenced to a fine or imprisonment or both, or detention in South Africa until the end of military operations there. The trial of these cases was assigned to a special tribunal consisting of three

[1] No. 11 of 1915.

judges of the Supreme Court. Those who were captured or who surrendered after the amnesty offered on November 12 had expired were, if not indicted, subjected, like all those indicted, to certain penalties, in the form of disqualification, for a period of ten years, for membership of Parliament, of a Provincial Council, or any local or educational authority, for holding any public appointment, serving on a jury or licensing court, or holding a licence to deal in or possess arms or ammunition. Any one included in this class might within a month appeal against his inclusion, and such appeals were to be heard by commissioners sitting in boards of three, each composed of a magistrate, a commissioned officer not below the rank of captain of the Defence Force, and an advocate or attorney. The leniency of the steps taken was obvious and creditable to the wisdom of the Government, and at the same time provision was made for meeting the losses suffered by loyalists at the hands of the rebels through looting, commandeering, or otherwise. In the Orange Free State state aid was rendered needless by the institution of associations, voluntary in character, which raised large sums to indemnify rebels and loyalists alike for their sufferings.

Mild as the procedure was, the Government took steps further to ameliorate it. On the meeting of the Parliament after the general election on November 30, 1915, it was proposed by Mr. Hertzog that the Government should give a complete amnesty to de Wet and all the other rebels. The Government, however, adhered to the doctrine that after the court had completed its work they would consider carefully what concessions could be made in the public interest without endangering the State. This policy received the wholehearted support of the majority of the House of Assembly, and in pursuance of it just before Christmas the Government released 119 rebels, including de Wet. The men were not released, however, until any fines imposed—£2,000 in de Wet's case—had been paid and they had given undertakings not to take part in politics until the date of the expiry of the sentences pronounced upon them, and even then 50 of the more dangerous ringleaders were left in prison, until a year later a general amnesty was accorded. It may be doubted if the generosity of the Government was fully appreciated by the rebels, who attributed their action to a desire to placate rather than to magnanimity.

The causes of the rebellion were in the main obvious. Allowance must be made for German intrigues, whose existence cannot be denied, but too much stress must not be laid on this factor. The desire of the Boers for independence was undoubtedly a strong motive with many of the more ignorant burghers as well as with some of the younger men, whose objection to the status in which they found themselves was based on the theories propagated so industriously by Mr. Hertzog above all. But a good deal of the rebellion was due to the blind following of trusted leaders by ignorant men with no political education, and to many of them at all events the rebellion was presented in the light not of revolt against the British connexion, but as an attempt to overthrow either Botha and Smuts, or the latter alone, Botha being represented as at heart devoted to the Boer cause. The spirit shown in dealing with it by Botha and Smuts was admirable, and their loyalty to their faith redeemed the Boers in South Africa from the discredit which else must have rested upon them for the rebellion. At the same time, a striking proof was given by General Smuts of his unwillingness to take advantage of the rebellion to impose disabilities on his political opponents by his action in securing the passing in 1919 of an Act (No. 46) providing that from the date of the termination of the war, as announced by the Governor-General in the Gazette, all the disqualifications imposed on persons implicated in the rebellion, whether convicted of high treason or not, should be removed. At the same time the wise step was taken of providing for the remission from the same period of the disabilities imposed on certain persons under the Indemnity and Undesirables Deportation Act, 1914, as the result of the grave labour troubles of that year in Johannesburg.

3. The Expeditions in the Western Pacific

On August 6, 1914, the Imperial Government suggested to the Government of the Commonwealth that a great and urgent imperial service would be rendered by the seizure of the wireless stations in New Guinea, at Yap in the Marshall Islands, and at

Nauru, but that it must be realized that any territory occupied must at the conclusion of the war be at the disposal of the Imperial Government for the purpose of an ultimate settlement.[1] The Commonwealth Government immediately accepted the duty, and, as soon as H.M.S. *Australia,* which had been engaged first in searching for the German vessels in the Pacific and then in escorting the New Zealand forces to Samoa, was available to act as escort, a small expedition of 1,200 men, including a contingent of the Naval Brigade, was dispatched to reduce the German possessions in the Western Pacific, while the light cruisers on the station were detached to put out of action the German wireless stations at Nauru and Anguar. On September 11 the Australian force landed at Herbertshohe, seized after some fighting the wireless station, which was destroyed, and occupied Herbertshohe itself. On the following day Rabaul was occupied without resistance, the German Acting-Governor having retired inland. The occupation of the island of New Britain was proclaimed on that day, and the British flag formally hoisted on the following day. The Acting-Governor had at first showed a disinclination to surrender, meditating apparently flight to Friedrich Wilhelmshafen, but the shelling of his place of retreat by the *Encounter* and the advance of a force under Colonel Watson induced him to change his mind, and on September 17 a formal capitulation was concluded. The terms granted were of the most generous type ; the Acting-Governor was to be free to return to Europe ; officers of the regular army were to remain prisoners of war, but all others, and all non-commissioned officers and men, were to be permitted to return to their usual occupations on taking an oath of neutrality ; civil officials, not required by the British administration or unwilling to take the oath of neutrality, were to be deported to Australia, but no obstacle was to be put in the way of their return to Germany, three months' salary and travelling expenses home were to be advanced and care taken to see that their wives and children accompanied them. Local laws and customs were to continue in operation, subject to military exigencies. All the German troops were to surrender with military honours, and the capitulation was to

[1] *Parl. Pap.* Cd. 7975.

extend to the whole group of islands known as German New Guinea.

If the British Administrator was excessively generous in his terms to an enemy who had no power of resistance, he was also both ready and able to secure the objects for which he had stipulated. On the departure of the Australian fleet on October 3 and 4, instructions had been left that the *Nusa* and *Sumatra*, two small vessels which they had captured, were to be dismantled and laid up, but the Administrator, hearing that the German vessel *Komet* was somewhere on the north coast of New Britain, countermanded the orders given, and appointed Lieutenant-Commander Jackson, who had been left to act as harbour master, to take over the *Nusa*, man her with men of the Naval Brigade from the expeditionary force, and capture the *Komet*, a feat cleverly effected on October 13. He had already on September 24 occupied Kaiser Wilhelmsland, and by November practically every point of importance in the group had been duly visited and brought under occupation, suitable arrangements being made for the conduct of the administration.

When the light cruiser *Melbourne* on September 9 landed at Nauru a party to destroy the wireless installation, the German Government representative there unconditionally surrendered, and was left at Nauru on parole. The island was worked by concession from the German Government for phosphate by a British Company, the Pacific Phosphate Company, and that Company, which also worked phosphates on the British possession of Ocean Island in the vicinity of Nauru, suggested that, as their vessel *Messina* was sailing for Ocean Island, it would be well if it could take on board a garrison at Rabaul and occupy Nauru. The proposal was approved on the understanding that the Company would make itself responsible for the provisioning of the island, and on November 6 a force was landed, the flag hoisted, and the British occupation proclaimed. The German Commissioner and twenty-five other Germans were deported to Sydney, and the island was placed under the control of a Deputy Commissioner for the Western Pacific, acting under the instructions of the High Commissioner for the Western Pacific, and not under the government of the Commonwealth. The distinction of treatment was important as it preluded the special treatment accorded to Nauru in the treaty of peace.[1]

To New Zealand, however, fell the honour of effecting the first capture of German territory in the Pacific.[2] Samoa had been shared between the United States and Germany in 1899, to the bitter disgust of New Zealanders, who did not realize that what they regarded as a disgraceful surrender of British interests by a heedless Government was really motived by the necessity of avoiding German hostility at a crisis of the war with the Boer republics, when disaster after disaster had met the forces in South Africa. It was known that the German islands were not formidably protected, but there was danger from the German cruisers *Scharnhorst* and *Gneisenau,* and a good deal of risk was run by the little expedition, which embarked on two of the passenger vessels of the Union Steamship Company, for as far as New Caledonia it had no more formidable convoy than three small British cruisers which were then in New Zealand waters, but which would have been themselves helpless against either of these cruisers. At New Caledonia the expedition came under the effective protection of the *Australia* and of the French warship *Montcalm.* From New Caledonia the expedition proceeded via Fiji to Upolu, and there found the German Governor unprepared to resist. The island and Savaii were surrendered and the Governor and the leading German merchants, officials, and planters were removed for internment in New Zealand. Colonel Logan, who had had command of the expeditionary force, was given charge of the administration, and the places of the German judges, magistrates, customs officers, and others were filled by members selected from the force. A moment of anxiety arose when the German cruisers appeared off the island after the departure of the *Australia* on her mission to escort the Australian troops to Rabaul, but the cruisers spared the islands a bombardment which could have effected no useful purpose, contenting themselves with raiding the cable station on Fanning Island.

[1] See below, Chap. VIII, § 2.
[2] *Parl. Pap.* Cd. 7972 ; L. P. Leary, *New Zealanders in Samoa* (1918).

4. The Dominion Naval Forces and the War

The valuable services which the *Australia* rendered to the two expeditions were performed under the final control of the British Admiralty, in accordance with the decision of the Commonwealth Government, formally carried into effect on August 10, 1914, to place the Australian navy at the disposal of the Admiralty for the period of the war. It was in 1909 that the momentous decision was taken to create an Australian navy, in lieu of continuing, after its expiry in 1913, the annual contribution of £200,000 first agreed upon by the Commonwealth at the Colonial Conference of 1902. The agreement then reached, at the Defence Conference of that year, contemplated the building for Australia of a fleet unit of one battle cruiser, three protected cruisers, six destroyers, and three (later altered to two) submarines, at a cost of £3,700,000 and an annual outlay of £750,000. The ships were ultimately to be manned in Australia, and some of them constructed there, trained artisans being sent to England to acquire skill in shipbuilding. Work was promptly begun, and in 1910 two destroyers, *Parramatta* and *Yarra*, were commissioned in England, and in 1912 a third destroyer, the *Warrego*, was sent out to Australia in parts and re-erected in the Commonwealth dockyard at Cockatoo Island, Sydney. The battle cruiser *Australia* was sent out to Australia in 1913, in which year two light cruisers *Melbourne* and *Sydney* also arrived, while the third, the *Brisbane*, was constructed at Sydney. The two submarines were received in 1914. A much increased expenditure was suggested by Admiral Sir Reginald Henderson, who visited the Commonwealth in 1911 at the invitation of the ministry to advise on naval defence; this contemplated a great scheme spread over twenty-two years, involving a capital cost for construction of £40,000,000, and an ultimate annual vote of £4,784,000, and provided a fleet of 52 ships with a personnel of 15,000 men. The scheme received the general approval of the Commonwealth Government, but the war intervened before much progress had been made with it.[1]

The relations between the Admiralty and the Commonwealth

[1] *Official Year Book of the Commonwealth*, xii. 1014, 1015.

naval forces were determined at the Imperial Conference of 1911, when the whole subject was carefully investigated.[1] It was conceded that the Commonwealth should in time of peace control entirely its naval forces, but that, if it transferred control in time of war—which was assumed as inevitable but not made obligatory —the forces transferred would be under the absolute control of the Admiralty for the term of the war. Provision was made for joint exercises, a definite station was marked out for the Australian navy's sphere of action in peace, arrangements to be made with the Admiralty when Australian ships were desired to go beyond that sphere. The Admiralty undertook to lend officers and men, and to make interchanges possible by ranking British and Australian officers according to seniority as one service, and it was contemplated that the same standards of discipline would be maintained. Legal power was given to the Admiralty to perform their share by the Naval Discipline (Dominion Naval Forces) Act, 1911, which became effective in Australia by an Act of 1912. From July 1, 1913, the full arrangement came into force and the Naval Board of the Commonwealth took charge of the Australian Fleet. A Naval College at Jervis Bay was established for the training of naval officers, open to competition by boys whose thirteenth birthday falls in the year in which the entrance examination is held, and the training ship *Tingira* was commissioned in 1912 to train boys from $14\frac{1}{2}$ to 16 years for the personnel of the navy, subject to an undertaking to serve until the age of 25.

It was this fleet which on August 10 *de iure* and earlier *de facto* passed under complete Admiralty control, a transfer rendered simple by the fact that the Admiral commanding was seconded from the British navy, and the officers had all served in that navy. The Naval Board, besides distributing the orders of the Admiralty, arranged for the supply of coal, oil, stores, munitions, &c., and for the dissemination of intelligence. It had foreseen its work, and, when the first warning of possible danger was received from the officers commanding the East Indies and China squadrons, it was prepared to bring into operation on

[1] Keith, *Responsible Government in the Dominions*, iii. 1247–52 ; *Imperial Unity*, pp. 310–29.

July 31 the war organization which had been drawn up. The *Australia* and *Sydney* had been barely nine months in Australian waters, and the squadron was off the Queensland coast; in four days it was ready for war, though most of the ships had to be sent to Port Jackson to refit. Immediately thereafter the fleet was sent on a search for enemy cruisers, but the *Australia* was shortly recalled to escort first the New Zealand expedition to Samoa, and then the Australian to Rabaul, and, after these operations were over, the light cruisers proceeded to escort the expeditionary forces to Europe, in the course of the voyage the *Sydney* having the good fortune to fall in with, and destroy, the *Emden*. The *Australia*, the *Encounter*, and three destroyers remained to deal with the menace of the German cruisers in the Pacific, and to ward off any attacks on Samoa or on Australian trade, and, on the destruction by Admiral Sturdee of the German cruisers at the Falkland Islands, the *Australia* was transferred to the Grand Fleet in the North Sea. Varied fields of activity awaited the other vessels of the fleet, and the yard at Cockatoo Island commissioned in 1915–16 three destroyers and a light cruiser, though naval construction in Australia proved to be both deplorably slow and extremely expensive. The dockyards, however, rendered valuable service in fitting up more than seventy transports with accommodation for 113,000 men and 17,000 horses, converted the *Komet* into the *Una* to patrol New Guinea, and provided gun platforms to sixty-four vessels for defensive purposes. Much care was spent on the wireless service, over 300 operators being appointed as additional operators to transports.

Admittedly the process of transfer worked admirably and the first experiment in the employment in time of war of a Dominion navy was a complete success, though it must remain open for argument whether it was a wise policy which found a battle cruiser of the value of the *Australia* on the Australian station on the outbreak of war. In point of fact it never had an antagonist of any strength to face, and it had the misfortune not to have any share in the decisive victory of the Falkland Islands. But it must be added that the experiment in this case proves little or nothing as to the merits of the plan when Dominion navies have fully developed and have acquired characteristics of their own. For all intents and purposes the Australian fleet in 1914 was merely an outlying section of the British fleet, from which it had only had a few months separate existence, and in whose traditions its officers and men had been trained. But it is legitimate to conclude that the success of co-operation between Dominion fleets and that of the United Kingdom will depend largely on the habit of co-operation in training and war exercises in time of peace, and for this ample provision is made in the agreement of 1911, which is followed in this regard in Lord Jellicoe's report on Dominion naval defence.[1]

By 1914 no other Dominion had any effective naval force. New Zealand had adopted by an Act of 1913[2] the principle of a local navy, and had acquired a small cruiser which came under Admiralty control during the war and did patrol work in the Indian Ocean, Persian Gulf, and Red Sea before being dismantled in 1916. The training ship *Amokura*, which had been stationed in Wellington harbour, rendered perhaps more important service by providing for a flow of recruits for the navy and for the mercantile marine. The *New Zealand*, the battleship purchased for the Imperial Navy by the Dominion, rendered valuable aid, but was an Imperial ship.

Canada at the outbreak of hostilities was no better situated than New Zealand, for she had failed either to develop a local navy, as was projected in 1909–11 by Sir Wilfrid Laurier, or to make a substantial contribution towards the Imperial navy in order to secure at once the construction of additional ' Dreadnoughts ' to counter the German menace, as proposed by Sir Robert Borden, in the latter case owing to the refusal of the Liberal majority in the Senate to consent to the reversal of their leader's policy. Nothing could, of course, be done during the war to undo the failures of the past. The *Niobe* and *Rainbow*, two vessels of insignificant value, which had been acquired by the Liberal Government, were handed over immediately on the outbreak of the war to the control of the Admiralty. As the war went on many small coastal vessels were manned by the

---

[1] See below, § 5.
[2] No. 45 ; see *Parl. Pap.* Cd. 7507, pp. 79–83.

Royal Canadian Volunteer Reserve, and some 1,700 Canadians were enrolled in the Imperial naval forces, a complete naval wireless service with forty-three coast stations on the Great Lakes was maintained, and the organization of a Canadian Naval Air Service was undertaken.[1] Newfoundland for her part was able to contribute over two thousand naval reservists to the Imperial forces, thanks to the arrangements which have subsisted since 1892 for the maintenance there of a branch of the Royal Naval Reserve,[2] and some reservists were also forthcoming from the Union of South Africa.[3] For all practical purposes, however, the defence of these Dominions from naval attack by the enemy and the safety of the sea routes connecting them with the United Kingdom were dependent on the efforts of the Imperial Navy, and it was thanks to the strength and effectiveness of the operations of that navy that throughout the Dominions not a single port was attacked, nor town held to ransom, nor British ships captured in their territorial waters, by the enemy.

5. The Future of Naval Defence

The question of naval defence did not come formally before the Imperial War Conference of 1918, either as a Canadian or an imperial question, but the Canadian Minister of Naval Service and others of the oversea representatives, while in England for the Conference, discussed various aspects of the problem with the Admiralty, and at one of these conferences the Prime Minister of Canada was present and took part. The Admiralty view, as set out in a memorandum of May 17, was naturally in favour of a single navy at all times under the control of a central naval authority, but this view did not commend itself to the Dominion Prime Ministers, who with the exception of the Premier of

[1] The Imperial Act of 1911 not having been applied to Canada, the validity of its legislation beyond territorial waters was doubtful, and application is accordingly now made for extended powers in this regard (cf. Acland, *Journal of Society of Comparative Legislation*, xviii. 15–25). In the meantime an Act of 1918 has rendered the Imperial Act of 1911 applicable to Canada, and it has so been applied by an Order in Council of June 20, 1920.

[2] Under the Imperial Acts, 22 & 23 Vict. c. 40 ; 59 & 60 Vict. c. 40 ; 2 Edw. VII. c. 5.

[3] Under Defence Act, 1912, ss. 22, 23, passed in accordance with Imperial Acts, 28 & 29 Vict. c. 14 ; 3 Edw. VII. c. 6 ; 9 Edw. VII. c. 19.

Newfoundland, after a meeting at the Savoy Hotel, London, agreed upon a common answer to the Admiralty views. Their decision as embodied in a memorandum of August 15,[1] rejected as impracticable the Admiralty scheme. It was admitted that, judged purely from the standpoint of naval strategy, there was strength in the arguments in the favour of a single navy under central control, but it was contended that the arguments were not unanswerable. The experience gained in the war had shown that in time of war a Dominion navy, like that of Australia, could co-operate with the highest efficiency as part of a united navy under one direction and command, established after the outbreak of war. It was thoroughly recognized that the character of construction, armament, and equipment, and the methods and principles of training, administration, and organization should proceed upon the same lines in all the navies of the Empire, and this policy had already been followed in the Dominions which had established naval forces. For this purpose the Dominions would welcome visits from a highly qualified representative of the Admiralty, who by reason of his ability and experience would be thoroughly competent to advise the naval authorities of the Dominions on such matters. As naval forces came to be developed by the Dominions on a considerable scale it might be necessary to consider at a later date the establishment for war purposes of some supreme naval authority, upon which each of the Dominions would be adequately represented. This reply in effect reaffirmed the Australian position as experienced during the war to be adequate for immediate needs, though it involved the surrender of control by the Commonwealth to the British Admiralty on the outbreak of war. At the same time it contemplated the possibility that the development of the strength of Dominion naval forces might render this position no longer acceptable without modification, which would take the form of permitting union of control, but securing for the Dominions concerned representation on the central body which should in time of war direct the movements of the British naval forces.

The outcome of this reply was delayed until the following year, when the condition of affairs permitted the sending of

[1] Canada, *House of Commons Debates*, June 14, 1920.

Admiral of the Fleet Viscount Jellicoe on a mission to the Dominions to consider questions of naval defence, and to advise the Dominion Governments on the needs of the case. In his reports to the Commonwealth and Dominion Governments Lord Jellicoe recognizes frankly the circumstances which render unattainable the Admiralty ideal of a single navy, as expressed consistently throughout the discussions, especially in 1909 with Australia.[1] He admits that experience has shown conclusively that responsibilities for naval defence are far more readily recognized and far more cheerfully met if the result of the efforts made is apparent to those making them, if in other words the ships provided are seen by the people paying for them and are manned by their own kith and kin. On the other hand due stress is laid on the weakness of Australia to stand by herself ; ' it must be recognized that Australia is powerless against a strong naval and military power without the assistance of the British fleet.' Australia, he insists, in common with the rest of the Empire, is dependent on the security of her sea communications, but Australia is also faced with the problems of invasion due to the attractions offered by the great potential value of the land and the very small population occupying it. The difficulty of defending Australia from invasion is greatly increased by the absence of strategic railways, the immense length of coastline, and the great distance from the United Kingdom with its naval and military support. Against these difficulties must be placed the advantage derived by Australia from her distance from other countries. The final decision of war must rest on the result in the main theatre of hostilities wherever that may be, and support to Australia would naturally be forthcoming if the situation in other respects permitted of it. None the less it is recognized that in certain circumstances great injury might be inflicted on Australia before aid from the United Kingdom could be sent. These are the considerations which justify military and naval preparations in Australia itself. But it is impossible to consider the naval requirements of Australia without taking account also of the naval requirements of the Pacific and Indian Oceans as a whole. The people of Australia and New Zealand are deeply

[1] *Parl. Pap.* Cd. 4948.

interested in sea communications in Indian and Chinese waters as well as in the remainder of the Pacific, and the people of India in their turn are interested in the safety of communications in the South Pacific and in China. Similarly the safety of the naval bases at Colombo and Singapore is of vital moment to Australia and New Zealand, and the safety of these bases and of Sydney and other bases in the South Pacific concerns deeply India. Even the prosperity of South Africa is associated, though in lesser degree, with these questions, and Canada is greatly concerned with the routes in the Pacific.

The Eastern naval problem is thus one which concerns the Empire as a whole and the only possible conclusion is that the Far Eastern Fleet should be provided by those constituent parts of the Empire, including the United Kingdom, for which it is a vital necessity, and that there should be the closest co-operation with unity of direction in war between the various squadrons composing that fleet. To effect these ends Lord Jellicoe suggests that the Admiralty should delegate the general direction of the operations of the Far Eastern Fleet to an officer of high rank residing at Singapore, and assisted by a strong staff. The Commander-in-chief afloat and the flag officers commanding the units of the Far Eastern Fleet should all come under his command in time of war, but in time of peace the Dominion navies would remain under Dominion control except when placed under the control of this officer for purposes of combined naval exercises. It would be the duty of the Admiral in chief command at Singapore to visit such places in the Pacific and Indian Oceans as might be of importance in time of war in order to acquire an intimate knowledge of the general situation. He should also visit the Dominions from time to time, and he would be in constant touch with the Admiralty and the officers commanding the British squadrons in China and the East Indies, and would be entitled to expect to be kept fully informed on naval questions by the Australian Naval Board and by the naval authorities of any other Dominion which might establish a naval unit of its own. The cost of his establishment would fall on Imperial funds, and would be a set-off against the expenditure necessary in Australia and New Zealand waters and in Canada to provide adequate docking and repair facilities.

The strength of the Far Eastern Fleet suggested by Lord Jellicoe during the next five years is considerable : 8 battleships of ' Dreadnought ' type, 8 battle cruisers, 10 light cruisers, 40 modern destroyers, 3 flotilla leaders, 2 dépôt ships for submarines, 36 submarines (excluding those stationed in Indian waters), 4 submarine parent ships, 4 aircraft carriers, 12 fleet minesweepers, 1 large seagoing minelayer, and 2 fleet repair ships.　The apportionment of cost and responsibility for the provision of these vessels raises grave problems, which Lord Jellicoe would solve as follows, taking into consideration at the same time the necessities of providing for convoys and for local defence.　As a striking force Australia should provide a unit consisting of 1 battle cruiser, 2 light cruisers, 6 destroyers, 4 submarines and 2 fleet minesweepers.　For the direct defence of trade she requires 4 light cruisers and 8 armed escort ships, assuming that similar provision is made by the other Governments. For harbour defence she requires 20 destroyers, 10 submarines, 82 minesweepers, of which 74 should be fishing trawlers, and 4 boom defence vessels.　New Zealand, for her part, would provide 3 light cruisers, 6 submarines, and 1 submarine parent ship. Canada, for her part, would have a double duty to perform ; in order to secure her safety, owing to the wide separation of the two coasts, each must have certain local defences, and in addition a naval force for the purpose of defending trade and the coast. The naval force which would be adequate purely for the protection of Canada's trade and Canada's ports under existing conditions would include 3 light cruisers, 1 flotilla leader, 12 torpedo craft, 8 submarines, and 1 parent ship, and certain auxiliary small craft.　If Canada, however, desired to aid in Imperial defence in any proportionate manner, much greater efforts would be requisite.　Lord Jellicoe suggests various alternative fleets which could be maintained for the sums of £5,000,000, £3,500,000, £2,000,000, and £1,000,000, the two latter serving merely for defensive purposes, and therefore leaving to the United Kingdom the burden of supplying the forces necessary to seek out and defeat the enemy fleets.　Either of the first two fleets would be a substantial contribution to Empire naval power in time of war. In this, as in his other reports, stress is laid on the necessity of having battle cruisers for serious modern defence. Millions of tons of cargo, and in times of war of men and stores also, are carried in ships and, until some other means of carrying these millions of tons over or under the ocean have actually materialized, it is, he argues, imperative that the British Empire should retain the command of the surface of the sea. This need will continue until, if ever, surface men-of-war lose their *métier*, and are displaced by aircraft or submarines. The capital ship is the strongest form of engine of war which exists for operating on the sea, and a series of inventions has succeeded in meeting with increasing effect the dangers to which battleships are exposed in time of war, whether from mines of various kinds, torpedoes, or, most recently of all, aircraft attack. The insistence on this issue in the report is, of course, easily explained by a reference to the history of naval opinion in the Dominions. Australia began its career in favour of a separate naval force on the theory that small craft like torpedo boats would be an effective and very cheap means of defence, and the development of the use of submarines and aircraft in the war has rendered widespread the belief that by the free use of these means the Dominions may protect their shores against attack, leaving it to the United Kingdom to supply the fleets necessary for offensive action at sea.

The fleet which could be maintained for £5,000,000 annually would comprise 2 battle cruisers, 7 light cruisers, 1 flotilla leader, 12 destroyers, 1 destroyer parent ship, 16 submarines, 1 submarine parent ship, 2 aircraft carriers, 4 fleet minesweepers, 4 local defence destroyers, 8 ' P ' boats, and 4 trawler minesweepers. For £1,000,000 8 submarines, 4 local defence destroyers, 8 ' P ' boats, and 4 trawler minesweepers could be supplied. At the least, however, in self-defence Canada should, it is suggested, provide and maintain a small force of light cruisers on her western seaboard for the protection of her trade in those waters, as well as a naval force on her eastern seaboard. South Africa's share should be that necessary to provide and maintain a squadron stationed at the Cape of Good Hope, having the primary duty of keeping open the trade route round the Cape, and protecting the trade on the west coast of Africa, leaving the trade to the eastward to the protection of the Far Eastern Fleet. India might provide a certain fixed sum annually in relief of the British estimates, say such an amount as would pay for the defence of her harbours and the upkeep (but not the prime cost or cost of replacement) of the East Indies squadron, comprising 5 light cruisers, 6 submarines, and 1 aircraft carrier, the probable total being £2,200,000 annually.

As a basis of financial apportionment Lord Jellicoe accepts the figures of population and seaborne trade as joint factors, and from these arrives at the conclusion that the whole Empire should in future share the cost of general naval expenditure in the following proportions : the United Kingdom 74·12 per cent., Australia 7·74 per cent., New Zealand 2·02 per cent., Canada 12·30 per cent., and South Africa 3·82 per cent. In practice he suggests that Australia and New Zealand should pay their proportion in the form of defraying a definite percentage of the cost of the Far Eastern Fleet, Australia bearing 20 per cent., New Zealand 5 per cent., and the United Kingdom 75 per cent. of the cost. The total for Australia would be £4,024,600 and for New Zealand £924,600, in 1926.

The obligations, financial and otherwise, which the acceptance of the principles laid down by Lord Jellicoe would impose upon the Dominions, are obviously considerable, though much smaller than they would have to assume if they were independent states. Not unnaturally there has been no haste to accept them in practice for the reasons expressly set out by the Canadian Government in a statement made in the House of Commons on March 25, 1920. Mr. Ballantyne said that, in view of Canada's heavy financial commitments and of the fact that the permanent naval policy of the United Kingdom had not yet been settled and the question of naval defence was down for discussion at the next Imperial Conference, it had been decided to defer in the meantime action towards the adoption of a permanent naval policy for Canada. The Government had decided to carry on the Canadian naval service on pre-war lines, and had accepted the British offer of one light cruiser and two torpedo-boat destroyers [1] to replace the obsolete training ships *Niobe* and *Rainbow*, which were acquired

[1] On June 14, 1920, Mr. Ballantyne added that a gift of two submarines had also been accepted.

before the war. In order to secure freedom of action in reorganiz-
ing the service on an economic basis orders had been issued for
the demobilization of all officers and naval ratings and for the
discontinuation of civil help at head-quarters and at the naval
dockyards at Halifax and Esquimalt. The Canadian officers who
were being paid by the Canadian Government would be recalled
and placed on duty with the Canadian naval service, and the
Naval College would be continued. In Committee of Supply on
June 14 he amplified the statement, explaining that eight cadets
from the College would be sent annually to be trained in the
Imperial Navy, and would be available for service on Canadian
ships when required. He laid stress on the necessity of new ships,
defended the appropriation of 2,500,000 dollars proposed, which
was small compared with the expenditure of Australia, and
suggested that Canada should, as an outcome of the Conference
of 1921, participate effectively in naval defence, probably on the
lines of Sir Wilfrid Laurier's policy in 1910, if on a more reduced
scale. The announcement caused no satisfaction to the Liberals.
Mr. Mackenzie King insisted that the German menace was over,
that the Government had adopted a policy already without
consulting Parliament, which could not refuse the ships which
it had already accepted, and that the expenditure was too heavy.
The Quebec spokesmen were more vehement ; Mr. Lemieux held
that in view of the change in the position of affairs since 1910
he could not support Sir W. Laurier's policy now ; Canada had
done enough and could not afford the expenditure proposed.
There was nothing to fear on the Atlantic, the alliance with
Japan was to be renewed as regards the Pacific, and Australia
was to have a unit on patrol there. Canada, in effect, on this
argument should rely for naval protection on the United Kingdom, the United States, Japan, and the Commonwealth, as
Quebec had relied during the war on the English-speaking people
of Canada.

Neither in the Commonwealth nor in New Zealand has the
Government accepted the suggestions of Lord Jellicoe ; in both
cases it is felt that the burden proposed is very heavy, that the
destruction of the German fleet and the existence of good relations
with Japan and the United States render the position for the

time being secure, and that the matter can stand over until the Conference. In the meantime both Governments are proceeding with the development along existing lines[1] of their naval forces, under the conditions determined at the Conference of 1911, which secure unity of control by the Admiralty in time of war, and close co-operation by exchange of personnel and joint operations in peace, a system which Canada also, according to the announcement of June 14, has decided to accept for the time being. As contributions to their defence the United Kingdom has presented to the Commonwealth 1 flotilla leader, 5 destroyers, 6 submarines, and 3 sloops, and to New Zealand a cruiser, while Newfoundland has been given a sloop and a trawler for service in connexion with her branch of the Royal Naval Reserve.

In the Union of South Africa an animated and important debate took place on July 22 and 23 on the proposal of Mr. Hertzog to omit the item of £85,000, included on the estimates as a naval subsidy in recognition of the service rendered by the Imperial navy to the Union. The item in question is a mere continuation of the total given by the Cape and Natal when they were colonies, and Mr. Hertzog himself was not very insistent on his objections to the item, though he explained that the Dutch, who had been menaced with the power of that fleet to bring British troops over to South Africa, could not be expected to feel the sentimental affection for the navy manifested by the British members of the House. Mr. Merriman, on the other hand, insisted on the meanness of the contribution in view of the protection of the £200,000,000 trade of the Union ; he renewed the suggestion of Mr. Hofmeyr in 1887 [2] that the Dominions should all contribute on the basis of their trade, a fact which would give the Dominions a real sense of interest in the navy. The Prime Minister recognized the inadequacy of the contribution ; he also recognized the propriety of the Union providing in some way for its own naval defence, but he insisted that Lord Jellicoe's reports showed how expensive the process was, and he pointed out that the Union had not been

---

[1] Under these arrangements neither Australia nor New Zealand now contributes anything to the cost of the British fleet. In the Commonwealth naval expenditure in 1920–21 has been drastically reduced, the battleship being placed in reserve with part of the other vessels.

[2] Keith, *Responsible Government in the Dominions*, iii. 1465.

visited by Lord Jellicoe, and that it would be impossible to frame any naval policy pending the Conference to be held in 1921. The leader of the Labour party also declared in favour of a local navy but ignored the question of cost.

In addition to detailed recommendations as to the construction of naval units Lord Jellicoe's reports are of importance in their insistence on the fundamental questions of naval administration. In order to secure true efficiency in the Dominion fleets he insists that there must be effective interchange with the Royal Navy, so that Dominion officers shall serve for part of their time on Imperial ships, and Imperial officers on Dominion ships. For that purpose he recommends that all officers of the military branch of all the navies of the Empire shall be borne on one general list, from which they would be promoted to the ranks of Commander and Captain by selection as is the case in the Royal Navy, a suggestion formally accepted by Canada and provided for in an Imperial Order in Council of June 20, 1920, under the Imperial Act of 1911 regarding naval discipline in its relation to Dominion navies. The control of the navy should be vested in a civil minister responsible to Parliament, but in technical matters he should essentially rely on the advice of a Naval Board composed of experts, and, to secure that the views of these experts should not be overruled lightly by the minister, it is suggested that the Chief of the Naval Staff should be empowered to present to the Prime Minister, in case of divergence of view, the case as seen by the naval members of the Board. The recommendation draws its special point from the fact that in the case of the report on operations in the Dardanelles the representatives of the Commonwealth of Australia and the Dominion of New Zealand, departing from the views of the rest of the Commission, laid down the doctrine that a naval or military expert was not entitled to express views which had not been approved by the minister under whom he was serving, while under British practice the rule is recognized that experts may at the Committee of Imperial Defence or analogous meetings freely express their own opinions, whether or not they are in harmony with those of their official superiors.

CHAPTER VII

THE PEACE CONFERENCE AND THE STATUS OF THE DOMINIONS

1. THE DOMINION SHARE IN THE PEACE NEGOTIATIONS.

Mr. Hughes's protest against armistice terms — Precedents as to Dominion representation — Dominion demand for new status — Recognition at Peace Conference — Dominion views as to peace terms — Separate signature of the treaties — Mode of ratification.

2. THE LEAGUE OF NATIONS AND THE STATUS OF THE DOMINIONS.

Position of the Dominions under the Covenant — The British Empire as a unit — Canadian view of Dominion status — Opinion in the Commonwealth and New Zealand — General Smuts on the reconstruction of the Empire — Nationalist criticisms — Revival of British War Delegation, June 1920 — Dominion representation at Geneva meeting of the League Assembly, 1920 — Treatment of German property in the Union.

3. THE DIPLOMATIC REPRESENTATION OF THE DOMINIONS.

Canadian Minister at Washington — Liberal opposition — Mode of communication between Dominions and League of Nations — Importance of Imperial consultation — International air convention — Persia and Mesopotamia.

1. THE DOMINION SHARE IN THE PEACE NEGOTIATIONS

As early as 1915 the Imperial Government had formally assured the Dominions that they would be consulted in the decision of the terms of peace, and both in communications with the individual Dominion ministers, who visited the United Kingdom in 1916, and at the War Cabinet meetings in 1917 and 1918, the questions for consideration included deliberation on the conditions on which the Empire in conjunction with her allies could assent to the termination of hostilities. It was doubtless due to the belief that these discussions had fulfilled the promise of consultation that the Imperial Government in the critical days preceding the armistice accepted formally, subject only to a reservation on the question of the freedom of the seas, the principles enunciated by the President of the United States as the basis on which the war should be concluded. The error in tactics was obvious, for the presence of Mr. Hughes in England precluded the possibility of contending effectively that it was impossible to consult the Dominion Governments in the time available, and the Prime Minister of the Commonwealth was not slow in protesting [1] against an action, which might, it was suggested, prevent the Commonwealth from attaining her aims as to the reparation due to her and her future security. It was obviously no effective reply to seek to distinguish between armistice and peace terms, but the fact that the Commonwealth Cabinet had telegraphed to the Prime Minister their objections to the proposals of the President some days before they were finally agreed to by the Imperial Government proves that Mr. Hughes had ample time to press his views on the Imperial Government, though it does not excuse the errors in procedure.

Precedent as to representation at the actual Peace Conference suggested that the Empire should be represented by a single delegation, on which ministers of the Dominions might serve as members or as advisers, but which would act as a unit.[2] Since 1870 at least the principle had been recognized that in matters vital to the Dominions the Imperial Government should not conclude treaties over their heads, and in the sphere of commercial treaties the rights of the Dominions had been steadily extended until in 1894 the Imperial Government recognized the right of the Dominions to have separate treaties negotiated for them, in the framing of which their representatives would take an important part, subject only to safeguards imperative to prevent the disruption of the Empire by such actions as the grant to foreign countries of more favourable terms than those conceded to other parts of the Empire. In 1907, at the instance of Sir Wilfrid Laurier, the further step was taken of leaving the actual negotiations solely in the hands of Dominion ministers, though a British minister or diplomat was associated in the signature of the treaty agreed upon. The authority of the Dominion representatives to sign and negotiate documents was conferred by the King on the advice of the Secretary of State for Foreign Affairs at the request of the Dominion concerned. In 1912, however, at the Radiotelegraphic Conference of that year the further step was taken of empowering the Dominion delegates to negotiate

[1] *The Times*, November 8 and 15 ; Governmental reply, November 9 ; Sir R. Borden's view, November 14, 1918.

[2] Keith, *Responsible Government in the Dominions*, iii. 1101–30 ; *Imperial Unity*, pp. 261–300 ; *Journal of Society of Comparative Legislation*, xviii. 47–57.

and sign for the King in respect of each of the Dominions separately while the British delegates signed for Great Britain and various British colonies and protectorates, and in 1914 the International Convention on the Safety of Life at Sea was signed by British representatives and also separately by Dominion representatives for Canada, Australia, and New Zealand. These conventions, therefore, had created a precedent for the separate representation of the Dominions, though the matters dealt with were in the wide sense of the term commercial, and only indirectly affected political issues. The precedent was followed; after full examination in the War Cabinet of other possibilities,[1] it was agreed with the hearty good will of the Imperial Government that the Dominions should be secured a position in the Peace Conference, which would at once place them on a footing of equality with the smaller powers and maintain their solidarity with the United Kingdom. The consideration which, it was felt, outweighed all others was the obvious fact of the great losses borne by the Dominions in the war on the one hand, and the reality of their self-government on the other. The Imperial Government had the power to involve them in liability to attack by her declaration of war; she had not the power to compel them to assist actively in the war, and when they did so they acquired the right to true national status.

The decisions arrived at between the several parts of the Empire had now to be made effective by international agreement. The Supreme War Council established by the allies fighting on the western front in February 1918, composed of the Prime Minister and one other minister from each of the powers concerned, had taken the preliminary decision that the great powers were to be represented at the Conference by five delegates each, and it had been contemplated that the British delegates would be the Prime Minister, Mr. Bonar Law as Leader of the House of Commons and of the Unionist wing of the Coalition Government, Mr. Balfour as Secretary of State for Foreign Affairs, Mr. Barnes as a representative—though since the general election not officially recognized—of Labour, and a representative of the

[1] While Canada pressed for separate representation (October 29 and December 4, 1918), Mr. Hughes found his Government reluctant to support him; Commonwealth *Debates*, 1920, pp. 2533, 2536.

Dominions or India changeable at discretion from meeting to meeting. It was necessary to alter this arrangement by expanding the scheme to admit the separate position of the Dominions. The final result, therefore, took the form of the retention of the right of the five powers, the United States, the British Empire, France, Italy, and Japan, to be represented by five delegates each ; Belgium, Brazil, and Serbia were allotted three delegates ; China, Greece, the Hedjaz, Poland, Portugal, Roumania, Siam, the Czecho-Slovak republic, Canada, Australia, South Africa, and India (including the native states), two each ; Cuba, Guatemala, Hayti, Honduras, Liberia, Nicaragua, Panama, Bolivia, Ecuador, Peru, Uruguay, and New Zealand were each represented by one delegate. Each delegation was entitled to set up a panel, from which the delegate present on any occasion could be selected, and the representatives of the Dominions and of India could, moreover, be included in the representation of the British Empire by means of the panel system. Newfoundland, though a Dominion, was obviously too small and unimportant to claim separate representation, and her case was in practice provided for by including her representative from time to time in the number of the British Empire delegation. The allocation was remarkable not merely in the privileges thus extended to the Dominions to enjoy double representation, but in the fact that the British Empire made its first appearance as a contracting body *eo nomine,* and that the decisions taken as to the attitude to be adopted by that delegation were arrived at in consultation with the representatives of the Dominions and India, the activity of the Imperial War Cabinet thus being continued on French soil.

For practical purposes this body of seventy delegates could not be made an effective instrument of negotiating peace, but the council of the delegates of the five great powers would equally have been unwieldy, and it never actually met. In its place the Supreme War Council, with its old membership of ten, now composed of the President and another representative of the United States and two representatives of each of the other four great powers, resumed its sessions. The spokesmen of the smaller powers and of the Dominions and India were called in when matters specially affecting their interests were under discussion, and the business to be considered by the Council of Ten was prepared for it by commissions, on which the minor states and the Dominions were represented. Thus Sir Robert Borden sat on the Commission dealing with Greece, his colleague, Mr. Sifton, on the commission as to international waterways, Sir Joseph Cook dealt with the affairs of Czecho-Slovakia, Mr. Hughes with the problem of reparation, General Botha with that of Poland, and Mr. Massey with the question of responsibility for the war. Moreover, though the reduction of the Council, from twenty-five to ten, enhanced the difficulty of Dominion representation upon it, Sir R. Borden on several occasions sat as the colleague of Mr. Balfour, while during the last month of the proceedings in Paris the additional compliment was paid to the Prime Minister of Canada of appointing him chairman of the British Empire delegation in the absence of Mr. Lloyd George.[1]

The decisions of the Council of Ten, though taken after receiving the advice of the Commissions, and after listening to the arguments of the powers affected, were arrived at by the agreement of the President and the Prime Ministers present, the foreign ministers obviously having no power to oppose decisions acceptable to their chiefs. But the procedure of the Council rapidly proved too formal and elaborate for the swift conclusion of peace, and in a short time the actual making of decisions was relegated to a Council of Four[2] comprising President Wilson, Mr. Lloyd George, M. Clemenceau, and Signor Orlando. No other procedure, it is obvious, was possible, and the interests of the Dominions fell to be secured by the continuous pressure which as members of the British Empire Delegation the Dominion representatives were able to exercise on the Council of Four. Neither the Dominions nor the minor powers precisely appreciated their relegation to this secondary place, as their protests showed. But the Dominions, it is certain, suffered far less from the arrangement than did the minor powers, secured as they were in a strong influence on the deliberations of the British Prime Minister, and the event fully justified their insistence on the principle that,

[1] Cf. Canada, *Sess. Pap.* 1919, No. 41 j.
[2] The Japanese Prime Minister did not come to Europe, and Japan disinterested herself in European affairs.

while they must be allowed a voice for themselves on a par with the minor powers, they must not be shut out of the right largely to influence the decisions of the Empire as a whole. It is not surprising, however, that the anomaly of the position should have been strongly felt by even the French and Italian Governments, or that, as an effort to mitigate what seemed an unfairness to the other members of the Conference, the rule should have been made that the Dominions were not to possess a separate vote from the British Empire in any case where formal voting was necessary. The restriction on the Dominion position, though not without importance in theory, was illusory; voting was only possible when the determinations of the Council of Ten or of Four were brought before the plenary conference for formal approval, and nothing could be agreed upon which did not commend itself in the ultimate issue to the Council of Four.

The special interests of the Dominions in the terms of the peace centred mainly in the treatment of the German oversea possessions; the Union was determined that South-West Africa should not return to Germany but should be annexed to the Union with which it had every natural bond of connexion; Australia was equally anxious to secure all the German islands in the Pacific, and New Zealand was resolved that the error of 1899 regarding Samoa should not be repeated. The Commonwealth claim raised a serious point of international interest; it aimed at preventing the establishment of Japan in the Caroline and Marshall islands, which she had occupied during the war under an agreement with the United Kingdom to which the Commonwealth had been unable to take exception in view of the urgent need to make certain of Japanese aid, and the naval advantages derived from the activity of the Japanese Navy in the hunt for the German vessels in the Pacific and in the convoy at the outset of the war of the Australasian forces. But, it was contended, the islands offered no scope for immigration, they were small atolls, with scanty population and little trade. Japan could need them only for strategic reasons, which the development of submarine warfare made extremely important. The United Kingdom sympathized heartily with the Australian demand for the retention of the German islands south of the Equator, but felt bound by the understanding with Japan to accede to her desire to retain those north of that limit. The United States, however, intervened in the interest of Australia, pressing that the systems of mandates should be made applicable to all the German possessions north and south of the Equator, and the mandate be allotted to Australasia. The mandatory system, however, was not welcomed by either Australia or New Zealand, who desired annexation pure and simple, and General Smuts, who was a keen supporter of mandates for the Ottoman Empire, Russia, and Austria-Hungary, was strongly opposed to the application of the system to German South-West Africa, which, he urged, ought to have been an integral part of the Union and which now should be granted its proper position as a part of that body. Strong objections were also raised by France to the mandate system as applied to Togoland and the Kamerun, where, it was argued, if free trade for all nations as contemplated in the mandatory system was accepted, the power accepting the mandate might incur great expense for the benefit chiefly of the trade of a former enemy. The result as usual was a compromise, and the evolution of a mandatory system of some complication.[1]

None of the other points at issue interested the Dominions so deeply. Mr. Hughes, however, distinguished himself by insistence on the necessity for reparation, the reimbursement of the whole of Australia's war costs and losses, the increase of the Australian Navy, war and mercantile, by additions from German captures, the transfer of German private property in New Guinea, the appropriation of sums obtained from the sale of enemy-owned stock, and the punishment of German officials who had treated harshly British-Australian soldiers. A plea was indeed preferred that in regard to reparation Australia had special claims owing to the exceptional dislocation of her trade and shipping by war conditions, and to the fact that unlike Canada she derived little profit from the manufacture of munitions. General Smuts, for his part, was anxious to secure the establishment in effective working of a League of Nations, and his views went to form the

---

[1] See below, Chap. VIII. Cf. General Smuts, *The League of Nations* (1918), p.15. For the wishes of the natives see *Parl. Pap.* Cd. 9210. The delay in determining the precise form of the mandates for the former German possessions was due to France. They had not by April 1921 been accepted by the United States.

final shape of the League, though that instrument was the work of many hands and in certain important respects did not conform to the wishes of the Premier of the Union. New Zealand was anxious that some steps should be taken to secure Gallipoli for the Empire, so as to substitute British for Turkish control of the graves of her heroic dead. It was hoped also in Australia that the conference would afford the means of terminating the unhappy state of affairs in the New Hebrides, where the condominium arranged between France and the United Kingdom in 1906, without adequate consideration of Australasian views, had failed to work satisfactorily from any point of view, but, as France was not prepared to surrender her claims, and as the United Kingdom could not surrender those of the Dominions, no settlement was achieved. An effort to induce France to surrender St. Pierre and Miquelon also failed. The Dominion representatives, however, took a keen interest in all the questions of the settlement, and as has been seen they were invited by the British Government to take a valuable and important part in dealing with the complicated issues of the politics of the new States in Central Europe. The procedure was undoubtedly of great value to them, as giving them practical experience of the issues which perplex European Governments and which have hitherto been so little appreciated in the Dominions, although some of them at least, like General Botha, were not enticed by the prospect of undertaking the duty of closer interest in such tangled diplomatic webs.

The mode of signature of the treaties concluded as the outcome of the labours of the Conference was based on that of the signature of the Convention regarding the Safety of Life at Sea [1]; in the list of High Contracting Parties in the treaty with Germany appeared the British Empire, forming along with the United States, France, Italy, and Japan the group of the Principal Allied and Associated Powers, and as representatives of His Majesty the King of the United Kingdom of Great Britain and

[1] Objection has been taken that each Dominion should have appeared as a distinct entity, not under the British Empire, but this would have meant a formal disruption of the Empire without consulting a single Parliament, clearly an impossible step. The form used was asked for by the Dominion Premiers in a memorandum of March 12, 1920.

Ireland and of the British Dominions beyond the Seas, Emperor of India, there signed Mr. Lloyd George, Mr. Bonar Law, Lord Milner, Mr. Balfour, and Mr. Barnes; Sir G. Foster and Mr. Doherty signed as representing the King for the Dominion of Canada; Mr. Hughes and Sir J. Cook for the Commonwealth; Generals Botha and Smuts for the Union; Mr. Massey for New Zealand; and Mr. Montagu and the Maharaja of Bikaner for India. The other treaties with the belligerents, Austria, Bulgaria, Hungary, and Turkey, were also signed on behalf of the Dominions and India, and the same process was applied to the treaties defining the relations between the allied States and Poland, Czecho-Slovakia, Roumania, Greece, and the Serb-Croat-Slovene State, those regarding Italian reparation payments, contributions to the cost of liberating the former Austro-Hungarian territories, the trade in arms and ammunition in certain parts of the world, that on the liquor traffic and the revision of the Berlin Act of 1885. To this rule one exception was made; the treaty of June 28, 1919, under which a definite obligation was undertaken by His Majesty, provided that a similar obligation was entered into by the United States of America, to support the French Government in the case of an unprovoked movement of aggression being made by Germany against France, was concluded on behalf of His Majesty by Mr. Lloyd George and Mr. Balfour and was not signed by any Dominion representative. But it was expressly provided that ' the present treaty shall impose no obligation upon any of the Dominions of the British Empire unless and until it is approved by the Parliament of the Dominion concerned '. The implication of the clause is clear; the conclusion of the treaty bound the Dominions, and it required an express exception in its terms to render that obligation null and void unless it was expressly approved by the Dominion Parliaments. The motive for the abstention of the Dominions is clear enough; what was needed by France to compensate her for the failure of the Conference to accede to her desire to control the territory on the left bank of the Rhine was an assurance of immediate aid from the United Kingdom and eventual support from the United States. The formal assurance of Dominion aid was not of first-class importance, whereas the undertaking of the obligation by the

Dominions would have involved the Prime Ministers in the possibility of difficulty with their Governments and Parliaments, which might have developed hostility to an arrangement which definitely placed on them the obligation of immediate recourse to war, while the procedure actually followed gave the Parliaments the free and unfettered right of deciding the issue.

After the signature of the treaty with Germany the Imperial Government, somewhat tactlessly, suggested that the ratification of the treaty could take place without the delay of referring the matter to the Dominion Parliaments for approval. Sir Robert Borden, in telegrams of July 9 and August 4, naturally and properly took the strongest exception to the suggestion, which, had it been carried out, would have placed the Dominions in a position of marked inferiority to the United Kingdom, the Parliament of which was formally consulted before ratification took place, an act for carrying into effect the treaty being passed by both houses. In all the Dominions, therefore, the terms of the treaty were formally approved by the passing of motions in favour of ratification, and the ratification of the British Empire was in due course deposited by the Secretary of State for Foreign Affairs.

In one point only did the proceedings in the matter of signature and ratification vary from the forms which would have been employed had the Dominions been independent States ; the Dominion plenipotentiaries were nominated and authorized to act for the Dominions by their Governments, but they received formal full powers to treat and sign from the King on the advice of the Secretary of State for Foreign Affairs, and the royal ratification for the Empire was signified on the advice of the Secretary of State. Thus in form the unity of the Empire was preserved, as in substance it was maintained, by the harmonious consultation and co-operation of all parties concerned in the negotiations.

2. The League of Nations and the Status of the Dominions

Apart from the signature and ratification of the treaties of peace on behalf of the Dominions, the Covenant of the League of Nations recognized in an unmistakable manner the new position of the Dominions. The original members of the League, enumerated in the Annex to the Covenant, include the British Empire, Canada, Australia, South Africa, New Zealand, and India, that is the Dominions and India, these names following immediately the specification of the British Empire. The grouping, however, does not indicate any diminution of rights; each of the units is a member of the League in its own right, possessing one vote in the Assembly of the League, and the right to be represented there by not more than three delegates. The Covenant, moreover, recognizes the possibility of other Dominions or Colonies attaining membership of the League, and treats them as units of international law, possessing international obligations. The British Empire, again, as one of the Principal Allied and Associated Powers, is entitled to permanent membership of the Council of the League and to have one representative at its meetings, but the Assembly is entitled to select from time to time in its discretion four other members of the League who shall have votes in the Council, and it was expressly agreed between the Prime Ministers of the United Kingdom, Italy, and France, and President Wilson, on May 6, 1919, that the Assembly was absolutely entitled to select a Dominion to have representation in the Council, if it desired to do so. The Council with the approval of a majority of the League may name additional members of the League whose representatives shall always be members of the Council, and may increase the number of members of the League to be selected by the Assembly, and the Dominions will be equally eligible for selection in this manner. It is true that in view of the position of the British Empire on the Council the selection of a Dominion to be represented there is little likely, but the same consideration would probably apply if the Dominions were independent states, for the same jealousy would probably subsist among other powers. Theoretically, of course, the representative of the British Empire might be a Dominion statesman, but there is obviously comparatively little likelihood of that result for a considerable period. But the Dominions have the great advantage that, if they are unlikely to be represented in the Council at any early date, they have the power of impressing on the Imperial Government the importance of any issues which may affect them. The value of this influence is notoriously established by the omission from the League of any clause requiring that members of the League should treat the subjects of other members on a most favoured nation footing; a provision to this effect would have been greatly desired by Japan, but the United Kingdom supported the United States in opposition to any provision which might seem to open the way to a claim for free entry into the Dominions or the United States by Japan. The issue, of course, is one which Japan has reserved the right to bring up again in the League, but it may safely be assumed that, whatever the attitude of the United Kingdom itself on the issue would be, the policy of the Empire will be dictated by the needs of the Dominions.

It is admitted that the Council of Four recognized explicitly the fact that, while the Dominions and India were members of the League, the British Empire also formed a unit. It does not appear, however, how far this admission must be deemed to affect the explicit terms of the League Covenant. On the strict reading of that document not only do the Dominions guarantee the territorial integrity and existing political independence of one another and of the British Empire and India, under Article X, but, if one of them resorted to war in disregard of its obligations under Articles 12, 13 or 15 of the Covenant, it would *ipso facto* be deemed to have committed an act of war against all the other members of the League, which would then be bound to apply to it measures of commercial and even military or naval constraint. Thus the Dominions might be bound to use hostile measures to the United Kingdom or *vice versa*. It is open to contend that these provisions are inapplicable to the Dominions and India, and in support of this contention the reference to ' existing political independence ' in Article X may be cited, as contemplating obviously only fully sovereign states, but the contention is subject to the obvious objection that it imports into the Covenant an element of uncertainty, which is unnecessary and therefore in all probability illegitimate. Moreover it is open to argue that the special relations of the Dominions and India and the United Kingdom are covered in spirit if not in letter by Article XXI, which provides that ' nothing in this Covenant shall be deemed to affect the validity of international engagements, such as treaties of arbitration or regional understandings like the Monroe doctrine for securing the maintenance of peace '. The constitution of the British Empire, however it may be varied from time to time, will always, even if the Dominions are regarded as in such a position towards it that agreements within the Empire are international engagements, be directed towards the maintenance of peace at least as effectively as the Monroe doctrine.

The conception of a League of Nations was warmly welcomed on the whole in the Dominions, if some of the Dominion statesmen—Mr. Hughes in special—were not precisely enamoured of it. But the reception accorded to it in the Dominion Parliaments when the proposals for the ratification of the treaty with Germany were brought forward indicated perplexities and anxieties as to the exact effect of the new arrangements on the future of the Empire, and the status of the Dominions. In Canada, somewhat to the surprise perhaps of the Prime Minister, who may have thought that he would have the approval of the Liberal party in treading the path of autonomy in which Sir Wilfrid Laurier so long walked, the Liberal party developed a considered criticism embodying a perfectly clear conception of the relations of Canada to the Empire far other than that contemplated by Sir R. Borden. Mr. D. D. Mackenzie,[1] Mr. R. Lemieux, and Mr. Fielding, in different form but in substantial agreement, held that the separate representation of the Dominion and the ratification on behalf of the Dominion were idle forms which added nothing to the validity of the treaty as binding on the Dominion through the action of the Imperial Government. Canada was not, and could not be, a nation under the constitution embodied in the British North America Act, and it was idle to contend otherwise. To seek representation in all matters of treaty relations and foreign affairs was neither necessary nor desirable ; the Imperial Government would look to these matters generally, and Canada would send representatives in cases specially affecting her as in the past—the doctrine enunciated by Sir Wilfrid Laurier in 1911. The League Covenant was open to specific objections. Article X imposed on Canada the necessity of entering into petty disputes in Europe at the decision of a Council sitting at Geneva in which the Dominion would have no representative. Article VIII, taken in conjunction with that Article, contemplated the obligation of Canada to maintain an armed force so as

[1] Canada, *House of Commons Debates*, September 2, 1919.

to be able to take her share in the enforcement of her international obligations in common with other members of the League.
Article XVI might even involve Canada in war with the United
Kingdom.   It might even be doubted, apart from the grave
objections to pressing for Canada's representation in international
matters—which had already caused serious difficulties in the
United States as to the approval of the peace treaty as a whole—
whether the Dominion Parliament had any right to pass legislation for carrying out a treaty not concluded simply by the Imperial
Government for the whole Empire, but by Canada as a separate
power.   The old status of the Dominion was preferable ;   under
it, to the satisfaction of Sir John Macdonald and Sir Wilfrid
Laurier alike, Canada had enjoyed full autonomy and had been
absolutely free to decide from time to time whether she would
take part in Imperial wars by the voting of men and money ;   now
she had lost her freedom of action ;   she would be bound by treaty
to intervene by commercial or military action in disputes which
did not concern her at the dictation of authorities other than her
own people and Parliament.

Mr. Fielding carried his objections to the shadowy status thus
claimed to the extent of moving an amendment to the resolution
for the approval of the Peace Treaty to the effect that ' in giving
such approval this house in no way assents to any impairment of
the existing autonomous authority of the Dominion, but declares
that the question of what part, if any, the forces of Canada shall
take in any war, actual or threatened, is one to be determined at
all times as occasion may require by the people of Canada through
their representatives in Canada '.   This amendment elicited a very
interesting exposition of his understanding of the League Covenant
from Mr. Doherty, Minister of Justice.   He enunciated the remarkable theory that Canada did not approach the allied or associated
powers or the United Kingdom to obtain nationhood. Nationhood
was a matter of fact ;   it was not derived from statutory enactment or from recognition by other nations.   When the signature of
the British Empire came to be affixed to the treaty it was necessary,
in addition to the signatures of the ministers of the United Kingdom, who represented that territory and the Crown colonies and
protectorates, that there should be affixed the signatures of the

statesmen of the Dominions and of India, because they were nations and with the other part of the British possessions made up the British Empire. The Labour Convention included in the treaty had been largely the work of the Prime Minister of Canada and the Minister for Public Works ; they had secured for Canadian employers and working men equal rights in regard to the representation of their interests with all powers save the five great powers, and these privileges had been won by the use of Canadian representatives, a fact which refuted the argument that it was sufficient to trust the statesmen of the United Kingdom. Article X had not the result of overruling the power of the Parliament of the Dominion ; between it and its operation the Dominion Parliament would operate as heretofore. The Article merely recognized the general principle that the territorial integrity and independence of each member of the League should be jointly guaranteed by the other members. The powers of the League Council regarding the fulfilment of the obligation were merely to advise as to the measures to be taken, and under Article V of the League any member not represented on the Council must be invited to send a member to any meeting of the Council during the consideration of matters specially affecting the interests of that member of the League. The decisions of the Council under Article IV must be unanimous, and accordingly, if Canada were asked to contribute men or money, then she would have the right to send to the Council a representative to express her views, and this representative would be able to veto any proposal not acceptable to the Dominion. On the other hand, it was impossible to accept the reservation proposed by Mr. Fielding, which would be equivalent to rejecting the treaty, and thus causing Canada to stand apart as no longer co-operating with the rest of the Empire. At the same time, he held that, if Canada should desire to withdraw separately from the League, there was no technical difficulty in doing so, and she would cease to be bound by any obligations under the League, though the British Empire remained a member.

The arguments of Mr. Doherty are obviously inconclusive ; by international law recognition by other nations is essential to give national status, and the new status of Canada is derived from the treaty of peace. Prior to it the ministers of the United Kingdom were wont to bind the Dominions without signature by the Dominion representatives, and the treaty for aiding France in event of German aggression was concluded for the whole Empire by the Imperial Government, though its operation in the Dominions was to be dependent on the action of their Parliaments, not, be it noted, their Governments. The services rendered by the Dominion ministers in regard to the Labour Convention might be recognized as of value without drawing the conclusion that constant representation with regard to treaties was desirable or necessary. The interpretation put on Article X clearly goes too far,[1] and is not in accord with the observations upon the clause by other ministers, who conceded that the Article imposes a real obligation on Canada which hitherto has not been borne by her, but which, they justly argue, is the necessary result of her attaining a new status. This, indeed, was the line of argument developed in the main by the spokesmen of the Government, and expressly set out by Mr. Rowell on March 11, 1920, in the debate on a resolution to approve the treaty with Bulgaria. His speech was interesting, because it was clearly intended to reply officially to the objections of the majority of the United States Senate to the representation of the Dominions in the League. He stated that the Imperial Government and the Government of the Dominion were agreed that, if a dispute arose between any part of the Empire and a foreign country and the matter, not being one suitable for arbitration or judicial determination, were referred by the Council to the Assembly for investigation and report, then in the voting in the Assembly on the issue no other part of the Empire, as being an interested party, could vote. Subject to this principle the Dominion stood for the precise observance of the rights which it had claimed and succeeded in obtaining. Thus in the case of the Labour Convention it had been proposed that no state plus its Dominions could have more than one member out of the twenty-four constituting the Governing Body of the International Labour Office, but Canada had objected to such a restriction on her status, and, with the concurrence of the other Dominions, had protested, with the result that the proposal was withdrawn and the

---

[1] At the Geneva meeting of the League in 1920 a Canadian amendment suggested the deletion of Article X from the Covenant.

only restriction imposed that none of the eight states of chief industrial importance, which had a right to send members to serve on the Governing Body to represent the Governments, should take part in the election of the remaining four governmental delegates who fell to be chosen by the other members of the League. The answer of Canada to the Lenroot amendment in the United States Senate to the treaty, declaring that the United States would not be bound by any decision of the League Council or Assembly in which any State with its Dominions had cast more than one vote, was that they could not consent to any impairment of the voting power of the Dominion, whose whole status was challenged by such a reservation. As regards the relation of the Dominion and the United Kingdom the time had arrived when complete autonomy and equality of status had been acquired by Canada, and it remained for a Constitutional Conference to meet, not for the purpose of creating any new Imperial organization, but for the purpose of developing a system of consultation and co-operation which would absolutely preserve the autonomy of the Dominions, and at the same time enable matters in which the Dominions were vitally concerned to receive that attention by the Dominions which, under the existing system, it was not possible to give them. Mr. Rowell's eloquence, however, failed to satisfy the Opposition, whose leader, Mr. Mackenzie King, deprecated any step to diminish the autonomy of the Dominion, and insisted on the absurdity of claiming that Canada was a sovereign power like the United Kingdom when it could not amend its own constitution, having, indeed, less power in this regard than either Australia or New Zealand. He criticized also the action of the Government in giving executive assent to the ratification of the treaties with the Serb-Croat-Slovene state and with Czecho-Slovakia on the ground that, if Canada was to have increased interest in foreign policy, it was necessary that there should be effective democratic control. On the other hand, on June 22 the House of Commons extended a sympathetic hearing to Sir Herbert Ames, Financial Director of the Secretariat of the League of Nations, who explained in detail the work of the League and appealed for a generous response from the Dominions to the financial appeal addressed to members of the League to enable the work of combating the typhus epidemic in Eastern Europe to be carried through successfully.

In addition to resolutions regarding all the treaties of peace, including the Polish treaty, and the arrangement regarding the occupation of the Rhine territory, Parliament agreed to Acts providing for the carrying out of the matters affecting Canada arising out of the treaties of peace, the cases of Germany and Austria being included in one measure. The Senate, indeed, proposed to make the one Act cover all the treaties, but as those with Bulgaria, Hungary, and Turkey were not yet ready, the Opposition objected to the suggestion, and the Government accepted the objection as valid.

In the Commonwealth of Australia approval was given to the treaty with Germany on September 10 with singularly little discussion on the effect of the treaty on the status of the Commonwealth, though the Prime Minister pointed out that the signing of the treaty gave Australia national status. He insisted, however, on the fact that the League of Nations would be of great value, but at the same time was clear that, as the Monroe doctrine was excluded from examination by the League, so the doctrine of White Australia must be deemed to be a regional understanding which was beyond any arbitration or enquiry by the League. He regretted the application of the mandatory system to the islands, and the failure to secure the annexation of them all to the Commonwealth, but this had proved impossible, and he had fought hard, with success, to secure that the islands should not be internationalized or left open to immigration. Australia was not hostile to Japan, but must insist on deciding whom to admit to her territories. He deplored also the acceptance of the President's views as to indemnities ; Australia had spent £364,000,000 in war costs which under the treaty were irrecoverable, and £100,000,000 represented her expenditure when capitalized on pensions and other recoverable costs ; he hoped for payment of from £5,000,000 before April 1921 and the rest in instalments in thirty years. The leader of the Opposition, Mr. Tudor, held that it was a matter of indifference whether Australia approved ratification or not, as the Imperial Government would in any event ratify, while Mr. J. H. Catts, another Labour member, pointed out that Australia's frontier had been extended to Rabaul, while that of Japan had come 3,000 miles south. Sir J. Cook, however, laid stress on the fact that under the mandate neither the Japanese nor the Australian islands could be fortified, which was a strong ground for anticipating peaceful relations. Mr. Hughes also moved the approval of the tripartite arrangement for the grant of aid to France in the event of German aggression; it was explained in the Senate that this would not mean necessarily the sending of armed aid to France; money or contributions in kind might be substituted. In Canada,[1] on the other hand, the Government more cautiously withheld action pending the decision of the United States, and thus evaded a decidedly controversial discussion. The Commonwealth, in addition to approving the other treaties of peace, legislated as in Canada for the carrying out of the terms regarding enemy debts contained in the treaties.

In New Zealand also, where the resolution in favour of ratification was passed on September 2, there was equally little exultation over the treaty of peace, though its constitutional import was recognized.[2] Mr. Massey's statement, indeed, was overshadowed by forebodings about Samoa which New Zealand had been obliged to accept in mandate, but which she would much rather have seen annexed to the Crown and administered by the United Kingdom. The indemnity to be obtained from Germany might reach £10,000,000 or £12,000,000, half their expenditure on pensions, &c., but when it would be received was uncertain. Sir J. Ward was yet more pessimistic, and Labour was wholly disappointed in the treaty, which it wished to see rejected. In addition to ratification resolutions in respect of the treaties, New Zealand legislated, as in Australia, both to carry out the economic terms of the peace treaties and to provide for the exercise of her mandatory powers.

In the Union of South Africa, the treaty discussions attained a high degree of interest and importance, General Smuts taking the opportunity to base on them a new conception of the British Commonwealth of Nations, much as he had advocated in his

---

[1] Canada, *House of Commons Debates*, April 8, 1920.

[2] Mr. Downie Stewart insisted on the possible dangers of sovereignty as disrupting the Imperial bond. See also Debates, September 23, 1920.

speeches in England in 1917. His enthusiasm for the League was evinced by his declaration, in moving on September 8 approval of the ratification of the treaty with Germany, that all he had done in his lifetime was as dust and ashes compared with the small effort he had been able to contribute towards building up this new organization for the future government of the world. The conclusion of the League compensated for the many sad disillusions he had experienced in respect to other parts of the treaty whose blots and blemishes he freely admitted, and the terms of which he did not ask the House to approve in detail. For South Africa the League accomplished two things : first, it afforded the possibility of world peace ; secondly, it provided additional recognition of the status of the Dominions by making them equal members of the Assembly of the League and entitling them to be elected to the Council, an honour which he held that some Dominion would speedily secure. On the other hand he had been anxious not to loosen the ties of Empire, and it was to avoid this result that places had been secured for the Dominions, thus removing the risk that with the advance in numbers and strength of the Dominions there would arise, in default of effective means of meeting natural aspirations, the decision to secede from the Empire. The new status brought responsibilities, but ' you cannot ask for recognition and admission among the nations of the world and still think you can sit on your antheap in South Africa '. The Labour charter was especially worthy of praise, while the reparation clauses had caused much anxiety to General Botha and would require drastic revision. The Nationalists denounced the treaty as fraudulent and hypocritical, and as worse than Germany's action in 1870, but their chief anxiety was to show, on the one hand, that the Union was not really free, as General Smuts contended, seeing that its Acts, if repugnant to British Acts, were invalid, or if the League Covenant was a reality, the Union must be entitled to declare its independence. General Smuts replied by insisting that the right of the Imperial Parliament to legislate for South Africa without the consent of the Union was absolutely gone. The debate was resumed on the Bill to enable the financial clauses of the treaty of peace to be carried out and to provide for the exercise of the Union mandate over South-West Africa, when the Prime

Minister [1] asserted the royal veto to be obsolete save in a case of a law for the secession of the Union from the Empire. The Nationalists endeavoured to secure an amendment asking for a referendum on the question in the Union and the South-West Territory, but this was defeated by 70 votes to 23.

On June 21 and 23, 1920, on the estimates for the Prime Minister an important discussion took place between the Prime Minister and his critics. The League of Nations was assailed on various heads, but especially because of the rash deeds of Poland and the economic boycott of Germany; it was also contended that the Union's share of the Secretariat expenditure (£20,000) was too high, and that the Union should have a representative on the Council of the League. General Smuts replied by regretting the difficulties which the League had to face, the defection of the United States; the tendency of the Supreme Council to usurp its functions; the rash offensive of Poland; but the force of public opinion might result in action by the League which would clear up matters. The Union was only entitled to representation on the Assembly of the League, and the expenses—based at present on the ratios of contribution to the Postal Union—would be revised shortly. Against the Imperial system Mr. Beyers protested that it denied independence to the Union; that South Africa under Article X of the League would be drawn into the whirlpool of European politics; that the King could veto Union Acts, and, despite the statements of the Prime Minister, was still quite likely to do so; that it allowed appeals to the Privy Council from the Appellate Division of the Supreme Court of South Africa; and that the Dutch language was denied its equal rights. He also contrasted the Prime Minister's assertions as to the unconstitutionality of secession with Mr. Bonar Law's and Mr. Chamberlain's assertions that a Dominion could withdraw from the Empire if it desired. Another Nationalist, Mr. Langenhoven, was anxious lest the position of the Union should be compromised without reference to the Parliament at any Constitutional Conference, and alluded with some anxiety to the views apparently held by Lord Milner in a speech in the House of Lords on June 17 [2] in favour of some more

[1] *House of Assembly Debates*, September 10, 1920.

[2] Cf. speeches reported in *The Times*, July 2, August 10, 1920. In July 1916 Lord Milner still advocated Imperial federation.

close link of connexion than that afforded by periodic conferences. General Smuts insisted in reply on the necessity of a constitutional conference to clear up the anomalies which had resulted from the new status of the Dominions on the one hand, and the continuance of old forms on the other. Correspondence through the Colonial Office was out of date. The position of the Governor-General should be assimilated to that of the King, and he should cease altogether to represent the Imperial Government and the Colonial Office. Then, as Canada had decided to have her own diplomatic representative at Washington, so every Dominion had the right to have its diplomatic representatives abroad, and this issue must be cleared up. They must also consider in what manner the Empire could speak with one voice in the affairs of the world, and thus preserve its due importance in decisions of foreign affairs. If, as it had been suggested, Lord Milner meant that there must be adopted the principle that the majority in an Empire discussion must be allowed to determine the issue, there would be an end of the freedom they had won ; the only principle must be that of Conference discussion and, if possible, agreement on a common line of action ; if no agreement could be come to, they must proceed without agreeing. Conference was essentially valuable for South Africa ; that country stood in a peculiar position, in part influenced by the continental, in part by the British point of view, and its contribution to Conference discussions would thus possess a special value. The true path for the greatness, freedom, and independence of South Africa was not, as he thought twenty years ago, through a republic ; it lay in preserving absolute autonomy and right of decision on all issues, but at the same time in co-operating with the other parts of the Empire. This explanation satisfied Mr. Langenhoven, but Dr. Malan still expressed deep anxiety regarding the possibility of the outcome of the Conference, deplored secret diplomacy of all kinds, and demanded the selection of the Governor-General by the Union and not by the Imperial Government.

The dialectical use of the utterances of Mr. Bonar Law made against General Smuts in the debate did not elicit from him a full exposition of his attitude. Mr. Bonar Law's description of Dominion Home Rule was evoked by the discussion on the Government of Ireland Bill of the Imperial Government on March 30, 1920, when he replied to the suggestion by Mr. Asquith of the grant to Ireland of that form of government. The Dominions, he argued, had control of their own destinies, of their fighting forces, of the amounts they would contribute to the general security of the Empire, and of their fiscal policy. ' But ', he added, ' it goes much further than that. To say that he [Mr. Asquith] is in favour of Dominion Home Rule means something much more. There is not a man in this House, and least of all my right honourable friend, who would not admit that the connexion of the Dominions with the Empire ' depends upon themselves. If the self-governing Dominions, Australia, Canada, chose to-morrow to say, " We will no longer make a part of the British Empire," we would not try to force them. Dominion Home Rule means the right to decide their own destinies.' The terms thus employed were, it must be remembered, used not in a considered discussion of the position of the Dominions, and it is not without significance that in the debate on the third reading of the Government of Ireland Bill on November 11 the Prime Minister guarded himself in his allusion to the possibility of granting Dominion Home Rule from asserting the inherent right of the Dominions to secede. The true interpretation of Mr. Bonar Law's words can be no more than that, if Canada or Australia resolved by the clear will of the majority of the people to sever its connexion with the Empire, the United Kingdom would not use armed force to prevent the consummation of its purpose. There is no suggestion, however, that the severance of union could be effected by a Dominion Act assented to by the Crown, and there is no possible reply to General Smuts' argument that the Crown could not constitutionally assent to any such Act by a Dominion legislature. The essential nature of such a legislature is that it is the legislature for a part of the British Empire, and, in enacting the severance of the connexion with the Empire, the legislature would be exceeding the powers allotted to it. The preambles to the Federation Acts of Canada of 1867 and of the Commonwealth of 1900 and to the Act for the constitution of the Union of South Africa in 1909 are conclusive on this score. The British North America Act is a measure for the federal union of the Provinces into ' one Dominion under the Crown of the United

Kingdom of Great Britain and Ireland ', the Commonwealth Act provides for the union of the Colonies in ' one indissoluble federal commonwealth under the Crown of the United Kingdom ', and the South Africa Act for the formation of a ' legislative union under the Crown of Great Britain and Ireland '. Parliaments, it is plain, cannot destroy the fundamental conditions on which they exist, and it rests with the Imperial Parliament alone to alter the constitutional dependence of any Dominion on the United Kingdom, and to recognize, if it deems fit, its position as an independent state of international law.

Even before the signing of the treaty with Germany it was found necessary for the Canadian Prime Minister to return to the Dominion, leaving Sir George Foster to act for Canada, and on the conclusion of the peace the effective action of the Imperial Delegation ended by the return of the Dominion representatives home, leaving further business to be conducted in large measure by telegraphic correspondence. Efforts, however, were made to secure a revival of oral discussions in London in preparation for the meeting at Spa to discuss with Germany the question of reparation, and a meeting was summoned at London at which Canada nominated Sir George Perley as her representative, Australia Mr. Watt, the Treasurer, New Zealand the High Commissioner, while South Africa was also to be represented. Mr. Watt, however, resigned office, and did not fulfil his commission, owing to disagreement with Mr. Hughes as to the extent of his authority to bind the Commonwealth. The outcome of the discussion was important for the Dominions, since it was followed at Spa in July by the agreement that the sums received from Germany by way of reparation should be divided in the proportion of 52 per cent. to France, 22 per cent. to the British Empire, 10 per cent. to Italy, 8 per cent. to Belgium, $\frac{3}{4}$ of 1 per cent. to each of Japan and Portugal, and the rest to the other powers entitled to receive reparation, but not signatories of this agreement. Comprehensive arrangements were also then agreed to on other reparation questions, the net outcome of the discussion being clearly to justify the doubts of Sir Joseph Ward as to the probability of any early return of money to any of the Dominions. The same view was expressed by Mr. Watt, who assured the Commonwealth Government that he was convinced of the futility of expecting the payment of a German indemnity as anticipated by the Prime Minister.

An important impetus to the renewal of Imperial consultation was afforded by the despatch to Europe of delegates to attend the meeting of the Assembly of the League of Nations at Geneva in November 1920. Canada sent as her three representatives Sir George Foster, Minister of Trade, and Mr. Doherty, Minister of Justice, together with Mr. Rowell, formerly President of the Council. It was announced that while in London the delegates would discuss with the Imperial Government the domestic topics of the amendment of the North America Act, the delimitation of the boundary between Canada and Newfoundland, and the problem of the naturalization of aliens. The Commonwealth of Australia selected Mr. Millen, who also undertook to deal in England with the establishment of a new machinery for promoting emigration to the Commonwealth. The Union of South Africa, by a gracious departure from custom, nominated as one of her delegates Lord Robert Cecil, in recognition of the distinguished part played by him in the framing of the Covenant of the League of Nations and his enthusiasm in its cause, and New Zealand sent her High Commissioner, Sir James Allen.

It is important to note that save for these occasions, and only then in a very imperfect manner, there has been no effort in 1920 to carry out the policy asserted at the Imperial War Conference in 1918 in favour of the holding of meetings of the Imperial Cabinet [1] from time to time, and that, since the necessity of constant co-operation for war purposes came to an end, the Dominions have done nothing to keep in touch with foreign policy by maintaining resident ministers in London. Even Canada, which from 1914 to 1919 had practically continuous representation by a minister, first Sir George Perley, then Sir Edward Kemp, has since the return of the latter to Canada in October 1919 had no ministerial representative, while even in 1918 opinion in the Commonwealth was not prepared to sanction the appointment of a minister

---

[1] On November 11 and 17, 1920, it was announced that an Imperial Cabinet would meet in June 1921, but that the Constitutional Conference contemplated by the Resolution of the War Conference of 1917 was postponed.

unless he could also perform the functions of the High Commissioner, who under existing legislation is by status an official. Though Mr. Massey on November 1918 declared his approval of the idea of a resident minister, in 1920 Sir James Allen was appointed only as High Commissioner without ministerial rank, and the Union of South Africa has never committed itself to approval of the principle.

The treaties of peace [1] authorize the retention by the Governments concerned of the property of enemy aliens within their territories, the value of which is to be reckoned in the computation of the total amount of reparation due by Germany. The situation of the Dominions generally in this regard is similar to that of the United Kingdom ; the sums owed by Germany far exceed the value of property in their hands. In the Union, however, the position is different ; the amounts which the Union can claim as reparation are comparatively small and the amount of German property relatively large. The governmental policy as decided on in July 1920 has been to repay to Germans in the Union property (value £3,000,000) which was taken into the control of the Custodian of enemy property during the war. As regards the property of Germans not domiciled in the Union the terms of the treaty will be adhered to. There will be paid out of the amount available all debts due to nationals of the Union, and further, if Germany does not repay the value of the property of nationals of the Union appropriated in Germany, these sums will be taken out of the fund. The claims on Germany on submarine account had been fixed at about £100,000, adopting the same basis of reckoning as that taken by the Imperial Government. This would give total deductions of £1,100,000. This would leave in the Custodian's hands about £10,000,000, which would be treated as a loan to the Union for thirty years at four per cent. It was added that, though the Union might appropriate German property in the South-West Territory, this would not be done ; *bona fide* concessions would be recognized and accrued diamond company dividends (£700,000) treated as a loan for thirty years. The settlement,

---

[1] Treaty with Germany June 28, 1919, ss. 119–23, and pt. x, ss. 296, 297 ; Treaty with Austria, September 10, 1919, ss. 248, 249 ; Treaty with Bulgaria, ss. 176, 177 ; Treaty with Hungary, ss. 231, 232.

which is one of remarkable generosity, was approved warmly by the House of Assembly, but it was of course only possible to adopt it in view of the lightness of the burden which the policy of the Union entailed on its people during the war, while the fact that separate treatment of the problem is possible in each Dominion exemplifies in the most striking manner the truth of General Smuts's assertion of the degree of autonomy attained by the Dominions.

3. The Diplomatic Representation of the Dominions

It followed as an immediate corollary from the separate representation of the Dominions at the Peace Conference that they were entitled, if they thought fit, to secure similar representation not merely at a great international conference but as a matter of course in foreign capitals. This was the sense in which Canada interpreted the situation, and she proceeded to put the new theory in operation by asking the Imperial Government to arrange for her diplomatic representation in the United States. The details of the discussions which followed were kept secret by the desire of both parties, but the difficulties which arose may easily be appreciated. In the first place, the refusal of the United States Senate to accept the Peace Treaty weakened the argument which might otherwise have been based on the fact that President Wilson at the Peace Conference accepted the new position of the Dominions, and there was therefore necessary diplomatic handling of the issue so as to secure that the United States would not be in a position to raise difficulties as to the reception of a Canadian envoy. The Canadian War Mission at Washington, which had rendered valuable services both to the Dominion and the Empire with regard to questions of war trade, had been expressly empowered, in order to avoid diplomatic difficulties, only to represent ' the Cabinet and the heads of departments ' at Ottawa, and to conduct negotiations with the ' heads of the departments or other administrative branches, committees or commissions, or other officials of the Government of the United States ', so that the change in status proposed was remarkable. On the other hand there already existed a treaty of January 11, 1909, regarding the boundary waters of Canada which recognized the peculiar position of

Canada with regard to the United States, though not introducing any absolutely new principle. That treaty provided for the establishment of an International Joint Commission of six members, three appointed by the President and three by the King on the recommendation of the Dominion Government. The treaty further provided that either the Government of the United States or the Dominion Government could refer to the Commission any matters of difference arising on questions affecting the common frontier, in which case the Commission might examine and report on the question, though without power to give a final award. On the other hand, Article X of the treaty authorized the reference to the Commission for final decision of any matters of difference involving the rights, obligations, or interests of the United States or of the Dominion either in relation to each other or to their respective inhabitants, the reference to be made, in this instance, by the Imperial Government with the consent of the Dominion Government, thus laying down the principle that the Imperial Government in such matters acted merely as the agent of the Dominion Government. The Commission had been active and had rendered valuable services, though in 1918 some difference of opinion arose between it and the Canadian Government as to the limits of its jurisdiction.[1] The interests of Canada and the United States had been closely linked in the war, and the partial abrogation of the old understanding of 1817 regarding the maintenance of warships on the Great Lakes, which would at one time have raised serious difficulty, caused no trouble. It was, therefore, possible for the United States to facilitate the acceptance of the desire of Canada, in a manner which at the same time met the other grave difficulty in the situation which presented itself. There was obviously every reason for deprecating the formal division of the Empire which would arise from the presence of two representatives at Washington of equal status, and the adoption of the general principle of separate representation, without the approval even of an Imperial Constitutional Conference, would have been difficult for both the Imperial and the Dominion

---

[1] *The Times*, September 12 and 27, 1918. On the Commission see L. J. Burpee, *Journal of Society of Comparative Legislation*, xvi. 5–12 ; *Canadian Annual Review*, 1919, pp. 118–20.

Governments. A compromise was therefore arrived at by which a Canadian nominee was to be accredited to the President as Minister at Washington, with the primary duty of dealing with all diplomatic questions arising between the British Crown and the United States affecting Canada only, acting upon instructions from and reporting direct to the Canadian Government. In the absence of the Ambassador the Minister would assume charge of the whole Embassy and of the representation of Imperial as well as of Canadian interests. It was explained in the official announcement of May 10, 1920, that the ' new arrangement will not denote any departure either on the part of the British Government or of the Canadian Government from the principle of the diplomatic unity of the British Empire '. It was also added that the motives for the change were that distinct Canadian representation would expedite matters and have the advantage derived from first-hand acquaintance with Canadian conditions. On May 17 the opposition took the opportunity to criticize both the method of making the appointment and its policy. Mr. Fielding insisted that there had been no resolution in Parliament or public discussion to justify the step, and it had been carried out in entire secrecy. It involved serious constitutional changes, and he moved an amendment on the motion for supply asking for full information on the subject, with copies of all correspondence and Orders in Council. Mr. Rowell defended the step taken as logical and likely to further Imperial co-operation ; where other than purely Canadian interests were involved the Minister and the Ambassador would co-operate. Mr. Lapointe, however, indicated the dangers of anticipating the results of the Constitutional Conference and the anomalous position of the Imperial Government with regard to responsibility for the actions of the Minister when representing the Ambassador. Sir R. Borden replied in a conciliatory speech in which he adduced the parallel of the International Joint Commission and of Mr. Fielding's mission to Washington to negotiate the Reciprocity Treaty in 1911—an ominous precedent. He insisted that the policy, though the details of the negotiations must remain secret, was not a hasty one ; he had discussed it in 1919 with British ministers and Dominion statesmen, and he was sure that the method of procedure followed was the best in the interest of Imperial unity. Mr. Mackenzie King, however, deprecated the arrangement by which a Canadian Minister would act for the Empire in the absence of the Ambassador, dealing with questions affecting Europe or arising out of the League of Nations, and indicated a clear preference for the rule that in matters between Canada and other countries Canada should manage her own affairs, and that in matters between the United Kingdom and other countries, the United Kingdom should manage her own affairs, always when necessary with co-operation and conference between the two. Mr. Lemieux reproached ministers with consorting so much with Imperial statesmen that they had forgotten their responsibility to their little Dominion, and were plunging the Dominion heedlessly into international difficulties. The precedent of Lord Alverstone's surrender of Canadian interests on the affair of the Alaskan boundary proved that association with the United Kingdom would not further Canadian interests. Recalling Mr. Asquith's pronouncement at the Conference of 1911, ' Do not ', he said, ' let us meddle in the affairs of the United mother country, and the mother country will let us govern ourselves.' Mr. Béland elicited from the Minister of Justice an important admission, that the appointment of the Canadian Minister would be made by the King on the advice of the Secretary of State for Foreign Affairs in the usual form, and not merely on the advice of the Dominion Government. But the Prime Minister insisted that the mode of appointment was not the vital point, but the fact that the appointment was made on the advice of the Dominion Government. The mode, however, remains of moment, since the necessity of Imperial intervention at once emphasizes the continued unity of the Empire in foreign affairs, and interposes a possibility of objection on the part of the Imperial Government. The procedure, therefore, follows that of the mode of ratification of the treaties of peace signed by the Dominion delegates. It is important to note that the amendment of Mr. Fielding was rejected by the small majority of 68 to 63.

The appointment [1] has naturally raised the definite issue of the action of the other Dominions. The Prime Minister of the Commonwealth has expressed the opinion that the Australian

[1] Though approved in principle, the post was left unfilled in 1920.

High Commissioner to the United States, a post the importance of which is recognized, should acquire equal status with the representative of Canada, and the Prime Minister of the Union has claimed that the Union possesses the same right of appointment as Canada. The issue is in his view to be dealt with at the Constitutional Conference, where also may be raised the kindred issue of according to the Governor-General authority to issue full powers to Dominion delegates to treat in international matters, thus eliminating Imperial intervention and accentuating the independent status of the Dominions, a step for which, however, public opinion in the majority of the Dominions is not yet ready.

A kindred question as to preservation of the unity of the Empire in diplomatic matters is raised by the issue of the mode of communication between the Council of the League of Nations and the Dominions. Should the annual reports, which the Dominions owe to the Council, as mandatories of the League, and any other representations to the League go direct or through the Secretary of State for Foreign Affairs ? Sir James Allen,[1] on behalf of New Zealand, has expressed himself as strongly in favour of the use of the Imperial Government as a channel of communication and the establishment of a Secretariat in which the several views of the Dominions could be focused. Clearly under the League Covenant the right to communicate direct exists, but it may be doubted if it should always be insisted upon. Yet to negative it might be held equivalent to derogating from the position of the Dominions in the League.

The question raises also the issue, whether, if communications are sent through the Imperial Government, that Government has any right to refuse to forward them. The answer, in this case, is clearly in the negative. There are clear advantages to be gained in the preservation of the forms of unity, but the functions of the Imperial Government and the Secretary of State for Foreign Affairs must as regards communications from the Dominions to foreign powers or the League be ministerial, and the requests of the Dominions complied with without reserve.[2] The advantage, however, of the use of this mode of communication would be that suggestions might be made before the Dominion definitely com-

---

[1] *The Times*, April 22, 1920.   [2] Keith, *The Times*, July 15, 1920.

mitted itself to any position. It is obvious that, if Imperial unity is not to disappear, each Dominion must keep the Imperial Government and other Governments informed of its views, and it would at least be convenient if no action on any issue were taken, whether by the Imperial Government or a Dominion Government, before opportunity for objections or suggestions had been afforded. The precise manner in which such consultation is arranged is only of secondary importance.

The need, however, of such consultation is strikingly exemplified by the case of the treaty with Japan of July 13, 1911, which was concluded after the Dominion Governments had been fully apprised of the international conditions which rendered the renewal and extension of the earlier engagements of the two countries essential. The two Governments by notes of July 8, 1920, have admitted to the League that the Agreement, as it stands, is not wholly consistent with the Covenant, and that the Covenant overrides the Treaty when the two documents differ. In the decision as to the necessary modifications the Dominions must concur, and it would certainly be acceptable to the Dominions if the suggestion approved by Colonel E. M. House were adopted of expanding the Treaty so as to include the United States and China in a compact for the preservation of peace and freedom of trade in the East.[1]

In one case, that of the Convention as to International Air Navigation,[2] the unity of the Empire has been combined in a curious manner with the right of separate representation. The British Dominions and India are given the status of states in express terms under the Convention, but on the International Commission for Air Navigation, which forms part of the organization of the League of Nations, while the United States, France, Italy, and Japan are assigned two representatives each, the United Kingdom, the Dominions, and India have, like the minor Powers, only one representative apiece. Moreover the voting power of the four great states is to be equal to that of the United Kingdom, the Dominions, and India combined, nor is there any

---

[1] *The Times*, August 8, 1920. For a criticism of Japanese policy, see A. M. Pooley, *Japan's Foreign Policies*, London, 1920.

[2] See Keith, *The Times*, September 24, 1919.

specification in the Treaty of the principles on which the British Empire vote is to be cast. Compulsory unity would clearly be contrary to the status of the Dominions as states for the purpose of the Convention, but apart from its obscurity the terms are strangely derogatory to the status of the Dominions and the United Kingdom alike, and it is difficult to account for them save on the hypothesis that they were determined upon before the full status of the Dominions had been appreciated. It may also have been felt by the other Great Powers that there was less objection to conferring on the Dominions and India the right to vote in the Assembly of the League, where votes would normally be unimportant, than to giving the right in matters where voting would have more immediate purpose.

The date of signature and perhaps the place account for the omission of signature for the Dominions in the case of the Treaty between the United Kingdom and Chile of March 28, 1919, for the reference to a Peace Commission for investigation and report of any dispute which is not otherwise adjusted. The Treaty is concluded in the old form for the whole of the British Dominions, but it expressly provides that in the event of the dispute affecting mainly the interests of a Dominion the British member of the Commission may be one representing the Dominion whose interests are specifically affected.

The new relations do not, of course, involve the necessity of the Dominions taking responsibility for the whole of the foreign relations of the Empire. Thus the Dominions were not involved in the responsibility for the conclusion of the Treaty of 1919 with Persia which, had it been accepted by the Persian Medjliss, would have involved important responsibilities for the United Kingdom in that country, nor have the Dominions any connexion with the quasi-protectorate *de facto* exercised by the Imperial Government over that territory. Similarly the Dominion Governments are not concerned directly with the British administration of Mesopotamia ; when the Prime Minister was asked whether in view of the decision to hold an Imperial Conference in June 1921 the question of the evacuation of Mesopotamia should be held over for discussion with the Dominion representatives he very properly declined to impose on the British taxpayer the burden of supporting military forces in Mesopotamia for any longer period than could possibly be helped.

The stage in the relationship of the members of the Empire which has now been attained has received singularly happy expression from Sir Robert Borden, himself so largely instrumental in bringing it about. In welcoming the Prince of Wales at Ottawa on August 29, 1919, he insisted on the tie of common allegiance. 'For each of these nations', he said, 'there is but one Crown, acting in each Dominion and in every Province or State upon the advice of ministers responsible to the people and invested with their mandate. Thus throughout the Empire there is created a direct and perfect relation between the Crown and the people.'[1] He laid stress on the effect of war as bringing about closer co-operation; 'equality of nationhood must be recognized, preserving unimpaired to each Dominion the full autonomous powers which it now holds and safeguarding to each, by necessary consultation and by adequate voice and influence, its highest interests in the issues of war or peace. For each nation complete control of its own affairs; for the whole Empire necessary co-operation according to the will of the people, in all matters of common concern.' It must be noted that the true intention of this language is not, as has been suggested, to indicate that the Empire should be dissolved into a set of independent states with distinct foreign policies, united only by a common allegiance; in internal affairs absolute autonomy is demanded, but in external affairs co-operation. The point of the Prime Minister's speech was admirably taken in the Prince of Wales's reply. In it stress was laid on the new status of the Dominions, but His Royal Highness added : 'At the same time the war has shown that the nations of the Empire can combine to act as a single state in defence of their common institutions and ideals. This was the feature least expected by our enemies and most effective in saving the liberties of the world. It must now be our aim to maintain our unity in the more complex conditions of peace, for on our unity depends not only the security of British institutions, but the peace of the world.'

[1] Cf. *Theodore* v. *Duncan*, [1919] A. C. 696, 706. See also Mr. Hughes, Commonwealth *Debates*, April 8, 1921.

CHAPTER VIII

THE MANDATORY SYSTEM AND THE MANDATED TERRITORIES

1. THE DOMINION MANDATES.
   Article XXII of the League Covenant — The Commonwealth and New Guinea
   — New Zealand and Samoa — The Union and South-West Africa.
2. THE NAURU ISLAND AGREEMENT.
   The Mandate to the Empire — Construction of Article XXII.
3. THE CONTROL OF THE LEAGUE.
   Powers of the Council and the Assembly — The annual report.

1. THE DOMINION MANDATES

IN the Commonwealth, New Zealand, and the Union it is
probable that the interest felt in the peace treaty with Germany
as a whole was negligible in comparison with that taken in the
mandatory system. As has been seen, the system was accepted
with the greatest reluctance by the representatives of all the
Dominions, and the United Kingdom loyally supported their
views in regard to the territories in which they were interested,
though it was prepared to concede the adoption of the system
for German East Africa, which had been reduced by forces under
Imperial control, though largely recruited from South Africa and
led by South African generals. The insistence of the President of
the United States secured the acceptance of the mandatory
system, but the protests of the Dominions prevailed to the extent
of a wholesale modification of the system when applied to the
territories in which they were specially concerned. It was laid
down in Article XXII of the Covenant of the League that the
well-being of peoples not yet able to stand by themselves under
the conditions of the modern world should form a sacred trust of
civilization, to which principle effect should be given by the
exercise of tutelage over such peoples by advanced nations, who
should exercise this tutelage as mandatories of the League of
Nations. The character of the mandate must differ according to
the stage of development attained by the people, their geographical
situation, economic condition, and other factors. In the case of

the Turkish Empire it might be enough to afford administrative advice and assistance ; but other peoples, especially those of Central Africa, were ' at such a stage that the mandatory must be responsible for the administration of the territory under conditions which will guarantee freedom of conscience and religion subject only to the maintenance of public order and morals, the prohibition of abuses such as the slave trade, the arms traffic, and the liquor traffic, and the prevention of the establishment of fortifications or naval and military bases, and of military training of the natives for other than police purposes and the defence of territory, and will also secure equal opportunities for the trade and commerce of other members of the League.' From this general principle, which was originally intended to apply equally to the territories mandated to the Dominions, an exception was made in the following terms [1] : ' There are territories, such as South-West Africa and certain of the South Pacific Islands, which, owing to the sparseness of their population, or their small size, or their remoteness from the centres of civilization, or their geographical contiguity to the territory of the mandatory and other circumstances, can be best administered under the laws of the mandatory as integral portions of the territory, subject to the safeguards above mentioned in the interests of the indigenous population.' The terminology of the addition is obviously vague, and it might be argued that free access of outside trade competition was one of the safeguards necessary for the natives, but the effect of the whole doubtless was meant to be that ascribed to it by the Prime Minister of the Commonwealth on September 10, 1919, when he asserted that it left the Commonwealth unfettered discretion save in so far that it must not permit the sale of arms or liquor to the natives, the carrying on of the slave trade, the raising of native forces for other than merely defensive purposes, or the erection of fortifications. He emphasized the concessions thus obtained from the original proposal, which would have compelled the Commonwealth to permit an open door for trade and goods, with the result that the control of the Commonwealth

---

[1] The actual terms of the mandates were settled only by the Council of the League in December 1920, and merely elaborated the language of the Covenant. The necessary assent of the United States is still withheld.

over trade and navigation would be gone, and that within eighty miles of Australia there could come pouring in those who, when the hour should strike, could pounce on the mainland. The attitude of Labour was critical; the administration of New Guinea already involved pecuniary burdens on the Commonwealth, and she had sufficient problems to face without adding to them the administration of native territories, which would have been far better left under international control.

Apart, however, from these considerations of preferable possibilities, the Commonwealth was not seriously embarrassed by the mandate; ever since the occupation of the German islands in 1914 the administration had been carried on smoothly and efficiently, with the result that no serious troubles had arisen, the position of the natives had been ameliorated, all remnants of servile conditions having been removed, and there was no doubt of the ready acceptance by the native population of transfer to the control of the United Kingdom. Further, no elaborate constitutional machinery was requisite; the conditions of the mandate could effectively be made operative by the mere application to the new territory of the system in force in Papua, while the right of the Commonwealth to legislate for the relations of Australia with the islands of the Pacific, or for any territory placed by the Crown under the authority of and accepted by the Commonwealth or otherwise acquired by the Commonwealth,[1] gave full power to the Parliament to apply such legislation as it deemed fit to the territory, which under the Peace Treaty was made over to the control of the Commonwealth. The chief point on which a Commission of three, including the Lieutenant-Governor of Papua, set up to advise as to the form of administration, differed, was whether the territory should be administered as part of, or in subordination to, Papua, as recommended by the Lieutenant-Governor, or as an independent unit, on the same basis as Papua.

The final form of the legislation determined upon by the Government and presented to Parliament in August 1920 adopts the plan of treating the German territories surrendered by the Treaty of Peace as a single unit, to be known as the Territory of

---

[1] Constitution, ss. 51 (xxx) and 122.

New Guinea, and the Act gives power to the Governor-General to accept the mandate for these territories when issued under the Covenant of the League of Nations. The administration is to be entrusted to an Administrator appointed by the Governor-General, who shall hold office at the pleasure of the latter. Except as specially provided in any Act the enactments of the Commonwealth Parliament shall not apply to New Guinea unless extended to it by Ordinance. For the meantime the power of legislation by Ordinance is vested in the Governor-General only, and no Legislative Council is created. Any Ordinance so issued must be laid before both Houses of Parliament within fourteen days after it has been made, and shall cease to have effect if either house passes a resolution disallowing the Ordinance. The mode of procedure thus ensures the full supervision by Parliament of the legislative authority which the Act vests in the Government of the Commonwealth, for, if it may be assumed that the Government may normally count upon the House of Representatives to support action taken by those who are its chosen representatives, it cannot assume that the Senate will approve its action if open to serious criticism.

The Act provides the necessary guarantees for the security of the native population contemplated by the League Covenant. Slave-trading is prohibited in the territory. No forced labour shall be permitted, even for essential public works and services, though this is permitted by the mandate. Traffic in arms and ammunition shall be controlled in accordance with the principles of the General Act of the Brussels Convention, 1890, or any Convention amending that Agreement. The supply of intoxicating spirits and beverages to the natives is prohibited. The military training of the natives, otherwise than for purposes of internal police and the local defence of the Territory, is prohibited. No military or naval base shall be established or fortifications erected in the Territory. Freedom of conscience and, subject to the provisions of any Ordinance for the maintenance of public order and morals, the free exercise of all forms of worship shall be allowed in the Territory. Finally, it is provided that the Governor-General shall make an annual report to the Council of the League of Nations containing full information as to the measures taken to carry out the requirements in regard to the guarantees, and as to the well-being and progress of the native inhabitants of the Territory.

The provisions thus enacted represent precisely the existing state of the law respecting Papua, save in so far as the necessity of a report to the League is concerned, and demonstrate how little difficulty there was in applying the system of the Covenant to the new territory.

For New Zealand the Samoan mandate involved much more serious difficulties. The power of the Dominion to legislate for Samoa without Imperial authority was held to be doubtful, and in accordance with this view the issue of an Imperial Order in Council was procured on March 11, 1920, authorizing the Dominion Parliament to legislate for Samoa, and pending such legislation conferring authority on the Dominion Government to legislate, subject to the terms of the Treaty of Peace. In the meantime the New Zealand Parliament had passed an Act in 1919 to provide for the acceptance of the mandate for Samoa and the approval of the issue of Orders in Council by the Government respecting the administration of the islands. It was then explained in the House of Representatives on October 17, 1919, that it had been desired to lay before the Legislature a Bill defining precisely the government of the islands, but this was rendered impossible by the delay in the issue of the mandate, whose terms could not definitely be defined before the ratification of the peace with Germany, and the constitution would, therefore, be determined later by Order in Council. There was a marked divergence between the Act of 1919 and the Imperial Order in Council regarding the source whence the mandate would be derived; the former measure treated the mandate as conferred on the King in right of His Dominion of New Zealand by the League of Nations; the latter, conforming precisely to the terms of the Treaty of Peace, recognized that, while the mandate was granted according to the Covenant of the League of Nations, it was accorded by the Principal Allied and Associated Powers, to which, and not to the League, the German territories were surrendered by the Peace Treaty (Article 119).

The actual constitution for the islands of Western Samoa is

laid down in the Samoa Constitution Order, 1920, which is based on the authority given by the Dominion Act of 1919 and the Imperial Order in Council of 1920. By it the Government of Samoa is vested in the King, as if the territory were part of His dominions, and is to be carried on subject to the control of the Minister of External Affairs of New Zealand by an Administrator. Elaborate provisions are made for the regulation of the public service and the employment of New Zealand officials in it. Departments of the Treasury, Police and Prisons, Education, and Public Health are provided for. The legislative authority in Samoa is to be exercised by a Legislative Council, consisting of the Administrator, four officials, and a like or smaller number of non-officials nominated by the Governor-General.[1] The powers of the Legislative Council are, however, limited ; it may not affect the royal prerogative or the title of the Crown to land in Samoa ; impose customs or export duties ; establish companies ; create municipal or local government authorities with rating, taxing, or legislative authority ; regulate currency ; or impose penalties exceeding one year's imprisonment or a fine over £100. It is further provided that it shall not be lawful for the legislative or executive Government of Samoa to establish or maintain military or naval bases or fortifications in Samoa ; to provide for the military training or service, otherwise than for the purpose of police, of the inhabitants of Samoa other than Europeans ; or to borrow money otherwise than from the New Zealand Treasury in accordance with the provisions in this regard laid down in the Ordinance. A High Court is created with civil and criminal jurisdiction, while the Supreme Court of New Zealand is to serve as a final court of appeal from its decisions, and also to exercise full jurisdiction over Samoa in all civil matters, and to try offenders against Samoan laws found in New Zealand. A criminal code and a code of criminal procedure are enacted, and the principles affecting Crown suits in force in New Zealand are applied to Samoa. Marriage, divorce, the treatment of insane persons, and public roads are regulated. English law as it existed on January 14, 1840, is made the law of New Zealand, subject to the restriction that no

[1] Two native chiefs will normally be on the Council, but in any case will have direct resort to the Government for advisory purposes.

English Act shall be operative unless operative in New Zealand on May 1, 1920, a provision intended to secure the application of the English common law to the Territory. New Zealand Acts shall not, unless expressly provided, be in force, nor the common law respecting the tenure of land by aliens, but a large number of New Zealand enactments, especially those dealing with commercial topics, are expressly declared to be operative. The question of intoxicants is dealt with drastically ; manufacture and importation and the giving of liquor to a Samoan are penalized, but the Administrator is permitted to import for medical, sacramental, and industrial purposes only. The land régime is assimilated to that of New Zealand ; in addition to Crown lands, there are European lands which are to be deemed to be held of the Crown in fee simple, and Native lands, that is land vested in the Crown, but held by Samoans on the customs and usages of the Samoan race, and by an Order of April 1, a Native Land and Titles Commission is set up, composed of the Chief Justice with two to four European assessors, and native advisors, to deal with claims to native lands. The courts are also required to observe native custom in matters of inheritance, and authorized to exercise discretion in enforcing contracts entered into by natives. Customs are regulated by an Order of April 20, under which a preference is given to British goods. Provision is made for loans from New Zealand as may be required, but it is hoped that there will be an annual surplus of ordinary revenue.

A Crown Estates Order of April 19 vests in the Crown in right of New Zealand the property of German subjects, as authorized by the Treaty of Peace, and the Crown takes over all the Government property in Samoa. A difficult question has thus arisen, for by 1914 about a sixth of the best land had passed, contrary to native law, into German hands. The prosperity of these plantations rested on the use of indentured labour, imported from the Solomon Islands and from China, for the Samoan will not work steadily on European plantations, and on his own land is but a negligent producer. By 1919, of the 2,200 Chinese and 850 Solomon islanders in Samoa in 1914, only 1,000 were left, indentured immigration being impossible from China during the war, while the Imperial Government and the Commonwealth

Government prevented the recruiting of Pacific islanders for service in Samoa. Chinese, when indentured, could on the expiry of their three years' term reindenture, but could never settle permanently in the islands, whence there grew up the problem of their children by Samoan women, who, on their fathers' repatriation, were left with their mothers' people. The Government, however, from the first declared that they would sanction indentured immigration, despite the protests of Mr. Ngata, a Maori member, and of Labour. A Parliamentary Labour delegation, which visited Samoa in the following year, acquired first-hand knowledge of the undesirable moral results of the system, but, on the renewal of the discussion of the topic of the Government of Samoa on the approach of the expiration of the operation of the Act of 1919, the decision to permit indentured labour was affirmed on July 31 by the House of Representatives by 33 votes to 11. The position of the Government and of Parliament was difficult; if they declined to continue the system, the islands would become a charge on the Dominion exchequer, and the plantations, now Government property, would become derelict, while, if it were continued, not merely would offence be caused to Labour, but the responsibility would fall on the Parliament of sanctioning a condition of affairs which the public opinion of the Dominion disliked, and approving a system which had been definitely abandoned as illegitimate by the Imperial Government as far as concerned the territories under its control. Under the new régime, however, married Chinese will be imported when possible with the aid of the Government of Hong-Kong.

Mention was made by Sir Francis Bell in the Legislative Council [1] of the fact that the terms of the proposed mandate contained an arrangement for the incorporation of the islands in New Zealand, if at any time the natives showed a desire to be annexed to the Dominion and the Allied and Associated Powers considered this desire to be deliberate and well founded. No such clause, however, appears in the mandate as approved by the Council of the League on December 17, 1920.

The mandate for South-West Africa was received without special enthusiasm in the Union; Mr. Merriman probably ex-

[1] Cf. *The Times*, June 6, 1919; *Parl. Pap.* Cmd. 1203.

pressed the prevailing opinion in arguing that what was wanted was annexation pure and simple. General Smuts explained the mandatory system and defended it ; he refuted also the argument of Mr. Hertzog as to the desirability of a referendum of the population of the territory by pointing to the obscurity of the term population ; the German population would prefer Union rule to any other save German ; the natives would prefer Imperial rule to Union rule. In the Act to approve of measures for the carrying out of the Peace Treaty with Germany, authority was included to permit of legislation by the Governor-General in Council for the South-West Territory, with authority to delegate the power to a subordinate officer. General Smuts, however, explained that, pending the arrival of the mandate, the territory must continue under military forms of administration, authority being exercised under martial law. But he proposed that steps should be taken to introduce under the powers given by the Act a form of civil administration. There would be no interference with peaceful German settlers,[1] land settlement and boring for water would be promoted, the interests of the natives and of coloured persons would be carefully safeguarded ; the existing deficit would disappear with the expansion of the diamond industry, which had been restricted in operations during the war.

Sir Thomas Smartt, for the Unionists, raised the question of securing the natives in the possession of their reserves, and not encouraging European settlement with undue precipitancy. It was explained by the Minister of Mines that the native population consisted of 90,000 Hereros and Damaras, a like number of Ovambos, 6,000 Hottentots, and 9,000 Rehoboth bastards ; when the Union took control, the Warmbad reserve of 100,000 morgen was occupied by Hottentots ; there was a reserve of 5,000 morgen at Bethany, and the whole of Ovamboland was a native reserve. Since that date there had been set aside reserves of 40,000 morgen in the Omaruru district, and of 50,000 morgen in the Windhuk district. The Government, however, were willing to accept an amendment to the Act which provided that no grant of any title, right, or interest in State land or minerals, or over the territorial

---

[1] In the Pacific territories German settlers have been repatriated in accordance with the authority given in the Peace Treaty.

waters of South-West Africa, should be allowed nor should any trading or other concession be conferred, without the approval of Parliament.   Power was, however, given to the Governor-General to apply to the Territory the Union Acts of 1912 and 1917 regarding land settlement, and the Crown Land Disposal Ordinances of 1903 and 1906 of the Transvaal, which include the power to grant to members of native tribes and to coloured persons in suitable cases individual title to land.   At the same time it was enacted that native reserves must not be alienated without the consent of Parliament.

In accordance with these principles, the Administrator was authorized to replace by proclamations issued under the authority of the Act such Martial Law Regulations as were of permanent interest, and at the close of the year proclamations were issued establishing Civil Courts, including a Superior Court and introducing Roman-Dutch law, in lieu of the German law hitherto in force, with effect from the beginning of 1920.   The Military Constabulary was transferred into the South-West Africa Police, organized on the same model as the Union Police.   When the repatriation of the German garrison and police was completed, the Protectorate Garrison Regiment was demobilized, and in December the same fate befell the Railway Regiment and other units, so that by May 1920 the Administrator could report that there was then no single military unit in the country, and the administration had been assimilated in all respects to administration in the Union. In November 1919 a Land Board subject to the control of the Lands Department of the Union was established, while a Commission was set up to examine the vexed problem of the many concessions which were alleged to have been granted by the German administration.

A marked effect on the settlement of the territory was produced by a visit from the Governor-General in September 1919, when Lord Buxton received representatives of all classes of the population, and emphasized the facts that in no circumstances would the territory be returned to Germany, and that the native policy must conform to the Union model.   The passing of the Union Act accepting the mandate in September also served to promote public confidence and to further trade, while the expansion of the diamond industry, in which the Government is interested to the extent of obtaining 66 per cent. of the profits, made the accounts of the Protectorate for 1919 show a surplus for the first time since the occupation, and presented the certainty of future prosperity. The most important result of the Union control, however, is the increased security granted to the native population; under German rule a policy of forced labour was carried into effect by the existence of legislation, which the Union has maintained in force, requiring all adult native males, save those with visible independent means of support, to be in employment, and by the further law—no longer in force—that no native might own any large or more than five head of small stock. The native was thus in a state of economic suppression, and when at work was liable to brutal ill-treatment—disgraceful details of which were published in a report compiled from official sources by the Administrator—both by his employers and by the Protectorate police. The native by 1920 had ceased to live in fear, but the process of adjustment to Union conditions was imperfect. There was serious shortage of labour; the Ovambos, the chief source of supply, refusing, as a result of past experience, to take work on farms, while the farmers pressed for the right of the police to inflict punishment on natives in the old fashion, a suggestion which the administration naturally declined to adopt. The natives, however, secure of receiving the wages for their work, were purchasing small numbers of livestock, and the contentment thus induced in a pastoral people was proved by the increase in the birth-rate.[1]

In June 1920 the Government asked for the extension for another year of the Act of 1919, which expired on June 20. The Prime Minister announced that the mandate terms had not yet actually been received, but that it was impossible to delay a settlement of the country indefinitely, and the Government would therefore proceed to devise lasting arrangements, for which purpose he would, on the prorogation of Parliament, visit the country and get in touch with all classes of the people.

[1] See Administrator's Report for 1920, U. G. 40, p. 5. The revenue for 1920–21 is put at £1,025,000, £800,000 of which is due to the diamond industry, and a surplus of £200,000 is anticipated. See also *Parl. Pap.* Cmd. 842.

In the course of this tour, General Smuts replied at Windhuk in September to representations which had been made on behalf of the German colonists. Their memorial is important as indicating the singular inability of the memorialists to appreciate the nature of the position created by the Peace Treaty. It was contended that the effect of the Peace Treaty was that South-West Africa must be administered as an independent province with an administration of its own and a separate budget, while the economic and political circumstances of the Protectorate differed so widely from those of the Union that they could not be supervised from Pretoria. The memorialists demanded the continuance of German institutions, the introduction of German capital, the return to German South-West Africa of Germans repatriated under martial law, the setting up of a German Consulate, the establishment of German as the official language, and other concessions. They insisted in special on the retention of the German Civil Code, asserting—it must be admitted with some ground—that the adoption of Roman-Dutch law was a retrogression of centuries. The Prime Minister's reply, though conciliatory in tone, explained in quite decided terms the true state of affairs, and urged the Germans to abandon the idea of looking to Germany for sustenance and support, and to recognize that their lot was indissolubly linked with that of the Union, under which they would enjoy vastly greater freedom than they had ever experienced under German rule.

The Government in June also secured the passing of a resolution in favour of the establishment of a representative Parliamentary Commission to inquire into the government of the Territory, in order to present a report not later than December 31, so that its terms might receive full consideration before the Parliament met in March 1921. An effort was then made to secure an instruction to the Commission to inquire into the past administration of the Territory, but this was negatived by 20 votes to 6. The debate was interesting, because the Prime Minister explained emphatically that the Territory fell in no way under the League of Nations, but would become an integral part of the Union for administrative purposes, while the mandate was derived, not from the League, but from the Allied and Associated Powers.

The report of the Commission, under the chairmanship of the Minister of Justice, suggested that, on the repeal of martial law, the Administrator should be afforded the benefit of the advice of a Council of six members appointed by the Governor-General, of whom five should represent farming, mining, commercial, and wage-earning interests, while the sixth, who might be an official, should represent native interests.

2. THE NAURU ISLAND AGREEMENT

While the decision of the Supreme Allied Council granted the mandates for the German Pacific Islands, Samoa, and South-West Africa to the Dominions, it conferred upon the British Empire the mandate for Nauru Island, which the Australian forces had occupied during the war, after it had capitulated to a naval attack. At the time of occupation the importance of the island lay in its enormous phosphate deposits, estimated at 80,000,000 tons, which were being worked under a German concession by the Pacific Phosphate Company, a British company in which there was a large German holding. Australia, which was wont to draw large supplies of phosphate from this source, laid claim to the mandate, but this was refused, and it was eventually agreed to apportion it between the United Kingdom, the Commonwealth, and New Zealand. The Company was to be expropriated, the sum of £3,500,000[1] eventually being fixed, while the German holdings were disposed of under the terms of the Treaty of Peace. The administration was to be carried on by an Administrator, subject to the usual terms provided in Article XXII of the League Covenant, with power to legislate by Ordinance, and it was agreed that in the first case Australia should appoint the Administrator for a period of five years, the two other Governments to appoint in turn later on. But the control of the extraction of phosphate was to vest in a Commission of three, one appointed during pleasure by each of the Governments, and of the output, 42 per cent. each was to be allotted to the United Kingdom and Australia, and 16 per cent. to New Zealand, subject to five-yearly readjustments, the object being to enable these Governments to supply

---

[1] This includes the company's interests in Ocean Island, which is British ; see the Company's report, *The Times*, July 16, 1920, and *Parl. Pap.* Cmd. 749.

phosphate to cultivators at cost price. If the United Kingdom did not require its full share, the amount was to be divided between the Commonwealth and New Zealand in the proportions of 42 to 16.

The ratification of the agreement took the shape of Acts in the three Parliaments ; in the Commonwealth doubt was expressed as to the financial result of the proposals, though the price of expropriating the Company was there underestimated, and the question whether the Commonwealth was constitutionally capable of entering into the agreement was mooted. In New Zealand, Mr. Massey expressed regret at the poor proportion assigned to New Zealand, but indicated that, as the purchase-price to the Company was to be paid in the same proportions, New Zealand would have a smaller burden to bear, while Sir F. Bell held, with strange oblivion of the Pacific cable agreement, that this was the first occasion of a working arrangement between Empire Governments. In the United Kingdom more vital criticism was offered. It was contended on the second reading on June 16 in the House of Commons that the measure ran counter to the principles of the Covenant both as regards the ' open door ' and the duty of trusteeship. The Administrator, it was pointed out, ought to be responsible for his action to the Imperial Government, since he represented the carrying out of a mandate to the Empire. The action of the Governments further amounted to a pure monopoly. Moreover, the right of the Governments to exercise the mandates at all was denied, in the absence of evidence that the terms of the mandate had been agreed upon by the members of the League or settled by the Council, in default of such agreement, in accordance with Article XXII of the League Covenant. To these representations a somewhat inconclusive reply was given by Mr. Bonar Law, and, though the second reading of the Bill was carried by 217 to 77 votes, an amendment was carried against the Government in the Standing Committee, under which clause 1 was made to read : ' The agreement is hereby confirmed subject to Article XXII of the Covenant of the League of Nations.' It was accepted in this form by the Commons and by the Lords, but in the latter on July 29, Lord Milner gave a reasoned defence of the agreement. He explained that the intervention of the

United Kingdom was due to the desire to mediate between Australia and New Zealand. The conferring of mandates rested with the Principal Allied and Associated Powers, and they had been allotted in 1919. But, though the terms of the mandate, which were merely an amplification of the terms of Article XXII of the Covenant, had been drawn up by a Commission under his chairmanship sitting at the offices in London of the League, through pressure of time they had not yet received the approval of the Supreme Allied Council nor been communicated to the Council of the League, with which would rest the duty of supervising their execution. He denied, however, that the terms required the approval of the Council of the League, though Mr. Bonar Law, in the Commons, had given assurances that they would be submitted for approval to the League Assembly. He further explained that the terms of Article XXII had been deliberately drafted so as not to make the condition as to the ' open door ' applicable to such cases as Nauru, though he also contended that, even if the case had been otherwise, as the Company could have sold to any persons it chose, the Governments which stood in its place could do so without interference with the principle of freedom of trade for all members of the League. Neither Lord Crewe nor Lord Emmott, however, accepted the situation as satisfactory.

3. The Control of the League

The discussion in the case of Nauru indicates clearly the elements of difficulty which exist in the situation. Lord Milner's contention that the terms of the mandate need not be submitted for the approval of the Council of the League is technically correct only on a forced [1] construction of the provision of Article XXII, that ' the degree of authority, control, or administration to be exercised shall, if not previously agreed upon by the members of the League, be explicitly defined in each case by the Council '. The ' members of the League ' would normally mean the Assembly, but it may be held to denote the members concerned, that is, those who have the power to dispose of the territories in question, and under the Treaty of Peace, this right clearly rested with the

[1] See Lord Robert Cecil, *The Times*, July 1, 1920.

Principal Allied and Associated Powers, to which Germany ceded the territories. But it is still clear that the Council of the League is entitled to examine any mandate to secure that it conforms with the terms of Article XXII of the Covenant, for the power of the Supreme Allied Council to dispose of the territories ceded by Germany is subject to the Covenant. Equally the Assembly has the right to examine the terms, and Mr. Hughes acted properly when he advised the Commonwealth to send a mission to determine on the proper form of administration for German New Guinea, in order that the necessary legislation should be passed and laid before the Assembly of the League in November 1920.

An annual report on the territory under its charge must yearly be rendered by the mandatory to the Council, and a permanent commission of that body is charged with the duty of receiving and examining these reports and of advising the Council on all matters relating to the observance of the mandates. The Council and ultimately the Assembly are thus given a vague and undefined right of intervention. But the administration is primarily a matter for the mandatory, and there is no doubt that there is no obligation on the mandatory to submit any proposed course of action, once the mandate is definitely settled, for the approval of the Council or the Assembly.

In connexion with the Imperial preference legislation of the United Kingdom in 1919, the issue was definitely raised whether it was consistent with the mandatory system to extend to mandated territories, of whatever category, the benefits of preference, and the Government emphatically upheld the propriety of such action, which, indeed, does not run directly counter to the terms of Article XXII, however much it may seem to contradict its spirit.

In addition to the terms of Article XXII of the Covenant, the conditions to be observed in regard to the mandated territories are regulated in the case of mandated territories in Africa by the provisions of the conventions relative to the trade in arms and ammunition, the liquor traffic, and the amendment of the Berlin Act of 1885 and the Brussels Act of 1890, which were concluded on September 10, 1919, and the general clauses of the first of these applies also to the Pacific mandates.

CHAPTER IX

COALITION GOVERNMENT AND NATIONALISM IN THE DOMINIONS

1. CANADA.
   Effect of the war on party politics — Liberal criticisms of governmental measures — Opposition of Liberals in Quebec to compulsion — Sir R. Borden's proposal of conscription in 1917 — Formation of Coalition Government — Victory at general election — Revival of Liberalism after the war — Political views of farmers — Resignation of Sir R. Borden and formation of a mainly Conservative Government in July 1920.

2. THE COMMONWEALTH OF AUSTRALIA.
   Liberal rejection of Labour overtures — Liberal defeat in general election — Question of constitutional alteration during war — Retirement of Mr. Fisher and premiership of Mr. Hughes — First referendum on conscription — Formation of new Government — Coalition of February 1917 — Defeat of second conscription referendum — Mr. Hughes's retention of office — Resentment of Labour and development of extreme Nationalism — Decisive defeat of Labour in December 1919 — Political position in 1920.

3. NEW ZEALAND.
   General election of December 1914 — Party disputes — Coalition of August 1915 — Break up of Coalition in 1919 — Politics in 1920.

4. THE UNION OF SOUTH AFRICA.
   State of parties in 1914 — General election of 1915 — Development of republicanism in Nationalist circles — Parliamentary discussion in 1918 — Nationalist Congress on deputation to Peace Conference, January 1919 — Parliamentary disapproval — Mr. Lloyd George's reply to Nationalist delegation — Renewal of dissension in South Africa — General election of March 1920 — Prime Minister's efforts to secure party co-operation — The expansion of the South African Party to contest Republicanism.

5. NEWFOUNDLAND.
   Co-operation of parties — Coalition of 1917 — Recrudescence of party politics in 1919 — Constitutional irregularities.

As in the United Kingdom the war did not immediately produce any attempt at the fusion of political parties into war Governments ; the advantages of coalitions to meet the needs of the crisis were recognized by certain politicians, but there was no adequate general recognition of the fundamental character of the alterations involved in the national life by the outbreak of war. This attitude was the more natural in that the Dominions had never been involved since they attained responsible govern-

ment in hostilities of any importance, with the exception of the
South African War, and that struggle, which affected largely the
trend of opinion in the United Kingdom, was not of vital importance to Canada or Australasia. It was the disappearance of the
early hopes of great success, which were far more prevalent in the
Dominions than in the United Kingdom, thanks to less accurate
sources of information as to the real nature of the contest, and
above all the needs of recruiting, which convinced political parties
in the Dominions that they could not secure the full strength of
the Dominions for war purposes, save by sinking questions of
internal concern and concentrating in coalition on the essential
problem of victory. Only South Africa remained to a certain
extent apart from this current of feeling ; accidents enabled the
Government, without surrendering any of its power, to obtain
co-operation from a party which on internal issues was by no
means in harmony with its aims. But the coalitions were essentially imperfect fusions ; they were dictated by war issues, and
they could not survive their cause ; the end of active hostilities
gave the signal for the disintegration of the unity which had been
created for war purposes, though the effect of coalition was seen
in the formation of new parties, in which some of those who had
been in close conjunction for war purposes united on a policy for
peace.

1. Canada

At the moment when war was declared, party feeling ran high
in the Dominion, and on either side there was eager interest in
the campaign which the Prime Minister on the one hand, and
Sir Wilfrid Laurier on the other, were to carry out in the West.
The immediate result of the war was the assurance given by
Sir Wilfrid Laurier to the ministry that he would co-operate in
the sending of troops and in any measures necessary to meet the
needs of the financial position, and in the short war session of
Parliament which followed, the Liberal Party lent whole-hearted
aid. There was indeed in certain quarters among the Conservative
Party a suggestion that a general election should be held, at which
the country could pronounce a verdict on the action of the Liberal
Party in securing in 1913 the rejection by the Senate of the
contribution of 35,000,000 dollars to the British Navy which

Sir Robert Borden had proposed, after learning when in England in 1912 the needs of the situation as a result of the attitude of Germany. But the Conservative Party, as a whole, was opposed to the suggestion, and the Liberals denounced it, laying stress on the view that, had the policy of a Canadian Navy, determined on by Sir Wilfrid Laurier in 1909, been permitted to develop, ships would actually have been ready for service in 1914, and not merely building as under Sir R. Borden's proposal.

At the same time, however, there appeared from the outset a marked line of discrimination between the Conservative and the Liberal impression of the way in which participation in the war would affect the destinies of Canada. The Prime Minister, the Minister of Justice, and other members of the Cabinet laid stress on the fact that the action of Canada and the other Dominions portended a revolution in Imperial relations. 'The hand that wields the sword of the Empire, justly holds the sceptre of the Empire ; while the mother country alone wielded the one, to her alone belonged the other. When as to-day the nations of the Empire join in wielding that sword, then must they jointly sway that sceptre,' said Mr. Doherty,[1] and Sir R. Borden was as emphatic, if less picturesque. Sir Wilfrid Laurier, however, remained true to his older faith. Canada was absolutely free to decide to aid the Empire or not ; ' this freedom is at once the glory and honour of England, which has granted it, and of Canada which uses it to assist England.' Concentration of authority under a federal system would convert what was voluntary into what was obligatory, and to such a change he was wholly opposed. The Parliamentary session of 1915 brought out more immediate points of divergence between the two parties ; the Government felt obliged to secure additional revenue by increasing the import duties by $7\frac{1}{2}$ per cent., or in the case of British imports 5 per cent., and the Liberals denounced the measure as unjust to Great Britain, and as unduly favourable to manufacturers in Canada, while they were active in exposing cases of extravagance and waste in the cost of equipping the first Canadian contingent. The suggestion in the Conservative ranks of a general election revived ; it was argued that the West was obviously absurdly under-repre-

[1] *The Round Table*, v. 428.

sented in the House of Commons, redistribution being due, and
that it was unfair to leave it in that condition, and that a governmental victory would be a sufficient ground for inducing the
Imperial Government to pass an Imperial Act altering the representation of Canada in the Senate, where Western Canada was in
a wholly unfair position, and where the Liberal majority was
strongly opposed to concede the increase desired by the Government, which, it was anticipated, would convert the majority into
a Conservative one. But there was no unanimity in the party,
and an accident, involving the destruction by fire of part of the
Parliamentary buildings at Ottawa and involving loss of life,
decided the issue. The necessary applications to the Imperial
Government for the passing of an Act extending for a year the
existence of the House of Commons were passed without dissent
in either House, and the Imperial Parliament immediately complied with the request.[1] But party spirit ran high over disclosures
made by a Commission appointed in 1915 by the Government to
investigate the charges then made by the Opposition of irregularities in the distribution of contracts and the purchase of war
supplies. The result of the report was embarrassing for the
administration, but Sir R. Borden acted promptly, and required
the resignation of their seats by two Conservative members
implicated. A strong attack was also developed on the Minister
of Militia on account of the transactions of the Shell Committee,
which, originally brought into being to make purchases for British
contractors, had become the purchasing agent of the War Office.
It was alleged that contracts had been placed by this Committee
in New York and not in Canada, and that out of these contracts
improper commissions had been made.[2] The Minister, recalled
from England to answer the charges, defended himself with
ability and vigour, but it was clear that subordinates, in whom he
reposed too great confidence, had been guilty of improper conduct,
and the position of the Government was undoubtedly impaired
by the episode, and by the friction which developed between the
Minister and his colleagues on questions effecting the control of

[1] 6 & 7 Geo. V. c. 19.
[2] See *The Times*, September 13, 1916 ; February 1, 1917 ; Canada, *House of Commons Debates*, January 31, 1917.

the Canadian forces, and which only terminated with his resignation in November from the Ministry. There was discontent also among the Liberals with the insistence of the Government on refusing to consider an income-tax or a land-tax as measures of raising the necessary revenue. But far more important was the controversy over the legislation of Ontario regarding the limitation of the teaching of French in the provincial schools.[1] Only the utmost efforts of the Prime Minister availed to prevent a split in his Government over the issue, which affected strongly the French-Canadians in the Cabinet, and the general election for the Provincial Legislature of Quebec, which followed shortly after the debate, showed a crushing defeat of the Conservatives in that province, only seven being returned out of eighty-five seats, which was a result far worse than had been hoped for, although it had never been expected that the Government of Sir Lomer Gouin, one of the ablest and most statesmanlike of French-Canadians, would be overthrown. More disappointment was created by the result in Nova Scotia, where some hope of winning the election had been entertained, and later in the year the Conservatives, who had held British Columbia by an overwhelming majority, were disappointed to find a Liberal Government returned with thirty-six supporters to ten Conservatives.[2] The defeat was mainly due to local issues, errors by the late Government in handling questions of the public lands, and in their dealings with railway companies, but the fall of the Government reacted on the Federal position. Nor was it felt safe by the Government to take any steps to fill vacancies occurring by death in the House of Commons ; they were ready to consent to elections if there were to be no contest, and the seat was to be allotted to the representative of the party which held it when the vacancy occurred, but they were not prepared to allow political contests to be carried on, though by this time there were nineteen vacancies in the Commons.

A definite sign of political divergence was afforded by the attitude adopted by the Liberals, especially Sir Wilfrid Laurier and Mr. Lemieux, when the decision of the United Kingdom to

---

[1] See below, Chap. XI, § 1.
[2] New Brunswick in February 1917 went Liberal by 27 to 21.

adopt compulsory service was announced. It was coupled with the propaganda of certain sections of British opinion to secure the federalization of the Empire, and it evoked strong protests against militarism from the Liberal leader; he regretted the British decision, which if in force before the war would have prevented the acquisition by the United Kingdom of the financial strength which made her able to endure the burdén of the conflict, and he protested vehemently against any consolidation of the Empire. Among the Nationalists of Quebec who had denounced Sir Wilfrid Laurier in 1909–11 for willingness to create a Canadian Navy there was increasingly violent opposition to the participation of the Dominion in the war; Mr. Bourassa reiterated in a thousand forms his protests against British militarism and imperialism, against the 'traders in human flesh, who, in England as in Germany, in France as in Russia, have brought the peoples to slaughter in order to increase their reapings of cursed gold'. Canada must be saved from the vortex of European militarism, and must not be stampeded into distant ventures of no direct concern to her. To speak of fighting for the preservation of French civilization in Europe, while endeavouring to destroy it in America, appeared to him an absurd piece of inconsistency, and 'free enlistment', he asserted, 'is now carried on by means of blackmailing, intimidation, and threats of all sorts'.

A definite decision was brought about by the return of the Prime Minister from the meetings of the Imperial War Cabinet in 1917 with the intention of introducing conscription in order to reinforce the Canadian troops at the front. The decision was accepted by the Cabinet, and the Prime Minister then announced his policy and made proposals for coalition. The mode of procedure was criticized, but it was deliberate, inspired by the view that Sir Wilfrid Laurier might feel it easier to enter a Government pledged to conscription than to become a member of a Government whose policy was still undecided. Subject to this, the terms offered were absolutely fair; Sir Wilfrid was to nominate half the ministers, exercise equal authority in council, and bear equal responsibility for the measures of the Government. Acceptance of the offer can hardly have been anticipated; the proposal of conscription alienated French Conservatives, and French Liberals and Nationalists, who had already co-operated in the elections for the Provincial Legislature in 1916, united in indignant protests. It was not to be expected that a man so devoted to his compatriots as Sir Wilfrid Laurier would deliberately set himself against their unanimous feeling. The most he could do was to urge the holding of a referendum in lieu of conscription, and the voting on his amendment, lost by 62 to 111 votes, was symptomatic of the divergence in view of his party; twenty-five English-speaking Liberals and one French Liberal supported conscription, only twelve English-speaking Liberals supported their leader, and of these only three represented constituencies in Ontario and the West. Though outside Quebec many Liberals favoured compulsion and were ready for coalition, the loyalty of the party at first remained firm; in August the Winnipeg Convention, representative of Western Liberalism, instead of declaring for union, endorsed their leader's position and negatived compulsion, even in the last resort. But this was the last triumph of the party machine; the Western leaders soon admitted their willingness to share in a national Government, but not under Sir R. Borden. The latter promptly summoned the Conservative Party in Parliament and offered to resign in favour of Sir George Foster, in order to secure union. Sir George resolutely declined, and the Western leaders waived their objection, but stipulated successfully for equal representation with the Conservatives in the Cabinet. The most notable addition to the Cabinet was Mr. N. W. Rowell, Liberal leader in the provincial politics of Ontario, who from the beginning of the war had favoured close co-operation with the Empire, and was an early convert to conscription, and who became President of the Council; Mr. A. L. Sifton, Premier of Alberta, became Minister of Customs; Mr. J. A. Calder, of Saskatchewan, Minister of Immigration and Colonization; Mr. T. A. Crerar, of Manitoba, Minister of Agriculture, and the other Liberal Ministers were all men of some note. Great unselfishness was shown by the Conservative Ministers whose retirement was rendered necessary by union. French Canada was represented but weakly by Mr. P. E. Blondin and Mr. A. Sévigny, Conservatives, in the portfolios of the Post Office and Inland Revenue.

Scarcely had the full number of the Ministry been made up,

than Sir Robert Borden announced on October 24 that two permanent Committees of the Cabinet had been formed. The first, the War Committee, an idea borrowed from the United Kingdom, was to co-ordinate the efforts of the several departments, to ensure the maximum of effort with the minimum of expenditure, and generally to throw the full power of Canada into the national endeavour. It was composed of ten members : the Prime Minister, Mr. Rowell, the Ministers of Militia (General Mewburn), Finance (Sir Thomas White), Marine (Colonel Ballantyne), Justice (Mr. C. J. Doherty), Public Works (Mr. F. B. Carvell), and Customs, a representative of the Oversea Military Service (the minister being stationed at London), and the Postmaster-General. The selection of portfolios was largely decided by the necessity for securing the proper representation of the parties in the Ministry. A second Committee of the Cabinet was to deal with reconstruction and development ; it was made up of the Prime Minister, Mr. A. K. Maclean as Vice-Chairman, the Ministers of Trade (Sir G. Foster), Finance, Railways (Mr. J. D. Reid), Immigration and Colonization—a new Ministry, Interior (Mr. A. Meighen), and Agriculture, and two Ministers without Portfolio ; Labour was found representation by the selection of a Parliamentary Under-Secretary in the Labour department.

The efforts of the Ministry were now concentrated on the general election, which the recent expiration on October 7 of the House of Commons rendered essential. Sir R. Borden had suggested in July that the term of Parliament might be extended for a year, but he made it clear that he would press this only if there were substantial agreement, and a majority of twenty in the House of Commons proved that such agreement was hopeless. The Government, however, despite Liberal opposition, which had hindered the conclusion of the arrangements for coalition, had secured the passing of two electoral acts[1] which disfranchised naturalized aliens of less than fifteen years' standing, gave the franchise to every Canadian soldier of whatever age, even if not resident in Canada before the war, and to nurses, wives, widows, mothers, and sisters of soldiers. Partly through this measure, the victory of the Government was overwhelming ; on the first results

[1] Military Voters Act, c. 34, and War Times Elections Act, c. 39 of 1917.

of the elections, excluding the soldiers' votes, which took time to collect and enumerate, the Government had a majority of forty-five, which was increased by the returns from the soldiers to seventy-two. The four Western Provinces returned only two members of the Liberal Opposition; Ontario but eight, New Brunswick and Nova Scotia four apiece, and Prince Edward Island two. Quebec, on the other hand, was almost wholly carried against the Government, only three Unionists being returned. The Ontario Liberals who survived nearly all owed this position to the votes of French or German elements in the constituencies. There was no satisfaction in the Liberal Party in the necessity of abandoning Sir Wilfrid Laurier, but there was widespread feeling that the interests of compulsion must come first. The two French Ministers were defeated, but their resignations were not pressed for.[1] Despite his defeat in the contest, Sir Wilfrid Laurier remained unperturbed, and rumours of his resignation of the leadership of the party proved unfounded. There was intense bitterness in the ranks of the Liberals who refused to become Unionists against the section of the party which did so, and Mr. W. Fielding, despite his strong patriotism, declined to join the Unionist party. Especial resentment was felt against Mr. Rowell, who had manifested himself as extremely critical of Quebec, the Roman Catholic Church, and the liquor interest, and who moreover was a newcomer into Federal politics. Mr. Rowell's influence was of special value to the Government; through him an electoral contest was avoided in Ontario, where the provincial Government was due to face the electors, with somewhat dubious prospects of success. The prolongation of the legislature for a further year, however, was now arranged, averting a severe strain on the cohesion of the new party.

The coalition had been created by one dominant issue, and from the first it was doubtful if it could have any future as a single party; a section of the Conservatives under Mr. Rogers denounced coalition, and pleaded for adherence to the protective tariff policy which was the standing aim of Conservatism, while the Liberals aimed at reconciliation with the Liberal Unionists other than

[1] Mr. Sévigny resigned on March 18, and in May Mr. Sifton became Minister of Customs and Inland Revenue. Mr. Blondin was made a Senator in July.

those in the Ministry. The Liberal Unionist Ministers thus lost gradually the strength due to support by Liberals, and the balance of the power tended more and more to pass over to the Conservative element. The decline of Mr. Rowell's influence with the Liberals of his own province was clearly seen at the Ontario Liberal Convention of June 1919, when his successor in the leadership of the provincial Liberal Party was decisively defeated by Mr. Dewart, who had remained faithful to Sir Wilfrid Laurier. The decline of Conservatism in the provinces was also marked ; in July, Prince Edward Island went Liberal by 26 to 4, and the Ontario election in October 1919 left the Conservative Party, dominant for fifteen years, in the third place with 25 seats to 29 of the Liberals and 45 of the United Farmers, whose advent to power marked the definite emergence of a new party in the Dominion. Their programme in Federal politics demands the immediate increase of the British preference from $33\frac{1}{3}$ to 50 per cent., the successive reduction of duties so as to render all British imports free in four years, and the acceptance forthwith by Canada of any offers of free trade in natural products or manufactures which might be made by the United States, thus expanding the proposals of the Liberal Government of 1911 which led to the fall of Sir Wilfrid Laurier. The Conservatives remained unable to meet this demand, for their strength rested on the eastern provinces, where high protection has always been demanded.

The position of the Liberals, however, was far from comfortable, for there was no unanimity on the issue of the tariff, since the Liberals of Quebec demanded protection, while the Liberals of the West approximated more and more to the position of the grain growers and farmers. Their difficulties were increased by the death of Sir Wilfrid Laurier, whose great qualities received just recognition throughout Canada on this occasion, and by the dispute as to his successor. The choice should have fallen on Mr. Fielding, but he had committed the sin, fatal in the eyes of Quebec, of having deserted Sir Wilfrid on the conscription issue. Mr. D. D. Mackenzie was appointed leader of the Parliamentary party for the remainder of the session, and the final choice of a successor to Sir Wilfrid was postponed to the Liberal Convention at Ottawa in August, when the choice of the party fell on Mr. W. L. Mackenzie-King, who had distinguished himself under Sir Wilfrid Laurier by his handling of labour questions. The Convention was emphatic in deprecating any change in the existing relations between the Dominion and the United Kingdom; it opposed any centralization of the Empire, and insisted on its loyalty to, and appreciation of, the effort of His Majesty during the war to promote harmony throughout his Dominions. It adopted a tariff policy of a fairly advanced character, demanding the increase to 50 per cent. of the British preference, the placing of wheat and the chief articles of food, agricultural and farming implements and machinery, mining machinery, fertilizers, oils, nets, and cement on the free list, and substantial reductions in the tariff on clothes, boots and shoes, and other articles of general consumption and raw materials. This, however, was not accomplished without opposition from representatives both of British Columbia and Quebec, and since the Convention, Mr. Pardee, chief whip under Sir Wilfrid Laurier, who deserted his chief on the conscription issue, but as soon as possible returned to the Liberal fold, has insisted that free trade is impossible for the Dominion, a concession necessary to meet the misgivings of Quebec.

The final disappearance of effective coalition was delayed by the illness of Sir R. Borden, who created the coalition and held it together by force of his personality; after prolonged absence from Parliament in the search for the restoration of health shattered by intense devotion to exacting duties, he finally resigned office, and was succeeded in July 1920 by Mr. A. Meighen, Minister of the Interior, who has sat for a Manitoba constituency since 1908. There was no doubt that he was the ablest Conservative available to fill the post; Sir Thomas White, the most expert financier whom Canada has ever had, had found it necessary at an earlier date to abandon his post for private reasons, and no other Conservative commanded sufficient support in Parliament or the country to be acceptable as leader. If ability had been the deciding factor, the choice should, in the opinion of some of the party, have fallen on Mr. Rowell, but he suffered from the fatal barrier of being a Liberal. Mr. Meighen's selection, however, in effect dissolved the coalition; the only Liberal Minister, indeed, who resigned was Mr. Rowell, the others remaining in the new National Ministry, which, as reconstituted, embraced all the old Ministers, save Mr. Rowell and Mr. Martin Burrell, who resigned the Ministry of Customs to become Parliamentary Librarian;[1] but the change of leader vitally affected the issue. The Conservatives at Toronto immediately impressed on their new leader their determination to adhere to the old traditions and to decline fusion with any party, and the farmers on the one hand and labour on the other manifested lively hostility to the new administration, while the Liberal leader started on a campaign in Ontario and the Western provinces, in which he denounced the administration as an autocracy determined to hold office in defiance of public opinion and as substantially the old Tory Party of high protection, despite the strong representation of Liberalism in the Cabinet. Perhaps, however, most significant of all is the widespread activity of the farmers' organization, with its resolute insistence on the effort to attain something approaching free trade, and in any case free trade with the United Kingdom, and its strong opposition to any change in the status of Canada, while Labour, which in May and June 1919 developed in Winnipeg and elsewhere a violence unprecedented in Canada, is now making definite preparations to seek political power. The result of the Ontario election of 1919, which returned the farmers at the head of all parties and gave twelve seats to Labour, is a remarkable index to the new forces which have been evolved during the war, and with which the new National or Conservative Government and the historic Liberal Party must reckon. In imperial policy it tends to demand full equality of status, with power to amend the constitution, abolition of the supremacy of Imperial legislation and of the power of disallowance, cessation of Privy Council appeals, and abstention from any centralizing movement such as implied in the War Cabinet conception. On the other hand it welcomes conferences and co-operation, with full publicity and discussion of all issues in the Dominion Parliament.[2]

[1] Three new Ministers from the Maritime Provinces were added, Mr. F. B. McCurdy, Minister of Public Works, Mr. R. W. Wigmore, Minister of Customs, and Mr. E. K. Spiney, without portfolio. Sir James Lougheed, who became Minister of the Interior, had been Minister of Soldiers' Civil Re-establishment under the Act of 1919. [2] O. D. Skelton, *Canada, The Empire, the League*, pp. 1–14.

2. The Commonwealth of Australia

In May 1913 the Liberal Party in the Commonwealth attained office by the margin of one vote in the House of Representatives with a minority of 7 to 29 in the Senate. An unhappy and vexed Parliamentary contest enabled them in June 1914 to secure from the Governor-General a double dissolution of the Federal Parliament on the ground of the rejection of measures proposed by them in the Senate.[1] Preparations for the elections were in full blast when war ensued, and elicited from the Labour leader, Mr. A. Fisher, the enthusiastic declaration that ' should the worst happen, after everything has been done that honour will permit, we Australians will help and defend the mother-country to our last man and our last shilling '. The Labour party then suggested that an election in war was to be avoided ; either, it proposed, the candidates of the parties holding seats should be unopposed in their constituencies, or the proclamation dissolving Parliament should be recalled—which was legally impossible—or the Imperial Parliament should re-establish the old Parliament. The offers, however, were refused, doubtless in the main because the Liberals felt that they had in the double dissolution a probable means of securing under the influence of the war a majority in either house. If this were the case, the event falsified materially their hopes ; Labour insisted on its merits in establishing compulsory service for home defence as the cause why it was possible at once to dispatch troops to the front, and promised a social Utopia, with the result that it increased its power in the Senate from 29 to 31, and secured 42 seats to 32 in the House of Representatives. The Ministry resigned, and Mr. Fisher on September 17, 1914, formed a Cabinet, the members of which were as usual chosen by the Parliamentary Labour Caucus ; the Cabinet was made up to eleven by the addition of three assistant Ministers. In July 1915 the Ministry of Defence was divided, a separate Ministry for the Navy being created,[2] which was handed over to the charge of Mr. Jensen, formerly an assistant Minister.

---

[1] Keith, *Imperial Unity*, pp. 106–112.

[2] Act No. 18 of 1915. One Minister died in December, so that Mr. Hughes's Cabinet was reduced to ten.

Coalition with the Liberal party was plainly impossible, but there was some measure of co-operation, an interesting experiment being tried under which a War Committee, containing six representatives of either party, was taken into the confidence of the Government on all topics regarding the welfare and security of the country, and was invited to advise the Cabinet on the issues. Unfortunately the Labour party felt bound to proceed with the proposed constitutional alterations, which they had submitted unsuccessfully to the people in 1911 and 1913, and which they now contended were essential if Australia were to play her full part in the war. The suggestion evoked bitter feeling among the Liberals, who regarded it as an effort, under the stress of war conditions, vitally to affect the constitution, though they did not deny that some changes were needful. But the party strife thus engendered was brought to a close by the decision of the Cabinet to appoint Mr. Fisher to be High Commissioner in London, in lieu of Sir George Reid, who had held the office since 1909. He, it was thought, by his intimate knowledge of Labour aims would be able effectively to represent the aspirations of the Commonwealth in London. Mr. Hughes, who took office on October 27, dropped the referenda in exchange for promises— imperfectly fulfilled by the States—to confer some of the necessary powers on the Commonwealth by legislation for the war period, and arranged also co-operation with the States in marketing their wheat and in finance. But as early as January 17, 1916, there were signs of discord between the Prime Minister and the extreme wing of the Labour movement, represented by syndicalists and the Industrial Workers of the World, whose activities in the Commonwealth were attaining some importance,[1] and a speech delivered on that date at Sydney town hall, in a recruiting campaign, evoked bitter attacks on Mr. Hughes as a traitor to Labour. His journey to England via Canada to consult with the Imperial Government further diminished his popularity with the section of his party which was frankly against the war.

It was, however, on Mr. Hughes's return from his visit to England that serious difficulties began. He had come resolved

[1] Efforts to suppress the movement were made by Acts No. 41 of 1916 and No. 14 of 1917, and in Canada by Order in Council (*Gazette*, October 5, 1918).

to secure conscription, if possible, in order to reinforce the Australian troops at the front, and he could persuade his Cabinet to do no more than agree to the people being asked if they wished to adopt for foreign service the principles agreed to for home service. Even to secure this result he had to accept the resignation of Mr. F. G. Tudor, Minister of Trade and Customs, on September 14. The result of the referendum was defeat, and its political consequences were considerable. Mr. Hughes did not at once resign ; he contended that the vote meant merely that the special method of meeting the crisis was not accepted, and he professed his intention of adopting other means to secure the necessary reinforcements for the front. When, accordingly, on November 14 the Parliamentary Labour Caucus held a meeting at which a motion of want of confidence in him was carried, Mr. Hughes left the meeting with only twenty-three adherents, placed his resignation at the disposal of the Governor-General, thus dissolving his former Cabinet, and then received a commission to form a new Government, composed of members of the Labour party who had remained loyal to him. The Governor-General, in accepting his advice to accord him a commission to form a Ministry, acted in harmony with the position he had adopted in 1914 that the Governor-General should assimilate his action to that of the Crown in the United Kingdom. Otherwise, no doubt, he would have sent for the leader of the Labour majority, and asked him whether he could undertake office.

The Ministry, which numbered ten, only one assistant Minister holding office, was chosen by the Prime Minister, and not elected by the Caucus, and was of more than average ability. But its Parliamentary position was obviously hopeless unless the Liberals would co-operate, and the invitation extended to Mr. Hughes by the newly-formed Coalition Government in England to attend the meeting of the War Cabinet gave the Prime Minister additional reasons to seek an accommodation with his former enemies in order to be able to go to England as the representative of a majority in the House of Representatives. Hence on February 17, 1917, his short-lived Labour administration was replaced by a National War Government in which sat eleven ministers ; the Liberals contributed Mr. J. Cook as Minister for the Navy,

Sir John Forrest as Treasurer, Mr. W. A. Watt, who had resigned the Premiership of Victoria to enter Federal politics as Minister for Works and Railways, Mr. P. M. Glynn as Minister for Home and Territories, and Mr. E. D. Millen as Vice-President of the Council, with Mr. L. E. Groom as honorary Minister; in September Mr. Millen received the newly-created Ministry of Repatriation,[1] and a couple of months later Mr. Groom was moved to his former office. Labour was comparatively feebly represented, for, though Mr. G. F. Pearce[2] retained his wonted portfolio of Defence, neither Mr. Jensen as Minister of Trade and Customs, nor Mr. W. Webster as Postmaster-General, nor Mr. E. J. Russell as honorary Minister, carried much weight in politics.

One part of the scheme at once miscarried; the Senate would not assent[3] to the passing of a resolution asking the Imperial Parliament to prolong the life of the Commonwealth Parliament so as to permit of Mr. Hughes visiting England and returning to take part in the general election which was due in 1917, and Mr. Hughes, doubtless wisely, felt assured that he must be present in Australia if his party were to triumph at the polls. A dissolution thus became necessary, and Mr. Hughes sacrificed the proposed visit to London. But a much more serious sacrifice followed when the dissolution of Parliament followed in March. Mr. Hughes had been in close touch ever since his return from England in 1916 with Mr. Holman, Premier of New South Wales, who, like himself, a leader of Labour, had found himself an object of suspicion to some of his party, and in November had been compelled to secure his retention of office by a bargain with the Liberals under Mr. Wade. The State Parliament's life was prolonged by legislation passed by this coalition majority, despite the protests of the Labour party, until the Premier dissolved it in February, when he judged that the coalition effected in the Commonwealth would help his electioneering prospects. The Ministry, however, found that their opponents were making great

---

[1] Acts Nos. 37 and 40 of 1917.

[2] Strong efforts had been made to have him removed from this office ; *The Sydney Morning Herald*, February 16, 1917.

[3] A dubious manœuvre to secure a majority caused much indignation against Mr. Hughes ; see *The Sunday Sun*, March 8, 1917 ; *The Australian Worker*, March 15, 1917.

play with the idea of the danger of conscription being furthered if Mr. Holman were returned to power, despite the fact that the State had no direct connexion with the issue, and they consented to give pledges that they would oppose conscription if a new referendum were taken. The same distrust of the people influenced the Commonwealth coalition, and they gave formal pledges that they would not, if returned to power, introduce conscription, but, if the war went against the Allies, would consult the people by reference of the issue to them, though Sir William Irvine protested against the pusillanimity of such an attitude. The tactics in either case succeeded, for Mr. Holman won a handsome victory, the unattached vote turning to him now that farmers were relieved of fears of the loss of labour and consequently of profits, and Mr. Hughes had the satisfaction on May 5 of winning the whole of the eighteen seats contested in the Senate, in which Labour was left with but seven, and materially increasing the strength of the coalition in the House of Representatives.

The position thus achieved was, in truth, delusive, for the Government which was selected on the strength of its promises to win the war had prevented itself from taking effective means to this end, and the Russian *débâcle* and the defeat of Italy brought about the necessity of seeking to restore the position. On November 7, therefore, the Government decided on a referendum, and five days later Mr. Hughes at Bendigo pledged himself and his colleagues to the doctrine that, if they were not given the power to compel men, they would not continue in office. The referendum of December 20 was not merely a failure ; it was decisively against the Government. The only honourable course to be followed was resignation, which would leave to Labour, which had defeated the conscription proposals, the burden of office and the responsibility for the share to be played by the Commonwealth in the war. But the same motives of anxiety for office and for their seats, which had induced the Government and its supporters to adopt the referendum in place of the honest course of appealing to the electorate to relieve them of their promises as to conscription, interposed a fatal obstacle to the taking of this course. A plausible argument was found for refusal to honour repeated, emphatic, and unambiguous pledges.

The Government, it was argued, had pledged themselves without the approval of the party, and to hand over the government to Labour would in the existing circumstances of industrial unrest and the position of the war be disloyal to Australian and Imperial interests.   Australia had, in fact, been suffering from a series of strikes involving wharf labourers, railwaymen, and other Unions ever since the advent to power of the Government, and the Labour party had ceased to take any really effective share in voluntary recruitment.   Hence at the Caucus meeting of the Liberal party in Parliament on January 3, 1918, when the defeat was undeniable, the leadership of Mr. Hughes was approved by an overwhelming vote.   On the following day Sir William Irvine with a few followers endeavoured to convince the party that they had no honourable alternatives save resignation, with the result that the Labour party must accept the duty of meeting the situation, or of accepting full responsibility for their policy, and dissolving Parliament in order to allow the electors to declare their minds.   Neither argument prevailed; the Caucus decided that nothing must be done to permit Labour to attain power, and that the matter must be left in the hands of the Government ' to take whatever steps it deems advisable with a view to giving honourable effect to the pledge given by it to the people of Australia '.

The Government's mode of interpreting this mandate was curious ; on January 8 Mr. Hughes tendered his unconditional resignation to the Governor-General, who, after consulting the leader of the Opposition, Mr. Cook, Sir J. Forrest, Mr. Watt, and three other gentlemen, notified on January 11 that he had commissioned Mr. Hughes to form a Government.   He rested his decision on the fact that the inquiries which he had made had resulted in the view that the Nationalist party would hold together, that no one but Mr. Hughes would have an effective majority, and that it was only legitimate for him to look to the parliamentary position without reference to matters outside Parliament.   The action of the Governor-General was in accordance with his interpretation of the duties of his position, and the responsibility for the events must rest with Mr. Hughes.   The Opposition on the meeting of Parliament sharply challenged the

Government for their breach of their pledges, and to this the administration had no effective reply. But the Labour party with their attack on this point mingled complaints of other matters, such as the prosecutions of public men under the War Regulations and the disfranchisement of citizens with alien connexions under the referendum rules, and thus the Government was secured of a decisive majority. The calamity involved, however, was not a slight one ; a Government pledged to effect great improvements in the national effort was, in fact, helpless to do anything. But the unfortunate effect of the breach of faith, as Labour regarded it,[1] was the widening of the cleavage between the Government and Labour, and the obvious predominance of extreme views in the Labour party. The result was plainly seen in the State elections, which, as usual, reflected conditions in the Commonwealth. The South Australian contest lay between Labour and a coalition of the Liberals and the National party, which represented those Labour men who, having supported the cause of conscription at the referendum of October 1916, fell under the ban of the majority of the party, and had coalesced to form a Liberal-National Government. The coalition won a decisive victory at the polls, securing a majority of 19 in the Legislative Assembly and 15 in the Council ; but not only did Labour improve its position, but it succeeded in defeating those moderate and able men like Messrs. Crawford Vaughan, J. Verran, and J. H. Vaughan, who formerly were its chief ornaments. In Queensland, where Mr. Hughes had conducted an extremely violent campaign, the result was a decisive and most unexpected defeat for the Nationalist party in the State which supported conscription and which had every reason to believe that on its domestic record the Labour Ministry which came to power in 1915 would meet with disaster. The actual results on March 16 were Labour 48 to Nationalists 24, and the attitude towards the problem of national service of the Ministry may be judged from the fact that one of the Ministry denounced England as ' a land of cant, humbug, and hypocrisy ', Irish Australians who enlisted as merely helping in the oppression of Ireland, and the Imperial Government as guilty of worse crimes in the suppression of the Irish rebellion of

[1] Commonwealth *Debates*, January 12 and 13, 1918.

1916 than the Germans in murdering Miss Cavell and Captain Fryatt. The President of the Central Political Executive of the Labour party in Queensland, the real governing body of Labour in the State, traced the war to imperialism and suggested that British and German imperialism were on the same footing.[1] The attempts of the Government to rally moderate Labour to their aid in recruiting proved a fiasco, and the resolutions of the Inter-State Labour Conference held at Perth in June 1918 showed marked hostility not merely to the capitalistic organization of industry and to conscription, but also to any measure for consolidating Imperial relations. It declared for complete Australian self-government, as in the British community, no Imperial federation, Australian policy and administration to be decided on the advice of Australian Ministers only, subject to the control of Australian Parliaments. All bills passed by Parliament must receive assent on the advice of Australian Ministers, and there must be no surrender of Australian self-government. The High Court should be the final court of appeal, excluding the Privy Council, and the practice of recommending Australian citizens for Imperial honours should cease. On the industrial side there developed further unrest, culminating in the strike of the seamen from May to August 1919, and in an ingenious and desperate, but by no means completely successful, endeavour to establish the principle of the ' One Big Union ' in the shape of the Industrial Workers' Union of Australia, a movement running parallel with the same phenomenon which resulted in Canada in the Winnipeg strike and its sequel. The Government were hampered in their dealings with the problems presented both before and after the Armistice by lack of any constructive industrial policy, which it was almost impossible to frame in view of the restricted powers in industrial and trade questions possessed by the Commonwealth. Moreover, the prolonged absence in London of the Prime Minister and Sir J. Cook in connexion with the peace negotiations weakened the power of the administration.

Mr. Hughes's return on August 22, 1919, was hailed by rejoicings of remarkable warmth and fervour, based largely on the belief that nothing but his strength of purpose had prevented

[1] See above, Chap. V, § 2.

the overlooking of Australian claims at the Peace Conference, the loss of the conquered German islands, and the acceptance by the League of Nations of the principle of free migration for all nations members of the League, thus overthrowing the doctrine of a 'White Australia'. No time was lost by Mr. Hughes in determining, after conferences between himself, Sir Joseph Cook, and the Central Executive of the Nationalist organization, on the definite formation of a new party to appeal in December to the country on a policy which included as two of its most important features measures to combat the cost of living and to deal with profiteering, steps which involved important changes in the constitution, which after enactment by Parliament would be submitted to the electors simultaneously with the general election. The reply of Labour asserted that it was not perturbed by 'subsidized shouting and electioneering antics', and that Mr. Hughes was trying to stampede Australia by rushing through Parliament a treaty of peace which would compel the Commonwealth to deport its young manhood to foreign battlefields, probably in support of Asiatic interests against the white race. At the same time Mr. Ryan, Premier of Queensland, entered the political arena as an aspirant for the leadership of the Federal Labour party on the plea that Mr. Tudor's leadership was lacking in vigour and too moderate in tendency. It may, however, be doubted whether his intervention served the party well; the general election of December 13 returned the Government to power with 40 supporters against 26 adherents of Labour and 9 candidates of the Farmers' Union, a new body, whose appearance in Federal politics is an interesting parallel to the similar movement to secure farming interests in Canada. In the Senate the Government were even more fortunate, for of the eighteen seats contested they secured all but one, making their majority, with the seats won in 1917, 35 to 1. But the referenda went against them, and they lost two ministers, Mr. Glynn, whose place as Minister for Home and Territories was taken by Mr. A. Poynton, and Mr. W. Webster, Postmaster-General, who was succeeded by Mr. G. H. Wise. Two new honorary Ministers were appointed to replace those thus promoted. In effect the election marked the end of the coalition of 1917–18; though Mr. Hughes still retained a minority of Labour colleagues, they had ceased to rely on Labour supporters, and had adopted the principles of the new party. The triumph was unquestionably a personal one ; in the absence of any minister of outstanding ability, the Commonwealth felt bound to repose its confidence in the one minister who had at least the merit of knowing what he wanted, and almost unbounded skill in devising means to retain authority. The defeat of the referenda was a severe blow, but the Government persisted in the decision to summon a convention representing the Parliaments and peoples of the States and the Commonwealth for the revision of the constitution. The cohesion, however, of the new Ministry was soon to be tested ; Mr. Watt, who had acted as Premier in Mr. Hughes's absence, and unquestionably is the ablest of his colleagues, proceeded to England on a mission to discuss with the Imperial Government outstanding financial questions. Shortly after his arrival in London he resigned office on June 9, and gave as his reason the fact that he was expected merely to act as a means of transmitting the Prime Minister's communications to the Imperial Government, while Mr. Hughes sent direct communications to the Imperial Government which were inconsistent with the terms of his proposals as communicated to Mr. Watt. Mr. Watt's place as Treasurer was filled by Sir J. Cook, while Mr. Laird Smith assumed the latter's portfolio of the Navy, but in April 1921 a Parliamentary crisis showed that Mr. Hughes had difficulty in adjusting himself to the co-operation with colleagues necessary in peace time, and that he had to face hostility from some of his old friends who with the representatives of farming interests had formed a Country Party.

In March the general election in New South Wales saw the downfall of the Nationalists, Labour securing 45 seats, the Nationalists 28, Progressives 15, and Independents 2, and, as the Speakership was assumed by Mr. Levy, a Liberal, Mr. Storey, the Labour leader, was commissioned to form a Government. Since assuming office he has been in somewhat violent contest with Labour extremists, who have failed to appreciate the readiness shown by him to advise the exercise of the power to release from imprisonment certain members of the organization of the Industrial Workers of the World, which had to be suppressed by the Commonwealth Government and Parliament in 1917. The men thus released somewhat inconsiderately responded by the delivery of inflammatory speeches urging class warfare.'

The persistence in the Commonwealth of the element of disloyalty in the extreme Labour party, which manifested itself during the war in the movement for a peace without victory, was curiously revealed in an incident in July 1920 regarding the deportation from the Commonwealth of Father Jerger, a German priest who had been confined in an internment camp during the war for repatriation on the occurrence of a suitable opportunity. A vehement agitation to prevent the deportation taking place was put on foot, while the Labour Unions endeavoured by diverse means to defeat the purpose of the Government to remove the priest from the country unless he was accorded a fair trial. The Government, however, persisted in their purpose, laying stress on the fact that the deportation order had only been confirmed after the most careful investigation of his case, and they expressed their willingness in the event of proceedings in the High Court being decided in favour of the priest during his absence to permit him to return to the Commonwealth. Another sign of the existence of disloyal elements in the Labour party was afforded by the decision of a conference of Labour Unions at Sydney to institute a policy of ' go slow ' and to carry on propaganda on board the Commonwealth warships, if the Government did not yield on the issue of deportations.

In the debate on a motion of censure in the House of Representatives on July 14, the Prime Minister effectively traced the decline in the prestige and power of the Labour party in the Commonwealth to their falling away in 1916 from the path of loyalty to the Empire, and he insisted that, unless the party changed its attitude, it could not hope to secure the confidence of the people of Australia. In October the result of the elections of Queensland afforded some confirmation of his views, for, though the Government of Mr. Theodore was returned to power, the majority was reduced to four. What, however, is more significant is that the time of the election was deliberately chosen by the Government when, by a display of striking enthusiasm for the Prince of Wales, they had removed the fears of many of the

electors as to their loyalty to the Empire, while they had on their
side the votes of the strong Irish and Catholic element in Queensland and the resentment widely felt against their opponents for
their responsibility in preventing the Premier obtaining a loan
for public works on the London market. Labour also failed
signally in the South Australian general election of 1921, winning
only 16 out of 46 seats.

In November a strange incident occurred, throwing vivid
light on the strain of vehement dislike of the Empire developed
in a section of Labour opinion ; Mr. Mahon, a former colleague
of Mr. Hughes in the Labour Ministry of 1916, was, on the motion
of the Prime Minister, expelled from the House of Representatives
on the ground of a violent speech which he had made at a public
meeting in which he denounced the ' accursed Empire '. The
leader of the Labour party, who opposed his expulsion, was
careful not to defend his attitude, but argued that the matter
was one to be dealt with by the courts, not to be used as a basis
for the expulsion of a member of Parliament.

A curious reflex from the perturbed condition of public affairs
in Australia and the rise of a movement contemptuous of order
and law was seen in the autumn of 1919 in the Northern Territory
of Australia, which is under the direct control of the Commonwealth and does not form any part of a State. Riotous protests
against the Administrator, Dr. J. A. Gilruth, led to his withdrawal
from office, and the Minister for Home and Territories then
established a local Advisory Council consisting of representatives
of the trade unions and of Government officials, the latter pre-
dominating. After a brief trial of this modified form of administration, the trade unionists, headed by the Mayor of Darwin, the
capital, waited upon Mr. Carey, the Director of the Territory,
Mr. Evans, the Government Secretary, and Mr. Bevan, the Judge,
and demanded their departure from the Territory by the first
available steamer, threatening in default riot and rebellion. The
officials agreed to do so, and telegraphed to the Minister, who
instructed them to remain at their posts. The industrialists,
however, five days later loaded a steamship and called upon the
officials to leave, menacing them with personal violence, and the
latter finally complied with the demand. The Government then

sent H.M.A.S. *Brisbane* to Darwin, and organized a police force to maintain order, but they also appointed Mr. Justice Ewing of Tasmania to inquire into the grievances which had induced the action of the townspeople.

3. New Zealand

On the outbreak of war the Reform party was in power in New Zealand, having ousted the Liberal Government in 1912, but the Liberals hastened to co-operate in the measures which at once were taken to enable New Zealand to play her part in the war. The general election was due in December, but the leader of the Liberals, Sir Joseph Ward, suggested that it might be postponed until February or March when the European situation might be cleared by the Allied victory which the Dominion confidently anticipated at any early date. The proposal was rejected by the Government, and on December 10 polling took place, the parties being divided on local issues only ; the result was all but a deadlock, 41 supporters of the Government being returned against 30 Liberals and 7 Labour members, the latter accepting a working agreement with the Liberals which placed Sir J. Ward in command of almost half the house. Moreover the situation was complicated by election petitions which menaced the safety of Government seats. When these were cleared out of the way without affecting the position, and Parliament met in June, practically no business could be transacted owing to disagreement on points of detail and criticisms of the Department of Defence, whose head, Colonel J. Allen, had incurred hostility by his effort in the preceding Parliament to secure the passage of a bill providing for the reading of the Bible in state schools, a cry which was absurdly enough made an issue in the general election. Happily on August 4, by dint of the informal and perfectly constitutional initiative of the Governor, the Earl of Liverpool, a National Government was formed, consisting of thirteen [1] members, six from each side, with a thirteenth representing, as usual, the Maori race. Mr. Massey retained, of course, the Premiership, while Sir J. Ward became Finance Minister and Colonel Allen retained the Ministry of Defence, in which he

---

[1] Act No. 15 of 1915 increased to ten the number of paid Ministers.

rendered great services. There was no fusion of parties or principles, but merely union for war co-operation.

The Coalition Government preserved its unity through the
difficult experiment of passing in 1916 a measure for conscription,
though in moderate terms, and the two leaders were united in
representing the Dominion at the War Cabinets of 1917 and
1918 and the Peace Conference. In 1918, however, there already
appeared signs that the Coalition was nearing its end. It had
failed to deal effectively with Labour unrest, coal strikes in 1917
and 1918 having been handled without dignity or competence,
and Labour had definitely veered into an attitude of strong
objection to compulsory recruiting whether for war or for national
service, which the Government enacted in 1918 as a clause in the
Finance Act, but never ventured to put in operation. Relations
between Capital and Labour steadily deteriorated, and the
Arbitration Court's decisions fell into disrepute. Politically the
discontent showed itself in the loss in 1918 in quick succession
of three by-elections, two to Labour, but one to an Independent
Liberal candidate who stood defying the coalition. Personal
reasons, however, seem to have been decisive in the step taken
by Sir J. Ward on August 21, after his return from the Peace
Conference, in announcing the termination of the coalition. He
asserted in reply to the protests of the Reform party that he had
not been invited to continue in unison with the Government of
Mr. Massey, and that decisions on questions of policy had been
taken without his concurrence. These charges were denied by
Mr. Massey, but there could hardly be any doubt that the two
statesmen had found it impossible to work effectively and har-
moniously with each other. A bid for the soldiers' vote was
immediately made by Sir J. Ward; returned soldiers were
insistent on the grant to them of a bonus of £75 for each year of
service, while the Government policy was to allow 1s. 6d. a day;
Sir J. Ward supported an amendment which would have made
the sum 2s., but this attempt to overthrow the administration
proved a failure, many of the Liberals having by this time come
to accept the views of the Reform section. It was naturally
thought that in the general election the split between the older
parties would tell in favour of Labour, whose aggressive tactics

had created the impression that it represented a strong body of opinion throughout the country as well as in industrial centres. The proposals of the two great parties as submitted to the electorate were not very dissimilar in terms, though Sir J. Ward was clearly in favour of nationalizing all the coal mines and generally advocated more advanced social and labour views than Mr. Massey. The result was a surprise probably to all parties ; the Reform Government was sustained by 48 seats being won, while Liberal members secured only 19 seats, Official Labour 8, and Independent Liberal Labour 5. Sir J. Ward was among those defeated, retiring definitively from politics as a result. It is probable that at no time was the alliance a happy one for either party ; it was only formed with difficulty and was due to the patriotism of either leader, and anxiety to co-operate for war ends, so that the termination of hostilities meant the end of the only motive which held the coalition together. There was obvious also, towards the close of the co-operation of the parties, a marked divergence between the aims of the two leaders on Imperial issues ; Sir J. Ward adhered to his belief in Imperial federation, and in special to his doctrine of the necessity of New Zealand avoiding the creation of a separate naval force, while Mr. Massey, under the driving force of Colonel Allen, was a stout supporter of the ideal of a New Zealand naval unit, to which encouragement is given by Lord Jellicoe's report. To Colonel Allen also was due much of the military effort of the Dominion, and his appointment as High Commissioner in 1920, in succession to Sir Thomas Mackenzie, who had held that office throughout the war, elicited fears lest the efforts of the Government should be relaxed in his absence, and the formation of a voluntary organization to further the plans which the Minister favoured. Other charges urged against the Government in the debate of July 1920 included failure to pass an effective electoral law and to deal with problems of high prices, housing, and coal shortage and industrial unrest, but the Government, which attributed its shortcomings to world conditions beyond their power of control, were upheld by 45 votes to 22, on a vote of confidence. An interesting effort was made by an Independent member of the House of Representatives to secure an expression of opinion from that body in favour of an elective executive, but the Prime Minister confessed that, though he had held the doctrine in his youth, he had recanted, and was convinced that the process of election by the majority party would not secure as effective a Ministry as the process of selection by the Prime Minister. The Opposition on September 1 suffered a severe loss in the death of Mr. W. D. S. Macdonald, who succeeded Sir J. Ward in the leadership of the Opposition. Mr. T. M. Wilford, selected to replace him, announced his adherence to the old Liberal policy of a contribution to the Imperial Navy in lieu of the maintenance of a fleet unit, submarines and aeroplanes being used for local defence.

4. The Union of South Africa

The declaration of war found political conditions in the Union of South Africa in a somewhat delicate position. When the four South African colonies agreed to merge in a legislative union it was anticipated by many politicians that the first Government of the new Union would be based on a coalition of the leaders of the several parties existing in the colonies before their merger. Considerations largely personal in character prevented the consummation of this ideal, and the Ministry formed by General Botha, who was commissioned by the Governor-General as Prime Minister, was chosen from the leaders of the Dutch parties in the Cape, the Transvaal, and the Orange Free State; in the case of Natal, where the population was overwhelmingly British, the Prime Minister's choice fell on politicians of moderate views. The British parties in the Cape and the Transvaal and some members from Natal united to form an Opposition, which, however, was divided on no very essential points from the views of the Prime Minister. The Government party, which took the style of the South African party, was from the first composed of two very different elements; of its numbers a considerable minority were representatives of the doctrine of Dutch racial supremacy, men who resented the overthrow of the independence of the two republics in 1899–1902 and who were determined to secure the predominance of the Dutch element. The other section, which included most of the Cape members of the party and many of the Transvaal members, accepted loyally the union of South Africa under the British flag, and had no desire to accentuate racial discriminations. The leader of the minority, Mr. Hertzog, one of the Orange Free State generals in the war, was determined to make his policy supreme in the councils of the party, and a sharp struggle between him and General Botha for the control of the position resulted in December 1912 in the reconstruction of General Botha's Ministry and the omission of Mr. Hertzog from its ranks. General Botha's action strengthened his Government in so far as it left him with a united following, but he had to face the constant criticism of the Nationalist party, the name adopted by Mr. Hertzog's followers, which was ready to seize any opportunity of suggesting that General Botha was betraying the interests of the Dutch element of the population and deferring unduly to the views of the British party, the Unionists. That party, representing as it did the mining and other industrial and commercial interests in the hands of the British elements of the population, was divided from the Government by its desire to promote British immigration, and by its views on the taxation of the mining industry. It also represented to some extent the views of the British mine-workers, but a small Labour party with distinctively socialistic views was just beginning to appear at the outbreak of the war, thus menacing the unity of the British vote.

Opposition to the war was immediately developed by the Nationalist party, doubtless partly on principle, partly because Mr. Hertzog saw in this issue an effective means of revenging himself on General Botha for his exclusion from office. A convinced supporter of Dutch domination in the political and social life of South Africa, Mr. Hertzog, though himself not willing to approve armed revolt, inspired the ideals of men such as de Wet, who took the field in an effort to overthrow General Botha, when that statesman, by accepting the suggestion of the Imperial Government for the occupation of German South-West Africa, had afforded them a plea for action, despite the fact that the Prime Minister's policy received the emphatic endorsement of an overwhelming majority in Parliament. From the suppression of the rebellion and from a brilliant campaign in German South-West Africa General Botha emerged to find that the hostility of the Nationalists was unabated. They ignored the generosity of his treatment of the rebels, and they denounced the policy of loyalty to the United Kingdom in the war on the ground that it must lead to national bankruptcy and to the imposition of compulsory service. The Government deferred to their views to the extent of intimating to the Imperial Government that, while it would organize volunteers from the Union, it would not pay for them, but even this did not satisfy the Nationalists, who poisoned the minds of the electors by insisting that the Government was favouring British interests at the expense of South Africa. The Government might have asked Parliament to prolong its life for a year, but this course would merely have postponed the issue, and have needlessly embittered public feeling against the Government and its supporters. The Labour party divided in sentiment ; the International Socialist element had succeeded, in the absence in German South-West Africa of Mr. Creswell and other patriotic members of Labour, in securing at the East London Conference in December 1914 a vote allowing each member to exercise his judgement as to his attitude towards the war, and, though the policy was reversed on the return from service of the loyalists, the mischief had been done, and in the general election the Rand, which was the natural stronghold of Labour and which had shown its sense by returning a colossal Labour majority in the provincial election of 1914, went almost solidly Unionist. In the country districts the Government suffered heavily, and would have lost more seats were it not for the practical understanding which prevented needless conflicts between Unionists and members of the South African party, where a conflict would merely let Labour or the Nationalists win the seat. In the result General Botha secured 54 seats, the Nationalists just half that number, the Unionists 40, Labour 3, and Independent candidates 6. Three ministers were defeated, including Mr. Burton, Minister of Railways, and Mr. de Wet, Minister of Justice, but seats were found for these two Ministers elsewhere. The most disquieting feature of the situation was the loss of all the seats of the South African party in the Orange Free State, which thus became— save for a single uncontested Unionist seat for Bloemfontein city—entirely a Nationalist preserve.

The result of the election thus made General Botha dependent on the forbearance of the Unionist party if he were to maintain power, unless he were prepared to sacrifice principle and accept union with the Nationalists. On the other hand the idea of a coalition was felt to be inadmissible ; to have accepted it would have meant that General Botha would have had to make personal enemies and weaken his party by discarding Ministers who had been loyal to him, and at the same time to alienate his Dutch adherents, who would have been convinced that he really was, as asserted by the Nationalists, working in the interests of the English-speaking population. The Unionists, in their turn, were prepared to place the interests of the Empire before party or personal considerations. Though, therefore, sorely tried by the renewed refusal of the Government to accept the proposal that the Union should bear the burden of increasing the pay of the Union expeditionary troops from the British rate of 1s. 2d. to 3s. a day, they declined to carry the point to a direct issue when assured that the step would involve the fall of the Ministry. On the other hand, the Ministry accepted legislation on topics of importance in the eyes of the party ; the session of 1916 saw the passing of an Act [1] regulating trading with the enemy in the teeth of the bitter opposition of the Nationalists, who claimed that the measure affected unjustly peaceful Germans settled in South Africa. The Nationalists appealed also to racial prejudice by declaring that the Government were degrading them by failing to provide sufficient carriages on the railways, reserved for native use. Though dependent, however, on Unionist support, the Government were careful to avoid any appearance of dependence on it, and when a Unionist vacancy occurred at Johannesburg the seat was lost to Labour, the Government contesting it against the Unionist candidate.

So far the Nationalist attitude had been one of acceptance of the relations between the United Kingdom and the Union, but of refusal to admit that this relation imported the grant of active assistance to the Empire on the occasion of a war, the attitude, in fact, adopted in 1911, when the doctrine of the neutrality of the Dominions had a strong vogue in the Union.

[1] No. 39 of 1916.

At the Nationalist Congress at Bloemfontein in August 1916, the Congress unequivocally accepted ' the position of the Union with regard to its connexion with the United Kingdom, resting as it does on the good faith of two nations ', and only laid stress on the point that it was essential that there should be absolutely no interference with the Union in its policy. The overt departure from this line of action was first seen in the following year when, basing themselves on the Allied reply [1] to the German Peace note, the chairman, Mr. Tielman Roos, and secretary, Mr. Poutsma, of the Transvaal Nationalists issued a declaration demanding the immediate restoration of the independence of the Transvaal and the Orange Free State in accordance with the Allied insistence on obtaining ' reparation for violated rights and liberties and recognition of the principle of nationalities and the free existence of small states '. The appearance of President Wilson's message to the Russian Provisional Government was the occasion for a declaration by *De Burger*, the Nationalist organ in Cape Town, that the Peace Conference, in carrying out the principles enunciated by the President, would have no option but to concede to the Union the right to cease to be part of the Empire. The Transvaal Nationalist journal, *Ons Vaderland*, introduced the claim for independence into the provincial elections, with results which showed that the loyalty of the South African party in the Transvaal had been seriously sapped since the Union election of 1915, while shortly after the Federal Council of the Nationalist party denounced any attempt to crush the Republican sentiment in South Africa. Mr. Hertzog, in addresses of May 4 and 11 to the students at Stellenbosch,[2] preached undiluted Republicanism, based on legal arguments. The allegiance of South Africa was due under the Treaty of Vereeniging to the King alone, and it was the King only who had any powers in the Union under the Union Act of 1909. The absurdity of these contentions was little appreciated in the Union, where they seemed plausible enough. Yet it was obvious that the King, to whom the surrender took place at Vereeniging, was not an individual, but a constitutional monarch representing the executive power of the United Kingdom and

---

[1] *Parl. Pap.* Cd. 8467.   [2] *Cape Times*, May 5 and 12, 1917.

the Empire, and the King of the Union of South Africa Act was in like manner a constitutional sovereign whose authority was that of the United Kingdom. The Union House of Assembly manifested on June 18, by a majority of 72 to 21 votes, its disapproval of the Republican propaganda, the minority consisting solely of Mr. Hertzog's supporters. The way was open for a coalition, and the Unionist party definitely desired in this manner to meet the approval of Republicanism given at Bloemfontein in July by the Nationalist Federal Council, but events were unpropitious; Mr. Burton, one of the ablest and most moderate men in the Government, fell ill, and had to leave work for a time, and the South African party was incensed against the Imperial Government by a dispute regarding the price to be paid for wool. The sum offered by the Imperial authorities represented an advance of 55 per cent. over the pre-war rates, but the prices of the year before had been far higher, and it was represented by the Nationalists that the markets of Japan and America were willing to pay far higher prices, but that the Imperial Government was using its control of shipping to compel the farmers to accept low rates, the suggestion—wholly contrary to fact—being that, if the Union had been a republic, there would have been shipping in abundance and a free market.

The strife was renewed in Parliament in the session of 1918, when the vote of £1,000,000, as a tardy and inadequate contribution by the Union to the cost of the Union expeditionary force, gave Mr. Hertzog fresh fuel for wrath, and elicited on April 18 from Sir P. Fitzpatrick a denunciation of Mr. Hertzog as preaching sedition and rebellion. General Botha intervened to press for moderation on both sides, and stated that if necessary he would introduce legislation to enforce peace. Mr. Hertzog yielded to the appeal to the extent that in a speech at Smithfield he warned the people against violence, but he also inveighed against the Government's subservience to the Imperial Government in the matter of the invasion of German South-West Africa, the purchase of wool, and the refusal of coaling facilities for Dutch shipping, and asserted that South Africa was menaced with the creation of a federation, and that a responsible British statesman has asserted that after the war no raw materials from the Union would be allowed to go to Germany until the United Kingdom and the Allies had been supplied, and on March 28 he had opposed bitterly in the Assembly the vote of thanks to Field-Marshal Haig and the Allied armies which the Government had proposed. Moreover, he persisted in asserting that the Imperial Parliament might enact conscription for the Union under the press of the emergency and send Union soldiers to Flanders, an insinuation denounced by the Government, and the more discreditable in that it was impossible to ignore the connexion between the renewed virulence of the Republican propaganda and the disasters in Europe. Nor was the Government wholly happy in its relations with the Opposition Unionists and Labour; it failed to carry its measure to prevent the increase of rents, which was badly needed in view of many cases of rackrenting, and to enable it to control the supply of mining stores and labour to the mines, though these powers were urgently required, in order to minimize the confusion on the Rand as the result of shortage of labour and material. The situation after the close of Parliament on May 8 was made more dangerous by serious strikes among white workers on the Rand, which were followed in June by efforts on the part of the natives to imitate the success of their European associates in holding up the community to ransom. The measures taken to suppress the natives' action, though in part legal, were far too harsh, while many unprovoked assaults were committed by Europeans on natives. The Government became panic-stricken, apparently on imperfect evidence, and declared in July that enemy agencies were at work in the country seeking to stir up strife among Europeans and natives; bodies of troops were held in readiness, and the native strikers overawed and induced to resume work by armed force, while three International Socialists were arrested on charges of inciting the natives to revolt. The Nationalists ridiculed the Government's assertions, but General Botha remained convinced that there had been seditious intent. At the Bloemfontein Conference of the Nationalists in August a resolution was adopted acclaiming the pronouncements of Mr. Lloyd George and President Wilson on the rights of nationalities, and demanding that ' these axiomatic principles be applied to South Africa, so that complete freedom and independence, including the right to determine the form of its own government, be put within the reach of this country'. It added, however, that the means to be taken for this end must be constitutional.

The defeat of Germany might have been expected—as indeed was the case in many circles in South Africa—to have put an end to the hopes of the Nationalists, but on the contrary they based on the principles enunciated by President Wilson the assurance that they would be admitted to the Peace Conference and given the power to withdraw from the British connexion. Fuel to the flame of their ill-feeling to the Empire was added by the tactlessness of the Imperial Government in selecting Lord Milner as Secretary of State for the Colonies, for the Dutch, even including General Botha, had never forgiven him his share in the Boer war or his administration of the conquered States after the war. A Nationalist Congress, summoned to meet on January 16 at Bloemfontein, resolved on sending a mission to Europe to secure the right of the four States to obtain their independence. Some doubt, however, arose as to the exact nature of the demand to be made; it was finally decided that the claim should be made on behalf of the Union as a whole, with the possibility of reducing the demand to the Transvaal and the Orange Free State, or even to the last alone if nothing else would be conceded. The difficulty felt by the Congress was due to the patent fact that Natal would not have independence at any cost, that the attitude of the people of the Cape was at least doubtful, that in the Transvaal the British element was absolutely opposed to the idea and was about numerically equal, and that in the Orange Free State alone could it be said that there was an absolute majority for independence.

The Unionists were not slow to take up the challenge; on February 11 Sir Thomas Smartt moved a resolution unequivocally condemning the Republican movement and insisting that its continuance must inevitably lead to civil war. The debate lasted for twelve days, 75 members spoke, and in the ultimate issue, by 78 votes to 24, the House adopted a resolution moved by the acting Prime Minister, ' that this house, while welcoming all constitutional development which will make the Union in the fullest sense a self-governing Dominion, emphatically condemns the present agitation for the disruption of the Union and the severance of the connexion between South Africa and Britain ', and expressed the opinion that ' this agitation is in its essence subversive of the fundamental principles of the constitution as laid down by the South Africa Act '. Mr. Hertzog stated his case at great length. He maintained that the two republics had lost their liberty by unjust acts, and *spoliatus ante omne restituendus*. In the second place he maintained his thesis that the position of the Union was really servile ; quoting the Federal argument, he laid down the doctrine that for true self-government there were no alternatives but Federal union with the United Kingdom or absolute independence ; the former was unacceptable to any Afrikander, and therefore all must and ultimately would agree to the latter course. In reply it was contended that, however wrong the annexation of the two republics, they were now part of a Union, and could not properly be torn apart from it. The Union Act represented a pact between British and Dutch South Africa ; it could not be varied in essentials as opposed to machinery except by the assent of a substantial majority of the people on either side. Moreover the case could be put higher ; the Union Act was a pact, the disruption of which was a matter in which the United Kingdom and the other Dominions forming the Empire had a right to be consulted. The debate was noteworthy also in addition to its value as setting out frankly and simply the British case, for it elicited the reiterated assertion of Mr. Burton that the Government, while insisting on autonomy, meant autonomy under the British flag, and that they were not, as the Nationalists insinuated, really in sympathy with them in everything but tactics. The patience of the Unionists with the Government was, however, much tried immediately afterwards, for renewed strikes on the Rand, with their inevitable accompaniment of native unrest and repression with needless violence, were dealt with for a time feebly and ineffectively by the administration.

The delegates sent to Europe had some difficulty in attaining their destination, owing to the objection of British seamen to carry them, and their refusal to accept the Spartan simplicity of the accommodation on board the British war vessel which the

Imperial Government courteously put at their disposal. The accomplishment of their journey brought, however, little satisfaction, since at Paris the Union of South Africa was already represented by a delegation commanding the confidence of the Union Parliament. On the request of General Botha they were received on June 5 by Mr. Lloyd George at Paris, and pressed on him a request, if not for the independence of the Union, at least for that of the Transvaal and the Orange Free State. It was admitted that the demand could not be based on actual interference by the Imperial Government with the people of the Union, and the Prime Minister countered directly the assertion of intolerance on the part of the British element of the population by pointing out that the Union Government since its inception had been predominantly Dutch in composition, and had been largely supported by British voters. The request must be refused because to grant it over the head of the Union Parliament and people would be an interference with the rights finally granted to South Africa when the Imperial Parliament in 1909 ratified the constitution drawn up by a convention of the South African people, and approved by the freely elected Parliaments of the four South African colonies. Moreover the disruption of the Union would be fatal to the interest of South Africa. The Governments of the two Boer colonies, though predominantly Boer, and their predominantly Boer Parliaments had never raised the demand for independence ; they had acquiesced in the new status, and they had freely agreed to unite with the Cape and Natal. This was a solemn pact which could not be broken. If it were to be conceded that the Boer populations might leave the Union, then the British must have the same right, and the Transvaal must be partitioned, while the natives would be equally entitled to make the same demand. On the other hand, the Union had acquired a new status of the utmost importance at the Peace Conference ; in the future League of Nations it would have the same membership and status as, and far more influence than, any of the other States outside the ranks of the few great Powers.

The effect of this reply was to evoke a meeting, mainly attended by Nationalists, at Somerset East, when suggestions for the reunion of the Nationalist and South African parties were mooted ; the idea of the promoters was to unite the Dutch parties on common interests, leaving Republicanism to be revived when a more favourable occasion offered. In the Cape the movement had some support, but in the Transvaal Mr. Tielman Roos was more rigid, refusing any idea of reunion unless the South African party accepted Republicanism. At this juncture the death of General Botha, very suddenly on August 26, deprived the South African party of its greatest statesman and the man in whom the rank and file placed their trust. The Governor-General, as was obviously right, commissioned General Smuts to form a Ministry, which he did without difficulty, succeeding in retaining the services of the other members of the Botha Cabinet, though rumours of friction were in circulation. The opportunity of forming a Coalition Government now presented itself ; General Botha was said to have contemplated it shortly before his death, and the dissolution of the Ministry by his death afforded an opportunity which a bolder man than General Smuts might have seized. On September 8 the Prime Minister introduced the motion for the ratification of the Peace Treaty with Germany, and there followed an animated discussion, protracted in duration, in the course of which it was conceded by Mr. F. W. Beyers, on behalf of the Nationalist party, that the reply given by Mr. Lloyd George had killed the movement for the separate grant of independence to the Transvaal and the Orange Free State, though the movement for independence would now proceed, taking as its aim the independence of the Union as a whole. General Smuts insisted that as a result of the new status of the Dominions the Parliament of the United Kingdom had no right to legislate for the Union ; and that the royal veto was obsolete with regard to Dominion legislation. To the last doctrine, however, he made one exception of the highest importance, in the case of a law proposing the secession of the Union from the British Empire ; such a law must be refused the royal assent, as the Crown could not divorce itself from the Union. The question was pressed later on by the Nationalists, because Mr. Bonar Law and others, in discussing Dominion status as applicable to Ireland, had asserted that it implied the right of secession, and the argument of the Prime

Minister obviously conflicted [1] with the views of British ministers, but General Smuts declined to surrender his doctrine; the Union could secede, but only by a revolution, and not, as his adversaries suggested, by the placid means of an Act of the Legislature, passed by a majority of Dutch representatives, severing the Union. He also turned the tables on Mr. Hertzog by asking him pointblank if he meant that ' it was the decided policy of the party to work for the secession of the Union from the Empire '. The demand staggered Mr. Hertzog, who asserted that his was a democratic party, and that it would be bound by the decisions of its Congress, but that Congress had not yet determined the issue. Later he recovered his more usual attitude of assuredness of his aims, and made it clear that he and his friends must adhere to their ideal of independence, though it was an open issue to what extent the claim was at once to be pressed. The sentiment of the Assembly was shown clearly enough by its approval of the ratification by 84 votes to 19, and the Senate by concurring in the vote by 30 to 5.

On September 17 the Prime Minister made, at the close of the session of Parliament, a striking demand for national unity. ' Peace ', he said, ' marks a great moment in our history; it is time to make a new beginning in a greater, wider, more solemn South African spirit.' To this end he enunciated the acceptance of three principles as essential: the agreement to abide by the British connexion; the principle of frank, honest, whole-hearted co-operation between the white races; and the necessity of industrial development. He suggested that on the basis of these principles there could be effective co-operation by all the parties to the common end. Sir T. Smartt welcomed the proposal from the Unionist point of view, and it was favourably received by Mr. Creswell for Labour, but the latter made it clear that he did not understand it as meaning coalition. Speaking at Cape Town on September 20 Mr. Hertzog interpreted the suggestion as meaning that the Nationalists must lay aside the ideal of ultimate independence, and, if that were the case, they could not accept

[1] The difference was largely formal; the British utterances contemplated the secession of a United Dominion, General Smuts the desire of a bare majority to secede; see above Chap. VII, § 2.

the proposal, though he hinted that the answer might have been other, if it were merely a question of dropping in the meantime the Republican propaganda. On October 3 the Nationalist Congress at Cape Town laid down that the existing relationship between the United Kingdom and the Union of South Africa was recognized, but ' the ultimate aim of the people of the Union must be full freedom and sovereign independence. The party therefore declares itself opposed to any policy of closing the door against attaining this aim '. At the Nationalist Congress of the Free State at Bloemfontein on October 16 the same resolution was adopted, but all reference was omitted to recognition of the existing position of the Union. Mr. Hertzog insisted that the choice before them was independence or declining to the status of a Crown colony. The time was not yet ripe for active steps to achieve independence, but they had the right to work until they could say ' The time has now arrived '. If the British Parliament passed an Act declaring the United Kingdom a republic, the King would be obliged to assent to it ; so, if the Union Parliament enacted such an Act, the United Kingdom would have no right to refuse assent. He recognized, but did not shrink from, the possibility of civil war. If the minority would not accept the decision of the majority to attain independence, the responsibility would be theirs. The Union constitution was nothing but a scrap of paper, declaring how the people of the Union desired to be governed ; as soon as the nation's will changed it was for the Government, Parliament, and the King to alter the scrap of paper accordingly. His views found full acceptance by the Congress which, beside asserting the right of the Free State to independence, suggested as a concrete step the withdrawal of the small naval subsidy [1] paid by the Union as a relic of the engagements of the Cape and Natal in pre-Union days.

It was not surprising if, at the Unionist Congress at Bloemfontein on October 21, Sir Thomas Smartt attacked the doctrine of a ' scrap of paper ' when applied to the Union Act, and reminded South Africa of the assurances of good faith then lavished by the Dutch leaders who now supported Nationalism. For his party he offered to consider any proposal by the Government for

---

[1] Keith, *Responsible Government in the Dominions*, iii. 1473.

the amalgamation of the parties, provided the principles of the Unionists were not compromised. General Smuts's reply, however, was not encouraging ; speaking at the Pretoria Congress of the South African party on October 30, he assured the Unionists that he did not meditate absorption of one party by another, but merely co-operation towards peace, and mining and agricultural development. A further speech by the Prime Minister at Bloemfontein in December caused dissatisfaction among Unionists, partly because of its insistence on the revolution which had occurred in the relations of the Union and the United Kingdom, partly because of the announcement of the intention to have a South African flag, and partly because of the intimation that khaki would not be the colour of the uniform of the Defence force, an allusion deemed derogatory to the services of the Union contingents during the war. A Reunion Commission endeavoured to find a bridge for the amalgamation of Nationalists and the South African party, the idea finding special favour in the Transvaal, where the South African party was unwilling to co-operate with the Unionists; but General Smuts remained firm in declining to meet delegates to discuss union, unless the Nationalists abandoned the secession movement and accepted the British connexion. On the other hand no acceptance was accorded by the Prime Minister to the suggestions of amalgamation which Sir T. Smartt made.

The result was that the elections of March 10, 1920, were fought by all the parties without any coalition. The event told heavily both on the Unionists, who secured but 25 seats, and on the South African party, which dwindled to 40 ; the Nationalists won outright 43 ; in one constituency the Nationalist candidate died, and in a second some votes were miscounted, and the South African party candidate who won the seat resigned it rather than take advantage of a technical victory ; Labour secured 21 seats and 3 went to Independents. The losses of the South African party, severe as they were, could hardly be considered abnormal, when it is borne in mind how much loyalty to General Botha weighed with Dutch voters ; the losses of the Unionists to Labour were perhaps less fully foreseen, and revealed the growing strength of the advanced labour element in the country. The

Prime Minister, despite the fact that he had no majority, decided that it was proper to remain in office, and on March 19 presented to the Assembly an elaborate programme of reform legislation. It included measures to meet high prices and profiteering, rack-renting, and the shortage of housing; it promised important native legislation, and laws on banking and currency. It included large measures of constructive development regarding railways, land, and irrigation, and the application to South African industries of the principles of the ' Whitley Council ' system and the enactment of measures regarding fair wages and hours. Issue was soon joined by the Nationalists over the question of the repatriation of enemy aliens and naturalized British subjects, who wished to leave the Union or whose deportation was recommended on grounds of public interest by a special commission, and the Bill could only be read a second time after the closure had been carried by 62 votes to 20. General Smuts in the meantime pursued his efforts at securing a *modus vivendi* in a Government representing all the parties ; Labour declined to co-operate, and the Nationalists offered conditions involving the exclusion of any other parties save the Nationalists and the South African party from office, a proposal which the Prime Minister rejected as involving the revival of racial strife, while the Nationalists insisted that co-operation in a Cabinet was impossible, since so many differences of opinion between the Unionists and the Nationalists existed on leading questions of practical politics. The Prime Minister, however, declined to accept the position as hopeless and reasserted his intention to work towards a union in government.

The Prime Minister's skill in leadership was vindicated by his remarkable success during the Parliamentary session, when he was faced by the desire of the Nationalists to secure the defeat of the Government on some vital measure by securing the withdrawal of Labour support. This was nearly accomplished on April 21 on the Profiteering Bill, which was not drastic enough to meet Labour views and which Labour desired to refuse a second reading. The Nationalists adopted the course of proposing reference to a Select Committee before second reading, while the Government was pledged to demand the second reading ; Labour prudently withdrew from the debate, leaving the second reading to be carried by 62 votes to 42, and no serious reverse of the Government took place during the rest of the session, which closed on August 17. Most important legislation was passed as to profiteering, rent speculation and housing, currency and banking, and native affairs, showing the possibilities of effective co-operation without needless party disputes. On August 16 General Smuts redefined his position towards the proposals for the reunion of his party and the Nationalists, declaring that no reunion could be accepted which excluded the English-speaking population of South Africa from co-operation, or which did not abandon Republicanism and accept the British connexion and the Union Act. The Nationalist leader observed throughout the session a studiously moderate attitude.

On August 31 the final results of the Transvaal Provincial elections showed 10 South African party returned against 21 Nationalists, while the Assembly elections showed 19 to 12. The value of these figures is uncertain ; provincial issues doubtless affected the voting, and they do not prove that the tide of Republicanism is rising.

The verdict of the Transvaal, however, appears to have strengthened Mr. Hertzog in his policy, and at the Free State Nationalist Congress at Cape Town in October, held after an effort to unite the South African and Nationalist parties had again ended in failure, a definitely Republican platform was adopted. On October 22 the Congress agreed to accept the following principles on the basis of their fundamental doctrine of ' South Africa First ' :

(1) The Nationalists acknowledge and will safeguard the sovereign will of the people of the Union. (2) The Nationalists acknowledge the right of the people of the Union to self-determination. (3) The Nationalists acknowledge the right of the people of the Union to secede from Great Britain and break any existing bond between the Union and Great Britain. (4) The Nationalists declare against and will oppose any attempt at a closer Imperial union. With regard to Republican propaganda the Congress is of opinion that no one may be hindered or prevented from a free expression of his convictions concerning the advisability of one form or other of government for the country. The Republicans

will not attempt to realize that ideal in any but a constitutional way. This Congress considers that no decisive step with regard to secession should be taken unless a majority of the people legally entitled to vote declare, by means of a referendum or otherwise, in favour of secession.

Mr. Hertzog, in defining his proposals, stated that the Nationalists did not necessarily mean to break away from the Empire, but they wished to emphasize their right to secede ; in any event the right was not that of his party, but of the South African nation. It is, however, important to note that the resolution contemplates that the matter might be decided by the mere will of the majority of the two Houses of Parliament, and does not require a referendum as the basis of action, though it is framed in such a manner as to suggest that this procedure should be adopted. Further, and the importance of this fact cannot be overlooked, the people to decide are the electors, to the exclusion therefore of the vast majority of the native population and of the British Indians, who form an important element of the people of Natal. The assumption that the electors can determine without consultation with the natives their future allegiance is signally dishonest.

The resolution had the merit of bringing to a head the decision of the Prime Minister on September 29 to cease the search for reconciliation with the Nationalists and to form a new party which should be strong enough to safeguard the permanent interests of the Union against the disruptive and destructive policy of the Nationalists, and the meeting of the South African party at Bloemfontein on October 27 was planned as the first step towards this end. General Smuts insisted in his address to the Congress that the Nationalists had become a purely Republican party bent on secession, and, while they talked of acting constitutionally, their ideas of what was constitutional were very elastic, nor could the constancy of their restriction of means be relied upon. He reminded his audience of the aims of General Botha and Messrs. Steyn and Hertzog when the Union was formed ; there had been no interference with the Union by Great Britain, and South Africa had, with the aid of the Imperial Government, attained a higher status, which would be lost by secession, quite apart from the separation of the white races on such an issue. A house divided against itself could not stand. There must be a strong non-racial party to guide South Africa through the dangers threatened, on the one hand, by a strong party working deliberately for political revolution, and, on the other, a smaller but growing party working for social and economic revolution, behind whom was the spectre of Bolshevism, which made even Labourites nervous. The natives, moreover, observing the divisions of European feeling, were beginning to talk of their South African Republic. He therefore proposed that the principle should be adopted, not of disbanding the party, but of extending it by the admission of all moderate men. He prophesied that even among the Nationalists there were many moderates who would join, and this view was corroborated by Professor Freemantle, up to then a strong supporter of the Nationalists, who stated that thousands of Nationalists who desired to respect both sections of the population, and maintain complete freedom without secession, and to build up a great nation, extended the hand of friendship to the South African party.

The resolution accepted by the South African party was open to one criticism; it called upon the Unionists to abandon their party designation in joining forces with the South African party, but, on the other hand, the South African party freely recognized the necessity of finding ministerial office for the Unionist leaders. The Unionist response to the appeal to form an effective barrier against Republican and Socialist propaganda was vindicated by a majority of 22 at the election of February 1921.

5. NEWFOUNDLAND

At the election of 1913 Sir Edward Morris was returned to power in Newfoundland, but the majority which he had possessed since his victory over Sir Robert Bond was severely shaken by a coalition of the regular Opposition with a newly created Fishermen's party under Mr. Coaker. The combined Opposition, indeed, succeeded in polling more votes than did the Government, but were seven seats short of its total. The advent of war, however, banished serious party contention, and the Opposition lent their full aid in the measures devised by the Dominion to send a regiment to the front and to maintain it there. It was not until 1917 that the need for formal change in the relations of the parties became evident. The election would normally have fallen due in October, and all parties desired to avoid it. On the other hand the Opposition were determined not to forgo an election unless given a share in the actual administration. A new Ministry was accordingly formed on July 17, 1917; the Cabinet was enlarged to twelve Ministers by the retirement of three of the normal nine and the addition of six representatives of the Opposition; the leader of that party, Mr. Lloyd, accepted the office of Minister of Justice. The arrangement, however, was only temporary; at the beginning of January Sir E. Morris retired, in order to prevent the outbreak of party strife, and on January 5, 1918, a new Ministry was formed, reduced to the normal nine members, under the Premiership of Mr. Lloyd. The general election, which, in 1917, had been avoided by the extension by agreement of the term of the Legislature for a year, was postponed a second time, and the Legislature passed a measure for compulsory service, found necessary to maintain the flow of recruits for the oversea force. The National Government, as thus reconstructed, remained in office until May 20, 1919, when the Minister of Finance, Sir M. Cashin, resigned office; as he had the support of the major portion of the supporters of the Government in the Assembly, Sir W. Lloyd placed his resignation in the Governor's hands. Sir M. Cashin, who then formed a Ministry, was not destined to have a long term of office; at the general election on November 2, which developed into a struggle on purely religious divisions, the Government suffered a severe defeat, and Mr. R. A. Squires became Prime Minister. The struggle had been peculiarly animated, and there were the usual allegations of electoral irregularities, but in one case, that of Mr. Woodford, who had been a Minister under Sir M. Cashin, the sequel was unusual. Challenged by an election petition he resigned his seat, but the Court before which the petition had been brought insisted on affidavits showing if there had been collusion. Mr. Woodford then deposed to an unlawful agreement made between himself, Mr. Squires, and a member of the Legislative Council, an offer of a governmental post having been made to him. Considerable excitement was caused locally by this allegation, but reliance was placed on the use by the Governor of his position, and his discretion in a case of emergency to secure that the allegations should be properly dealt with. Accordingly on June 29 it was announced in the Assembly by Mr. W. Warren, Minister of Justice, that the Governor had appointed a Commission, consisting of two judges of the Supreme Court and a member of the Legislative Council, to investigate the charges brought by Mr. Woodford.

The strangeness of the episode is not, however, without parallel in Newfoundland, the scanty population of which prevents the full development of the institutions of self-government. In 1917 a strong sensation was caused in the Dominion when a statement by Sir W. D. Reid, long head of the Reid-Newfoundland Company, made in a letter to Sir T. Shaughnessy of Canada, became public, as it asserted that he had financed the general elections of 1908, 1909, and 1913, had worked in conjunction with Sir T. Shaughnessy to promote the union of Newfoundland and Canada, had brought about the retirement of Mr. A. B. Morine from politics to smooth the way for the coalition of Sir. E. Morris's Government with the Opposition under Messrs. Lloyd and Coaker, and had arranged for the latter, as President of the Fishermen's Union, to tour through the United States and Canada in 1917 in order to study the possibility of federation. A prosecution at the instance of Mr. Coaker ensued, and the other parties concerned denied the charges made, but on April 1 a grand jury refused to allow the case to proceed. The episode, however, is of interest as a record of the deep anxiety of a section of the leading men of Newfoundland and Canada to complete the destiny of the Dominion by the incorporation within it of Newfoundland, as was contemplated by the British North America Act. The prospect was not formerly attractive to the Canadian Government, which feared the embarrassments resulting from the French and United States' fishing rights in Newfoundland waters, but since the treaty of 1904 reduced to moderate limits French privileges, and the Atlantic Fisheries arbitration of 1910 gave a binding interpretation of the United States' rights, the way is paved for the inclusion of Newfoundland in Canada, if and when the people of Newfoundland so desire. In the period 1918–20, however, the issue was not prominent in public life, and on November 11, 1920, a final agreement was come to to expedite the decision by the Privy Council of the disputed question of the boundary between Newfoundland and Canada on the mainland of Labrador.

Less important, but perhaps not less unprecedented, was the procedure on the ejection of Sir W. Lloyd from office. When Sir M. Cashin rose to move that 'the Government as now constituted does not possess the confidence of the members of this House', the Premier rose to explain the circumstances in which the resignation of Sir M. Cashin had taken place, but was reminded by the Speaker that his explanation was out of order, as the motion had not been seconded. The Premier resumed his seat, but, as the House continued to sit in silence, after a brief interval rose again and formally seconded the motion, which then passed without a vote, the Leader of the Opposition declaring himself in favour of it. The task of forming the new Ministry was then given by the Governor to Sir M. Cashin, and not to the Leader of the Opposition, on the ground that the motion on which the Government was declared not to have the confidence of the House was proposed by the former.[1]

[1] In *Commercial Cable Co.* v. *Government of Newfoundland*, [1916] 2 A. C. 610, the Privy Council asserted the inability of the Government to bind the Dominion by a contract made without the approval of the House of Assembly.

CHAPTER X

CONSTITUTIONAL DEVELOPMENTS IN THE DOMINIONS

1. THE CONSTITUTIONAL POSITION OF THE GOVERNOR.
Obsolescence of discretionary power — Recall of Governor of New South Wales — Advantages of new status — Difficulty in case of nominee upper houses : swamping of Queensland Council in 1920 — Proposed local appointment of Governors — Royal princes as Governors.

2. THE DISUSE OF THE POWER OF DISALLOWANCE.
Obsolescence of the veto — Refusal to disallow Queensland Acts in 1920 — Possibility of arbitration in disputes between Dominion and Imperial Governments.

3. TERRITORIAL LIMITATIONS ON THE POWERS OF DOMINION LEGISLATURES.
New Zealand legislation for Samoa — Union legislation for South-West Africa — Canadian application for extended powers.

4. RESTRICTIONS ON THE LEGISLATIVE AUTHORITY OF THE IMPERIAL PARLIAMENT.
Views of General Smuts — Peculiar case of Canadian constitution — Indemnity Act, 1920.

5. THE POWERS OF THE LEGISLATURES.
Validity of defence legislation — Extension of duration of Parliaments.

6. THE FRANCHISE AND REPRESENTATION.
Female suffrage — Disabilities on former enemy subjects — Changes in representation.

7. TITLES OF HONOUR.
Responsibility for grant of honours in Dominions — Canadian disapproval of hereditary honours — Representations to Imperial Government.

8. APPEALS TO THE PRIVY COUNCIL.
Growing objections in Dominions to appeals — Mr. Hughes's suggestion of an Imperial Court of Appeal — Arguments for and against appeals.

1. THE CONSTITUTIONAL POSITION OF THE GOVERNOR

PRIOR to the war, though there had been in operation a tendency to assimilate the constitutional position of the Governors-General and Governors of the Dominions and States to that of the King in the United Kingdom, the process was far from complete. While it had become an essential part of the theory of the British constitution that the King could perform no political action save on the authority of a Minister, it was still open to a Governor to form conclusions contrary to those of his Ministry, and to offer them the alternatives of deference to his wishes or resignation.[1] The Governor could not, of course, carry on the business of the state save through Ministers, and if he forced a Cabinet to resign he must be prepared to secure other Ministers who would work with him, and who would defend in Parliament his action, accepting *ex post facto* full responsibility for it. Occasions on which a Governor could risk the resignation of a Ministry were naturally rare, but a request for a dissolution on a reverse in the lower house of the Legislature almost invariably entailed upon the Governor the obligation of arriving at a decision on his own responsibility. Public opinion demanded this exercise of an independent judgement on his part, with the inevitable result that Premiers who might have hesitated to advise a dissolution, had the ultimate responsibility for action rested upon them, as it would have done in the United Kingdom, were ready enough to make requests which it would have been wrong to grant.

It was natural to expect that the outbreak of war would enhance the independence and importance of the position of the Governors-General[2] and Governors as direct representatives of the Imperial Government and the channel of communications of the highest importance. Events, however, proved that this anticipation was founded on false assumptions. Considerations of speed and efficiency led to the adoption of direct communication between the naval and military authorities of the Dominions and the British Admiralty and War Office, and, though political correspondence continued to pass through the Governors-General, in the last year of hostilities their function in this regard was diminished in importance by the decision of the Imperial War Cabinet[3] of 1918 that communications on matters of Cabinet importance might pass direct between the Premiers of the Dominions and the Prime Minister of the United Kingdom. The decision was one of considerable constitutional importance, for the Imperial Government at the Imperial Conference of 1911 had

---

[1] Keith, *Responsible Government in the Dominions*, iii. 1627, 1628 ; *Journal of Society of Comparative Legislation*, xvii. 227–32. The normal rule of ministerial responsibility is laid down in *Theodore* v. *Duncan*, [1919] A. C. 696, 706, per Lord Haldane ; *A. G. for N. S. W.* v. *Williams*, [1915] A. C. 573, 580, 581, per Lord Fletcher Moulton. See above, p. 179.

[2] The Governor of New Zealand was granted the style of Governor-General by Letters Patent of May 11, 1917. [3] See above, Chap. III, § 1.

remained firm to the doctrine that the normal channel of communication between the United Kingdom and the Dominions must be the Governor-General, whose duty it was to use his personal influence with Ministers in any matter on which the Imperial Government sought their co-operation. The alteration of practice is a definite intimation that the functions of a Governor-General are to suffer material change. In the past he has combined the duties of an ambassador from the Imperial Government and the constitutional head of the administration ; in future other methods of disposing of matters in which the Imperial and the Dominion Governments have common interests are to be adopted, and the Governor-General will be restricted to the performance of those duties which belong to the head of the state.

The process of evolution was practically inevitable, as soon as the war had created topics of immediate and burning interest to both the Imperial and the Dominion Governments. As in the case of relations between the Allied Powers in Europe direct communications between responsible Ministers were found more efficacious than correspondence through ambassadors, so, in the case of the Dominions, Ministers who were undertaking the responsibility of co-operation in a great war felt pressing need to come into immediate contact with one another. The personalities of the Governors-General lent themselves to a change which was in itself unavoidable. The Governors-General of the Commonwealth and of New Zealand, Sir Ronald Munro-Ferguson and the Earl of Liverpool, were content to second the patriotic efforts of their Premiers ; in South Africa Viscount Buxton had as his chief advisers two men of the outstanding position of Generals Botha and Smuts, while in Canada the Duke of Connaught, as a prince of the blood royal, was precluded from any action which might seem to suggest any desire to impose his personality on his Ministers. Occasions, indeed, presented themselves in the progress of events, both in Canada and in the Commonwealth, when a Governor-General of the ardent spirit of Earl Grey might have sought by his personal action to influence the course of events, and occasional suggestions were made by critics of Governments that the representative of the Crown was permitting the usurpation of the functions of his office. But the self-effacement of the

Governors-General was generally approved, and reflection confirms the wisdom of their action. Nothing was more essential than the avoidance of any suggestion that pressure was being exercised on the Dominion Governments by the Imperial Government, and the rigid abstention of the Governors-General from any action not based on ministerial advice rendered it impossible to bring any effective charge against the United Kingdom of interference in Dominion politics. At the same time the full confidence which existed between Ministers and the representatives of the Crown enabled the latter to fulfil with exceptional success the unusually heavy burden of duties which the war entailed.

It was not unnatural, however, that the public should have misunderstood the position, and that, when the news of the decision of the Imperial War Cabinet as to the mode of conducting correspondence was announced in the Dominions, the suggestion should have been made that the time had come for the appointment of Governors-General to cease as a needless and expensive office, which had ceased to fulfil any useful function when it was possible for the Prime Ministers of the Dominions to enter into effective communication with the Prime Minister of the United Kingdom. It is doubtful whether those who adopted this point of view had given any serious consideration to the issues involved or in what manner they conceived the place vacated by a nominee of the Crown should be filled. The appointment of the Chief Justice or other official to discharge the formal functions of the Governor-General was mooted in some quarters, and no doubt it would not surpass reasonable ingenuity to devise a system which would work adequately enough. But the suggestions made ignored the function of the Governor-General of acting as a visible and dignified embodiment of the royal authority which forms the one assured bond of connexion between the United Kingdom and the autonomous Dominions, and as a constant reminder of the unity which still is present in the Empire.

The only derogation which took place in the Dominions during the war from the strict following of ministerial advice by the Governors-General arose from the fact that the Crown possesses war prerogatives which extend, as has been seen, over all the Dominions, and had not been delegated to Dominion Governments in the period before the war. Instances of such prerogatives are such cases as the right to requisition neutral merchant vessels in British harbours, which as a right arising out of a state of war could be exercised only by a Governor-General under specific delegation from the Crown and did not pass to him as a matter of course with the normal delegation of the royal prerogative in respect of the Government of the Dominion contained in the Constitution Acts and the Letters Patent constituting the office of Governor-General in each Dominion.[1] Again, the prerogative of mercy, which is delegated to each Governor-General, applies, properly speaking, to offences against the Dominion laws, and not to such an offence as trading with the enemy under the common law of the Empire. In such instances the question arose whether the power should be exercised on the advice of the Dominion Ministry or on the advice of the Imperial Government ; [2] the strict principle would have been the adoption of the latter view, which had the obvious advantage of securing uniformity of action, but this attitude, if pressed, would have resulted in undesirable friction with Ministries.

Even in the case of the States of Australia, although their Governments were less directly affected by the war, circumstances told in favour of the aggrandizement of the powers of the Ministry at the expense of the independence of the Governors. In 1916 [3] there arose in New South Wales a divergence of opinion between the Governor, Sir Gerald Strickland, who had exceptional experience in that capacity, and the Premier, Mr. Holman. Owing to an alteration in the grouping of parties, as an outcome of the controversy on conscription which, illogically enough, had been imported into the politics of the State, though the matter was one which under the Constitution concerns the Commonwealth, Mr. Holman's Government was unable for the time being to command a majority in the lower house on a question of confidence. Negotiations for a readjustment of parties were in progress when

[1] Keith, *Responsible Government in the Dominions*, i. 105. The wide extent of the prerogative is illustrated by *Bonanza Creek Gold Mining Co.* v. *The King*, [1916] A. C. 566, according to which it includes the right to grant charters of incorporation. Cf. *A.G. for N.S.W.* v. *Williams*, [1915] A.C. 573 ; 16 C.L.R. 404.

[2] Sir R. Borden in *Parl. Pap.* Cd. 8566, p. 59. Cf. [1915] A. C. 580, 581.

[3] See *The Sydney Morning Herald*, November 13, 1916.

the Governor, interpreting the position as indicating that neither in Parliament nor in the country was Mr. Holman in command of a majority, signified to the Premier his inability to regard him as possessing the right to his unqualified support. The issue was complicated by the fact that Mr. Holman's Government were anxious to secure the assent of the Governor to a Bill extending the life of Parliament, and the Governor was doubtful both as to his legal power to accord assent to so grave a change in the constitution of the State, and as to the propriety of sanctioning the proposal in the face of the opposition of the Labour party in Parliament and in the country, which contended, with much show of reason, that the result of a general election at that juncture would be to secure its return to power in lieu of Mr. Holman's party. The intervention of the Governor was in one sense decidedly opportune ; Mr. Holman hastened to come to terms with the supporters of Mr. Wade, and so recovered a majority in the lower house. But, though the action of the Governor was amply justified by precedent and by its result in composing differences which were paralysing the activities of the State, Mr. Holman resented his intervention, and the Secretary of State for the Colonies, yielding to his representations, recalled the Governor, after authorizing him to assent to the Bill for the extension of the life of Parliament. The action of the Secretary of State not un-naturally met with severe criticism from Labour in New South Wales, and it was alleged that the intervention of the Imperial Government had been motived by the desire to further Mr. Hughes's efforts to secure conscription in the Commonwealth by co-opera-tion with Mr. Holman.

Disregarding, as is right, these controversial amenities, it may fairly be deduced from the episode that the Governor who acts on his own responsibility cannot expect, if his action involves him in controversy, support from the Imperial Government, and that accordingly he should adopt in his conduct the rules by which the King is guided in his relation to his Ministers in the United Kingdom. The advantages of the position are plain. Independent action on the part of a Governor inevitably bears the appearance of interference by the Imperial Government in the affairs of the State or Dominion, although in point of fact the Governor has acted on his personal responsibility. Moreover, the possibility of such action on the part of the Governor is a real barrier to full confidence between the Ministry and the representative of the Crown ; Ministers fear to display their weaknesses, in case knowledge of them may embolden the Governor to decline on some issue to accept their advice as binding. The possibility of the Governor's refusal to act on advice weakens dangerously the sense of ministerial responsibility, and encourages them to prefer requests which they themselves could not justify if they were bound to take full responsibility for them. Nor is it compatible with the ideal of the equality of status between the Dominions and the United Kingdom asserted at the Imperial War Conference of 1917, that a Ministry which represents the choice of Parliament and the constituencies should be subject to control in their action by a nominee of the Imperial Government, even though his action is taken on his own initiative.

Yet the abandonment of the discretionary use of the authority of the Governor is obviously not without difficulty so long as public opinion has not accepted definitely the position that its use is undesirable. The political education of the Parliaments of the greater Dominions is more complete than that of the Parliaments of the States or of Newfoundland, and a convention which is established regarding the Governments of Canada, the Commonwealth, New Zealand, and the Union of South Africa may be more tardy in acceptance in other cases. As late as 1918 the Premier of Victoria unsuccessfully asked the Governor, the Hon. Sir Arthur Stanley, for a dissolution of Parliament which the latter could not have accorded without inflicting needless loss of time and expense on the people of the State. In the small community of Newfoundland the general election consequent on the close of the war resulted in the bringing against the leaders of the victorious party of charges of conduct which would have rendered them unworthy of the confidence of the Governor, upon whom accordingly devolved the duty of arranging with his advisers the appointment of a Commission to investigate the allegations made. Incidents of this type are, however, rare and a mere indication of an imperfect political development whose passage is but a matter of time. A curious example of the refusal of advice by an acting Governor is the refusal of Sir J. Pope Cooper in August 1920 to appoint Mr. W. Lennon a member of the Legislative Council of Queensland as a protest against that gentleman's action as Lieutenant-Governor in swamping the upper house. In the sequel Mr. Lennon, on reassuming his functions as acting Governor, from which he had been temporarily incapacitated by illness, was advised to appoint, and did appoint, himself to the Council.[1]

The adoption of the Imperial rule in these matters must not, however, be misunderstood as implying the total surrender of discretion on the part of the Governor-General or Governor. Even in the United Kingdom in certain cases the right of independent judgement on the part of the Crown is admitted to exist. Of these the only clear case is the right of the Crown to choose the person who is to receive a commission to form an administration, when, by the resignation or death of the Prime Minister, that office is vacated. Curiously enough, in the Dominions, while the discretion of the Governor in other matters has remained wider than in the United Kingdom, in this respect it has been less freely exercised in the Dominions. The practice has there been followed in many cases that the outgoing Premier should advise the choice of his successor, though according to every logical principle the fact of his resignation deprives him of any right to advise an action subsequent to it. Remarkable instances of this usage were seen in the Commonwealth in regard to the formation of Mr. Hughes's administrations in November 1916 and in January 1918. On both occasions the Prime Minister, on resigning his position in the Governments immediately preceding, advised the Governor-General to recommission him to form a Ministry, and the Governor-General acted on this advice. Yet it is clear that on the British usage the outgoing Premier would normally not even have been asked to suggest a successor, and in no case would have tendered advice. In Ontario, also, on the announcement of the result of the general election of 1919, which resulted in the Government party, the Conservatives, having only 25 members to 29 Liberals and 45 of the United Farmers' party, a strong claim was made by the leader of the Liberal party that he should,

[1] *The Times*, August 21, 1920.

as a matter of course, be called upon to form a Government in his capacity as the leader of the larger of the two established parties, since it was quite possible that, if commissioned, he might be able to arrange for the carrying on of the Government. The Lieutenant-Governor, however, repelled this contention, declared his un-fettered right of action, and chose Mr. Drury, the most prominent among the representatives of the farming interests. A similar discretion was exercised by the Governor of New South Wales, when the election of 1920 resulted in almost a tie.

The other case in which personal action may still be possible is in the event of a Prime Minister defying the Constitution with the aid of a majority in the Legislature. The possibility of such a case cannot be denied,[1] but it is obvious that nothing but grave necessity would justify any departure from the rule of the Crown acting on ministerial advice in the United Kingdom, and that the same principle should be applied in the Dominions.

In two cases, however, the relaxation of the authority of the Governor creates a problem of constitutional interest. The Legislative Councils of New South Wales and of Queensland, whose constitution follows the old colonial model, are nominee bodies, the right of nomination being exercised by the Governor on behalf of the Crown.[2] Hitherto it has been possible for the Governor to protect in some measure the authority of the upper house as a legislative body by declining to add members to it at the pleasure of Ministers. Thus in 1907 Lord Chelmsford refused to accept the advice of Mr. Kidston as Premier to put pressure in this manner on the Legislative Council of Queensland, and, though the Ministry of Mr. Philp, which took office on Mr. Kidston's resignation of office in consequence of the Governor's refusal, was badly defeated at the ensuing general election, Mr. Kidston on his return to power recognized the disadvantages of ' swamping ' as a mode of procedure. An Act was therefore passed in 1908

[1] Several regrettable cases of ministerial corruption were revealed in the Canadian provinces during the war, especially in New Brunswick and Manitoba ; serious charges were made in 1917 against Mr. Rogers, Dominion Minister of Public Works, who soon after resigned office. In 1920 severe strictures were passed on the late Minister of Lands in Ontario by a judicial Commission.

[2] Keith, *Responsible Government in the Dominions*, i. 559 ff ; *Imperial Unity* pp. 398–401.

providing for the reference to the electors of Bills twice in successive sessions rejected by the upper house or amended in a manner unsatisfactory to the Legislative Assembly. In New South Wales, however, nothing had been done by the outbreak of war to secure the position of the upper house. The advent to power under war conditions of Labour Governments in either State produced strained relations between the two houses, and in New South Wales and Queensland alike the Labour parties pronounced themselves in favour of the abolition of the upper houses. In New South Wales large concessions by the upper house, influenced by a desire to avoid its overthrow as an independent branch of the Legislature, averted the menace of open swamping, but Queensland was not so fortunate in the issue. In 1917 the Labour party, acting in strict accordance with the Act of 1908, secured the reference to the electorate of a Bill for the abolition of the Legislative Council, with the unexpected and unwelcome result that a decisive majority of 63,000 votes pronounced in favour of the retention of the upper house. No further attempt to raise the issue was made during Mr. Ryan's Premiership, but on his resignation in order to engage in Federal politics, his successor, Mr. Theodore, induced the Governor of the State, Sir J. Hamilton Goold-Adams, to secure the appointment as Lieutenant-Governor of the State of Mr. W. Lennon, a member of the Labour party, who, after holding office in the Ministry, had for a brief period been Speaker of the Assembly. The selection for this office, important in that on the departure of the Governor from the State the administration of the Government devolved on its holder, of a political partisan was unprecedented, the normal rule being to appoint the Chief Justice of the State or the President of the Legislative Council, and the action of the Secretary of State for the Colonies, with whom rested the responsibility for the approval of the nomination, must have been actuated, in accepting the proposal, by the view that it was no part of his duties to investigate the motives for the Ministry's action. The aim of the appointment was seen in February 1920, when a Lands Act Amendment Bill, which had been previously rejected by the Legislative Council on the ground that its provisions were a repudiation of contracts entered into by the Government of Queensland, was reintroduced in the Council, after a rapid passage through the Legislative Assembly. On February 10 the Opposition having notified its intention of rejecting the Bill on the second reading, the debate was adjourned until the following day, when the Secretary for Mines intimated that, as the motion for the adjournment on the preceding day had been carried against the Government, he did not propose to force another division on the subject. On February 19, however, the motion for the second reading of the Bill was unexpectedly revived, fourteen new members having been added in the meantime to the Council by Mr. Lennon, whom the absence of the Governor had left in charge of the administration of the Government, on the advice of Mr. Theodore. The measure then passed through its remaining stages without amendment, and Mr. Lennon assented to it in the name of the Crown on March 9.

The action of the acting Governor was clearly unconstitutional,[1] for the Act of 1908 had indicated the proper method of solving differences of view between the two houses, and the people of Queensland had indicated in unmistakable terms in 1917 their desire that the upper house should continue to function as an integral and independent part of the Legislature. If the upper house is swamped to suit the purpose of one political party, it is obvious that when the Opposition obtain power there will be put forward a claim for the further swamping of the Council in order to undo the mischief of the past, and that no just ground can be adduced for refusing such a claim. The inevitable conclusion is that, as in the United Kingdom by common consent [2] the time has come when the constitution of the House of Lords must be revised and its relations to the lower house redefined, so in the case of the two States the time has come when the principle of nomination must give way to that of election. This has been recognized in the case of New Zealand where, by an Act of 1914, provision is made for the substitution of election for nomination as the method of constituting the Council, and rules are laid down as to the relations which are to subsist between the two houses. This measure, whose operation was postponed during the war by

[1] Keith, *The Times*, May 27, June 2 and 9, 1920 ; *contra*, Mr. Theodore, May 28, June 4, 1920.　　　　[2] *Parl. Pap.* Cd. 9038.

Acts of 1916 and 1918, was by a proclamation of December 23, 1919, to be brought into operation with effect from January 31, 1921, but an Act of 1920 postponed the operation of the Act until a date fixed by proclamation.

In Newfoundland, also, the Council is nominee, but the power of swamping it does not reside with the Governor, as the action of the Crown on the advice of the Secretary of State is necessary for the making of new appointments. Accordingly, when in 1917 there was friction between the two houses of the Legislature on financial policy, the necessary addition of members to secure the Government a majority for their proposals in the upper house was carried out not by the Governor, but by the Crown on the initiative of the Newfoundland Government. The proposal of the Government was motived by reasons which were unanswerable ; it claimed that it was not legitimate to allow a nominee body to interpose difficulties in the way of the carrying out of the financial policy which had been resolved upon by the Government, and that the practice of the United Kingdom must be made applicable to the Dominion. When the necessary majority of the Government in the upper house had been secured, a second session of the Legislature was held in August 1917, at which the tax on all trade and business profits over 3,000 dollars, which the upper house had thrown out in the first session, was passed, and an Act carried under which the upper house may not interfere with or reject a Bill certified by the Speaker to be a money Bill.[1]

In Canada also the right to add on an emergency a number of Senators to solve a deadlock—the increase being limited to six until increased to eight, with effect from the next general election following the date of the Act, by Imperial legislation in 1915 [2]—is vested in the Crown, acting on the recommendation of the Governor-General, a provision which throws a direct responsibility on the Imperial Government. It may, however, be held that under the status of the Dominion, as now established, the power of the Crown would fall to be exercised automatically if the Governor-General recommended the adoption of the course, while it is clear that on the now recognized theory of that officer's

---

[1] Acts 1917, 2nd Session, cc. 1 and 2. Cf. Keith, *Responsible Government in the Dominions*, ii. 598, 599.   [2] 5 & 6 Geo. V, c. 45.

authority, he would be bound, whatever his personal opinion, to make the recommendation if it were desired by his Government. Happily, though the use of the power was under consideration during the first two years of the war when the Senate was still under the control of a Liberal majority, any serious necessity for its application did not arise, and when the general election of December 1917 took place, the Government were, under the Act of 1915, enabled to make fresh appointments to the Senate for the western provinces, which secured, with the filling of vacancies due to the death of Senators, a Conservative majority. The problem may be revived on the change of régime probable at the next election.

In the case of elective upper chambers the Governor-General or Governor is relieved from any personal responsibility of the kind involved with nominee chambers.

The reduction of the functions of the Governor-General or Governor to those of a constitutional sovereign raises a question which has been discussed with considerable vivacity in the Australian States. Is there, it is asked, any valid reason why the choice of the representative of the Crown should not be left to the State Government, whose selection would normally, if not always, fall upon a local man? The argument is supported by the practice of leaving the Lieutenant-Governors, often for considerable periods, to act in the absence of the Governors on leave of absence, or in the interregnum between the departure of one and the arrival of another Governor, and by considerations of economy as well as the analogy of the appointment of local men to the Lieutenant-Governorships of the Canadian Provinces. The analogy, however, is irrelevant, as, though local men are appointed, the selection lies with the Dominion and not the Provincial Government in each case, and the proposal chiefly favoured in the States is that the selection should lie with the local Government. The matter is one on which no agreement has yet been found possible,[1] and the attitude of the Imperial Government has also shown signs of uncertainty. When the Government of Victoria, on the retirement of Sir Arthur Stanley after a successful tenure of

[1] The Premier's Conference of May 1918 favoured retention of Imperial selection.

office, suggested that no successor from the United Kingdom should be sent out in his place, the reply of the Secretary of State seemed to indicate sympathy with the view, but in August 1920 an Imperial selection was announced. On the other hand, when in 1920, as the sequel of Mr. Lennon's action in swamping the Legislative Council of Queensland, a deputation representing pastoralist industries in the State proceeded to England to ask the Secretary of State to appoint without delay a Governor from the United Kingdom, and thus to remove Mr. Lennon from the office of acting Governor, the proposal met with acceptance, Sir Matthew Nathan being selected for the post. The decision of the Secretary of State elicited a strong protest from the acting Premier, Mr. Fihelly, who took exception,[1] not to the personality of the new Governor, but to the fact that the appointment had been made without the concurrence of the State Government. Logically, indeed, there is no answer to the argument that the choice of the Governor should rest primarily with the State Government, subject to the approval of the Crown, and the transition stage to this consummation already exists in the rule that, while the Imperial Government reserves the initiative in nomination, it will not press any appointment to which a Dominion or State Government offers objection, and it is prepared to consider, without binding itself to accept, suggestions as to suitable appointments from the Governments concerned.

The appointment of Prince Arthur of Connaught to succeed Viscount Buxton as Governor-General of the Union of South Africa is, indeed, sufficient proof that the rule that the holder of the office should be nominated by the Union Government, proposed by Dr. Malan, a leading Nationalist in the Union Parliament, is in large measure effectively in operation. The selection of a royal prince is plainly intended to emphazise the doctrine so ably expounded by General Smuts that the Governor-General should not be the representative in any sense of the British Government or the Colonial Office, but should be the representative of the King and nothing else. The same idea has underlain the suggestion, mooted from time to time, that the offices of Governor-General should regularly be assigned to

[1] *The Times*, July 17, 1920.

members of the royal family, but the proposal has met with little general acceptance, as is shown by the contemporaneous decision to appoint Lord Forster, formerly Financial Secretary to the War Office and a distinguished cricketer, to the Governor-Generalship of the Commonwealth.

2. THE DISUSE OF THE POWER OF DISALLOWANCE

A tendency parallel to the obsolescence of the right of the Governor to exercise a personal discretion is the practical surrender during the war by the Imperial Government of the right of disallowing the Acts passed by Dominion or State Governments. From the earliest days of the grant of responsible government to the colonies there had been in force the principle that Imperial interference with colonial enactments was to be restricted within the narrowest limits, and by the outbreak of the war interference with such enactments had become rare, though as late as 1911 the Imperial Government had refused to consent to the coming into operation of a New Zealand measure which aimed at excluding British Indians from employment on ships trading with the Dominion.[1] The war, however, increased indefinitely the difficulty of Imperial intervention ; the fact that the Dominions spontaneously lent all their power to aid the United Kingdom in the contest rendered the suggestion of overriding the decision of their legislatures unattractive in the highest degree, while the stress of war conditions was such as to justify any legislation which might commend itself to the judgement of the different legislatures.

The question whether the control which had been in abeyance during the war should be revived was brought to a definite issue by the passing in 1920 of two Acts by the Parliament of Queensland, both of which were open to the objection that they repudiated in some degree contractual arrangements entered into under the authority of earlier legislation. The more far-reaching of these measures, the Lands Act Amendment Act, repealed sections in the Land Act of 1910 which provided that, on periodic reappraisement by the Land Court of the rents of pastoral holdings and grazing selections held by tenants of the Crown, the rate of

[1] Keith, *Responsible Government in the Dominions*, ii. 1009 ff. ; *Imperial Unity*, pp. 143, 145, 590.

increase ordered by the Court must not exceed fifty per cent. of the former assessment. This provision was not unnaturally denounced by those affected as confiscatory, and stress was laid on the fact that the holders affected were assured of this limitation by an Act of 1905, and that this assurance had been deliberately renewed by a Parliament in which Labour had a controlling voice in 1910. The strongest protests were also made on behalf of British companies which had advanced large sums of money to pastoralists on the faith of the terms of their leases, and which were now confronted with a serious impairment of the value of the security on the faith of which their advances had been made. The Labour party, on its part, contended that the pastoralists were making an insufficient contribution to the revenue of the State, and that the needs of the development of Queensland justified the revision of earlier provisions. Prior to 1920 the resistance of the Legislative Council frustrated the efforts of Labour to secure the passing of the measure, but in that year, through the appointment of Mr. Lennon to administer the Government of the State, and his compliance with Mr. Theodore's request for the swamping of the Legislative Council, the Bill was forced through the Council, and received the royal assent. The action of the acting Governor in assenting was open to criticism, for under the Royal Instructions he was required to reserve for the consideration of the Imperial Government any Bill of an extraordinary nature and importance by which the rights and property of British subjects not resident in the State might be prejudiced, and the measure in question might fairly be held to fall under this category.

The other Bill which was passed into law by the same methods was an Act providing the terms on which the Government could acquire the tramway system of the City of Brisbane, which was the property of a British Company and had been constructed under earlier legislation of the Queensland Parliament. The Act, among other provisions of an unusual character, conferred on the Government the right of paying for the tramway system in debentures in lieu of cash, and of appropriating without any payment whatever any part of the system which might have been constructed without formal authority, however necessary it might be to the successful working of the system as a whole. The failure of the acting Governor to reserve a Bill of this character was a glaring instance of disregard of the Royal Instructions.

The pastoralists in Queensland deputed a delegation, consisting of Sir R. Philp, an ex-Premier, Sir A. Cowley, a former Speaker, and Mr. Walsh, to proceed to the United Kingdom in order to secure the disallowance of the Land Act under the power of disallowance reserved to the Crown in the Constitution Act of 1867. The delegation received support from the British companies interested in the leases and the Brisbane Tramways Company presented a formal request for disallowance to the Secretary of State. In neither case, however, was any action taken by the Secretary of State, whose attitude implied in effect that even in respect to measures prima facie confiscatory the power of disallowance must be deemed to be obsolete.

The agitation, however, which had been carried on in London, had untoward effects on the interests of the State. The Premier, Mr. Theodore, who was in England in June and July on a mission to secure a loan of £3,000,000 for important projects of public works and settlements, found it impossible, in view of the distrust created by the acts of repudiation of his Government, to raise the sum desired. The acting Premier immediately announced the abandonment of the governmental schemes and denounced the delegates for their action in preventing the raising of the loan, on the strength of which an appeal to the country was precipitated with a very moderate amount of success.

The episode served to draw public attention prominently to a problem of considerable importance affecting investors in the stocks of the Dominions and States. These stocks were made available for trustees to invest in by an Act of 1900 which gave the Treasury power to determine what conditions must be satisfied before trustees could invest in them. Of these conditions the most important, as laid down by the Treasury, is the requirement that the Government concerned must place on record a declaration of opinion that any Act which would impair the value of the security on the faith of which investors had purchased the stock would properly be disallowed by the Imperial Government. The value of this declaration was obviously seriously impaired if the power of disallowance were practically obsolete as asserted by the Premier, and apparently admitted by the Secretary of State. A suggestion was put forward during the controversy [1] that the principle of arbitration should be accepted as applicable to such cases, so that if the Imperial Government considered that a prima facie case of repudiation of a contract by a Dominion or State Government to the detriment of British subjects resident in the United Kingdom had been made, it could ask the Dominion or State Government to submit the point in question to arbitration. A similar procedure would, of course, have been available in any case where British subjects resident in a Dominion or a State had a grievance against the Imperial Government, and a suitable tribunal would be found in the Privy Council, from which a panel including Imperial and Dominion representatives could easily be selected. The suggestion was not formally accepted by the Premier,[2] but it is obvious that no other means exist in the long run to decide questions at issue between Governments of different parts of the Empire, now that equality of status has been claimed for and conceded to the Dominions.

3. TERRITORIAL LIMITATIONS ON THE POWERS OF DOMINION LEGISLATURES

A further development of the authority of Dominion legislatures has arisen directly from the terms of the treaty of peace with Germany, under which mandates for South-West Africa and Samoa have been conferred on the Union of South Africa and on New Zealand. In neither case was the new territory to be annexed in the accustomed manner to the Dominion, though it was to fall under its full control. The question, therefore, immediately presented itself as to the power of the Dominion legislatures to legislate for mandated territory, in view of the general rule [3] that the legislative authority of a Dominion Parliament extends only to the territorial limits of the Dominion, thus differing from that of the Imperial Parliament, which can legislate

[1] Keith, *The Times*, May 27, June 2 and 9, 1920 ; *Imperial Unity*, pp. 165, 166. Cf. a similar suggestion of the Attorney-General of Ontario, *The Times*, September 3, 1920.   [2] *The Times*, May 28, June 4, 1920.

[3] Keith, *Responsible Government in the Dominions*, i. 372–401; *Journal of Comparative Legislation*, i. 9–11 ; ii. 328, 329.

without regard to territorial restrictions. In the case of the Commonwealth, which was accorded a mandate for the territory formerly German New Guinea and other Pacific islands, no difficulty of this kind arose, for under the constitution of the Commonwealth the Parliament is expressly empowered to legislate regarding the relations of the Commonwealth with the islands of the Pacific and any Territory acquired by it, an authority wide enough to cover any action necessary under the mandate.

Divergent views of the position were taken in the Union and in New Zealand. In the latter Dominion there had long been a conflict of judicial opinion as to the extent of the legislative authority of the Parliament. The Chief Justice, Sir Robert Stout, had held that the power of the Parliament to legislate for the peace, order, and good government of New Zealand gave it authority to bind New Zealand British subjects even beyond the limits of the territory. In 1919 the question was brought to a direct issue on the trial of a New Zealand soldier,[1] who being already married, went through a form of marriage with a girl in England, where he was stationed while on war service. The New Zealand Crimes Act, 1908, following the provisions of the British law of bigamy, enacted penalties for any British subject who entered into a second marriage, during the subsistence of his first marriage, wherever the second marriage might take place, but it was contended for the defence that, while the Imperial legislature had power to pass such an enactment, no such authority was vested in the Dominion Parliament, whose legislative sphere was restricted to New Zealand. This contention was repelled by the Chief Justice, who held that power to punish a New Zealander for such an offence followed as a natural consequence from the right to make laws for the peace, order, and good government of the Dominion, but the other judges of the Court of Appeal agreed that the New Zealand Act was invalid in so far as it purported to penalize actions taking place beyond New Zealand limits.

In face of this decision of the highest tribunal in the Dominion, it was natural that the Dominion Government should hold that the Dominion Parliament had no power without Imperial authority

---

[1] R. v. Lander, [1919] N.Z.L.R. 305. Cf. Delaney v. Great Western Milling Co., 22 C.L.R. 150, 161 ; McLeod v. A. G. for New South Wales, [1891] A.C. 455.

to enact legislation applicable to New Zealand. Steps were accordingly taken to secure the issue of an Imperial Order in Council of March 11, 1920, made under the Foreign Jurisdiction Act, 1890, which recites that under the peace treaty the islands of Western Samoa were to be administered by His Majesty in his Government of his Dominion of New Zealand and that by treaty His Majesty has jurisdiction in the islands, and enacts that the Parliament of New Zealand may make laws for the peace, order, and good government of the islands of Western Samoa subject to and in accordance with the treaty of peace. The power of the Dominion to legislate for Samoa thus rests ultimately on an Imperial Act, and is not derived directly from the mandate.

In the case of the Union of South Africa circumstances existed which rendered the question apparently easier of answer. The question of the right of the Union Parliament to legislate for South-West Africa was raised by a Nationalist member in the House of Assembly on September 8, 1919, when General Smuts asked leave to introduce the Bill to give effect to the treaty of peace and the mandate for South-West Africa. The Prime Minister contended that the Union Parliament had repeatedly passed Acts affecting the Union beyond its borders, and would continue to do so. He also laid stress on the fact that the treaty contemplated that South-West Africa should be administered by the Union as an integral part of its territory, so that the laws of the Union would naturally apply to it as they would do to any territory formally annexed to the Union. The Speaker ruled in favour of the right of the Union Parliament to legislate. Germany, which had possessed the right to do so, had renounced all its authority, and this authority had been transferred under the treaty with certain limitations to the Union. He alluded to the precedents of legislation by the Cape of Good Hope for Kaffraria and other territories beyond its limits, and he also argued that, if the Union declined to act on the mandate, a source of danger would arise on the border of the Union, due to the neglect of Parliament to comply with the spirit, if not the letter, of the Act of Union, requiring it to legislate for the peace, order, and good government of the Union.

The reasoning adduced in favour of the authority of the Union was perhaps not very cogent ; the precedent adduced from the history of the Cape was by no means strictly relevant, and it was impossible effectively to assimilate mandated to annexed territory. It was, however, open to justify the right on a different ground,[1] the new status acquired by the Union through its participation in the signature of peace and its admission as a member of the League of Nations. It could fairly be argued that in virtue of these facts the Union acquired a semi-sovereignty which was adequate ground on which to base a claim to a right to legislate for a mandated territory. The action taken in the case of New Zealand, on the other hand, is open to the criticism that it implies that New Zealand, despite the conferring on her of the mandate, was unable to exercise it effectively without the authority of the United Kingdom, and accordingly in subordination to the United Kingdom, which in some sense must thus remain responsible for the actions of New Zealand, seeing that it would have authority to disallow New Zealand Acts.

Apart, however, from the issue of mandates, the same question of the restrictions on the territorial extent of Dominion legislation has been raised in the Dominion of Canada. It has been claimed by high authorities [2] on the Canadian constitution that the right to legislate with extra-territorial effect must be inherent in the powers of the Dominion, since otherwise it would have no power to provide for the discipline overseas of its military forces or the regulation of its naval forces beyond the territorial waters of Canada. The first argument, however, is invalidated by the fact that the Imperial Army Act authorizes the extra-territorial application of Dominion legislation on this topic, and the second by the fact that the same purpose is aimed at as regards Dominion navies by the Imperial Naval Discipline (Dominion Naval Forces) Act, 1911. The Courts of the Dominion have indeed upheld the validity of the section of the Canadian Criminal Code [3] which penalizes bigamy committed outside of Canada, but, though their decision [4] was not based on this fact, the Act itself restricts the

---

[1] See Keith, *The Times*, October 24, 1919.

[2] Lefroy, *Canadian Constitutional Law*, p. 80 ; Clement, *Canadian Constitution*, pp. 65–115.   [3] Revised Statutes, 1906, c. 146, s. 275.

[4] In re *Criminal Code Sections relating to Bigamy*, 27 S.C.R. 461. Cf. Mr. Justice Riddell *Canadian Law Times*, xl. 500–2.

penalty to cases in which a British subject resident in Canada quits the Dominion for the purpose of committing the offence, and such an enactment is clearly within the powers of the legislature. The High Court of the Commonwealth of Australia has been emphatic in its expression of the view that the legislative power of the Commonwealth is territorial in the absence of express words extending its power of action.[1]

The Government and Parliament of Canada have finally decided to secure the extension of the powers of the Dominion by requesting an amendment of the British North America Act so as to confer on the legislation of the Dominion extra-territorial effect to the same extent as belongs to legislation of the Imperial Parliament. One immediate ground of seeking this power was afforded by the desire of the Government to legislate regarding aircraft registered in Canada when flying beyond the strict limits of the Dominion. The decision, however, raises a difficulty since the power of regulating the actions of British subjects beyond British territory, hitherto the sole prerogative of the Imperial Parliament, must be shared with the Dominions. To obviate conflict of jurisdiction it is clearly necessary that each Parliament should confine its authority in actual exercise to those British subjects who by birth or residence are identified with its territory. A precedent for such action exists in the case of merchant shipping, since each Dominion is now expected to regulate British shipping registered in its territory, and the immigration laws of the Dominions have recognized the right of a native of the Dominions or a settler who has effectively established there his home to re-enter his native land or adopted home without complying with the conditions exacted from other British subjects. It will, however, still be necessary for the Imperial Parliament to legislate in certain cases for all classes of British subjects, for instance as regards the legal position of all British subjects resident in places where the Crown exercises extra-territorial jurisdiction such as China and Persia or the Ottoman territories.[2]

---

[1] Compare *Clark* v. *Union Steamship Co. of New Zealand*, 18 C.L.R. 142; *Australian Steamships Ltd.* v. *Malcolm*, 19 C.L.R. 298; *Delaney* v. *Great Western Milling Co.*, 22 C.L.R. 150, as explained by Chapman, J.. [1919] N.Z.L.R. 330, 331.

[2] Keith, *Journal of Comparative Legislation*, iii. 132–4, and the Canadian Bill of 1920 defining Canadian nationals for League of Nations purposes.

4. Restrictions on the Legislative Authority of the Imperial Parliament

The extension of the territorial ambit of Dominion legislation has an important bearing on the exercise of the power of the Imperial Parliament to legislate for the whole of the British dominions. From the first grant of responsible government to the colonies, the tendency has been more and more narrowly to restrict the use of Imperial legislation where the end could be effected by legislation in the colonies,[1] and the removal of the territorial limitation will render Imperial legislation less necessary than ever. The claim that the exercise of the legislative authority of the Imperial Parliament is obsolete as regards the Dominions has most emphatically been expressed by General Smuts,[2] who in discussing the peace treaty in the Union House of Assembly declared that the Union Parliament stood exactly on the same footing as the British Parliament, which had no legislative power over the Union. Whatever laws had to be passed for the Union must be passed by the Union Parliament. The doctrine that the British Parliament possessed sovereign legislative power was no longer valid. Without the consent of the Union it could not pass any law binding South Africa without a revolution.

The doctrine enunciated by General Smuts is an obvious corollary to the principle of the equal status of the Dominions and the United Kingdom, but the logic of his position is slightly vitiated by the implicit admission that the Imperial Parliament may still legislate for South Africa with the assent of the Union.[3] If the admission of the Union to membership of the League of Nations be treated as conferring a species of sovereignty on the Union, it may be held that the right of the Imperial Parliament to legislate for the Union has definitely passed away by the destruction of the colonial status, hitherto assigned by international law to the Union. But it is hardly consistent with this view to accept the possibility of the Imperial Parliament legislating even with consent regarding South Africa. But the validity of the conclusion is clear, whatever the precise argument by which it

[1] Keith, *Responsible Government in the Dominions*, iii. 1316–28.
[2] Cf. Mr. Hughes in *Parl. Pap.* Cd. 9177, p. 212 ; Mr. Burton, *ibid.* p. 213.
[3] Explicitly recognized by Sir R. Borden, *ibid.* pp. 212, 213.

is supported. Imperial legislation can apply to a Dominion only with the full assent of that Dominion, which normally will be expressed by a resolution of its Parliament.

The problem of Imperial legislation presents itself with special acuteness in the case of Canada, for the federal Parliament has no power to vary in essentials the constitution provided for it in the British North America Act. It is, therefore, only possible to obtain changes in the constitution when they are supported by the clear wish of the vast majority of the people of Canada as attested by addresses from either house of the Dominion Parliament, and the lack of opposition from the provincial Governments. When in 1907 important changes were made in the subsidies granted by the Dominion to the provinces, the Imperial Government consented to obtain the assent of Parliament to the alterations desired only when they secured assurances that the provinces were willing that the federal compact should thus be varied and an express admission was made that the constitution could not be changed without general assent. In 1915 very necessary changes in the representation of the various parts of the Dominion in the Senate were similarly effected by an Imperial Act after the concurrence of the Senate in the alterations had been procured by concessions made by the Government to the Opposition on matters of importance, including the postponement of the operation of the change until the next general election of the Canadian House of Commons.[1]

The position in Canada is therefore irksome and inconvenient; changes in the constitution are possible only when they are non-contentious; any serious difference of opinion would merely result in the refusal of the Imperial Parliament to legislate, and important alterations would inevitably excite sufficient opposition to secure their being left in abeyance. The situation of the Dominion thus compares very unfavourably with that of the Commonwealth, which has ample power of change of constitution, although like Canada its constitution is federal in principle. It

[1] Keith, *Responsible Government in the Dominions*, ii. 757–9 ; *Imperial Unity*, pp. 390 ff. In addition to wider powers of legislation Canada seeks power to secure the removal of judges on account of age or infirmity, contrary to British North America Act, 1867, s. 99. This is provided for at age 70 by New South Wales Act, No. 9 of 1918.

has naturally, therefore, been a subject of consideration in the Dominion to discover a basis on which to effect agreement on a method of altering the constitution in which the aid of the Imperial Parliament need not be invoked. So far, however, the attempts made have not been successful, Quebec in particular deprecating any change in a system which assures her the fullest protection for her peculiar position in the Dominion.

A curious problem is presented as to the validity of the exercise of the paramount power of Imperial legislation by the passing of the Indemnity Act, 1920, of the Imperial Parliament. That enactment forbids the institution in any court of an action for any proceedings by officers of the Crown or persons acting by their orders in certain circumstances, whether the matters concerned took place within or without His Majesty's dominions. The enactment at first sight would appear to apply to all courts in the Empire, but this interpretation is negatived by the power given in section 7 to apply the Act to any part of His Majesty's dominions except the self-governing Dominions, so that the indemnity has no application directly to matters coming before the courts of these Dominions. On the other hand, the enactment has an indirect effect; had it not been passed an action could have been brought in England in respect of an illegal act done in one of the self-governing Dominions, unless an Act of Indemnity applicable to the action in question had been passed in the Dominion. But, though the Act does not attempt to interfere with the jurisdiction of Dominion courts, it expressly forbids the British courts to treat as illegal an action done in a Dominion, even if the action is not validated by legislation in that Dominion. In a much more direct manner there is an invasion of what might be claimed as a sphere of Dominion action in sections 5 and 6 of the Act, which validate sentences passed by courts administering military law in territories occupied by His Majesty's forces during the war, and legislative measures passed by the authorities administering such territories pending the establishment of lawfully constituted authorities. These sections aim at meeting a real difficulty arising out of the war, affecting both territories which were directly occupied by British forces, such as portion of the Cameroons, Togoland, and East Africa, and territories occupied by Dominion forces, such as Samoa, New Guinea, and South-West Africa. In all of these it was necessary to establish military courts to try offences committed during the occupation and to lay down regulations to be observed by the people while the occupation was in force. It was contended that the legislation necessary in the case of the territories occupied by Dominion forces should be passed by their legislatures alone, but in the opinion of the Imperial Government Dominion legislation might be held to be ineffectual for the purpose. The Dominions, on this view, were only able to legislate for the territories after they received formally the mandates necessary, and therefore could not ratify acts done when they had no legislative power. The argument was obviously convincing, and the action taken relieves the officers concerned in the occupation of any risk of proceedings against them either in British or Dominion Courts. The indemnities also given by Dominion legislation are valuable but not strictly speaking essential.

5. THE POWERS OF THE LEGISLATURES

The enactment of compulsory service was responsible for a curious anxiety to depreciate the powers of legislation vested in Dominion Parliaments, and that too by parties whose aims were nationalist and who, therefore, should *a priori* have been inclined to support the widest possible extension of the legislative powers of the Dominions. In Canada and in New Zealand the same argument was adduced ; the power to legislate, as conferred by the Imperial Acts constituting the constitutions of the two Dominions, gave them authority only to legislate for the peace, order, and good government of the Dominions ; how, therefore, could they legislate to send troops overseas, and therefore beyond the limits of the Dominion ? In Canada a direct issue on the point was avoided, but in New Zealand the issue was faced by the Court of Appeal, with the courage normal in that court, which is refreshingly free from the inclination to evade difficult problems. The point was, as a matter of fact, only incidental in the cases which were under review, and which arose under War Regulations penalizing utterances or acts prejudicial to recruiting ;[1] there

---

[1] *The Round Table*, vii. 630, 827, 828. Cf. the Quebec case, *Fournier* v. *Price*, R.J.Q., 60 S.C. 489.

was no doubt of the validity of the Regulations or of the statute under which they were made, but the case for and against the Act providing for conscription was elaborately argued, and on the express invitation of the Solicitor-General the four judges expressed the view that the Act was *intra vires* the Dominion. The power of the Parliament was, they held, ample to enable the Government to dispatch a force and to compel men to serve in it beyond the territorial limits of New Zealand. The Chief Justice thought the matter plain on the wide wording of the constitution which authorized legislation for ' peace, order, and good government '. Chapman, J., pointed out that the argument involved the assumption that the Parliament could not provide for discipline in a naval expedition which Parliament authorized the executive to send to attack some naval base in the Pacific which was a growing menace to New Zealand. On the same view a colony with a land frontier would be compelled idly to watch a menace growing; before it could send troops against the enemy, they must have passed the boundary. The conclusion of the Court,[1] which was delivered on April 4, 1917, and was received with much approval in the Dominion, was doubtless sound, though the arguments are not all of them equally convincing, for the authority to control troops beyond the limits of a Dominion rests in reality on the Imperial Army Act,[2] which gives when needed extra-territorial application to Dominion legislation, and the power to maintain discipline on a naval expedition sent from New Zealand may be traced to the Naval Discipline (Dominion Naval Forces) Act, 1911, and not to the inherent authority of the Dominion legislatures. In the Union of South Africa the same argument cropped up in a different form. In his efforts to justify his treason to the Union General Beyers maintained that the consultation of Parliament by the Government before they entered upon the war with German South-West Africa was not sufficient, as the power of the legislature referred to internal matters only, and that in regard to an offensive against German South-West Africa the people should have been consulted.[3]

---

[1] *Semple* v. *O'Donovan*, [1917] N.Z.L.R. 273. See [1919] N.Z.L.R. 331, 339.
[2] See Keith, *Responsible Government in the Dominions*, iii. 1320.
[3] *Parl. Pap.* Cd. 7874, p. 39.

The Courts also took the most favourable view throughout
of the wide extent of the authority conferred by Acts of Parliaments dealing with War Measures or War Precautions, enactments
to this effect being held in all the Dominions to authorize the
passing of regulations of the greatest variety and scope.   Doubtless in their decisions the Courts were actuated, as in the United
Kingdom, by reluctance to seek to fetter the discretion of the
executive in time of stress, when the Government must often
act without certain knowledge, and occasionally run the risk of
committing an injustice rather than endanger the security of the
State.   The licence granted reached, perhaps, its farthest limit
in the case of the Commonwealth, where under the War Precautions
Acts, 1914–16, the Government, as the Prime Minister explained
on December 10, 1919, was practically endowed with a vast
power of legislation on any topic which in their opinion served to
further the cause of the war.   Under this power they entered into
elaborate arrangements regarding the control of butter, wool,
sheepskins, flax, and wheat, and their sale to the British Government, no less than they regulated the more obviously defence
matters of control of aliens and naturalized persons.[1]

Moreover, some of the Parliaments made use of the extraordinary power exercised by the British Parliament in the war
of prolonging the term of their existence so as to avoid elections
in war time.   On the outbreak of war the Labour party in the
Commonwealth suggested that in order to avoid an election which
was then due, a dissolution of both houses having been granted
before the war, the Imperial Parliament might be asked to extend
the life of the Commonwealth Parliament, but the Government,
expecting a triumph at the polls, negatived the suggestion.   The
point rose again in 1917 when on forming his coalition Government Mr. Hughes was determined not to proceed to England for
the Imperial War Cabinet meetings, unless the Opposition was
prepared to concur in resolutions asking the Imperial Parliament
to extend the life of Parliament to permit of his presence in
England and return to the Commonwealth before the election
was held, but this device failed owing to objections in the Senate,
where Labour possessed a majority.   In Canada in 1916 agreement

[1] See *Official Year Book of the Commonwealth*, xi. 1034–43 ; below, Chap. XI, § 2.

was attained for the passing of an Imperial Act extending the duration of Parliament by a year, but in 1917, when conscription had been determined upon, an attempt to secure another prolongation was abandoned by Sir Robert Borden when it was only carried by a majority of twenty in the House of Commons. In either case an Imperial Act was necessary because, though the Commonwealth constitution could have been altered, the process involved a referendum to the people which was absurd, and in Canada no legal means existed save a reference to the Imperial Parliament with general assent.

In other cases local Acts were possible, though these raised the grave constitutional question how far it was right for a legislature to deprive the electorate of the right of recording its choice in due season. In Newfoundland a year's extension was granted in 1917 and 1918 with general agreement, and in New Zealand there was no very determined opposition to extensions in 1916 and 1918, the second expiring in the following year. In the Union General Botha preferred, after the war in German South-West Africa and the rebellion, to face the electorate and not undergo the charge of seeking unjustly to perpetuate his authority. In New South Wales the most bitter controversy arose in 1916, when Mr. Holman in his support of the recruiting schemes of Mr. Hughes incurred Labour hostility to an extent which would have caused his defeat but for negotiations with Mr. Wade which ended in the appointment of the latter to be Agent-General in London, and secured the former the support of Mr. Wade's followers in extending the life of Parliament. Reference has been made to the Governor's natural misgivings as to his right to assent to a measure which was denounced by the Labour party and which defrauded the electors of their right to record their votes in the interest of particular individuals. The case was made the more unsatisfactory because, once the crisis over, Mr. Holman found no difficulty in dissolving Parliament when he, correctly, judged that he could secure success in the election. But the authority then given by the Secretary of State for the Colonies to the Governor to assent may be interpreted as the verdict of the Colonial Office that in such cases the legal right of the Parliament may be exercised. Similarly it may be noted that the action of the legislature of Ontario in 1918 in prolonging its existence was passed by the Dominion Government as within the constitutional powers of the province and not therefore a suitable ground for disallowance.[1] The cases are of interest as emphasizing the paramount power of the Dominion and State legislatures within the limits of their constitutions. A minor illustration of the same fact is the increase of members' salaries to 4,000 dollars in Canada, £500 in New Zealand, £600 in South Africa, and £1,000 in Australia, effected in 1920 without any prior consultation of the electors, though not without protest from public opinion.

6. The Franchise

As in the United Kingdom the exigencies of the war effected in some matters a complete revision of conceptions of the right of women to exercise the franchise. Though it had long been conceded throughout Australasia, there was no clear sign that the movement was making much progress in Canada. But in 1915 the new spirit manifested itself widespread throughout the prairie provinces ; in Manitoba, Alberta, and Saskatchewan alike the grant of the suffrage was promised, and in due course in 1916 accorded. British Columbia followed suit, and Ontario did like-wise in 1917. The Dominion was now confronted with a position of some difficulty ; if it admitted the right of women to vote in the provinces, where they had been enfranchised, in the federal elections they would create the anomaly that in some provinces there would be female voters, in others none. The actual step taken was in 1917 [2] to admit the principle of the voting throughout Canada of the wives, widows, mothers, daughters, and sisters of serving soldiers only, excluding those other women who in certain provinces were enfranchised, and the women's vote thus accorded added materially to the completeness of the governmental success in the general election. In 1918 [3] the logical step was taken of a general admission of women at age 21, amendments suggested in the Senate raising the age to 30 or imposing an educational

---

[1] The action of the British Columbia legislature in 1916 in prolonging for a brief period its existence was criticized, and in 1917 a new legislature ratified its Acts. On constitutional change cf. *McCawley* v. *R.*, [1920] A. C. 691.

[2] C. 39. By c. 34 nurses were given the franchise.   [3] C. 10.

test being defeated by the Government. In the same year Nova Scotia, which had earlier rejected the proposal, fell into line with Ontario and the western provinces. In 1919 New Brunswick followed suit.

In South Africa the progress of the movement during the war was extremely marked : in 1912 a Bill to enfranchise women was rejected by 70 to 30 votes in the Assembly ; in 1917 a motion to the same effect failed by 63 to 28, but in 1918 an amendment to the electoral Bill of that year which would have conferred the franchise on women was only rejected by 54 to 39, though there were various technical grounds which made the amendment inexpedient. In 1919 a motion in favour of the grant by Mr. Wyndham was passed in the Assembly by 44 votes to 42, and on April 20, 1920, a motion to the same effect by Mr. Brown was carried by 64 votes to 39, the minority consisting mainly of South African party and Nationalist supporters of the more old-fashioned type, who predicted dire evil from the vote or asserted that Dutch women did not want it, or, like Mr. Hertzog, that they could not go to the poll. Action, however, to carry out the policy approved by the Assembly could not be taken in the session of 1920.

The distinction of being the first British legislature actually to have women as members was attained in the session of 1918 by Alberta when two women had seats, but the principle of admitting women as members even when the suffrage is conceded is not universally accepted ; [1] thus efforts to induce the Legislative Council of New Zealand to accept the proposal of the eligibility of women were resisted by that body, which insisted that any such proposal could originate only in the Council itself.[2]

The war was also responsible for several curious innovations both as regards the franchise and the mode of recording votes. In the session of 1914 the New Zealand Parliament authorized the men who were to proceed to England in October to record their votes for the party which they preferred, Government, Opposition, and Labour, and assigned to the Premier, the leader of the Opposition, and two members of the Labour party, the duty

---

[1] New South Wales Act No. 50 of 1918 opens the Assembly, not the Council, to women.   [2] Act No. 16 of 1919, but see No. 59 of 1914, s. 18.

of deciding to which candidates the vote should be assigned. In the following year elaborate, but as the event proved, not wholly satisfactory provision was made by the Canadian Parliament for that end.[1] Of much greater importance was the decision of the Dominion in the War Times Election Act, 1917, which only passed its third reading in the Commons by 53 votes to 32, to disfranchise Doukhobors and Mennonites who came to Canada on the undertaking that they would not be liable to military service, and all naturalized voters, natives of enemy countries, who had been less than fifteen years in the Dominion. The number thus affected was large, for, according to the quinquennial census in the three prairie provinces, of the men between 20 and 34 the British and Canadian born numbered only 169,685 to 111,304 of other stock, chiefly German and Austrians of Slav race. The proposal was strongly criticized by the Liberals, including those who favoured conscription, on the ground that the naturalization accorded should be respected in any case in which the naturalized subject had throughout the war shown himself orderly and obedient to authority; the Conservatives, on the other hand, maintained that Germans, at any rate, despite their naturalization remained subject to German nationality, and should not be permitted to endanger the safety of Canada by votes which might be dictated, not by consideration of the needs of Canada, but by loyalty to another allegiance. Further, the franchise was extended to all members of the expeditionary force and to nurses attached to the force. Conditions of residence were of course waived in these cases, minors were permitted to vote, and persons who had not been resident in Canada were authorized to vote, their votes being counted according to the place of their enlistment. The Government Bill had authorized the Government to decide how the votes were to be counted in such cases, but this proposal was dropped in view of the tendency to fraud offered by it. The votes had to be cast either for the Government or the Opposition, since it was deemed impossible that the electors could make any intelligent choice among candidates of whom they knew nothing.[2]

[1] So in Alberta Act 1916, c. 5.

[2] In Alberta (1917, c. 12) and Saskatchewan (1917, c. 4) extra members were added to the legislature to be elected by soldiers oversea. In the former case one of the two elected was a nurse.

In the Commonwealth an Act of 1917 made similar provision for voting by members of the forces overseas for ministerial or opposition candidates and it disfranchised all naturalized British subjects born in an enemy country save those serving in the forces overseas, Syrian or Armenian Christians, and certain relatives of men serving in the forces.

The Commonwealth Electoral Act, 1918, confers the franchise on every natural born or naturalized British subject who has lived for six months continuously in Australia, not under twenty-one years of age, but the last qualification is waived in the case of any member of the forces, for a period up to three years after the war. It established also a system of preferential voting for the House of Representatives, each voter being required to record his preferences in order, and in the following year the same system was applied with some modifications to Senate elections. The need in their case for alteration was obvious ; under the former law the three places normally vacant every third year were filled by the votes of the whole State, each elector having three votes, so that minorities were rarely if ever represented at all. Under the new system each voter must indicate his preference for one more than double the number of candidates to be elected. Provision is made also for the grouping of candidates of the same party and for postal voting in lieu of the former system of absent voting, which is unworkable when taken in conjunction with the preferential system, when an elector is outside his own State.

On March 11, 1920, the Canadian Government brought forward a measure of the highest importance in the shape of an Elections Bill to provide a simple and uniform franchise, under which any British subject by birth or naturalization, aged at least twenty-one, who has resided in Canada for a year and in an electoral district for two months preceding the issue of the electoral writ, is given the franchise. The only exceptions of importance are those accepting the disqualification for the franchise under provincial laws as disqualifying for the federal franchise also, save for persons who served in the Dominion forces in the war, and providing that a person, whose nationality is British only by reason of marriage [1] or change of allegiance or naturaliza-

---

[1] A wife becomes British by marriage to a British subject.

tion [1] of another person, shall not be qualified to vote, unless born in the North American continent or himself qualified for naturalization and only debarred from the right by being already a British subject. The measure adopts the voters' rolls of the provinces but gives power to add or delete names where necessary, and allows advance voting in the case of such persons as railway employees. Women as well as men are eligible for election to Parliament. Nothing in the measure directly penalizes subjects of former enemy countries, but the Naturalization Act, 1920, forbids for ten years as a rule the naturalization of former enemy subjects and excludes them from the possibility of obtaining the franchise for that period. Under the measure women of enemy alien nationality by marriage with British subjects will not be able to obtain the franchise for ten years, since until then they could not themselves attain naturalization.

Apart from the increase by four members on redistribution of the House of Assembly of the Union of South Africa, one change only of importance has taken place in the representation in the Dominion Parliaments. The Dominion constitution provides for the periodic change of representation in the House of Commons based on the possession of 65 members by Quebec, and in 1914 an Act was passed adapting the representation in that House to the census of 1911. The number of the House was thus increased to 235 while Ontario and the maritime provinces lost eight and the western provinces gained 22 members. The constitution, however, gave no power to increase the representation of the provinces in the Senate, and the unfairness of the distribution had been obvious. Political differences, however, rendered action difficult. Sir R. Borden's Government was anxious that the new Senators allotted to the west should be added forthwith, while the Liberal majority in the Senate, which feared the loss of its position, desired that the addition should be postponed until the next general election, when the new members for the House of Commons in the west would be elected. The necessity of securing an Imperial Act to amend the constitution determined the Government to concur in this view, and the Houses passed an

[1] A child of a person naturalized became under the law up to 1914 naturalized if residing while a minor with his parents in Canada.

address[1] to the Crown asking for the change desired, to which effect was given by an Imperial Act on May 19. Under it the total number of the Senate is raised from 87 to 96 by the grant to each of the four western provinces of 6 members, in lieu of the four each (three in the case of British Columbia) formerly assigned to them. These provinces are also grouped as one unit, beside Ontario, Quebec, and the maritime provinces, and in the case of a deadlock the Crown is authorized to summon two from each unit to increase the number of the Senate, in place of two from each of the older three units. Newfoundland if admitted to the Union will also have six Senators. At the same time, in deference to the urgent request of Prince Edward Island, backed by the maritime provinces, it was provided that no province should ever have fewer representatives in the House of Commons than she has Senators ; had the strict rule of population been rigidly adhered to in the Canadian Act of 1914 its representation would have been diminished from four to three.

Proportional representation made distinct progress in 1918 when it was adopted in New South Wales,[2] five and three member constituencies being established. The result at the general election held under it was all but a deadlock, only the acceptance of the Speakership by a Liberal permitting a Labour Government to be formed. The repeal of the measure has therefore been suggested by the Labour party in the State. In 1918[3] the Labour legislation in the Transvaal Provincial Council of 1914 was undone, proportional representation in municipal elections being revoked, and a return made to the method of three-member constituencies. Aliens who were enfranchised in 1914 were excluded from the vote.

The war was responsible for interesting constitutional legislation in the Union of South Africa. Under the constitution of 1909 a quinquennial census was requisite of the European male adults in the Union with a view to determine whether any increase in the number of members of the House of Assembly was necessary, the number of such members to be allocated to each province, and any redistribution of seats in the provinces as an outcome

---

[1] *Parl. Pap.* Cd. 7897 ; 5 and 6 Geo. V. c. 45.

[2] Act No. 40 of 1918. A New Zealand Bill in 1919 was dropped, and a motion in favour of it defeated in 1920, the Prime Minister energetically denouncing the idea.   [3] Ordinance No. 11 of 1918.

of the increase. The first census should have been taken in 1916, but the absence of so many men on service rendered the taking of a census undesirable. In 1918, however, it was held to be necessary, in view of the improbability of an early termination of the war, to hold a census, while providing at the same time for the holding of another in 1921, and allowing for the inclusion in the enumeration of the European male adults absent on service at the date of the census.[1] The enumeration took place on May 5, 1918, showing a total of about 280,000 in the Union, and 18,478 on service. In order to permit the numbers of men serving overseas to be included when calculating the redelimitation of constituencies, it was necessary to effect an amendment in the constitution[2] which excludes from the franchise members of His Majesty's regular forces on full pay, a provision which of course when enacted contemplated only the cases of the Imperial garrison in the Union. The South Africans oversea, however, were serving as part of the regular British forces under the Army Act, receiving British pay, and accordingly it was decided by the Electoral Redelimitation Amendment Act, 1918, to alter the constitution for the sole purpose of the redelimitation[3] to be carried on after the census of 1918.

Under the constitution, while large powers of alteration are conceded, it is requisite that in certain cases, including the qualification of voters, any change made must be approved by a Bill passed by both Houses of Parliament sitting together, the third reading of the Bill being agreed to by not less than two-thirds of the total number of members of both Houses at such a joint sitting. The measure in question was therefore referred to such a session, convened by the Governor-General by message to both Houses, and presided over by the Speaker of the House of Assembly. The Bill received on the third reading the necessary approval by 143 votes in favour, there being no opposition. Both this Bill and the Electoral Census Bill, as containing constitutional alterations, were duly reserved as required by the constitution, and received the royal approval by Order in Council on the advice of the Secretary of State for the Colonies.

---

[1] Act No. 15 of 1918.   [2] 9 Edw. VII, c. 9, s. 34.
[3] Union *Parl. Pap.* U.G. 58 of 1919.

The question of the constitution of the Senate was also discussed in the Union, but save a measure declaring that the tenure of the existing members extended to October 31, 1920, doubt on that point existing under the terms of the constitution, no change was made.

7. Titles of Honour

The war brought to a definite issue in Canada a tendency which had been in operation prior to its outbreak, but which might not have resulted in a definite issue save for the circumstances resulting from the war. It is an unquestioned part of the royal prerogative to confer titles of honour which are valid throughout the Empire; it was even contemplated by the framers of the Quebec Act of 1791 that there should be established a hereditary upper house in Canada. Though that project came to nothing, in the obvious absence of the possibility of creating such a class under Canadian conditions, the bestowal of knighthoods on men prominent in the public life of Canada was not rare. The responsibility for selecting those worthy to receive such honours rested ultimately with the Imperial Government, but naturally it had to rely in increasing measure on the recommendation of the Governor-General, and he in his turn was bound in his action in this regard to have in mind the views of his Prime Minister.[1] In 1902 the question of recommendations obtained greater definition through the suggestion of Sir Wilfrid Laurier to the Imperial Government that titles should be granted in Canada only on the advice of the Dominion Government. The attitude adopted by Mr. Chamberlain as Secretary of State for the Colonies was that the Canadian Government should have the sole right of deciding what persons should be nominated for honours in respect of services of a political or administrative character in Canada, but that in the case of persons whose claims rested on Imperial or municipal services or on charitable, literary, or scientific work, the Governor-General should be at liberty to make recommendations, subject to the rule that he should submit, for any observations which they might desire to offer, the names of his nominees to the Dominion Government. The rationale of this decision is

---

[1] Keith, *Responsible Government in the Dominions*, iii. 1299–1315; *Imperial Unity*, pp. 54–62, 74, 75; [*Journal of Comparative Legislation*, i. 11–13.

clear ; as the titles were of Imperial validity, the final decision must rest in the hands of the Imperial Government, but it was right that that Government should defer to the judgement of the Dominion Government on the question whether political or administrative services in Canada were worthy of recognition.

Under this arrangement comparatively few titular distinctions were granted each year in the Dominion, chiefly to ministers of the Dominion, Premiers of the provinces, high judicial and civil officials, or men distinguished in the commercial, scientific, or journalistic life of the Dominion. As early as 1914, however, a protest had been made in the House of Commons at Ottawa against the practice of conferring titles on Canadians, and proximity to the United States had been a factor in producing a dislike of titular distinctions, especially as it was always possible in any given case to urge that men of greater merits and distinction had been passed over. The war, however, was responsible for an innovation, the grounds of which have never been sufficiently disclosed. A baronetcy was bestowed on a Canadian who had been under continuous attack in the press as drawing excessive profits from the business in which he was engaged,[1] and a peerage was conferred on the owner of a newspaper published in Montreal. At the same time it was understood that two or three hundred decorations of various classes of the newly-established Order of the British Empire were available for distribution in Canada. Public feeling in 1917 rose to a height ; the subject was debated in provincial legislatures, and at conventions of church organizations, grain growers, farmers, and trade unionists, resolutions were adopted asking the newly-formed Government at Ottawa to refrain from recommending Canadians for titles of honour. A special attack was made on hereditary honours as manifestly out of harmony with the social, political, and economic conditions of Canadian life.

The popular outcry found formal expression in the Dominion House of Commons on April 8, 1918, when Mr. W. F. Nickle introduced a motion against the grant of further hereditary titles in Canada. The temper of the House of Commons proved to be

[1] *The Round Table*, viii. 623–6, 843–6 ; E. Porritt, *Evolution of the Dominion of Canada*, pp. 365–8.

decisively unfavourable to the practice. Sir Wilfrid Laurier, who had accepted with some reluctance a G.C.M.G. on the occasion of Queen Victoria's jubilee in 1897, offered to make a bonfire of his order, and invited his fellow knights to take the same course. The Government, it turned out, had foreseen the course of events, and disarmed criticism by communicating to the House the terms of a request which had been prepared for transmission to the Imperial Government. This request expressly recognized the right of the Imperial Government to decide what number of titles or honours should be allocated to Canada from time to time, but it insisted that no honour of titular distinction (save those granted for military services during the war, or those ordinarily conferred by the King *proprio motu*) should be conferred on any British subject ordinarily resident in Canada except with the approval of, or upon the advice of, the Prime Minister of Canada. It asked also that no hereditary title should henceforth be conferred on a British subject ordinarily resident in Canada, and that steps should be taken by legislation or otherwise to secure that no title of honour held by a British subject then or thereafter ordinarily resident in Canada should be recognized as having hereditary effect.

The demand of the Dominion as regards the bestowal of honours in future has, of course, been accepted by the Imperial Government, and no Canadian appointments have been made to the Order of the British Empire. But it has not yet been possible to deal [1] with the request that steps should be taken to extinguish the operation of hereditary titles already conferred, and the position has been rendered decidedly more difficult by the action of the Dominion Parliament in 1919, when the controversy of 1918 was renewed with fresh vigour, at a time when it had been hoped that the governmental proposals had removed the issue from the sphere of political controversy. The matter was again raised in an able speech by Mr. Nickle, and his suggestion that no more honours should be bestowed on persons domiciled in or living in Canada was supplemented by Mr. R. L. Richardson's suggestion that steps should be taken to ensure the extinction of hereditary titles at present in existence in the Dominion at

[1] A Canadian Act could effect the result for Canada, but not for the Empire.

the death of their present holders. Sir Thomas White, on behalf
of the Government, explained that the question of making recommendations for the recognition of work done by civilians during
the war in Canada had been under the careful consideration of
the Government, and that on January 3 the Prime Minister had
telegraphed suggesting that the whole question of civil honours for
war services and of titles in general should be submitted to a select
committee of the House of Commons. The governmental proposal
of a select committee was carried by only 71 to 64 votes. The report
of the Committee was adopted on May 14, and was drastic in
terms; it was debated with some warmth in the Commons, where
an effort was made to secure acceptance of the principle of conferring honours, provided due care were observed; Sir Thomas
White defended honours, but admitted ' that in all the British-
speaking countries the bestowal has been on altogether too
generous a scale, and has not proceeded upon the principle that
it should have proceeded '. The attempt to change the Committee's report failed by 43 votes to 96, and the House of Commons
accordingly adopted an address to the Crown, going considerably
beyond the limits of the Order in Council of 1918. The address
asks that the King may be pleased ' to refrain hereafter from
conferring any title of honour or titular distinction upon any of
your subjects domiciled or ordinarily resident in Canada, save
such appellations as are of a professional or vocational character,
or which appertain to an office ', and ' to provide that appropriate
action be taken by legislation or otherwise to ensure the extinction of a hereditary title of honour or titular distinction, and of
a dignity or title as a Peer of the Realm on the death of a person
domiciled or ordinarily resident in Canada at present in enjoy-
ment of a hereditary title of honour, or titular distinction, or
dignity or title as a Peer of the Realm, and that thereafter no
such title of honour, titular distinction, or dignity or title as
a Peer of the Realm shall be accepted, enjoyed or used by any
person or be recognized.' The Committee also reported against
the acceptance or use in Canada of foreign titles, but it recognized as legitimate the award of military or naval decorations,
such as the Victoria Cross, for exceptional valour and devotion
to duty, and it approved the continued use of the styles ' Right

Honourable' and 'Honourable', proper to members of the Imperial Privy Council and to members of the Dominion and provincial executives.

Very real difficulties undoubtedly exist as to the mode of terminating the hereditary character of peerages already existing on the ground that their holders are or may become ordinarily resident in the Dominion. Responsibility for the impasse, however, cannot be borne wholly by the British Government, though the decision to confer hereditary honours was an unwise one. It is not asserted that the action taken was adopted without the assent of the Dominion Prime Minister, and the episode has brought into prominence the grave objections which have existed to the procedure hitherto adopted. Under the milder proposals of 1918 the responsibility for any title of honour bestowed on a Canadian would rest with the Dominion Government, which therefore could be challenged in the House of Commons for its action, and must be prepared to justify it. In the past it has been possible for ministers to declare that the matter is one which does not rest on their responsibility, and to shelter themselves behind the royal prerogative.

In the other Dominions the question has not assumed the acute form in which it has appeared in Canada.[1] The conferring of a peerage in 1918 on Sir John Forrest, distinguished for services as Premier of Western Australia and as a minister of the Commonwealth, was disapproved by Labour, but the issue was not pressed, as it was recognized that the peerage would lapse on the death of the holder—then imminent—without an heir. Labour ministries have taken the view that they cannot recommend for titles of honour of any kind, but they have not hitherto pressed their objections to the extent of demands that no honours should be granted, and, while the Labour organizations throughout the Commonwealth disapprove the grant of honours, other parties see no objection to the grant of such honours as are not hereditary, there being more or less general agreement on the point that it is

[1] The protests of the Conference of State Premiers in June 1918 dealt with the lack of consultation of the Governments on British Empire awards, the view being taken that the matter was federal ; cf. Keith, *Responsible Government in the Dominions*, ii. 808. The Labour Government of New South Wales disapproved of the grant of any hereditary title (April 28, 1920).

an error to seek to create hereditary dignities in democratic societies. The injury done to the political prestige of Sir Joseph Ward by his acceptance of a baronetcy in 1911 has been a warning to statesmen in New Zealand of the dangers of violating public sentiment on this score, and the Union of South Africa alone has shown little or no feeling on the subject of the practice of bestowing baronetcies on its leading men, a fact fully explained by the social conditions of that territory. The Nationalists, indeed, disapprove wholeheartedly of such honours, but on republican rather than on democratic grounds.

There is, however, little doubt that the tendency of Dominion sentiment is more and more definitely against titles of honour, and the feeling has been strengthened by the somewhat lavish distribution of decorations of the Order of the British Empire, accompanied as it has been by grave errors both of selection and omission.

8. Appeals to the Privy Council

Fresh importance has been attached by the development of the status of the Dominions to the question of the retention of the right to appeal from Dominion courts to the Judicial Committee of the Privy Council. That body itself has shown no anxiety to extend its jurisdiction; it has on the contrary affirmed the principle that only on cases of the highest importance will it hear appeals from the Union of South Africa,[1] so that for practical purposes the appeal from the Union is a matter of mere theoretic interest. It has similarly declined to exercise its technically valid right to hear criminal appeals from Canada, even in so interesting a case as that of the Winnipeg rioters whose condemnation raised bitter political feeling in the Dominion.[2] It has also shown great reluctance to grant leave to appeal in any Australian case not of the first importance. It may, therefore, be held that the jurisdiction, though still in active exercise and though still of the highest importance as regards cases on the Canadian constitution, is in process of obsolescence, and that the way is paved for its extinction unless steps are taken to revise the basis on which it

[1] *Whittaker* v. *Mayor and Councillors of Durban*, (1920) 36 T. L. R. 784; contrast *Marshall's Township Syndicate* v. *Johannesburg Investment Co.*, [1920] A. C. 421.

[2] *Russell* v. *R.*, The Times, June 22, 1920 (Appellate Court of Manitoba).

rests. The feeling in Canada in favour of the retention of the appeal is growing weaker, as is evinced by the proposal in 1920 of the Ontario Government to secure the abolition of appeals from the courts of that province to the Judicial Committee. The proposal was ultimately dropped, and it is plain that it was *ultra vires* the provincial legislature, as the right of the Committee to grant leave to appeal rests on the Imperial Act of 1844, so that while the legislation of Ontario might successfully bar the prerogative right to grant leave, it could not invalidate the statutory right or the Order in Council as to appeals from Ontario made under the Act.[1]

Mr. Chamberlain in 1900 was responsible for an effort, then without result, owing largely to hostility in the United Kingdom and the colonies alike to any change, to secure the merger of the House of Lords in its judicial capacity with the Judicial Committee of the Privy Council in a single appellate court of the highest standing for the whole Empire.[2] The suggestion was taken up again by the Prime Minister of the Commonwealth at the Imperial War Conference of 1918, when he urged that the common share of the people of the Dominions in the war entitled them to expect to share a common final appellate court. It should, he urged, be constituted of the Lord Chancellor of the United Kingdom; persons who had held certain high judicial offices; and other persons specially selected from the United Kingdom, India, the Dominions and the colonies to serve as members. The tenure of office of all the members should be during good behaviour, and their salaries should be equal, and should be defrayed from the Imperial Exchequer. Appointments of Dominion judges should be made in consultation with the Dominion Governments, but there should be no formal rules as to the representation of Dominion judges on the tribunal; the adoption of the principle that the fittest man to fill each vacancy should be appointed, it being understood that familiarity with the subjects likely to come before the tribunal was an element of fitness, should be relied upon to secure for the Dominions, not formally but practically, the same degree of representation on the supreme tribunal as that enjoyed by Scotland or Ireland.

[1] Keith, *Journal of Society of Comparative Legislation*, xvi. 218.
[2] Keith, *Imperial Unity*, pp. 379–81.

The essence of the new scheme was the substitution of effective and continuous service by Dominion judges on the final tribunal of appeal on the same footing as the other members of the court, in lieu of the present system under which Dominion appeals are dealt with by a court of inferior status to the House of Lords, and one on which, though the presence of Dominion judges is possible, they sit only for the hearing of a few cases, chiefly those from their own Dominions, and receive no remuneration for their work. The suggestion, however, received little support at the Conference ; the Lord Chancellor saw many practical difficulties in the way of success ; Sir Robert Borden hinted that Canada would like to see a reduction of appellate courts, and the representatives of South Africa, India, and Newfoundland were unable to commit themselves to approval of the creation of one final court of appeal.[1]   Finally, a compromise resolution was arrived at, which commended to the prompt consideration of the Imperial Government the question of the replacement of the existing dual system of appeal by the creation of a single Imperial Court of Appeal, and invited the Lord Chancellor to prepare and circulate to the Dominions and India a memorandum of any proposals which the Imperial Government felt able to support. It was, however, clear from the trend of the discussion as from the absence of further developments in the United Kingdom or the Dominions that, though the question was left over for further consideration at the next Imperial Conference, there was little prospect of any serious progress in this regard. It is of special importance that Sir Robert Borden suggested that Canada should undertake the decision of all her constitutional questions, and that even Mr. Hughes was prepared seriously to consider the final abolition of the appeal. Such a step would, of course, harmonize well with the independent status now attained by the Dominions, but Mr. Hughes's proposal is obviously equally compatible with that status, and a Court of Appeal of the type indicated by him would serve as a very real link of unity within the Empire, while the practical difficulties caused by distance could

[1] *Parl. Pap.* Cd. 9177, pp. 134–53, 202–8, 210, 211, 243, 244.   A recent case of divergence between the Lords and the Committee is *London Joint Stock Bank* v. *Macmillan*, [1918] A.C. 777, as against *Colonial Bank of Australia* v. *Marshall*, [1906] A.C. 559.

be mitigated by the dispatch of panels of the Court of Appeal to hear appeals from time to time in the Dominions.

The arguments against the perpetuation of the right of appeal to the Privy Council may be put succinctly [1] as the inferiority of status which it implies ; the suggestion that Dominion judges are deficient in character or judicial capacity ; and from time to time the failure of the Court effectively to deal with legislation passed in the Dominions to meet commercial or other conditions of a peculiar character ; decisions of the Court on native lands in New Zealand, on the power of the Commonwealth to create Royal Commissions, and on the respective authority of the provinces and the Dominion in Canada in respect to companies, have elicited criticisms in the Dominions which, if by no means wholly justified, have had some foundation in truth. On the other hand some of the arguments adduced in favour of the continuance of the appeal are hardly of serious weight ; the impression that there is something of special value in the idea of a suppliant having the right to ask the King to do him justice, which has been refused in the Courts of the Dominion, has really very little applicability to a procedure which enables wealthy corporations to inflict grave difficulties on poorer litigants, and which is practically not effectively available to a poor litigant. Nor is there much more force in the argument that the Judicial Committee tends to secure a uniformity of law, for so many inroads have been made in the Dominions into the common law that this function is of no great importance, and in Quebec and the Union of South Africa English law is not the common law. There is greater validity in the contention that the Court serves to maintain the true doctrine of the royal prerogative, a subject especially difficult for Dominion Courts to deal with, and that its overruling authority preserves the supremacy of Imperial over Dominion legislation, where the two conflict. But the fact that the Commonwealth High Court not unsuccessfully interprets the Commonwealth constitution indicates that there are few questions with which the local courts cannot effectively deal, and that there is no sufficient ground to justify the retention of the present system of appeals.

[1] Manitoba *Free Press*, September 24, 1919 ; cf. W. E. Raney, *Canadian Nationality*, pp. 5, 6 ; Keith, *Journal of Comparative Legislation*, ii. 331, 332.

CHAPTER XI

THE FEDERAL CONSTITUTIONS UNDER WAR CONDITIONS

1. THE DOMINION AND THE PROVINCES.

The French language in Ontario — Agitation in Quebec — Decision of the Privy Council — Dissatisfaction of Quebec — Divorce legislation — Disallowance of Provincial legislation — Unconstitutionality of initiative and referendum in the Provinces — Dominion war measures regarding Provincial and municipal finance.

2. THE COMMONWEALTH AND THE STATES.

The proposed referenda of 1915 — Abandonment of the referenda — War powers of the Commonwealth Parliament — The referenda of 1919 — Grievances of the States.

1. THE DOMINION AND THE PROVINCES

THE outstanding effect of the war on federal government in the Dominion was the recrudescence in an exaggerated form of the latent opposition between the French-speaking people of Quebec and the English-speaking people who constitute a considerable minority in that province, and an undisputed and often overwhelming majority in the other provinces of the Dominion. The divergence of view which made the English element of the population enthusiastic for a war which was a matter of indifference or positive dislike to a considerable proportion of the French population was inevitable. The average countryman of Quebec knew absolutely nothing of foreign politics ; he had no feeling against Germany, and emigrant priests had convinced him that France was atheistic, and opposed to the just rights of the Papacy. Unfortunately, too, there was already in existence, when war broke out, hostility against the Government and people of Ontario, for what was asserted to be a deliberate effort to overthrow the position of the French language in that province.[1]

The British North America Act, 1867,[2] gave official equality to both the French and the English languages in Quebec and the

[1] G. M. Wrong in *The New Era in Canada*, pp. 229–59.

[2] 30 & 31 Vict. c. 3, s. 133. This was applied to Manitoba by the Canadian Act, 33 Vict. c. 3, s. 23.

business of the federal Parliament and the federal courts. This express declaration left it to be inferred that English alone was to be the official language of the other provinces, until in 1870, when the new province of Manitoba was created out of lands formerly under the Hudson Bay Company, both languages there were accorded equal rights, a fact due to the existence in the territory of a population largely French-speaking; but in 1890 the legislature of Manitoba, in which the English-speaking population had outgrown the French, repealed the privileges granted to French. It was natural, however, for the people of Quebec to overlook the fact that French had no claim to official recognition outside Quebec and in federal business, and to feel that any neglect of the French language was contrary to the spirit of the federation, though it cannot be admitted that there was any just ground for the contention.

The British North America Act,[1] however, did contain a provision as to education which gave denominations certain rights. It conferred on the legislatures of the provinces the sole right of legislation on this topic, but it enacted that ' nothing in any such law shall prejudicially affect any right or privilege with respect to denominational schools which any class of persons have by law in the province at the Union '. The words of the enactment were wide and vague, and it is easy to see how very different interpretations might honestly be put upon them. Such school privileges appertaining to denominations existed in Ontario at the time of Union. An Act [2] passed before the Union had provided that any number of people, not less than five, being Roman Catholics, might convene a public meeting of persons who desired to establish a separate school for Roman Catholic children, and that trustees might be elected to manage such schools. The Act gave to these trustees the status of bodies corporate, and authorized them to impose rates on, and collect subscriptions from, persons sending their children to the schools or willing to contribute to their maintenance, and gave them the same powers with regard to these separate schools as were possessed under the Common Schools Act of 1859 of Canada by the trustees of common schools. These powers included the right to acquire school sites

[1] s. 93.　　　　　　　　　[2] 26 Vict. c. 5.

and premises, to determine the kind and description of schools to be established, the teachers to be employed and the terms of their employment; but an obligation was imposed on the trustees to see that the text-books should be a uniform series of authorized text-books, and that all schools under their charge were conducted according to the regulations authorized by the Government from time to time.

The boundary between Ontario and Quebec is artificial, and French are naturally to be found there, especially in the counties of Prescott and Russell, bordered by the Ottawa river, which forms the boundary, but also in the west at Sandwich. For twenty years after federation no attempt was made to press the learning of English in those areas where the French predominated, and where separate schools accordingly flourished. But the Orange influence is strong in Ontario, and apart from this the English-speaking Roman Catholics of the province were anxious that in Ontario they, and not French-speaking Catholics, should control the counsels of the Church. By 1885, therefore, the Government were induced to act, and the rule was laid down that in all schools in the French and German districts the pupils should be taught to read English, and in 1890 efforts were made to train bilingual teachers to facilitate the process; but the movement was not particularly successful, for the salaries paid were absurdly low, and the demand for bilingual persons in other occupations considerable. The controversy continued its process, but in 1905 the fall of the Liberals from power brought into office a Conservative Government, which dealt more effectively with the issue. A Commission was appointed to investigate the question, and the report showed that in many schools there was no effective teaching of English, that the education given was ineffective and the attendance bad. The result was the issue in June 1912 by the Ontario department of education of an Instruction No. 17 effecting radical changes in the position, though in a reissue of August 17, 1913, some modifications in detail were made. The effect of the new rules was that English must be taught to every pupil as soon as he entered the school, and that, while French might be used as a medium of instruction for the Form I period of a child's school life, after that English must be the medium, though the Inspector of any school was authorized to permit the continued use of French for this purpose, where the children did not understand English. At the same time it was made clear that the teaching of French, as distinguished from its use as a medium of study, was normally to be restricted to an hour a day unless the Inspector ordered otherwise, and it was alleged that the Instruction meant that French could only be taught in schools where it had been taught before the issue of the Instruction, and that, if new schools were opened, French could not be made a subject of instruction. This interpretation, however, was denied by the department, which pointed out that under other regulations the teaching of French or German was permitted in schools, old or new, if the Inspector recommended it and the department approved. But obviously the position of the French language was seriously affected, and Quebec was much moved. It had already been divided seriously in sentiment from the rest of the Dominion by the determination of Sir Wilfrid Laurier, as a result of the Defence Conference of 1909, to establish a Canadian Navy, and at the general election of 1911 the leaders of Quebec Nationalism opposed him bitterly. When in 1913 Sir R. Borden adopted instead the policy of contribution of 35,000,000 dollars to the British Navy in order to permit of an immediate increase in the number of its capital ships, Sir Wilfrid Laurier opposed the suggestion, and through his influence the Senate, which still contained a Liberal majority, rejected the proposal, a fact which stimulated bitterness in Ontario, which showed itself in renewed insistence on the Government carrying out its policy as to education. The issues of defence and education were of course vitally distinct ; the former was federal, the latter provincial, but logical considerations were of no import in such a case.

The outbreak of war gave additional fuel to the strife ; Mr. Bourassa claimed that Quebec had no interest in the struggle, the Empire should look after its own affairs, British navalism was as bad as German militarism, British domination as objectionable as German, and Britain tyrannized over the Boers, the Irish and the French Canadians whose language was denied its just rights. The divergence between French and English speakers increased even among Roman Catholics ; in 1915 a final step was taken in the gradual process, which had substituted French-speaking teachers for English in the Roman Catholic University of Ottawa, through the dismissal of all English-speaking professors, thus forcing English-speaking students to seek elsewhere the secondary and university training which they had hitherto gladly sought there. The split spread to the west ; in Manitoba in 1916 the newly elected Liberal Government made the teaching of English compulsory in the schools, and on the death of the Archbishop of Winnipeg, Mgr. Langevin, the see was divided between a French-speaking and an English-speaking bishop. It was at Ottawa, however, that feeling ran highest, a fact easily explained by the special circumstances of the city. The presence there of the Federal Government and the use of French on an equality with English in official business, and the proximity of Quebec, which meant that many workers in Ottawa lived over the border, where their children were educated in schools where French was the only language in use, made the claim of the Government to restrict French teaching seem not merely harsh, but a defiance of the constitution. The Board of Trustees of the Roman Catholic Separate Schools, therefore, determined to defy the Instruction of 1912 ; it declined to permit inspection by any but its own inspectors ; it got rid of its costly lay staff in favour of the cheaper services of members of religious orders, some of whom did not possess the qualifications necessary under Ontario regulations for school teachers, and it sought to borrow money to open new schools in which French would be taught and used in defiance of the Instruction. In this policy, however, it had not merely the Government to fear, but the English members of the Board, who objected, though themselves Roman Catholics, to measures which, they contended, had nothing to do with their faith but concerned the domination of the French members of the Board only. On April 29, 1914, these members of the Board obtained from the Supreme Court of Ontario an injunction forbidding the Board to pay or employ teachers not legally qualified, and to borrow money, so long as the provincial regulations were not obeyed. The Board replied by an act of defiance ; it dismissed its staff, closed its schools, and left seven or eight thousand children in Ottawa without instruction. The case in the Courts proceeded to final judgement,[1] which, delivered on September 11, 1914, ordered the Board to reopen the schools and to employ only duly qualified teachers, and on July 12, 1915, the Appellate Division of the Supreme Court affirmed this judgement.

In the meantime the Legislature had been moved to further action to meet the issue. It enacted in 1915 an Act which expressly provided that the Instructions of the department were binding on the Board, and which proceeded to the strong step of authorizing the provincial government to withdraw for such time as it thought fit the rights of the Board and to confer them upon a Commission nominated by the Government. Accordingly, three Commissioners were appointed on August 4, 1915, who proceeded to carry on the schools, removing those teachers who were not duly qualified to teach. On the Misses Deloges thus being required to desist from teaching, their pupils withdrew with them, and angry mobs of women sought to prevent children attending schools where teachers named by the Commission were employed. The Legislature of Quebec, quite unconstitutionally, decided that it was interested in the contest, and authorized municipalities to make grants out of the parish taxes for the purpose of supporting the agitation against Ontario. The St. Jean Baptiste Society, the national organization of French Canadians, took up the struggle; efforts were made to have the Act disallowed by the Dominion Government, but the request was refused on the sound ground that the measure was clearly within the powers of the province to enact. The matter was carried into federal politics, though plainly the question lay without the sphere of the Federal Parliament. Mr. Lapointe, a Liberal member for Quebec, moved, and Sir Wilfrid Laurier seconded, a motion ' that this house, especially at this time of universal sacrifice and anxiety, when all energies should be concentrated on the winning of the war, would, while fully recognizing the principle of provincial rights and the necessity of every child being given a thorough English education, respectfully suggest to the Legislative Assembly the wisdom of making it clear that the privilege of the children of French parentage of being taught in their mother tongue be not interfered with '. The constitutionality of the legislation of the province was not

[1] *Mackell* v. *Ottawa Separate School Board*, 32 Ont. L.R. 245.

seriously disputed in the debate, and the Prime Minister rested his opposition to the suggestion on that ground, while neither approving or disapproving the substance of the resolution. In the ultimate issue it was defeated by 107 to 60 votes ; their distribution is interesting : a suggestion that Sir Wilfrid Laurier would resign his leadership of the Liberal Party, if the Ontario Liberals voted against the motion, kept all but one loyal to their leader; but the Liberals from Manitoba, Saskatchewan, and Alberta voted solidly against it, and an intimation by the Prime Minister that he would advise a dissolution, if the French members of his Cabinet voted for it, prevented a split in the governmental party.

The constitutional rights of the case were eventually, on November 2, 1916, decided by the Judicial Committee of the Privy Council,[1] in a manner satisfactory to Ontario, if rather disconcerting in detail. They analysed the legislation affecting the issue, and laid it down that the trustees were bound to carry out any regulations affecting their schools dealing with the language of instruction, unless it interfered with a right or privilege accorded by the Act of 1867, that is a right or privilege attached to denominational teaching, and that the question of language was not such a right or privilege. But at the same time they held that the Act authorizing the substitution of a Commission for the Board of Trustees was not within the powers of the local legislature, on the ground that it did affect prejudicially the privilege enjoyed by any five or more Roman Catholics who desired to have separate schools and to elect managers for them. The result, therefore, was that the Board of Trustees alone was entitled to manage the schools, but that it must comply with the regulations of the Government, including those affecting the teaching of languages and the employment of qualified teachers. The Commission at once handed over the control of the schools, and there the litigation might have ended with profit to all parties. Unfortunately, the Board decided to carry it further ; the Commission had raised during its management of the schools a rate of 84,000 dollars, and obtained from the Quebec Bank 97,000 dollars, and from the Bank of Ottawa 71,000 dollars more. The Board,

---

[1] *Ottawa Separate Schools Trustees* v. *Mackell*, [1917] A.C. 62 ; *Ottawa Separate Schools Trustees* v. *Ottawa Corporation*, [1917] A.C. 76.

thereupon, sued the Quebec Bank [1] for the 97,000 dollars which had been expended from the funds standing to the Board's account in the bank, the Bank of Ottawa for 37,000 dollars which had been transferred to it from the funds obtained from the Quebec Bank and held by it as a sinking fund to meet certain debentures issued by the Board, and the Commissioners for the sum raised by the rate. The whole proceeding was obviously vindictive ; the monies had been admittedly expended on education of Roman Catholic children in accordance with the law, and that either the banks or the Commissioners individually should be made liable would have been extremely unjust. The Supreme Court, however, felt itself bound to allow the claims, but subject to the deduction in the case of the Commissioners of such sums as they could show to have been properly expended on the conduct of the schools. The legislature, however, had intervened before the actions were tried by an Act which expressly provided that the payments made by the Commissioners were to be deemed for all purposes to have been made by them at the request of the Board, and that they were entitled to be indemnified by the Board in respect of them, while the liability of the Board to the Bank of Ottawa for the loan of 71,000 dollars was expressly affirmed. The Act was given fuller effect by the Appellate Division of the Supreme Court and by the Judicial Committee, which agreed that it was valid, and that it did not in any way prejudicially affect rights of denominations in Quebec.

The decisions of the Judicial Committee at the same time made the position perfectly clear regarding the duties of the Board. They pointed out in their judgement of November 2, 1916, that not only was the Board subject to legal process if it declined to carry out its obligations, but that their decisions in no way affected the principle of compulsory free primary education enacted in the Schools Act of 1859. If, therefore, the Board failed to carry out the duties imposed upon it in connexion with the privileges granted to Roman Catholics, the result would be that the children would be compelled to attend the common schools, and thus be deprived of the privileges regarding religious education desired for them.

[1] *Ottawa Separate Schools Trustees* v. *Quebec Bank*, [1920] A.C. 230.

The pronouncements of the Privy Council undoubtedly effected a simplification in the issue, and the leaders of the Catholic hierarchy with much wisdom did their best to calm ruffled feelings and secure the carrying out of the rules laid down by the Government. But the resentment of Quebec was profound, and, when the angry feelings were about to subside, the issue between the province and the rest of the Dominion was revived by the decision of the Dominion Government to pass a measure for compulsory service, to which French Canada was bitterly opposed. The opposition of Quebec was as bitterly resented in the English-speaking provinces, and the conflict of feeling led to a suggestion in the Quebec legislature of the adoption of a motion that ' this house is of opinion that the province of Quebec would be disposed to accept a rupture of the federation pact of 1867 if in the opinion of the other provinces it is believed that the said province is obstructive to the union, progress, and development of Canada '. More hotheaded partisans suggested absurd ideals of an independent French Quebec, possibly on a Republican basis, possibly under the British Crown, but wholly free from connexion with the rest of the Dominion. Nothing serious came of the proposal, which was set down for discussion on January 18–23, 1918, for the Premier, Sir Lomer Gouin, treated the topic with good sense and judgement, and his influence also was effective, after the deplorable rioting in Quebec against the enforcement of the military service levy in April, in securing the acquiescence of Quebec in the necessity of obeying the levy. Yet the bitterness of feeling regarding the position of the French language has by no means diminished in intensity if its demonstrations have been modified in form. M. Rodophe Lemieux, who won considerable distinction in Sir Wilfrid Laurier's Government, has pressed the topic as one on which the influence of other parts of the Empire might justly be brought to bear on the public feeling of Canada,[1] and strong arguments have been adduced in favour either of introducing French as a normal subject of teaching in all provincial

[1] Cf. Mr. N. A. Belcourt in Canadian *Senate Debates*, April 7, 1920. An effort was made in April 1918 in the Senate to amend the railway Bill to compel trainmen on local trains in Quebec to speak both languages. In 1919 Saskatchewan adopted legislation similar to that of Ontario regarding the use and teaching of French.

schools, or at least of improving the teaching of French where it already is taught, and extending its use where there is any desire to learn it. It must not, however, be forgotten that in parts of the west of the country it is not French but German or a Slav speech which commands many speakers, and that, if the English-speaking provinces do not encourage the learning of French, Quebec certainly does not encourage the learning of English.

A further sign of the diminished influence of Quebec on Dominion politics during the war is seen in the attitude adopted by the Federal Government towards divorce. The constitution of the Dominion accords to the Dominion Parliament legislative authority in matters of divorce, but it did not interfere with powers already vested in the courts of the provinces to grant divorce. Such powers existed in the case of Nova Scotia, New Brunswick, and British Columbia, but it was generally held that none of the other provincial courts had power to grant divorces. It was obviously the duty of the Dominion to provide courts which could dissolve marriages in other provinces, but the Dominion would not confer this jurisdiction on any provincial court. The reason was simple ; Quebec was determined to object to any divorce legislation of this kind, and no administration was prepared to face the hostility of that province. The result was that, as divorces could not absolutely be denied, divorce by Parliamentary enactment became usual, and the duty of investigating such applications was ascribed to the Senate, a body with no special qualifications, it need hardly be said, for so difficult a task. The House of Commons, however, did not abandon the right of examining the decisions of the Senate, though it exercised it but rarely.

The first breach in the system arose from the discovery, which was confirmed by decisions of the Judicial Committee of the Privy Council,[1] that in the western provinces, Manitoba, Saskatchewan, and Alberta, the courts had the right to grant divorces, though it had not been realized that legislation prior to confederation had endowed their courts with jurisdiction in divorce. The ground for the misunderstanding was simple enough ; the powers granted

---

[1] See *Canadian Law Times*, xxxvii. 687–705 ; xl. 337–43 ; *Board* v. *Board*, [1919] A.C. 956 ; *Walker* v. *Walker*, ibid. 947.

to the courts were in general terms conferring on them jurisdiction possessed by English courts at the time when the provincial courts came into being, and the general impression was that the jurisdiction created in England by the Imperial Act of 1857 regarding divorce was of so special a character that it did not pass under a general grant of authority, a doctrine now finally dispelled. Thus an incurable breach had been created in the divorce jurisdiction of the Dominion Parliament, and the absurdity of continuing to deny Ontario a divorce court was made manifest. But these considerations could hardly have prevailed, had Quebec possessed her old authority in the Dominion, and it was the comparative eclipse of her dominion in Parliament that permitted the Government to approve the principle that Parliament should establish a regular system of divorce throughout Canada.

It was Quebec also which brought into prominence the vexed question of the disallowance of provincial legislation[1] on the authority of the Dominion Government. The constitution accords the right without qualification to the Dominion, and in the early days of the federation it was exercised without hesitation in any case where the Dominion Government were dissatisfied with the provincial action. But this state of affairs gradually died out, and under Sir Wilfrid Laurier's last administration the rule was in effect laid down that disallowance would not be used save on the ground that the measure impugned was unconstitutional, and that the provinces must be the judges of what measures within the limit of their legal authority they would enact. The doctrine thus enunciated was not, however, accepted in its entirety by Mr. Doherty, Minister of Justice in the Conservative administration, and in 1912 he asserted the right of the Dominion to intervene ' for the purpose of preventing, not inconsistently with the public interest, irreparable injustice or undue interference with private rights or property through the operation of local statutes *intra vires* of the legislatures'. The adoption of this position entailed obvious difficulties, such as the appeal from Quebec for the disallowance of the Ontario Act of 1915 regarding the supersession of the Board of Trustees of the Roman Catholic schools there, and

[1] Keith, *Responsible Government in the Dominions*, ii. 725–49 ; *Imperial Unity*, pp. 432–6.

on one ground or other the principle, though from time to time reiterated by its author, remained a *brutum fulmen* until May 30, 1918, when the Dominion Government formally disallowed an Act of the legislature of British Columbia on the ground that it was an invasion of valuable proprietary rights.[1] It must, however, be added that in this instance the Dominion had more than a merely general concern. The statute was held to derogate from an arrangement with regard to the lands in the railway belt of British Columbia into which the Dominion along with the provincial government had entered in 1883 with the Esquimalt and Nanaimo Railway Company, so that acquiescence by the Dominion in the legislation might have been held to involve it in the same condemnation for repudiating an agreement as the provincial government and legislature.

The revival of the control of the Dominion over provincial legislation is naturally not acceptable to the provinces, which on the other hand have been accorded by decisions of the Judicial Committee on the complex and confused topic of company law a wider sphere of power than the Dominion had contended for, and had generally been deemed to appertain to the provinces.[2] Moreover the western provinces other than British Columbia have claimed that the appropriation of the control of their lands by the Dominion, which has been in force since they attained provincial status, is, if not *ultra vires* of the Dominion,[3] at least unconstitutional, and that the Dominion constitution implies that all the provinces should be on the same footing, and not subject to Dominion ownership or control of their public lands. The Conservative Government was under a vague pledge to give effect to the desires of the provinces in this regard, but the undertaking has not matured in action. But this and other considerations have raised more and more definitely the feeling that the time has come for the existing provisions of the constitution to be revised. A legal difficulty, however, here intervenes in the absence of any method other than an Imperial Act to alter the British North America Act of 1867, and the impossibility of securing

[1] *Canadian Law Times*, xxxviii. 445–9, 584 ; Act 1917, c. 71.

[2] T. Mulvey, *Canadian Law Times*, xxxix. 79–101 ; *Great West Saddlery Co.* v. *R.*, 37 T.L.R. 436.

[3] B. Thompson, *Canadian Law Times*, xxxix. 494–508 ; xl. 101–21.

legislation from the Imperial Parliament, save on a matter in which there is agreement in substance between not only the parties in the Federal Parliament, but also between the provinces and the Dominion. The position of Quebec renders solution difficult, for any power given to the Canadian people to change the constitution might result in an impairment of the self-determination of Quebec.

The existence of an important and perhaps unsuspected limitation on the powers of the provinces was revealed by the decision of the Judicial Committee against the validity of the Initiative and Referendum Act of 1906 of Manitoba.[1] The measure provided that legislation might be initiated, even connected with supply, by electors not less in number than 8 per cent. of the votes cast at the last general election ; the legislature was given the power of passing the Bill desired at the session during which it was submitted, but, if it failed to do so, the Bill fell to be submitted to a referendum contemporaneously with the next general election or to a special referendum if desired by the petitioners. If it received a majority of the votes cast, it then became law, ' subject, however, to the same powers of veto and disallowance as are provided in the British North America Act or as exist in law with respect to any Act of the Legislative Assembly.' Similarly electors, not less in number than 5 per cent. of the votes at the last general election, might petition for the repeal of an Act, and, if it were not repealed by the legislature, the same procedure became applicable with the difference that, if a majority of votes favoured repeal, the Act became *ipso facto* repealed. The measure obviously affected vitally the position of the legislature of the province, and it might be doubted whether on general grounds it could be held that a legislature might divest itself of its functions to such an extent. The grounds, however, on which the Act was held by the Judicial Committee to be *ultra vires* were more technical. Apart from the fact that under the British North America Act supply measures can be initiated only on the motion of a minister of the Crown or with the sanction of the Crown, the Act affected in a vital point the office of Lieutenant-Governor,

---

[1] Keith, *Journal of Comparative Legislation*, ii. 111–15. An Initiative and Referendum Bill was introduced in New Zealand in 1919 but went no further.

which is excepted from the general powers of provincial legislatures to alter the constitution, by depriving him in the case of the repeal by the referendum of an Act of the right to withhold his assent which belongs to him in respect of all Bills of the legislature, and in the opinion of the Judicial Committee it was even doubtful whether he retained the right of withholding assent in respect of measures enacted by the referendum.[1] With the Manitoba Act must, it seems, fall the Alberta Act for the same purpose, though that measure is more guarded in its terms. Seemingly, therefore, if these devices are to be introduced into the provincial constitutions, an amendment of the British North America Act will be essential.

The strength of the feeling for autonomy in Quebec was seen on the passing on December 22, 1917, of an Order in Council which prohibited the issue of securities by provinces, municipalities, and companies without the consent of the Minister of Finance for the Dominion. Against this Order, Quebec, with the support of Saskatchewan, protested in violent terms, declining to recognize its validity. The minister met the criticisms of the provinces by pointing out that, if the Dominion were held not to have the power claimed with regard to the provinces, it would equally be unable to exercise them in respect of municipal issues, while control and regulation were essential to secure that the Canadian money market should be conserved for the issue of absolutely necessary securities, and liquid capital should not be diverted to unnecessary public works or unproductive enterprises. The objections of the provinces were ultimately met by amending on January 9, 1918, the regulations so as to allow the minister to authorize or approve issues after they had been placed on the market, while the Dominion Government consented to make advances to the provinces, to enable them to meet obligations maturing abroad without issuing loans in Canada. In the main, however, the emergency Orders in Council of the Federal Government were accepted as legitimate exercises of the extraordinary authority conferred by the War Measures Act, under which the economic measures adopted in the Dominion were given legal validity.

[1] [1919] A.C. 935. Compare British Columbia Act, 1919, c. 21.

2. The Commonwealth and the States

In Australia no less than in Canada the war complicated and rendered more urgent questions of the relations of the Commonwealth and the States. The constitution of 1900 was framed on strictly federal basis by men who chose as their model the constitution of the United States and who were prepared, even if not in all cases anxious, to see responsible government in the British sense replaced by the system of a non-parliamentary executive. On the whole since the constitution came into operation the tendency of Australian thought has lain rather in a desire to secure greater unity; there is not, it is contended, sufficient political ability in the Commonwealth to man seven legislatures effectively; there are no such distinctions of character among the people as to render provincial autonomy necessary or desirable; devolution of powers to subordinate legislative bodies by a central sovereign legislature would secure all that was necessary in the way of efficiency and avoid the endless contests in the courts as to the limits of State and federal powers which leave as many issues undecided as they solve, and impose unreasonable limitations on the powers of both the central and the local legislatures. On the other hand local feeling and conservatism have told in favour of the States, and the somewhat vehemently Labour character until lately of the Senate has rendered men unwilling to entrust undue authority to the Parliament of the Commonwealth. The Senate indeed has admittedly proved to respond but very imperfectly to the ideal of a chamber representing State interests, for the Labour Senators have proved in the main completely superior to State considerations, when these conflicted with the principles of the Labour party.

The obvious difficulties in the way of securing complete unification led the Labour party to seek to effect their result piecemeal, by securing such changes in the constitution from time to time as seemed to be necessitated by actual experience of the difficulties involved through the absence of such powers. In order to effect a change of the constitution a Bill must be passed by an absolute majority in either house of Parliament, and then submitted within six months to the vote of the electorate, becoming law if approved by a majority of electors in a majority of States, and by a majority of all the votes cast.[1] The first referendum to extend the powers of the Commonwealth was held on April 26, 1911, with a negative result ; the same proposals were submitted again by Labour on May 31, 1913, but on this occasion also without success, while at the same time, the voting proceeding contemporaneously with a general election, the Labour party suffered defeat by a bare margin. The election which took place in 1914, however, returned them to power, and in the session of 1915 they secured the passage by Parliament of six laws to confer very important powers on the Commonwealth. Under the constitution the Commonwealth has power only as to foreign and inter-State trade and commerce, leaving to the States the control of all trade and commerce so far as it is confined to the limits of any one State, and it was now proposed to extend the power of the Commonwealth to deal with all forms of trade and commerce, without indeed depriving the States of their power, but granting paramount authority to the Commonwealth. A second law dealt with corporations, the Commonwealth power under the constitution being restricted to foreign corporations and trading or financial corporations formed within the limits of the Commonwealth and as judicially interpreted being of small extent even with regard to such corporations. The new measure, accordingly, extended the Commonwealth jurisdiction to corporations generally, including ' (a) the creation, dissolution, regulation, and control of corporations ; (b) corporations formed under the law of a State, including their dissolution, regulation, and control, but not including municipal or governmental corporations, or any corporation formed solely for religious, charitable, scientific, or artistic purposes, and not for the acquisition of gain by the corporation or its members ; and (c) foreign corporations, including their regulation and control '. Even more important was the proposal to substitute new powers for the very narrow right of legislation for ' conciliation and arbitration for the prevention and settlement of industrial disputes extending beyond the limits of any one State '. It was proposed to grant in lieu the control of ' industrial matters, including (a) labour ; (b) employment and unemployment; (c) the terms and conditions of labour and employment in any

---

[1] Constitution, s. 128. See also J. Quick, *Legislative Powers of the Commonwealth and States of Australia* (1919).

trade, industry, occupation or calling; (d) the rights and obligations of employers and employees; (e) strikes and lockouts;
(f) the maintenance of industrial peace; and (g) the settlement of
industrial disputes '. A fourth law proposed to take away from the
States their sole right to control the conditions of service on their
railway services by empowering the Commonwealth to legislate for
' conciliation and arbitration for the prevention and settlement
of industrial disputes in relation to employment in the railway
service of a State '. Fifthly, power was granted entirely *de novo* to
regulate ' trusts, combinations, monopolies and arrangements in
relation to (a) the production, manufacture or supply of goods, or
the supply of services; or (b) the ownership of the means of production, manufacture, or supply of goods, or supply of services.'
Finally the Commonwealth was to be authorized to nationalize
on just terms the industry or business of producing, manufacturing,
or supplying any specified goods or of supplying any specified
services if both Houses of Parliament in the same session had
declared by absolute majorities that the industry or business was
the subject of a monopoly.

The attitude of the Liberal opposition[1] to these proposals was in
large measure that while, in part at least, they were necessary and
valuable in themselves and might suitably be passed during a time
of peace, when their merits and demerits could be calmly criticized
and weighed, it was wholly contrary to the best interest of the
country that referenda should be taken on December 11 as proposed by the Government. It was essential rather that the whole
strength of the country should be devoted to the business of winning the war, and distraction by domestic issues was utterly vain.
Labour, on the other hand, after stressing the fact that it was the
Liberal party which had refused at the opening of the war to drop
party strife, argued that the alterations were vital if the country
were to do its best in the war. To effect the mobilization of the
resources of Australia the Commonwealth must have control of all
the resources of the country and of all the men; they must be able
to dictate to capital and labour; to regulate prices and prevent
profiteering; to combat trusts and monopolies; to preserve
industrial peace by compelling capitalists to accept the awards of

[1] See P. M. Glynn, *Federal Constitution, The Proposed Amendments* (1915).

courts and not to seek to circumvent them by legal devices. The war would be a long one, and the country could not produce its most effective effort if the people could not be secured their just rights. To the argument that the powers might be misused and were too great to trust to a Government, they replied by the argument that, before using any of them, they would pass a Bill providing for the initiative and referendum which would place it in the power of the electors to veto any use of the powers which they might deem dangerous.

The argument against raising at such a moment an issue so contentious had strong supporters, and when, on Mr. Fisher's resignation of the leadership of the Labour Government to take up the office of High Commissioner in London, Mr. Hughes attained office as Premier, an important change of policy took place. A conference with State Governments elicited agreement on the principle that the State Parliaments should for the period of the war and one year thereafter confer on the Commonwealth the powers included in the referenda proposals with certain minor changes, and that in return the proposal to hold the referenda should be dropped. On November 4 the arrangement was announced and the referenda abandoned, but the State Parliaments showed no haste to redeem the undertakings on the strength of which the referenda had been dropped; only in New South Wales was the requisite Act[1] passed, and, as the scheme was only to be operative in the event of legislation by all six States, it fell to the ground. But the need of such legislation for war purposes became less essential in the course of time as a result of the decisions of the High Court, with which the interpretation of every constitutional question affecting the relations of the Commonwealth with the States or the States *inter se* rests,[2] unless it sees fit to allow—which in practice is extremely rare—recourse to the Judicial Committee of the Privy Council. The High Court had earned, before the referenda were due to be voted on, the dislike of the Labour party by its decision that it was within the legal power of a State to acquire wheat compulsorily, as did the New South Wales Government under an Act of 1914, and to provide for its sale and distribution, despite the rule of the con-

---

[1] No. 65 of 1915. In Western Australia the Bill was not even brought forward.
[2] Const., s. 74; *Jones* v. *Commonwealth Court of Conciliation*, [1917] A. C. 528.

stitution that trade, commerce, and intercourse among the States shall be absolutely free. It was contended that the New South Wales Act was a violation of this principle since it rendered it impossible to carry out contracts previously entered into for the export of wheat to Victoria. But the High Court overruled this objection ; every owner of goods, it pointed out, was at liberty to enter into such contracts as he thought desirable for the transport of goods from one State to another, and no State law could forbid, in view of the constitution, the making of such contracts. But, as soon as the State law operated to prevent the owner any longer possessing ownership by the transfer of ownership to the State, the provision of the constitution ceased to be applicable.[1] This judgement was regarded with dislike by Labour, partly because of its economic effects, partly because they deemed it to be, despite the reasoning of the court, a derogation from the doctrine of the economic unity of the Commonwealth. But the High Court showed no disposition to diminish Commonwealth rights, if it was not prepared to deny the States their rights. When the New South Wales Parliament passed the Meat Supply for Imperial Uses Act, 1915, under which it was enacted that all stock and meat in any place in New South Wales ' shall be held for the purposes of, and shall be kept for the disposal of His Majesty's Imperial Government in aid of the supplies for His Majesty's armies in the present war ', the High Court found that the enactment was invalid if it purported to prevent persons of Queensland domicile, who had purchased pigs in New South Wales, removing them from the State to Queensland.[2] In another case [3] the validity of regulations under the War Precautions Act, 1914–15, of the Commonwealth was challenged on the ground that the regulations impugned could not validly fall under the Commonwealth powers of legislation as to naval and military defence or as to naturalization and aliens. Under the rule in question authority had been conferred on the Minister for Defence to order any naturalized person whom he had reason to believe to be disaffected or disloyal to be detained in

---

[1] *The State of New South Wales* v. *The Commonwealth*, 20 C.L.R. 54.

[2] *Foggitt, Jones & Co.* v. *State of New South Wales*, (1916) 21 C.L.R. 357. The State had not acquired property in the stock.

[3] *Lloyd* v. *Wallach*, (1915) 20 C.L.R. 299 ; cf. Keith, *Imperial Unity*, pp. 357, 358 ; In re *Beranek*, (1915) 33 O.L.R. 139 (Canada War Measures Act, 1914).

military custody during the war. This decidedly drastic enactment was pronounced valid by the High Court, which went on to hold that the minister was not bound to give his reasons for the belief he professed, thus conferring upon him an extremely wide and even dangerous power over the liberty of naturalized persons. It must, it may be added, be remembered that naturalization was conferred before the war on fairly easy terms by the Commonwealth.

The most important sign of the attitude of the High Court to the powers of the Commonwealth in war time was afforded by the decision in the case of the right of the Commonwealth Parliament during the war under the powers granted by the War Precautions Act, 1916, to fix the prices of the necessaries of life, the contention being that such a power manifestly appertained to the States and to the States alone, and that the States had exercised the power. The Act of 1916 authorized the Government to make regulations prescribing the conditions of the disposal of property, goods, &c., and under it a regulation was made fixing the price of bread. On a conviction being recorded for a breach of the regulation by overcharging the matter was carried on appeal to the High Court, which by a majority of five justices to two held that the regulation was *intra vires*, on the ground that it was a matter of military defence, the minority on the other hand declaring that the right appertained to the States alone.[1] The decision, of course, was far more important than in its immediate application ; it established beyond doubt that practically any authority could be exercised by the Commonwealth during the war, if only it was honestly intended to serve the purpose of promoting the defence of the country in the widest sense of the term.[2]

The close of the war renewed the necessity of the consideration of the extent of Commonwealth powers, and on October 1, 1919, the Government introduced a Constitution Alteration (Legislative Powers) Bill which was passed on October 10. The measure contained four proposals for the amendment of the constitution so as to confer on the Commonwealth extended powers as to trade and commerce, corporations, industrial matters, and trusts and mono-

[1] *Farey* v. *Burdett*, (1916) 21 C.L.R. 433.
[2] For instances of such regulations see above, Chap. IV, § 2.

polies following the terms of the four Bills passed in 1915 but never submitted to the people. A separate Bill provided power for the nationalization of monopolies, but an important alteration was made in the terms of the measure as compared with that of 1915. It repeated the exclusion from the operation of the power of any industry or business conducted by a State Government or a public authority constituted by a State, and it provided that in any case the power of nationalizing a business, the subject of a monopoly, could only be exercised after the two houses of Parliament had referred to the High Court for report by a Justice the question whether the industry or business was really the subject of a monopoly, and on the Justice's report being received had declared that a monopoly did exist, the action of the houses in referring the question and in deciding it to be taken by an absolute majority. A further concession was made in both cases : the legislation was not in any event to be permanent ; it was to be passed for three years only at most, with the intention of the Commonwealth constituting before the end of that period a Convention to consider the recasting of the constitution and securing the approval of the recasting by the people. The enactments were then to cease to take effect, but it was expressly provided that if the Commonwealth Government failed to convene the Convention by December 31, 1920, the enactments would lapse on that date. These complicated provisions were, it was thought, likely to induce more ready acceptance of the proposals. In course of the passing of the Bills through the Parliament, the Government accepted two amendments to the first from the Senate. They abandoned the power to deal with ' the creation, dissolution, regulation and control of corporations ' on the substantial ground that, as the power was to last only for three years at most, and as it dealt only with corporations created by the Commonwealth, it was unnecessary to insist upon it, and they accepted the exclusion from the power to deal with State corporations in the case of educational corporations, as it was suggested that the power might be used to affect the State Universities, a proceeding which would have been extremely unpalatable to the States. The arguments for the Bills were based emphatically on the need of the powers in question to deal with the problems created by the war, among which profiteering took first place ; industrial unrest must be put down, and as matters stood the Commonwealth Court of Arbitration had no power to regulate the conditions of industry, had no power to lay down a common rule or provide for collective bargaining, and was helpless unless a dispute spread beyond the limits of a State. It was not proposed to supersede the State tribunals and wage boards, but to harmonize and assist their action. Monopolies again must be fought, and at present the Commonwealth was helpless, and it was ludicrous that the power to control trade stopped at the customs house. The high cost of living and scarcity of material could not be fought unless the powers asked for as a war measure were conceded. In the Senate Mr. E. J. Russell mentioned, as proof that further powers were urgently required, the doubtful validity of the carrying on of the manufacture of wool in the Commonwealth woollen mills, nor was it at all clear that the Commonwealth would have power on the expiry of the War Precautions Acts to combine in such commercial undertakings as the butter pool. The only opposition to either measure came from the Labour party, which argued that the terms of the Bills should have been more drastic ; exception was taken to the dropping of the proposal to take power to regulate the working and rates of State-owned railways, and to the provision for an inquiry by a Justice of the High Court before any industry or business could be pronounced a monopoly, but amendments to include these provisions were defeated.

Despite, however, the strong arguments in favour of the Bills and the unanimity of Parliament, on the referendum of December 13, 1919, both were rejected.

It must, however, be remembered that, if the Commonwealth feels aggrieved by its impotence in many directions, the States are equally aggrieved by what they regard as defects of the Commonwealth constitution,[1] and certain of these defects were made painfully prominent, in their opinion, by the war. The Commonwealth has deprived Western Australia of the revenue which she derived from customs prior to the advent of inter-State freedom of trade, and the war measures of the Commonwealth admittedly did some injury to her commerce and industry ; the export of her metallic

---

[1] *The Round Table*, ix. 798–807.

ores to markets abroad was prohibited in the interest of the smelting industry in the eastern States, while she was forbidden to import sugar in order to foster the sugar industry in Queensland, which, worked as it is by white labour, requires all the governmental support that can be spared to make it profitable. Tasmania in the war suffered similarly from her lack of importance; the Commonwealth did not find it worth while securing a fruit ' pool ', while in the case of the wheat and wool very effective arrangements were made for marketing the produce on good terms. Tasmania also has been eager for years for a proper shipping service, which many Governments have promised her, but which does not materialize. New South Wales again suspects the Commonwealth Government of being unduly affected by the influence of Melbourne, which has effectively prevented progress with the construction of the federal capital at Canberra, and much feeling arose between the State and the Commonwealth in 1919 when the influenza epidemic ravaged Australia and induced New South Wales to adopt drastic means of closing its borders to immigration of men or goods from the bordering States. The action taken was alleged to be an infringement of the Commonwealth power as to quarantine, but feeling in the State ran so high that the Commonwealth authorities did not press their point of view for the time being.[1] The question is, of course, complicated by the problem of the meaning of the provision of the constitution providing for freedom of trade, commerce, and intercourse among the States.

The States, moreover, are in the unhappy position that the Surplus Revenue Act, 1910, which allots to each State 25s. per head of population as a compensation for the loss of customs and excise can now be varied, and the proposals of the Commonwealth Treasurer in 1919 meditated the reduction of the amount by 2s. 6d. annually until it fell to 10s. in 1926, at which figure it would stand for five years. The States are thus in a certain measure dependent on federal goodwill, and it is this consideration which has given value to the decision of the Commonwealth Government as an outcome of the failure of the referendum to seek at any rate to secure the meeting of a convention which can

---

[1] A Bill to assert the supremacy of the Commonwealth law was brought in in 1920 and passed into law.

discuss the revision of the constitution as a whole. Labour, which has never regarded the States with favour, mainly in the first instance because of the power there exercised by the upper houses, which in Victoria, South Australia, Western Australia, and Tasmania are elective and anti-Labour, has developed an extreme policy which would abolish the Senate and reduce the Commonwealth Parliament to a unicameral legislature of a hundred members, while the States as sovereign entities would disappear and would be replaced by thirty-one district Councils each of ten members, which would, like the provinces of South Africa, be allotted certain defined powers, subject always to the paramount authority of the Commonwealth Parliament. This proposal involves the disappearance of the State Governors, and it was the fact that the abolition or diminution of the status of the Governors is an essential part of proposals for the lessening of the powers of the States that made the Conference of State Premiers in 1918 abandon what had been expected to be a unanimous vote in favour of locally appointed Governors.

In the meantime the Commonwealth High Court, which, in its inception inclined to a rigidly federal interpretation of the constitution, has by reason of changes in its personnel come to adopt an attitude far more generous to the authority of the Federal Parliament, has pronounced in August 1920 a judgement whose effect is likely to be far-reaching. Overriding earlier decisions which held that the Commonwealth Parliament could not, under its power to legislate as to conciliation and arbitration in cases where disputes extend beyond the limits of a State, affect the control by the States of their railway employees,[1] it has decided in a case where the Amalgamated Society of Engineers was claimant and a large number of business concerns, including trading concerns of the Government of Western Australia, were defendants, that it has jurisdiction as regards the relations of the minister controlling these concerns and the employees, and that there was no distinction to be drawn between railways and trading concerns. Mr. Justice Duffy dissented from so wide an extension of the powers of the Commonwealth. The question naturally arose whether interest on State loans was liable for federal income tax, but the

---

[1] See Keith, *Responsible Government in the Dominions*, ii. 837.

Federal Government has not committed itself on that head, pointing out that the reasonable expectation of the lender of money to the States must be borne in mind.

In *Joseph* v. *Colonial Treasurer* [1] the High Court pronounced the important decision that the Government of a State could not exercise the war prerogative of the Crown even in so far as that pertained to a Dominion Government, but that the power to do so rested with the Commonwealth as entrusted under the constitution with the defence of Australia.[2]

[1] 25 C.L.R. 32, overruling the decision of the New South Wales Supreme Court, 17 S.R. (N.S.W.) 624.

[2] See *Welsbach Light Co. of Australasia* v. *The Commonwealth*, (1916) 22 C.L.R. 268, affirming the validity of the Trading with the Enemy Act, 1914, No. 9, s. 2; (1917) 33 T.L.R. 382.   For the power of the Commonwealth to pass *ex post facto* legislation of the nature of the Crimes Acts No. 12 of 1914, and No. 6 of 1915, see *R.* v. *Kidman*, (1915) 20 C.L.R. 425.

CHAPTER XII

THE DOMINIONS AND INDIA

Admission of India to the War Cabinet and Conferences — Indian disabilities in the Dominions — Conference resolutions in 1917 and 1918 — Imposition of new disabilities in South Africa in 1919 — New Zealand Immigration Act, 1920 — The position in Canada.

THE Colonial Conference of 1907, in framing a constitution for the Imperial Conference, excluded from its membership India on the technical ground that India did not possess responsible government, and therefore should not have a place at a meeting of heads of responsible administrations, the assumption being that the Imperial Government would secure that due regard was had in the deliberations of the Conference to the necessities of India. In the case of the Conference of 1911 the exclusion of India was not a matter of moment, for its interests were presented on the one case where they were seriously involved, the anti-Asiatic shipping legislation of New Zealand, by Lord Crewe, whose experience as Secretary of State for the Colonies gave him wide authority. It is, however, remarkable that the Indian Government and the India Office should have acquiesced in the arrangement, and that the Indian legislature should have let it pass indicates how feebly the national spirit of India had been awakened. The growth of Indian nationalism was, however, rapid after 1911, and public feeling rose to considerable vehemence over the disabilities inflicted in South Africa on resident British Indians, and the refusal not only of the Union but of the other Dominions, especially Canada, to grant Indians entry. Supported by Indian opinion, the Indian Government became more effective in its protests, and the Imperial Government engaged in long negotiations with the Union Government with a view to remove what was plainly becoming a source of deep alienation of feeling between India and the Dominions and in a less degree the mother country, which ought, it was urged in India, to exercise effective control over the legislation and administration of the Dominions. The efforts of the United Kingdom in 1913 and

1914 happily succeeded in inducing the Union Government to come to a settlement with the Indians in South Africa, who had the advantage of the leadership of Mr. Gandhi. In Canada, however, matters went less satisfactorily. Apparently on the instigation of agitators engaged in machinations against the British Empire, endeavours were made to land large numbers of Indians in Canada, and nothing but the firmness of the Dominion Government foiled the attempt, which had an unhappy sequel, as some of those who were prohibited entrance, on their return to India, broke out in revolt and caused some loss of life before they were overpowered.[1]

Happily the readiness of the people of India as a whole to lend their aid in the war, and the valuable services rendered in France in the early days of hostilities by the Indian troops sent thither, resulted in the establishment of better feelings both in the Dominions and India, based on the respect due to a common loyalty and comradeship in arms. Already in 1915 the necessity of rescinding the resolution of 1907 was pointed out, and, though the suggestion was not immediately acted upon, when the summons was issued in December 1916 to call an Imperial War Cabinet into being, India was invited to send three representatives to aid the Secretary of State in stating the views of India on the subjects to be dealt with by the meeting. It was inevitable that the opportunity of pressing Indian claims to the treatment which her imperial services rendered due could not be lost, and at the meetings of the Imperial War Conference held contemporaneously with the Cabinet there were brought under discussion the two questions of the future position of India in regard to the Imperial Conference and the status of Indians in the Dominions. The former proved capable of solution, though by a method somewhat absurdly cumbrous; on the plea that the Conference was not the regular Imperial Conference—though its composition was identical—the resolution of 1907 was not modified, but it was agreed to recommend that the assent of the Governments should be obtained to its modification, so as to permit of the inclusion of India in the next regular Conference meeting.[2]

[1] Keith, *Imperial Unity*, pp. 194–213.
[2] *Parl. Pap.* Cd. 9005, pp. 22, 23.

The other problem [1] proved harder of settlement. It was pointed out in a note by the India Office that immigration of Indians into all the Dominions save Newfoundland, whose rigorous climate forbids Indian immigration, was effectively prevented by legal restrictions. In Australia and New Zealand exclusion was effected by a language test, so administered as to exclude every uneducated Indian and at pleasure every educated Indian. In South Africa power was taken to exclude immigrants of any race deemed unsuitable, and instructions secured that Indians were so deemed save in an infinitesimal number of cases of specially qualified men, whose admission formed part of the agreed settlement of 1914. In Canada similar power existed, but was not exercised, the exclusion of Indians resting in practice on the rule that an immigrant must come from his place of origin by a continuous voyage on a through ticket, which was impossible as there was no direct steamer communication ; and an Asiatic must possess 200 dollars, unless he belonged to a country with respect to which there was special statutory provision—as in the case of China, or with which a special agreement was operative as in the case of Japan. The outcome of this rule was to differentiate in a marked manner between Indians and Japanese, for the latter, under a special arrangement between the Japanese Government and that of Canada, were permitted to enter to a number not exceeding four hundred in all yearly, subject to their falling within certain categories, which included the families and domestic servants of Japanese already resident in the Dominion, and to their receiving permits from the Japanese Government, which thus made itself responsible for them. Under the compromise of 1914 Indians in the Union were permitted to introduce, if not already having a wife in the Union, a wife and her minor children, but no such concession was made in any other Dominion, though Canada was prepared to forgo the requirement of the possession of 200 dollars in the case of a wife, if she could comply with the condition of entry by a continuous voyage. In Canada tourists, students, and certain other classes of educated persons were not subject to the immigration laws ; but in the other Dominions even these persons required special

---

[1] *Parl. Pap.* Cd. 9005, pp. 117–21, 159–62.

permits, and the formalities involved were irksome and a cause of discontent.

Attention was also called to the complaints made by domiciled Indians of unjust discrimination against them. It was admitted that the grant of the franchise in Parliamentary elections in South Africa would be difficult, involving as it did questions of the rights of native Africans to vote, but it was pointed out that the withholding of the municipal franchise was a real injustice, especially as the grant of trading licences was largely in the control of the municipalities. To forbid domiciled Indians to introduce their wives and children was conducive to producing the risk of miscegenation and moral wrongdoing, which might be expected to result from a condition of affairs where family life was rendered impossible.

Stress was laid on the importance of consulting Indian feeling on the matter, and concrete suggestions were made to secure agreement. Domiciled Indians should be allowed, subject to the rule of monogamy, to introduce a wife and minor children, and Indians desiring to enter for labour or settlement should be allowed to do so on terms not inferior to those conceded to any other Asiatic race. If this were not possible, then arrangements might be made on the basis of mutuality for the exclusion of persons desirous of entering for purposes of settlement or labour, while provision was secured for the entry of tourists, students, and persons engaged on temporary business other than labour.

The arguments and suggestions of the India Office were reinforced at a private meeting arranged by Sir Robert Borden when Sir Satyendra Sinha, representing educated Indian opinion, explained the case for India moderately but effectively. At the official discussion on April 27, therefore, the proceedings were formal : the Conference accepted the principle of reciprocity of treatment and commended the views of the India Office to the favourable consideration of the Dominions.

The resolution shared for the time being the usual fate of Conference resolutions which require more than executive action. But India returned again to the charge at the Imperial War Conference of 1918, when Sir S. Sinha presented a memorandum [1]

---

[1] *Parl. Pap.* Cd. 9177, pp. 245-8.

in which he pressed for the grant of greater facilities for temporary residence in the case of students, tourists, and bona fide merchants, and for the grant to the Sikhs domiciled in British Columbia of the right to introduce their wives and children. But the main part of his memorandum dealt with the more difficult topic of the treatment of domiciled Indians in the Union, troubles having arisen there since the enactment of the Indians Relief Act, 1914. The difficulties in the Union are made far more real than elsewhere in the Dominions, since the policy of the other Dominions has rendered the numbers there negligible : according, however, to the census of 1911 there were 6,606 Indians in the Cape, 10,048 in the Transvaal, 106 in the Orange Free State, and 133,031 in Natal, and the increase since then cannot be less than 10,000.

The grievances of the Indians in the Union were mainly as regards the issues of licences to trade, and as to land rights, apart from the general grievance of the refusal of the Parliamentary franchise and of the municipal franchise in the Transvaal and the Free State, though in the other two provinces Indians had shown their capacity for the satisfactory exercise of the franchise. Trading licences are under recent legislation [1] controlled mainly by municipalities and appeals from their decisions are only allowed in certain cases ; thus an applicant for a licence in Natal can only appeal to the Provincial Division of the Supreme Court on a question of procedure, while an applicant for a mere renewal has an appeal on the facts as well. It was suggested that in all the provinces and in every case an appeal should be allowed on the facts and the law, on the ground that the trade rivals of the Indians used their authority on the municipalities to prevent the grant of new trading licences to Indians. The land question arose only in effect in the Transvaal, where the old Republican law no. 3 of 1885 forbade Indians to own fixed property. This provision from an early date was evaded by the device of nominal European ownership, but in 1914 this cumbrous and expensive method was superseded in favour of the principle of registering a company all whose members were Indians which,

[1] See Cape, Natal, Orange Free State Ordinances of 1914 ; Cape Ordinance No. 14 of 1916.

possessing a distinct juristic personality, was capable to hold land. The principal use made of these methods was to enable Indians to carry on business in townships where the Gold Law, 1908, or local regulations forbade the sale of stands to Indians, with the result that but for these means of evasion Indians would have been driven to reside and trade in special locations, the policy of the Republican Government against which the Indians carried on a spirited struggle even before the annexation of the Transvaal. It was suggested that, so far from opposing the possession of land by Indians, their right should be freely recognized by the repeal of the Act of 1885, which placed them in a position inferior even to Africans and was wholly without excuse. Complaint was also made of recent regulations regarding accommodation on the railways which rested on a racial base and were insulting to Indian self-respect.

The subject received more effective consideration by the Conference than in 1917, Sir R. Borden again using his influence to secure a favourable issue. It was agreed to give effect to the resolution of 1917 and to lay down the inherent right of each part of the Empire to exercise complete control of the composition of its population by restricting immigration from other parts. Visits of British citizens to other parts of the Empire should be permitted for purposes of pleasure or commerce, including temporary residence for educational purposes. Such visits should be regulated on the basis of passports or permits issued by the country of domicile and subject to visé there by an official of the country to be visited, if so desired by that country, and the right should not apply to visits or temporary residence for labour purposes, or to permanent settlement. India should have the right to subject British citizens domiciled in any other British country to the same conditions in visiting India as those imposed on Indians desiring to visit that country. Indians domiciled in any part of the Empire should be allowed to bring in their wives and minor children, provided that only one wife and her children could be admitted for each Indian, and that each individual so admitted should be certified by the Government of India as being the lawful wife or child of the Indian in question. The other points raised by the representatives of

India were commended to the early consideration of the Dominions concerned.[1]

On this occasion the outcome was more rapid. Canada, though not without uneasy protests, proceeded to arrange for the concession desired by the Sikhs as to the admission of their wives and children,[2] though in many cases the Sikhs had no intention of permanent settlement in Canada and merely desired to make money there. In Australia and New Zealand assurances were given that no difficulties existed in the way of the exercise of the right, which indeed was of negligible importance in view of the paucity of resident Indians. The necessary legislation based on reciprocal treatment which had been prepared in India in 1908 was presented to the Legislative Council in 1920. But the favourable consideration which had been hoped for in respect of the disabilities of Indians in the Union was destined to complete disappointment. On the contrary the outcry against the holding of trading licences by Indians and their use of the registration of companies to hold land became so strong that the Government capitulated and enacted a measure still less favourable to Indians than the existing law. The Transvaal Ordinance No. 9 of 1912 [3] gave the power to municipalities to grant trading licences, but allowed an appeal to a magistrate from a refusal, and in Krugersdorp in 1918 three cases occurred in which appeals were allowed, thus rousing angry temper among the competitors of the Indians. At the same time attention was concentrated on the use of companies to hold land, the number of Indian companies having increased from 3 in 1913 to 370 in 1919 with a capital of £480,000, carrying on a large trade in the East Rand area. Their rivals accused them of living in unsanitary premises, cutting prices, and other malpractices, while for the Indians it was argued that their methods were as honest as those of their competitors, and that the latter were not of any high status, being mainly Jews or other immigrants. The latter, however, had votes, and their views prevailed in the Act No. 37 of 1919. The effect of this measure is that in mining areas, which are, of course, the places

[1] *Parl. Pap.* Cd. 9177, pp. 195-201.

[2] Order in Council, March 26, 1919. An Order of June 12, 1918, exempted British Indians from military service.

[3] The Gold Law, No. 35 of 1908, forbade residence in gold areas.

where Indians desire especially to trade, no new trading licences may be issued after May 1, 1919, save in respect of businesses already established; that in other areas, which are of minor importance, no change is made; and that after the same date the devices by which Indians have managed to evade the law prohibiting their holding land are to be illegal.

It is hardly surprising that these new disabilities, occurring at a time when the status of India had been markedly increased by the determination to confer upon it a new constitution, created deep indignation in the Indian community, which already suffers from the complete neglect of the Government to provide for it educational facilities or proper housing accommodation, factors which are largely responsible for the defects found in the community. Appeals were made to the Government of India and the Secretary of State to secure the disallowance of the measure by the Imperial Government, but Mr. Montagu [1] pointed out that the step taken would be deeply resented by the Union Government, which had just proclaimed its perfect autonomy in language which suggested a warning against interference. Nor could he see much prospect of relief through reciprocal legislation in India, for South Africans are hardly ever resident there in any number. He, therefore, urged the Indians to take advantage of the offer of the Union Government to set up a commission to investigate the grievances of the Indians, and arrangements were made that Sir Benjamin Robertson, who was instrumental in presenting the Indian case in the negotiations of 1914, should proceed to the Union, not to sit as a member of the commission, but to give evidence and to aid it with his advice. The discussion was acerbated by allegations of bad faith, made by leaders of the Indians, who declared that the Government had repudiated an understanding arrived at with Mr. Gandhi when the settlement of 1914 was attained, while the Indian case suffered from the unhappy connexion of Mr. Gandhi first with the passive-resistance movement which evoked the Punjab disorders, and then with the Caliphate endeavour to discontinue co-operation with the Government of India. Yet the justice of the Indian claims is hardly open to serious con-

[1] *The Times*, September 3, 1919.

tention, however great the practical difficulties of giving them effect. But the commission's report does not promise relief.

In New Zealand also events have tended to render more difficult the position of British Indians. Alarm spread in 1920 on the ground that the number of Indians who successfully passed the language test for entrance into the Dominion was increasing, Indians, it was said, learning during a brief sojourn in Fiji sufficient English for this purpose. As a result the Government proceeded to introduce fresh immigration legislation of a curious character. Under it persons of British birth or parentage (except criminals, lunatics, and those suffering from certain diseases) can settle in the Dominion on taking the oath of allegiance. Other persons may visit New Zealand for business, health, or pleasure purposes, but those who desire to enter the Dominion in order to settle there are required to make a previous application in writing from their country of residence, setting forth in detail their qualifications for settlement. If the Minister of Customs is satisfied of the desirability of the proposed settler, he may grant a permit for entry, and the Governor-General by proclamation may exempt nations and peoples from the operation of the rule, but otherwise no settler, not of British parentage or origin, may enter the Dominion without a permit. The enactment would, of course, be ineffective to achieve its purpose if ' British ' included British Indian or Chinese subjects, and accordingly it is made clear that these British subjects as aborigines of Asia [1] are reckoned for the purposes of immigration as foreigners. The mode of procedure is unfortunate, and offends against imperial sentiment, and it is a very minor advantage that it enables the Government to dispense with the provisions of the law of 1908 requiring thumb-marks of Chinese immigrants to be taken, an arrangement against which the Chinese representative in New Zealand has protested energetically to the Dominion Government. When it is remembered that in the Commonwealth of Australia it has been found possible by a language test, ingeniously employed, to exclude every undesirable immigrant, it is strange that New Zealand could not adopt the same device.

[1] All British subjects by naturalization, and aboriginal natives of British possessions, are placed in the same position ; Act No. 23 of 1920.

In Canada also the situation has become less easy in 1920, partly in sympathy with the Californian movement to exclude Japanese immigration and to secure the gradual elimination of Japanese settlers. Undoubtedly during the war, especially in 1918, there was some increase in the Asiatic population in British Columbia, for the Chinese immigration was promoted by employers of labour, and Japan was entitled to allow some four hundred of her subjects to enter, and strict enforcement even of that limit was rendered difficult under war conditions. The matter is complicated by the fact that Asiatic labour is urgently demanded by fruit farmers and by employers who need domestic servants or laundry workers, while Labour regards with much hostility any movement which may perpetuate competition in wages. Moreover, rumours of the intention of Japan to form strong settlements in America, spread without a due sense of responsibility, tend to create a feeling of hostility to all Asiatics, which affects British Indians as well as Japanese or Chinese. The position is embarrassing for the Dominion Government, which could not extend to British Indians the same treatment as it allots to Japanese, without raising a storm of political feeling which it could not well face, while to deprive the Japanese of the privilege which they now enjoy would be internationally an extremely delicate step. The Dominion indeed is already embarrassed in its dealings with the Japanese settled within its limits by the attempt of British Columbia to defy its authority in treaty matters by insisting on the exclusion of Japanese from employment in certain forms of labour. Under the treaty by which the commercial relations of Japan and Canada are governed, it is provided that the Japanese shall not be differentially treated in this regard, and, as the treaty has been made operative throughout the Dominion by a Dominion Act, passed under the federal power to carry out the treaty obligations of Canada, the Dominion Government are clearly right in holding that the provincial legislation which runs counter to the treaty is so far null and void. One matter of satisfaction may, however, be recorded ; when the Dominion Government in their Franchise Bill in 1920 provided for the exclusion from the franchise of persons who, otherwise eligible, would be excluded under provincial laws from the provincial franchise, thus excluding British Indians in British Columbia, there were protests from the Liberal party which deprecated the attempt to refuse the right to vote on such a ground. But whether as regards Canada or Australasia it is impossible to gainsay the declaration of Senator Earle on March 12 in the Australian Senate : ' There cannot be any natural feeling of fellowship between Asia and Australia. Our principle of a White Australia, by which we must stand or fall, necessarily embitters the Asiatic peoples ; and, except for diplomatic reasons, there can be no real friendship between the peoples of Australia and the millions of Asia.'

These considerations explain the doubts felt in the Dominions as to the wisdom of renewing the Anglo-Japanese alliance of 1911. The Premiers of Australia and New Zealand alike, however, have asserted their belief in the wisdom of renewal, subject to due security being obtained for the policy of reserving the Dominions for white settlement and for the avoidance of any obligation tending to support of Japan in a controversy with the United States, with which power the Dominions are anxious to establish close relations of amity and co-operation. In Canada public opinion tends in the same direction. Australia has a special interest in the attainment of cordial relations between the United States and Japan, for her unfettered power to control immigration and trade in the islands mandated to her was conceded by Japan on the understanding that similar rights would be hers in regard to the former possessions of Germany north of the Equator, including the island of Yap, and if Japan should fail to secure her aims, she would have some title to ask for the reopening of the whole issue.[1]

---

[1] To neither desire of the Dominions does there appear to be any unsuperable obstacle; the treaty of 1911 expressly contemplated (Article IV) that, if either party concluded a general treaty of arbitration with a third power, nothing in the treaty would impose upon it the obligation of going to war with that power, and it has been generally conceded that the Peace Commission treaty of September 15, 1914, between the United Kingdom and the United States, fulfils the condition envisaged in the treaty of 1911. Compare Canada *House of Commons Debates*, April 27, 1921.

CHAPTER XIII

THE DOMINIONS AND NATIVE RACES

Native loyalty in the war — Enfranchisement of Canadian Indians — The natives of Australasia — Native unrest in South Africa — The policy of segregation and the colour bar — The Native Affairs Act, 1920.

THE war brought most satisfactory proof of the loyalty of the native races of the Dominions to the British Crown. The American Indians of Canada, the Maoris of New Zealand and the people of the islands under her administration, and the natives of South Africa showed eagerness to render whatever services they could in the war. The Maoris pressed their right to enlist in the fighting forces until it had to be conceded, and, though they were not included automatically in the Act of 1916 establishing the draft system, the power to apply it to them was given by the measure, though its application did not prove to be necessary. Even more remarkable was the enthusiasm of the Cook Islanders, whose remoteness from the affairs of the world was no barrier to the expression of their determination to serve in numbers remarkable in view of their scanty population. In Canada some Indians raised the question whether, in view of their special status, the application of compulsory service to them could be justified, but there was no lack of loyalty in this attitude. In South Africa enlistment of men for military service was negatived by considerations of internal policy, but large bodies were recruited for labour service overseas and regrettably many of these labourers perished by accident and epidemic while rendering excellent services to the Empire.

The fruits of Indian loyalty in Canada were seen in the introduction of a Bill in March 1920 to improve the status of the Indian population, which numbers about 106,000, settled in 1,625 reserves throughout the country. The measure aims at attaining the better education of Indian children and the elevation of Indians to the status of fully qualified British subjects. The Government is authorized to establish day, industrial, and boarding schools for Indian children of any reserve or district designated by the Superintendent-General, and every Indian child between the ages of seven and fifteen who is physically able must attend school, due regard being paid to his religion. The process of enfranchising Indians is simplified : such enfranchisement may be granted on the report of an official appointed by the Superintendent-General ; on it being granted the Indian, his wife and children, are placed on the same plane as other British subjects in the Dominion. Patents may be issued for their lands to enfranchised Indians, and Indian bands as a whole may be enfranchised, and severe penalties are imposed on gambling, drinking, and the possession of liquor in an Indian reserve. Any Indian woman who marries any person other than an Indian ceases to be subject to the regulations affecting Indians.

In New Zealand the Maoris unquestionably achieved for themselves an increase of public respect by their war services, while their economic condition has been furthered by measures of co-operative labour applied to the working of their lands. The addition of Samoa to the charge of New Zealand eventuated in a long-needed reform ; an Act of 1919 created a new ministry, that of External Affairs, and a department of External Affairs, and charged it with the administration of the dependencies of the Dominion including the Cook Islands and Samoa. Hitherto it had been impossible effectively to manage the affairs of the dependencies through the dispersal of the business connected with them over several departments, and the new minister was accorded the opportunity of effecting the necessary changes in the island administration, but in 1920 the Cook Islands were taken from the minister's control. The Civil Service of the Cook Islands, like that of Samoa, is to form part of the Civil Service of New Zealand, a reform which is of high importance.

In the Commonwealth there is no native population comparable with that of New Zealand in development, and the war prevented any great expenditure on the development of the resources of Papua, though the importance of oil evoked at the end of hostilities an arrangement for the undertaking by the Anglo-Persian company of researches in order to ascertain and make available Papuan oil. In Australia itself no progress was

made in dealing with the question of the aborigines, but a somewhat significant titular change in November 1916 denoted the
recognition in the Commonwealth that the style of Minister for
External Affairs was inappropriate as denoting a minister whose
chief duty was the supervision of the administration of the territories of the Commonwealth. The title was then dropped in
favour of the name Minister for Home and Territories, and in
lieu of the old name of Minister for Home Affairs was adopted the
designation of Minister for Works and Railways.

In the Union of South Africa, however, the effects of the war
on the native population have been far reaching, and the results
will deeply influence for all time the history of the country.
The wider experience gained by the war, the visits of many to
European countries, reports of the extreme efficiency of the
African troops armed by Germany, increased education and
freedom from tribal conditions have created in the native desires
of which he was previously without experience. But the seeds of
the dissatisfaction now prevalent throughout South Africa were
sown before the war, especially by the Natives Land Act of 1913.[1]
The measure was prompted by the conception that a policy of
segregation between the natives and Europeans was possible,
and that it was to be carried out by defining throughout the
country areas in which natives could purchase lands, while in all
other lands such purchases were made illegal. The leasing of
lands by natives on the share system was also prohibited ; under
it prior to the Act many natives had squatted on private farms,
or lands held by large companies, or on Crown lands, paying to
the farmers in the case of private lands rent in the shape of
a share in their produce and labour. This now became illegal,
and farmers, though permitted to renew existing tenancies on
this basis, preferred to grant mere contracts of service. The
acquisition of lands by Europeans within native areas was forbidden, but this was little comfort to the natives, who derived
practically no benefit from it. An alleviation, however, was
secured as regards the Cape, for the Supreme Court held that
the terms of the Act were inoperative in that province, since if

[1] Keith, *Imperial Unity*, pp. 180–9 ; *Parl. Pap.* Cd. 7508 ; *The Round Table*,
ix. 403–10 ; General Smuts, *Journal of African Society*, xvi. 278–82.

operative they would have violated the provision of the Union Act which preserves the native franchise in the Cape by limiting the native's possibility of obtaining the land qualification for the vote.

The demarcation of areas was entrusted to a Commission under Sir William Beaumont which reported in 1916. The terms of the report caused great dissatisfaction among the natives; it was admitted by Sir W. Beaumont that he would have liked to set aside for the natives large compact areas, but this course proved impossible, as objections were constantly raised to the inclusion of European-owned farms in native areas, and accordingly the Commission carved out artificial areas. Moreover the relative distribution of land evoked much bitterness; 87 per cent. of the land was to be reserved for 1,250,000 Europeans, the rest for 4,500,000 natives, whose numbers were increasing at a much more rapid rate than those of the white population. On this report was framed the Native Affairs Administration Bill of 1917, which aimed at carrying out the policy of 1913 by assigning definitely certain areas, as suggested in the report, to the natives, and excluding them from any other areas. Protests were at once made that the lands thus to be granted were neither in extent sufficient to allow a native to have a reasonable chance of acquiring land, nor in quality and position suitable for making a satisfactory living upon. The Unionist party objected strongly to the proposal, which was eventually laid aside for the time being, but left the natives convinced that the aim of the Government was to allot to them such small amounts of land that they would be compelled to work in a quasi-servile condition for Europeans if they were not to starve.

At the same time the situation was aggravated by the Labour unrest in the Transvaal which resulted in the white workers acquiring higher wages while nothing was done for the natives. As early as February 1918 the natives on the East Rand had boycotted certain stores by reason of the high prices charged, and though a special inquiry was held and also an investigation by the Commission on the Cost of Living nothing was done to secure an increase of the wages of the natives. When, therefore, the municipal employees at Johannesburg, by means of a strike in March to May, secured very large increases of wages from the municipality, the natives, who had an equal right to consideration and received nothing, adopted the same method, only to find that under the Riotous Assemblies and Criminal Law Amendment Act, 1914, they were guilty of an offence, as they had broken their contracts, whereas the European employees, being under daily engagements, had avoided a technical crime. Severe sentences were imposed, and bitter indignation created, resulting in agitations and protests by Churches and missionary societies. The Government, unhappily so long quiescent, felt it necessary to move, especially as they feared that enemy agents were instigating revolt; on June 29 General Botha appealed to the loyalty of the natives, suspended the sentences, and appointed the Chief Magistrate of the Transkeian territories to inquire into their grievances. On July 11 he met a representative gathering of natives who protested against the increased cost of living; the lack of educational facilities; the operation of the pass law, admittedly unjust and inequitable; the defective provision made for compensation in respect of miners' phthisis, death, or disablement; and the colour bar. Under the governmental regulations issued in terms of the Mines and Works Act, 1911, certificates of competency cannot be granted to coloured persons in the Transvaal or the Free State, and certificates granted in other provinces are not available outside the province. Thus a native, however efficient, is for ever barred from becoming a skilled labourer, and his rights as an unskilled labourer were at the same time assailed by the Miners' Union, 60 per cent. of whose members were Dutch, and who demanded that coloured drill sharpeners should be dismissed, while the Johannesburg municipality had approved the practice of paying unskilled white workers at enhanced wages, thus barring employment in that avenue also to the natives. General Botha warned the delegation of the danger of listening to agitation, dwelt on the prevalence of world high prices, and the difficulties of Parliamentary action, and, though the trouble was tided over for the moment, the causes of unrest were left untouched. Accordingly in February 1919 the difficulties again came to a head, the natives, under the pressure of high prices, claiming increased wages and the appointment of a native wages board. Riots took place in native compounds, and on February 28 a native meeting was followed by racial riots, apparently due to the fault of the Europeans in Vrededorp, in which eight natives were killed. The disorders were repressed with, as usual, little regard to the just complaints of the natives, who remained discontented and sullen, resenting deeply both their economic depression and the unfair operation of the pass laws, which are kept in operation because they aid in rendering the natives amenable to control. A passive resistance movement, or even a strike, was advocated in 1919 on this specific ground. The abolition of the colour bar was suggested by Mr. Jagger, but nothing has been accomplished generally to make this effective even as regards the coloured as opposed to the native workers; the Labour party maintain that they would agree to its removal if the law provided that the same rates must be paid to workers whatever their colour, but otherwise they will not relax their attitude.

The obvious gravity of the situation has not been underestimated by the Government. When opposition developed to the action taken in 1917, the question of adopting Sir W. Beaumont's report was referred to four committees, one in each province, which reported as to the changes desirable in the report. The divergences were such as to preclude action, and on May 26, 1920, accordingly the Prime Minister introduced a measure based on the recognition that the time was not ripe for any decisive demarcation of areas. The new measure, as passed, provides for the establishment of a Native Affairs Commission under the chairmanship of the Minister for Native Affairs, to consider any question relating to legislation or administration (other than routine administration) in connexion with the natives. The Commission will make recommendations to the minister; if he does not accept them, they may require that the question be decided by the Governor-General in Council, and as a final resort require the laying before Parliament of all the papers on the issue. The plan is based on the proposals scheduled to the South Africa Act, 1909, regarding the administration of native territories at present under the Crown if handed over to the Union, and aims at the adoption of a continuous and well-thought-out policy on native affairs. In the second place, the Governor-General is authorized to establish a local council for areas where aboriginal natives predominate, with power to provide for the maintenance of roads, drains, dams, and furrows, water supply, suppression of stock diseases, destruction of noxious weeds, sanitation, hospitals, methods of agriculture, and educational facilities, for which purpose they may levy a rate of £1 annually on each adult male. Rules may be made for the consultation of the natives before the members are nominated, and for their period of office and remuneration ; each council will be presided over by a permanent civil servant. Thirdly, the Governor-General may on the advice of the Commission summon an assembly of native chiefs, members of native or local councils, and prominent natives, with a view to ascertaining the sentiments of the native population of the Union. This proposal is based on the power given to the Governor in the Transvaal constitution of 1906 and the Free State constitution of 1907, but in neither case was it acted upon. On the other hand the appointment of councils is an extension of a system which, applied in the Cape under the Glen Grey Act,[1] had worked very advantageously.

In explaining the Bill the Prime Minister dwelt on the growing estrangement of the natives, laying stress on the fact that the tribal life was breaking up and the native had entered industry only to find that the European workers interposed barriers to his further progress. He urged that careful study of the situation was necessary, and this could be performed by a Commission, which might at once take up the problems of racial segregation, native education, native life in urban and industrial areas, native taxation, and the operation of the pass laws. Very divergent views were expressed by the different parties. Colonel Creswell, for Labour, declared his belief in the real segregation of natives and Europeans, the former to be given adequate lands and sufficient aid in making them productive to make it needless for them to leave their reserves, while the Europeans should labour as elsewhere with their own hands, and not depend on native workers. Similar sentiments were expressed by Colonel-Commandant Collins, of the South African party, who held that, if a

---

[1] No. 25 of 1894.

native were to have property, it must be apart from the white man, and by Dr. Malan, a Nationalist, who argued that the only courses open were oppression or fusion, which American experience showed to be thoroughly bad, or segregation, under which the native could develop his characteristic qualities, though neither of these speakers emphasized the necessity of large additional areas being granted. A young Nationalist, Mr. Van Hees, revived the traditions of the Boer Republics by insisting that the problem must be viewed solely from the point of view of the protection of the white man without regard to justice to the native, and demanded the elimination of Portugal from Mozambique, of Belgium from the Congo, of the British South Africa Company from Rhodesia, and of the Imperial Government from Basutoland, Bechuanaland Protectorate, and Swaziland. Mr. Feetham, a Unionist, described the policy as one of brutal Prussianism which would be fatal to the white man in South Africa, and reminded the House that under Article XXIII of the League of Nations Covenant members of it undertake to secure the just treatment of the native inhabitants of territories under their control. Sir T. Smartt held that segregation in the full sense was impossible as it would involve the handing over of too large areas and paralysing the industries of the country; but he held that native education could be improved, and the natives permitted to develop in the social scale without breaking down the social divisions between the races. The debate, however, revealed plainly the extraordinary difficulty of the issues and suggested no clear or easy solution.

One decidedly ominous feature of the situation is the growing influence of sedition mongers among the natives, who, encouraged by the possibility of civil war in the Union, have begun to preach the doctrine of a Republic for the African race, and the extreme class consciousness of many of the natives was vividly exhibited in rioting arising from wage claims at Port Elizabeth in October 1920.

BIBLIOGRAPHY

GENERAL

The Journal of the African Society, London, 1914–20.

The Journal of the Parliaments of the Empire, London, 1920.

The Journal of the Society of Comparative Legislation (renamed *The Journal of Comparative Legislation and International Law*), London, 1914–20.

The Round Table, London, 1914–20.

United Empire, The Royal Colonial Institute Journal, London, 1914–20.

British Dominions Year Book, London, 1915–20.

The Times History of the War, London, 1914–20.

The Times Documentary History of the War, London, 1916–20.

The Oxford Survey of the British Empire, Oxford, 1914.

Canada : Acts of Parliament and of the Provincial Legislatures, Debates, and Sessional Papers, 1914–20.

J. C. Hopkins, *The Canadian Annual Review of Public Affairs*, annual issues from 1914–19, Toronto, 1915–20.

G. M. Wrong (ed.), *Review of Historical Publications relating to Canada*, Toronto, 1915–19.

A. Shortt and A. G. Doughty (ed.), *Canada and its Provinces*, Edinburgh, 1914.

Commonwealth of Australia : Acts of the Commonwealth and State Parliaments, Debates, and Parliamentary Papers, 1914–20.

Federal Handbook prepared in connection with the Meeting of the British Association held in Australia, August 1914, Melbourne, 1914.

The Official Year Book of the Commonwealth of Australia, nos. 7–12, Melbourne, 1914–19.

The Year Book of Australia, Sydney, 1915–20.

New Zealand, Acts, Debates, and Parliamentary Papers, 1914–20.

The New Zealand Official Year Book, Wellington, 1915–19.

Union of South Africa : Acts, Debates, and Parliamentary Papers.

The Official Year Book of the Union of South Africa, nos. 1–3, Pretoria, 1918–20.

Newfoundland : Acts.

Dominions Royal Commission. First Interim Report (Cd. 6515).[1]

  Second Interim Report, relating to Australasia (Cd. 7210).

  Third Interim Report, relating to South Africa (Cd. 7505).

  Fourth Interim Report, relating to Newfoundland (Cd. 7711).

  Fifth Interim Report, relating to Canada (Cd. 8457).

  Final Report on the Natural Resources, Trade, and Legislation of Certain Portions of His Majesty's Dominions (Cd. 8462).

  Minutes of Evidence and Papers laid before the Commission :

    London, 1912–17 (Cd. 6516, 6517, 7173, 7351, 7710, 8460).

    New Zealand, 1913 (Cd. 7170).

    Australia, 1913 (Cd. 7171, 7172).

    Union of South Africa, 1914 (Cd. 7706, 7707).

    Newfoundland, 1914 (Cd. 7898).

    Maritime Provinces of Canada, 1914 (Cd. 7971).

    Central and Western Provinces of Canada, 1916 (Cd. 8458, 8459).

---

[1] Publications followed by numbers in brackets are Parliamentary Papers of the United Kingdom, issued by the Stationery Office, London.

CHAPTERS I–III

Lord Birkenhead, *The Story of Newfoundland*, London, 1920.
M. Cohen (ed.), *An Empire Symposium on Important Imperial Issues*, Dunedin, 1916.
C. W. Boyd, *Mr. Chamberlain's Speeches*, London, 1914.
J. M. Creed, *My Recollections of Australia and elsewhere*, London, 1918.
C. H. Currey, *British Colonial Policy, 1783–1915*, Oxford, 1916.
L. Curtis, *The Commonwealth of Nations*, Part I, London, 1916.
  The Problem of the Commonwealth, London, 1916.
H. E. Egerton, *Federations and Unions within the British Empire*, Oxford, 1911.
H. d'Egville, *The Empire and the War*, London, 1916.
J. Hight and H. D. Bamford, *The Constitutional History and Law of New Zealand*, Christchurch, 1914.
A. Hurd, *The Defence of the British Empire*, London, 1917.
P. Hurd and A. Hurd, *The New Empire Partnership*, London, 1915.
R. Jebb, *The Imperial Conference*, London, 1911.
  The Britannic Question, London, 1913.
A. B. Keith, *Responsible Government in the Dominions*, Oxford, 1912.
  Imperial Unity and the Dominions, Oxford, 1916.
  Selected Speeches and Documents on British Colonial Policy, 1763–1917, London, 1918.
  Dominion Home Rule in Practice, London, 1921.
Z. A. Lash, *Defence and Foreign Affairs*, Toronto, 1917.
C. P. Lucas, *Historical Geography of the British Dominions*, vol. ii, part ii, *South Africa : History to the Union of South Africa*, Oxford, 1915.
J. A. Macdonald, *Democracy and the Nations*, Oxford, 1915.
A. Mackintosh, *Joseph Chamberlain : an Honest Biography*, London, 1914.
J. S. Mills, *The Future of the Empire*, London, 1918.
Lord Milner, *Manchester Speeches*, London, 1919.
A. P. Newton, *The Old Empire and the New*, London, 1917.
J. Pope, *Memoirs of Sir J. A. Macdonald*, London, 1894.
E. Saunders, *A Self-supporting Empire*, London, 1918.
E. Scott, *A Short History of Australia*, Oxford, 3rd ed., 1918.
O. D. Skelton, *The Canadian Dominion*, New York, 1919.
G. M. Theal, *South Africa*, London, 1917.
C. Tupper, *Recollections of Sixty Years*, London, 1914.
  Political Reminiscences of the Right Honourable Sir Charles Tupper, London, 1914.
B. Willson, *The Life of Lord Strathcona and Mount Royal*, London, 1915.
W. B. Worsfold, *The Empire on the Anvil*, London, 1916.
Imperial Problems. Opening Addresses delivered at Conferences between Representatives of the Home and Dominion Parliaments, London, 1916.
Recommendations of the Economic Conference of the Allies held at Paris on June 14, 15, 16 and 17, 1916 (Cd. 8271).
Resolutions passed by the Committee on Commercial and Industrial Policy after the War, on the Subject of Imperial Preference, 1917 (Cd. 8482).
Final Report of the Committee on Commercial and Industrial Policy after the War, 1918 (Cd. 9035).

Imperial War Conference, 1917. Extracts from the Minutes of Proceedings ;
and Papers laid before the Conference (Cd. 8566).
Extracts from Discussions on the Admission of Canadian Cattle into the United
Kingdom (Cd. 8673).
War Cabinet. Report for 1917 (Cd. 9005).
Report for 1918 (Cmd. 325).
Imperial War Conference, 1918. Resolutions agreed to by the Conference ; Extracts
from Minutes of Proceedings ; and Papers laid before the Conference (Cd. 9177).
Empire Settlement. Report of the Committee appointed to consider the Measures to
be taken for Settling within the Empire Ex-service Men who may desire to
Emigrate after the War (Cd. 8672).
Oversea Settlement Committee. Report for 1919 (Cmd. 573) ; *for 1920* (Cmd. 1134).
British Empire Statistical Conference, 1920, Reports and Resolutions (Cmd. 648).
Report on the Imperial Entomological Conference, 1920 (Cmd. 835).
British Empire Forestry Conference. Resolutions passed July 22, 1920 (Cmd. 865). ·

CHAPTER IV

E. B. Biggar, *The Canadian Railway Problem*, Toronto, 1917.
J. Castell Hopkins, *The Book of the Union Government*, Toronto, 1918.
Canada at War, Toronto, 1918.
A. Shortt, *Early Economic Effects of the War upon Canada*, Toronto, 1918.
R. E. Spence, *Prohibition in Canada : A History of the Temperance Movement*,
Toronto, 1919.
Manitoba Grain Growers : *Annual Report and Year Book*, Winnipeg, 1917–19.
Reports of the Minister of Agriculture, Ottawa, 1915–19.
Report on Cold Storage in Canada, by Mr. W. F. O'Connor, Ottawa, 1917.
Report of the Royal Commission on Mr. O'Connor's Report, Ottawa, 1917.
Report of the Canada Food Board, Ottawa, 1918.
Report of the Royal Commission on Railways and Transportation, Ottawa, 1917.
Reports of the Minister of Railways, Ottawa, 1915–19.
Reports of the Minister of Marine, Fisheries, and Naval Service, Ottawa, 1915–19.
Report of the Women's War Conference, Ottawa, 1918.
Report of the Advisory Committee for Scientific and Industrial Research, Ottawa,
1918.
Report on Munition Resources, Ottawa, 1918.
Publications of the Commonwealth Bureau of Census and Statistics.
Annual Reports on Prices, Purchasing Power of Money, Wages, Trade Unions,
Unemployment, and General Industrial Conditions, Nos. 6–9, Melbourne,
1915–19.
Bulletin on Production, 1917–18, Melbourne, 1919.
The Private Wealth of Australia, together with a Report on the War Census of
1915, Melbourne, 1918.
Price Indexes, their Nature and Limitations, Melbourne, 1918.
Local Government in Australia, Melbourne, 1919.
Reports of Central Wool Committee, Melbourne, 1918–19.
Department of Works and Railways. *Digest, No. 26, and Statements regarding*
Cost of Construction, Revenue, and Expenditure of Trans-Australian Railway,
Melbourne, 1918.
Department of Shipping. *Commonwealth Line of Steamships, Return of Voyages,*
&c., and *Merchant Shipping and the Submarine*, Melbourne, 1917–18.

New Zealand. *Reports of the Board of Trade under the Cost of Living Act, 1915,* Wellington, 1916–19.

Union of South Africa Government Publications, Pretoria.

Report on Cost of Living, by Mr. G. Owen-Smith, 1916.

Report of War Stores Commission, 1916.

Report of State Mining Commission, 1918.

Report of Commission on Low Grade Mines, 1919–20.

Report of Industries Advisory Board and Scientific and Technical Committees, 1918.

Reports of Cost of Living Commission, 1918–19.

Report of the Select Committee on the Cost of Living Commission Reports, 1919–20.

See also the Year Books given under GENERAL.

CHAPTER V

(a) CANADA

F.-M. Earl Haig, *Despatches,* 2nd ed., London, 1920.

W. M. Aitken, *Canada in Flanders,* vol. i, London, 1916.

Lord Beaverbrook, *Canada in Flanders,* vol. ii, London, 1917.

C. G. D. Roberts, *Canada in Flanders,* vol. iii, London, 1918.

J. D. Craig, *The First Canadian Division in 1918,* London, 1919.

J. W. Dafoe, *Over the Canadian Battlefields,* Toronto, 1919.

J. C. Hopkins, *Canada at War,* Toronto, 1919.

J. F. B. Livesay, *Canada's Hundred Days : With the Canadian Corps from Amiens to Mons,* Toronto, 1919.

W. H. Merritt, *Canada and National Service,* Toronto, 1918.

G. C. Nasmith, *Canada's Sons and Great Britain in the World War,* Toronto, 1919.

F. Roy, *L'Appel aux Armes et la Réponse Canadienne-Française,* Quebec, 1917.

H. Steele, *Canadians in France, 1915–18,* Toronto, 1919.

A. Sullivan, *Aviation in Canada, 1917–18,* Toronto, 1919.

J. G. Adami, *The Official War Story of the Canadian Army Medical Corps,* Toronto, 1919.

H. A. Bruce, *Politics and the Canadian Army Medical Corps,* Toronto, 1919.

Canada in the Great World War, Toronto, 1918.

Report of the Minister for the Overseas Military Forces of Canada, London, 1919.

Canada's War Effort, 1914–18, Ottawa, 1918.

Report of the Director, Military Service Branch, Ottawa, 1918.

(b) AUSTRALASIA

J. W. Barrett and P. E. Deane, *The Australian Army Medical Corps in Egypt,* London, 1919.

E. Dane, *British Campaigns in the Nearer East,* vols. i and ii, London, 1918–19.

W. Dyson, *Australia at War,* London, 1918.

A. D. Ellis, *The Story of the Fifth Australian Division,* London, 1920.

H. G. Gullett and C. Barrett, *Australia in Palestine,* London, 1920.

I. Hamilton, *Despatches from the Dardanelles,* London, 1918.

S. de Loghe, *The Straits Impregnable,* London, 1917.

W. T. Massey, *Allenby's Final Triumph,* London, 1920.

J. Monash, *The Australian Victories in France in 1918,* London, 1920.

A. Murray, *Despatches*, London, 1920.
P. F. E. Schuyler, *Australia in Arms*, London, 1916.
A. T. Strong, *Australia and the War*, Melbourne, 1915.
C. H. Weston, *Three Years with the New Zealanders*, London, 1918.
Reports of the Dardanelles Commission (Cd. 8490 and 8502 ; Cmd. 371).
New Zealand at the Front, London, 1917.

(c) AFRICA

J. Buchan, *The History of the South African Forces in France*, London, 1920.
A. Buchanan, *Three Years of War in East Africa*, London, 1919.
J. H. V. Crowe, *General Smuts' Campaign in East Africa*, London, 1918.
R. V. Dolbey, *Sketches of the East Africa Campaign*, London, 1918.
Von Lettow-Vorbeck, *Um Vaterland und Kolonie*, Berlin, 1919.
F. B. Young, *Marching on Tanga*, 2nd ed., London, 1919.
H. H. Johnston, *The Black Man's Part in the War*, London, 1917.
Treatment by the Germans of British Prisoners and Natives in German East Africa,
    1917 (Cd. 8689).

(d) NAVAL

Earl Brassey and J. Leyland, *The Naval Annual*, London, 1919 and 1920.
H. C. Ferraby, *The Imperial British Navy*, London, 1918.
G. Fiennes, *Sea Power and Freedom*, London, 1917.
R. H. Gibson, *Three Years of Naval Warfare*, London, 1918.
Viscount Jellicoe, *The Grand Fleet*, London, 1919.
    Reports to the Governments of Canada, Australia, and New Zealand on his
    Naval Mission of 1919.
W. Wood, *Flag and Fleet : How the British Navy won the Freedom of the Seas*,
    Toronto, 1919.

CHAPTER VI

E. Dane, *British Campaigns in Africa and the Pacific, 1914–18*, London, 1919.
H. C. O'Neill, *The War in Africa 1914–17, and in the Far East, 1914*, London, 1919.

(a) THE PACIFIC

F. S. Burnell, *Australia versus Germany : the Taking of German New Guinea*,
    London, 1915.
L. P. Leary, *New Zealanders in Samoa*, London, 1918.
L. C. Reeves, *Australians in Action in New Guinea*, Sydney, 1915.
H. C. Smart, *Australia and the War*, London, 1916.
*Correspondence respecting Military Operations against German Possessions in the
    Western Pacific*, 1915 (Cd. 7975).
*Correspondence relating to the Occupation of German Samoa by an Expeditionary
    Force from New Zealand*, 1915 (Cd. 7972).

(b) SOUTH-WEST AFRICA

H. A. Gibbons, *The New Map of Africa*, New York, 1917.
R. Hennig, *Deutsch Sud-West im Weltkriege*, Berlin, 1920.
K. Morris, *A Great Soldier of the Empire : Botha's Wonderful Conquests*, London,
    1917.
W. S. Rayner and W. W. O'Shaughnessy, *How Botha and Smuts conquered
    South-West Africa*, London, 1916.
M. Ritchie, *With Botha in the Field*, London, 1915.
J. P. K. Robinson, *With Botha's Army*, London, 1916.

H. F. B. Walker, *A Doctor's Diary in Damaraland*, London, 1917.
W. Whittal, *With Botha and Smuts in Africa*, London, 1917.
Union of South Africa. Correspondence respecting Proposed Naval and Military Expedition against German South-West Africa, 1915 (Cd. 7873).
Union of South Africa. Report on the Outbreak of the Rebellion and the Policy of the Government with regard to its Suppression, 1915 (Cd. 7874).

CHAPTER VII

G. B. Adams, *The British Empire and a League of Peace*, London, 1919.
B. M. Baruch, *The Making of the Reparation and Economic Sections of the Treaty*, London, 1920.
V. Bartlett, *Behind the Scenes at the Peace Conference*, London, 1919.
R. Borden, *Addresses on Canada at War*, Ottawa, 1918.
J. Boyd, *The Future of Canada : Canadianism and Imperialism*, Montreal, 1919.
G. Butler, *A Handbook to the League of Nations*, London, 1919.
E. T. Dillon, *The Peace Conference*, London, 1919.
S. P. Duggan, *The League of Nations*, London, 1920.
C. E. Fayle, *The Fourteenth Point : a Study of the League of Nations*, London, 1919.
H. D. Hall, *The British Commonwealth of Nations*, London, 1920.
H. W. Harris, *The Peace in the Making*, London, 1920.
A. F. Hattersley, *The Colonies and Imperial Federation : an Historical Sketch, 1754–1919*, Pietermaritzburg, 1919.
J. M. Keynes, *Economic Consequences of the Peace*, London, 1919.
R. Lansing, *The Peace Negotiations*, London, 1921.
B. Pares, *The League of Nations and other Questions of Peace*, London, 1919.
F. Pollock, *The League of Nations*, London, 1919.
J. Smuts, *The British Commonwealth of Nations*, London, 1917.
The League of Nations : a Practical Suggestion, London, 1918.
H. W. V. Temperley, *A History of the Peace Conference of Paris*, London, 1920.
C. Walston, *The English-Speaking Brotherhood and the League of Nations*, 2nd ed., Cambridge, 1920.
W. B. Worsfold, *The War and Social Reform*, London, 1919.
Treaty of Peace betewen the Allied and Associated Powers and Germany, June 28, 1919 (Cmd. 153).
Protocol supplementary to the Treaty of Peace with Germany, June 28, 1919 (Cmd. 220).
Treaty respecting Assistance to France in the Event of Unprovoked Aggression by Germany, June 28, 1919 (Cmd. 221).
Agreement between the United States of America, Belgium, the British Empire, and France and Germany with regard to the Military Occupation of the Territories of the Rhine, June 28, 1919 (Cmd. 222).
Treaty of Peace between the United States of America, the British Empire, France, Italy and Japan and Poland, June 28, 1919 (Cmd. 223).
Treaty of Peace between the Allied and Associated Powers and Austria, September 10, 1919 (Cmd. 400).
Treaty between the Principal Allied and Associated Powers and the Serb-Croat-Slovene State, September 10, 1919 (Cmd. 461).
Treaty between the Principal Allied and Associated Powers and Czecho-Slovakia, September 10, 1919 (Cmd. 479).

Treaty of Peace between the Allied and Associated Powers and Bulgaria, November 27, 1919 (Cmd. 522).

Treaty between the Principal Allied and Associated Powers and Roumania, December 9, 1919 (Cmd. 588).

Treaty of Peace between the Allied and Associated Powers and Hungary, June 4, 1920 (Cmd. 896).

Treaty between the Principal Allied and Associated Powers and Greece, August 10, 1920 (Cmd. 960).

Treaty of Peace with Turkey, August 10, 1920 (Cmd. 964).

Tripartite Agreement between the British Empire, France and Italy respecting Anatolia, August 10, 1920 (Cmd. 963).

Peace Commission, Treaty between the United Kingdom and Chile, March 28, 1919 (Cmd. 518).

League of Nations. International Labour Conference. Draft Conventions and Recommendations adopted by the Conference at its First Annual Meeting, October 29–November 1919 (Cmd. 627).

Convention for the Regulation of Aerial Navigation, October 13, 1919 (Cmd. 670).

Agreement between His Britannic Majesty's Government and the Persian Government, August 9, 1919 (Cmd. 300).

Convention revising the General Act of Berlin, February 26, 1885, and the General Act and Declaration of Brussels, July 2, 1890, September 10, 1919 (Cmd. 477).

CHAPTER VIII

A. F. Calvert, *South-West Africa during the German Occupation, 1884–1914*, London, 1915.

H. Clifford, *The German Colonies : a Plea for the Native Races*, London, 1918.

W. Eveleigh, *South-West Africa*, London, 1915.

P. Giordani, *The German Colonial Empire* (trs. by G. W. Hamilton), London, 1917.

J. H. Harris, *Germany's Lost Colonial Empire*, London, 1917.

E. Lewin, *The Germans and Africa*, London, 1915.

E. D. Morel, *Africa and the Peace of Europe*, London, 1917.

E. Zimmermann, *The German Empire of Central Africa* (trs.), London, 1918.

Papers relating to Certain Trials in German South-West Africa, 1916 (Cd. 8371).

Report on the Natives of South-West Africa and their Treatment by Germany, 1918 (Cd. 9146).

Correspondence relating to the Wishes of the Natives of the German Colonies as to their Future Government, 1918 (Cd. 9210).

Union of South Africa. South-West Protectorate. Report of the Administrator for 1919, Cape Town, 1920.

Convention relating to the Liquor Traffic in Africa and Protocol, September 10, 1919 (Cmd. 478).

Convention for the Control of the Trade in Arms and Ammunition, September 10, 1919 (Cmd. 414).

Union of South Africa. The Mandate for South-West Africa and Draft Conventions, Cape Town, 1919.

C. B. Fletcher, *The New Pacific*, London, 1919.

G. H. Scholefield, *The Pacific, its Past and Future*, London, 1919.

Nauru Island. Memorandum, 1920 (Cmd. 749).

Correspondence with the Government of New Zealand relating to Chinese Labour in Samoa, 1920 (Cmd. 919).

Late German New Guinea.   Interim and Final Reports of the Royal Commission,
    Melbourne, 1920.

CHAPTERS IX AND X

C. A. Bernays, *Queensland's Politics during Sixty Years, 1859–1919*, Brisbane,
    1919.
R. Borden, *The War and the Future,* London, 1917.
H. Bourassa, *Que devons-nous à l'Angleterre ?* Montreal, 1915.
    Hier, aujourd'hui, demain : Problèmes nationaux, Montreal, 1916.
J. Christie, *Manual of the War Legislation of New Zealand,* Wellington, 1917.
L. Crawford, *The Statesman,* Toronto (monthly).
L. O. David, *Laurier : sa Vie ; ses Œuvres,* Beauceville, 1919.
H. V. Evatt, *Liberalism in Australia,* London, 1918.
J. S. Ewart, *Kingdom Papers,* No. 21.   *Imperial Projects and the Republic of
    Canada,* Toronto, 1917.
    The Canadian Nation (monthly).
L. Gouin, *The True Spirit of Quebec : an Address,* Quebec, 1918.
N. Levi, *Jan Smuts,* London, 1917.
P. McArthur, *Sir Wilfrid Laurier,* Toronto, 1919.
H. Mitchell, *The Grange in Canada,* Kingston, 1917.
M. Nathan, *The South African Commonwealth,* Johannesburg, 1919.
C. W. Peterson, *Wake up, Canada,* London, 1919.
D. Sladen, *From Boundary Rider to Prime Minister : Hughes of Australia,* London,
    1916.
H. Spender, *General Botha,* 2nd ed., London, 1920.
J. Willison, *Reminiscences : Political and Personal,* Toronto, 1919.
The Farmer's Platform (ed. by Canadian Council of Agriculture), Winnipeg, 1917.
The Grain Growers' Guide, Winnipeg (weekly).
Mr. Hughes, a Study, London, 1918.
Manual of Emergency Legislation, Commonwealth of Australia, Melbourne, 1916.
Northern Territory Administration.   Report of Royal Commission, Melbourne, 1920.

CHAPTER XI
(a) CANADA

J. T. M. Anderson, *The Education of the New Canadian,* Toronto, 1918.
E. R. Cameron, *The Canadian Constitution,* London, 1915.
W. H. P. Clement, *The Law of the Canadian Constitution,* 3rd ed., Toronto, 1916.
J. C. Hopkins, *The Book of the Union Government,* Toronto, 1918.
W. P. M. Kennedy, *Documents of the Canadian Constitution, 1759–1915,* Oxford,
    1918.
A. H. F. Lefroy, *A Short Treatise on Canadian Constitutional Law,* Toronto, 1918.
W. H. Moore, *The Clash : a Study in Nationalities,* Toronto, 1918.
P. F. Morley, *Bridging the Chasm : a Study of the Ontario-Quebec Question,* Toronto,
    1919.
E. Porritt, *The Evolution of the Dominion of Canada,* New York, 1918.
W. R. Riddell, *The Constitution of Canada in its History and Practical Working,*
    Oxford, 1917.
A. Savard and W. E. Player, *Quebec and Confederation,* Quebec, 1918.
W. S. Scott, *The Canadian Constitution historically explained,* Toronto, 1918.
C. B. Sissons, *Bi-lingual Schools in Canada,* Toronto, 1917.

The Federation of Canada (Four Lectures by G. M. Wrong, J. Willison, Z. A. Lash, and R. A. Falconer), Toronto, 1917.

The New Era in Canada (ed. by J. O. Miller), London, 1917.

Reports of the Supreme Court of Canada.

The Canadian Law Times.

(b) AUSTRALIA

E. J. Brady, *Australia Unlimited*, Melbourne, 1918.

J. W. Barrett, *The Twin Ideals : an Educated Commonwealth*, London, 1918.

P. M. Glynn, *The Federal Constitution : the proposed Amendments*, Adelaide, 1915.

C. H. Northcott, *Australian Social Development*, New York, 1918.

J. Quick, *Legislative Powers of the Commonwealth and the States of Australia*, London, 1919.

R. P. Thomson, *A National History of Australia and New Zealand and the Adjacent Islands*, London, 1917.

C. Wade, *Australia : Problems and Prospects*, Oxford, 1919.

H. L. Wilkinson, *State Regulation of Prices in Australia*, Melbourne, 1917.

Commonwealth Law Reports.

CHAPTER XII

The Aga Khan, *India in Transition*, London, 1918.

J. J. Doke, *M. K. Gandhi, An Indian Patriot in South Africa*, Madras, 1919.

K. M. Panikkar, *The Problems of Greater India*, Madras, 1916.

Union of South Africa. Correspondence relating to the Indians Relief Act, 1914 (Cd. 7644).

Report of Select Committee on the Disabilities of British Indians in the Transvaal, 1919.

CHAPTER XIII

M. S. Evans, *Black and White in South-East Africa*, London, 1911.

Black and White in the Southern States : a Study of the Race Problem in the United States from a South African Point of View, London, 1915.

J. H. Harris, *Africa, Slave or Free?* London, 1919.

C. T. Loram, *The Education of the South African Native*, London, 1917.

A. J. Macdonald, *Trade, Politics, and Christianity in Africa and the East*, London, 1916.

S. M. Molema, *The Bantu, Past and Present : an Ethnological and Historical Study of the Native Races of South Africa*, Edinburgh, 1920.

E. D. Morel, *The Black Man's Burden*, London, 1920.

S. T. Plaatje, *Native Life in South Africa before and after the European War and the Boer Rebellion*, London, 1916.

P. Salkin, *Études Africaines*, Brussels, 1920.

E. J. C. Stevens, *White and Black : an Enquiry into South Africa's Greatest Problem*, London, 1914.

L. Woolf, *Empire and Commerce in Africa*, London, 1920.

Union Government Publications. *Cape of Good Hope Local Native Lands Committee*, 1918.

Orange Free State Local Native Lands Committee, 1918.

Eastern Transvaal Native Lands Committee, 1918.

Western Transvaal Native Lands Committee, 1918.

Natal Native Lands Committee, 1918.

Reports of Select Committees on Native Affairs, 1915–20.

INDEX

Acworth, W. M., 56.

Admiralty, relations to Dominions, 132–45.

Advisory Committee on Food Supplies, South Africa, 71.

Advisory Council for Scientific and Industrial Research, Canada, 55.

Aircraft, legislation for, in Canada, 265.

Air Force, Canadian, 85.

Alberta, 59, 273, 274, 298, 302.

Alderson, General, 78.

Aliens, 20, 21, 41 n. 1 ; disfranchisement of naturalized aliens of enemy origin, 275, 276.

Allen, Hon. Sir James, 110, 170, 171, 176, 220, 222.

Allied command, unification of, in March 1918, 34.

Alverstone, Lord, surrender of Canadian interests by, 175.

Amendment of constitution, Canada, 8, 162, 267, 300, 301 ; Australia, 303–10.

Amendment of Covenant of the League of Nations, Article X, suggested by Canada, 161 n. 1

Ames, Sir Herbert, 162.

Amokura, 135.

Anderson, Sir R., 101.

Anglo-French-United States treaty of 1919, 154, 155, 164.

Anglo-Japanese treaty of 1911, 177, 324.

Anguar, German wireless station at, 129.

Appeals to the Privy Council, 166, 207, 215, 285–8.

Arbitration, in disputes between Imperial and Dominion Governments, 261.

Army Act, Imperial, 12, 78 n. 1, 87, 97, 103, 264, 270.

Asquith, Rt. Hon. H. H., 17, 31, 167, 175.

Astraea, 114.

Atlantic Fisheries Arbitration, 242.

Australia, 129, 131, 132, 134.

Australia, formation of Commonwealth, 2 ; constitution, 3 ; senate, 4, 277, 278 ; constituent powers of legislature, 8 ; naval defence, 13 ; economic activities during the war, 60–6 ; prohibition, 69, 70 ; military forces in the war, 86–96, 106, 108 ; post-war organization, 110 ; occupation of German New Guinea, 128–31 ; naval forces, 132–5, 140, 142, 143 ; share in peace negotiations, 146–55 ; mandate for New Guinea, 180–4 ; coalition government, 208–20 ; extra-territorial legislation, 263, 264 ; franchise and representation, 273, 274, 276, 277 ; Commonwealth and States, 303–13 ; attitude to India and Japan, 316, 324 ; question of aborigines, 326, 327.

Australian Defence Act, 87.

Australian Labour Party, 88, 94, 96, 110, 208, 216, 218, 219, 284, 305, 307, 310, 312.

Australian Metal Exchange, 61.

Australian Wheat Board, 62.

Austria-Hungary, 20, 154.

Austrians, disfranchised in Canada, 275 ; in Australia, 276.

Autonomy of Dominions respected during the war, 20–2 ; views on character and extent of, 158, 160, 162, 163, 164, 165, 166, 167, 207, 215, 230–9.

Balfour, Rt. Hon. Arthur J., 10, 13, 148, 150, 154.

Ballantyne, Col. Hon. C. C., 142, 203.

Barnes, Rt. Hon. G. N., 148, 154.

Beaumont, Sir William, 328.

Béland, Dr. Hon. H. S., 175.

Belcourt, Hon. N. A., 297 n. 1.

Belgium, 148, 169.

Bell, Hon. Sir F. H. D., 187, 193.

Bennett, R. B., 79.

Berlin Act, 1885, revision of, 154.

Berrangé, Col., 115.

Bevan, Judge, 219.

Beves, Col., 114.

Beyers, F. W., 166, 233.

Beyers, General, 120, 121, 122, 123, 124, 125, 126.

Bi-cameral legislatures, 3, 4.

Bigamy, powers of Dominion legislatures to punish, if committed outside their territorial limits, 262, 264, 265.

Bloemfontein, Nationalist Congress at, in August 1916, 227 ; in July 1917, 228 ; in August 1918, 229 ; in October 1918, 235 ; South African party meeting at, in 1920, 239.

Blondin, Hon. P. A., 202, 204 n. 1.

TABLE OF CASES CITED

OUTLINE OF PLAN

FOR THE

ECONOMIC AND SOCIAL HISTORY OF THE WORLD WAR

I

EDITORIAL BOARDS
(Further arrangements to be announced later.)

GREAT BRITAIN

Sir William Beveridge, K.C.B., *Chairman.*
Mr. H. W. C. Davis, C.B.E.
Professor E. C. K. Gonner, C.B.E., M.A., Litt.D.
Mr. Thomas Jones.
Mr. J. M. Keynes, C.B.
Mr. F. W. Hirst.
Professor W. R. Scott.
Professor James T. Shotwell, *ex officio.*

FRANCE

Professor Charles Gide, *Chairman.*
M. Arthur Fontaine, *Vice-Chairman.*
Professor Henri Hauser, *Secretary.*
Professor Charles Rist.
Professor James T. Shotwell, *ex officio.*

BELGIUM

Dr. H. Pirenne, Belgian Editor.

AUSTRIA-HUNGARY

Professor James T. Shotwell, *ex officio, Chairman.*
Professor Dr. Friedrich von Wieser, *Honorary Secretary.*
Professor Dr. Clemens von Pirquet, *Honorary Treasurer.*
Dr. Gustav Gratz.
Dr. Richard Riedl.
Dr. Richard Schüller.

ITALY
Professor Luigi Einaudi, *Chairman*.
Professor Pasquale Jannaccone.
Professor Umberto Ricci.
Professor James T. Shotwell, *ex officio*.

THE BALTIC COUNTRIES
Professor Harald Westergaard (Denmark), *Chairman*.
Professor Eli Heckscher (Sweden).
Mr. N. Rygg (Norway).
Professor James T. Shotwell, *ex officio*.

THE NETHERLANDS
Professor H. B. Greven, Editor for the Netherlands.

MONOGRAPHS IN COURSE OF PREPARATION

(This list includes only those at present in course of preparation, and will be added to from time to time.)

GREAT BRITAIN

British Archives in Peace and War, by Dr. Hubert Hall.

Manual of Archival Administration, by Captain Hilary Jenkinson.

Bibliographical Survey, by Dr. M. E. Bulkley.

The War Government of Great Britain and Ireland with special reference to its economic aspects, by Professor W. G. S. Adams, C.B.

War Government in the Dominions, by Professor A. B. Keith, D.C.L.

The Mechanism of Certain State Controls, by Mr. E. M. H. Lloyd.

Rationing and Food Supply, by Sir William Beveridge, K.C.B., and Professor E. C. K. Gonner, C.B.E.

Prices and Wages in the United Kingdom during the War, by Professor A. L. Bowley.

Food Statistics of the War Period, by Professor E. C. K. Gonner, C.B.E.

Taxation during the War, by Sir J. C. Stamp, K.B.E.

The General History of British Shipping during the War, by Mr. E. Ernest Fayle.

Allied Shipping Control ; an Experiment in International Administration, by Mr. J. A. Salter, C.B.

The British Coal Industry during the War, by Sir Richard Redmayne, K.C.B.

The British Iron and Steel Industries during the War, by Mr. W. T. Layton, C.H., C.B.E.

The Wool Trade during the War, by Mr. E. F. Hitchcock.

The Cotton Control Board, by Mr. H. D. Henderson.
Food Production, by Sir Thomas Middleton, K.B.E.
English Fisheries during the War, by Professor W. A. Herdman, C.B.E.
The Labour Unions; Transport trade unions (excluding railways), Mining trade unions, Workshop organization, Railway trade unions, Relation of skilled and unskilled workpeople; by the Labour Research Department (Mr. G. D. H. Cole).
Labour Supply and Regulation, by Mr. Humbert Wolfe, C.B.E.
The Agricultural Labourer during the War, by Mr. Arthur Ashby.
The Health of the Civilian Population during the War, by Dr. A. W. J. Macfadden, C.B.
The Clyde Valley during the War, by Professor W. R. Scott and Mr. J. Cunnison.
Scottish Agriculture during the War, by Mr. H. M. Conacher.
Scottish Fisheries during the War, by Mr. D. T. Jones.
Scottish Textiles (jute) during the War, by Dr. J. P. Day and Dr. R. C. Rawlley.
Source Materials of Relief Organizations in Scotland, by Miss N. Scott.
The Effects of the War on the Economic and Industrial Development of Ireland, by Professor Charles H. Oldham.

FRANCE

Bibliographical Guide to the Literature concerning France for the Economic History of the War, by Dr. Camille Bloch.
Administrative and Constitutional Changes caused by the Economics of the War in France, by M. Chardon.
French Industry during the War, by M. Arthur Fontaine.
The Organization of War Industries, by M. Albert Thomas.
Government Control—National and International, by M. Etienne Clementel.
Rationing and Food Control, by M. Adolphe Pichon.
Price Fixing, by Professor Charles Gide.
Statistical Study of Prices during the War, by M. March.
French Commercial Policy during the War, by Professor Henri Hauser.
The Blockade, by M. Denys-Cochin.
Changes in French Commerce during the War, by Professor Charles Rist.
French Merchant Shipping during the War, by M. Paul Grunebaum-Ballin.
Internal Waterways, Freight Traffic, by M. Pocard de Kerviler.
Reorganization of French Ports, by M. Georges Hersent.
French Railroads during the War, by M. Marcel Peschaud.
Supply of Coal and Petroleum, by M. Peyerimhof.
Metallurgy and Mining, by M. Pinot.
The Chemical Industries, by M. Mauclère.
Aeronautic Industries, by Colonel Dhé.

The Development of Hydraulic Power, by Professor Raoul Blanchard.
Forestry and the Timber Industry during the War, by General Chevalier.
French Agriculture during the War, by M. Augé-Laribé.
Labour during the War, by MM. Oualid and Picquenard.
Unemployment during the War, by M. Crehange.
Women in Industry under War Conditions, by M. Frois.
Syndicalism, by M. Roger Picard.
Foreign and Colonial Labourers in France, by M. Nogaro.
Problem of Housing during the War, by M. Sellier.
Statistics of Population, by M. Huber.
The Cost of the War to France, by Professor Charles Gide.
War Costs : Direct Expenses, by Professor C. Jeze.
War Finances, by M. Truchy.
The Money Market and French Banks, by M. Aupetit.
The Movement of Exchange, by M. Decamps.
Questions of Public Health and Hygiene, by Professor Leon Bernard.
The Economic Redivision of France (Regionalism), by Professor Henri
    Hauser.
The Invaded Territory of France, by M. Demangeon.
The Refugees, by M. P. Caron.
The Organization of Labour in the Invaded Territories, by M. Boulin.
The Economic History of French Cities during the War, by MM. Sellier
    (Paris), Herriot (Lyon), Brenier (Marseille), Levainville (Rouen), etc.
The Colonies, by M. Giraud.
Northern Africa, by M. Aug. Bernard.
The Allied Armies in France, by M. Dolleans.
Alsace-Lorraine, by G. Delahache.

BELGIUM

The History of Belgium after the Armistice, by Dr. H. Pirenne.
The Deportation of Belgian Workmen and the Forced Labour of the
    Civilian Population during the German Occupation of Belgium, by
    M. Fernand Passelecq.
The Food Supply of Belgium during the German Occupation, by M. Albert
    Henri.
German Legislation with Reference to the Occupation of Belgium, by
    M. M. Vauthier and M. J. Pirenne.
Unemployment in Belgium during the German Occupation, by Professor
    Ernest Mahaim.
The Social History of Belgium during the German Occupation, by
    M. J. Pirenne.
Destruction of Belgian Industry by the Germans, by Count Kerchove.

AUSTRIA-HUNGARY

Austria-Hungary:

Bibliography of Printed Materials, by Dr. Othmar Spann.

Survey of the Economic Situation in Austria at the Outbreak of the War, by Dr. Richard Schüller.

War Government in Austria-Hungary, by Professor Dr. Joseph Redlich.

The Economic Use of Occupied Territories: Russia and Roumania, by Dr. Gustav Gratz and Dr. Richard Schüller.

The Economic Use of Occupied Territories: Serbia, Montenegro, Albania, by General Kerchnawe.

'Mittel-Europa': the Preparation of a new Joint Economy, by Dr. Gratz and Dr. Schüller.

The Exhaustion and Disorganization of the Hapsburg Monarchy, by Professor Dr. Friedrich von Wieser.

The Break-up of the Monarchy, by Dr. Richard Schüller.

Empire of Austria:

The Economic Situation of Austria before the War, by Dr. G. Stolper.

Regulation of Industry in Austria during the War, by Dr. Richard Riedl.

Food Control and Agriculture in Austria during the War, by Dr. H. Löwenfeld-Russ.

Kingdom of Hungary:

General History of the War Economics of Hungary, by Dr. Gustav Gratz.

Public Health and the War in Austria-Hungary:

General Survey, by Professor Dr. Clemens von Pirquet.

Military Survey, by Colonel Georg Veith.

(Others to follow.)

THE UNITED STATES

Guide to American Sources for the Economic History of the War, by Mr. Waldo G. Leland and Dr. N. D. Mereness.